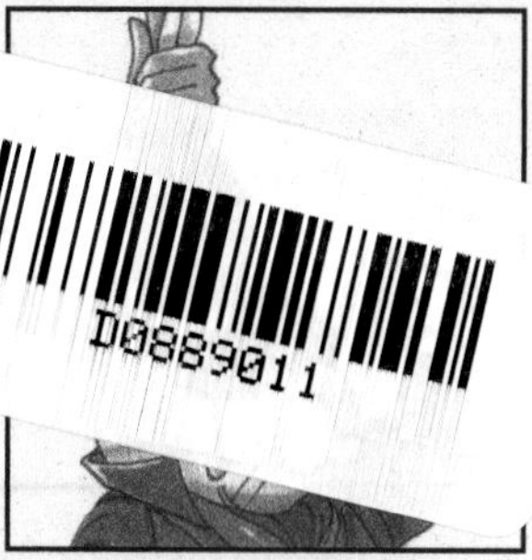

"Most congenial of innkeepers,
Your customer has entered.
Where would you like me to sit?
Those who must sit by the entrance
Cannot be at ease."

It's got a nice ring to it, doesn't it?
A song from the pirates of northern Europe.

—Eiichiro Oda, 1997

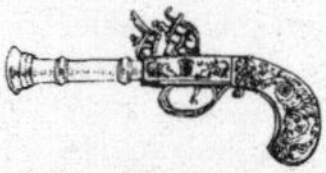

Eiichiro Oda began his manga career at the age of 17, when his one-shot cowboy manga **Wanted!** won second place in the coveted Tezuka manga awards. Oda went on to work as an assistant to some of the biggest manga artists in the industry, including Nobuhiro Watsuki, before winning the Hop Step Award for new artists. His pirate adventure **One Piece**, which debuted in **Weekly Shonen Jump magazine** in 1997, quickly became one of the most popular manga in Japan.

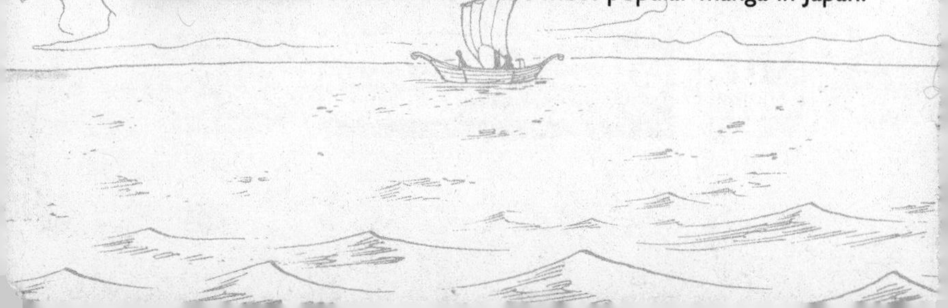

ONE PIECE VOL. 2
EAST BLUE PART 2

SHONEN JUMP Manga Edition

This graphic novel contains material that was originally published in English in **SHONEN JUMP** #5 and all of **SHONEN JUMP** #6–9.

STORY AND ART BY EIICHIRO ODA

Translation/Andy Nakatani
English Adaptation/Lance Caselman
Touch-up Art & Lettering/Bill Schuch
Graphic & Cover Design/Sean Lee
Senior Editor/Jason Thompson
Graphic Novel Editor/Shaenon K. Garrity

Printed in the U.S.A.

Published by VIZ Media, LLC
P.O. Box 77010
San Francisco, CA 94107

20
First printing, October 2003
Twentieth printing, August 2018

SHONEN JUMP MANGA

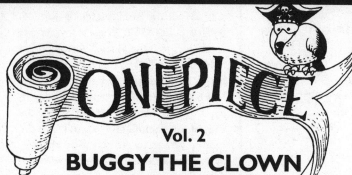

ONE PIECE

Vol. 2

BUGGY THE CLOWN

WANTED

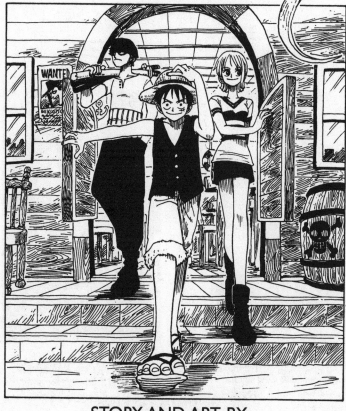

STORY AND ART BY

EIICHIRO ODA

THE STORY OF ONE PIECE
Volume 2

It is the Golden Age of Piracy. Countless pirates sail the seas, searching for legendary pirate Gold Roger's mysterious treasure, the "One Piece." Among them is Monkey D. Luffy, who grew up listening to the wild tales of buccaneer "Red-Haired" Shanks and dreaming of becoming a pirate himself. Having eaten the fruit of the Gum-Gum Tree, Luffy has the bizarre power to stretch like rubber—at the cost of being unable to swim!

Monkey D. Luffy

He ate the fruit of the Gum-Gum Tree, gaining stretchy powers. He wants to become King of the Pirates—and find his hero, "Red-Haired" Shanks.

"Red-Haired" Shanks

A pirate captain. He saved young Luffy's life, losing his own arm in the battle, and taught Luffy a love of the sea.

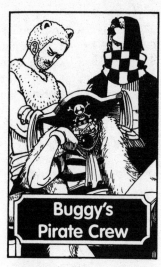

Buggy's
Pirate Crew

Mohji Buggy Cabaji

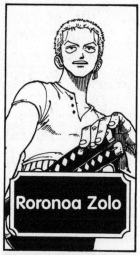

Roronoa Zolo

Although he's won fame as a pirate hunter, his true dream is to become the world's greatest swordsman.

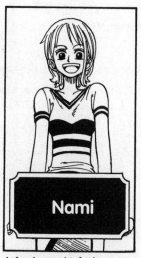

Nami

A freelance thief who targets pirates for her robberies.

Now Luffy's quest to become the King of the Pirates has begun. He's found an unlikely friend and crewmate in the fearsome pirate hunter Zolo. But Luffy and Zolo are separated and run afoul of the ruthless pirate Captain Buggy and his gang. Meanwhile, Luffy meets Nami the thief, who specializes in robbing pirates. With an untrustworthy thief at his side and enraged pirates on his tail, Luffy's career on the high seas is already in big trouble. And he's about to learn the terrible secret of Captain Buggy's success...

Vol. 2
BUGGY THE CLOWN

CONTENTS

Chapter 9:
FEMME FATALE

READ THIS WAY

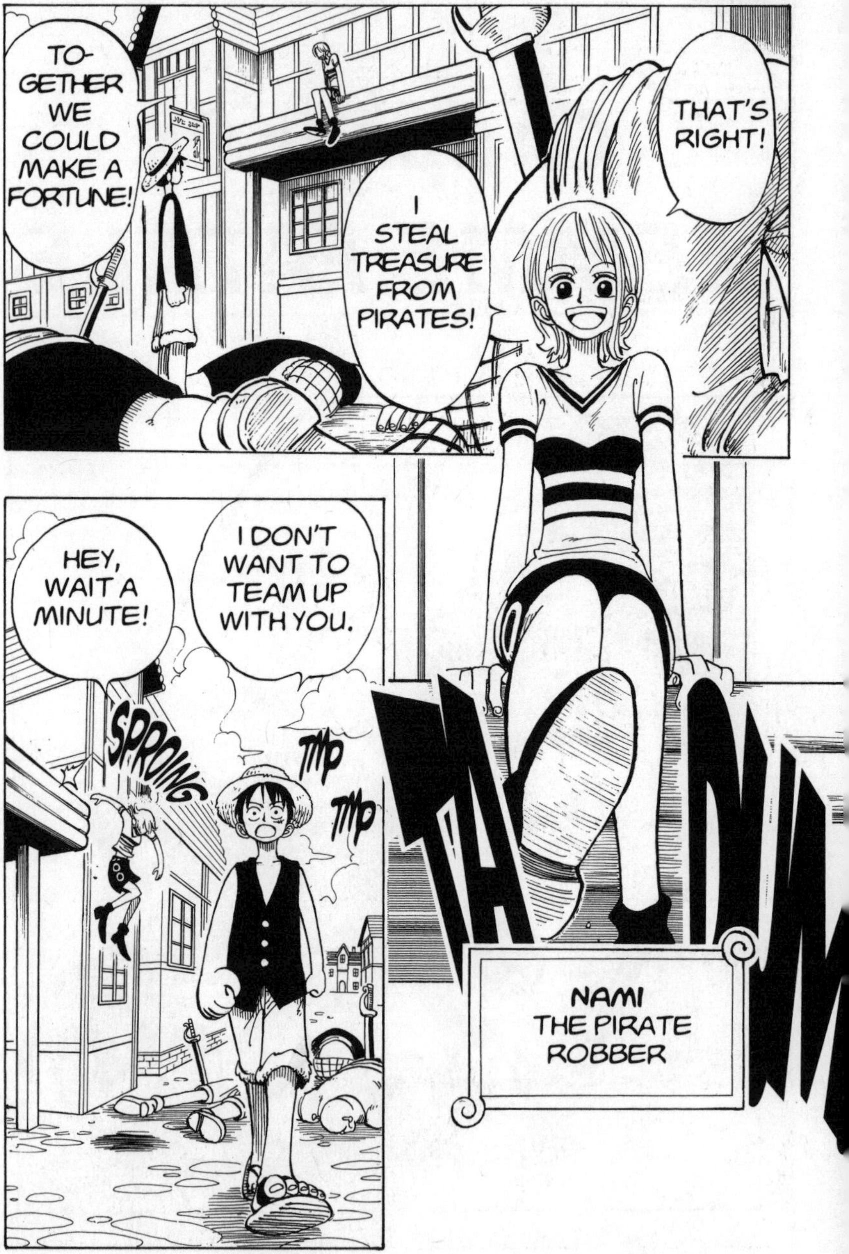
THAT'S RIGHT!
I STEAL TREASURE FROM PIRATES!
TO-GETHER WE COULD MAKE A FORTUNE!
NAMI THE PIRATE ROBBER
I DON'T WANT TO TEAM UP WITH YOU.
TMP
TMP
HEY, WAIT A MINUTE!
SPROING

READ THIS WAY

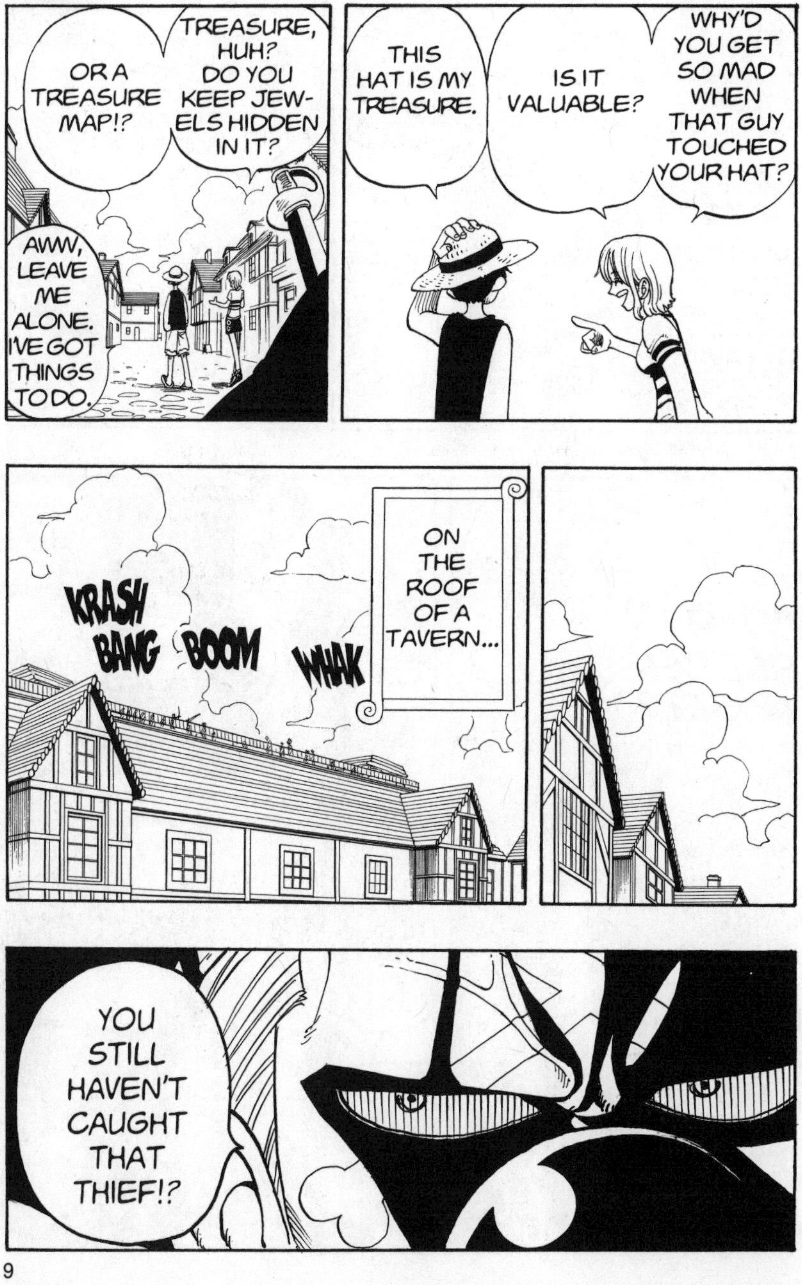
WHY'D YOU GET SO MAD WHEN THAT GUY TOUCHED YOUR HAT?
IS IT VALUABLE?
THIS HAT IS MY TREASURE.
TREASURE, HUH? DO YOU KEEP JEW-ELS HIDDEN IN IT?
OR A TREASURE MAP!?
AWW, LEAVE ME ALONE. I'VE GOT THINGS TO DO.
ON THE ROOF OF A TAVERN...
WHAK
KRASH
BANG
BOOM
YOU STILL HAVEN'T CAUGHT THAT THIEF!?

READ THIS WAY

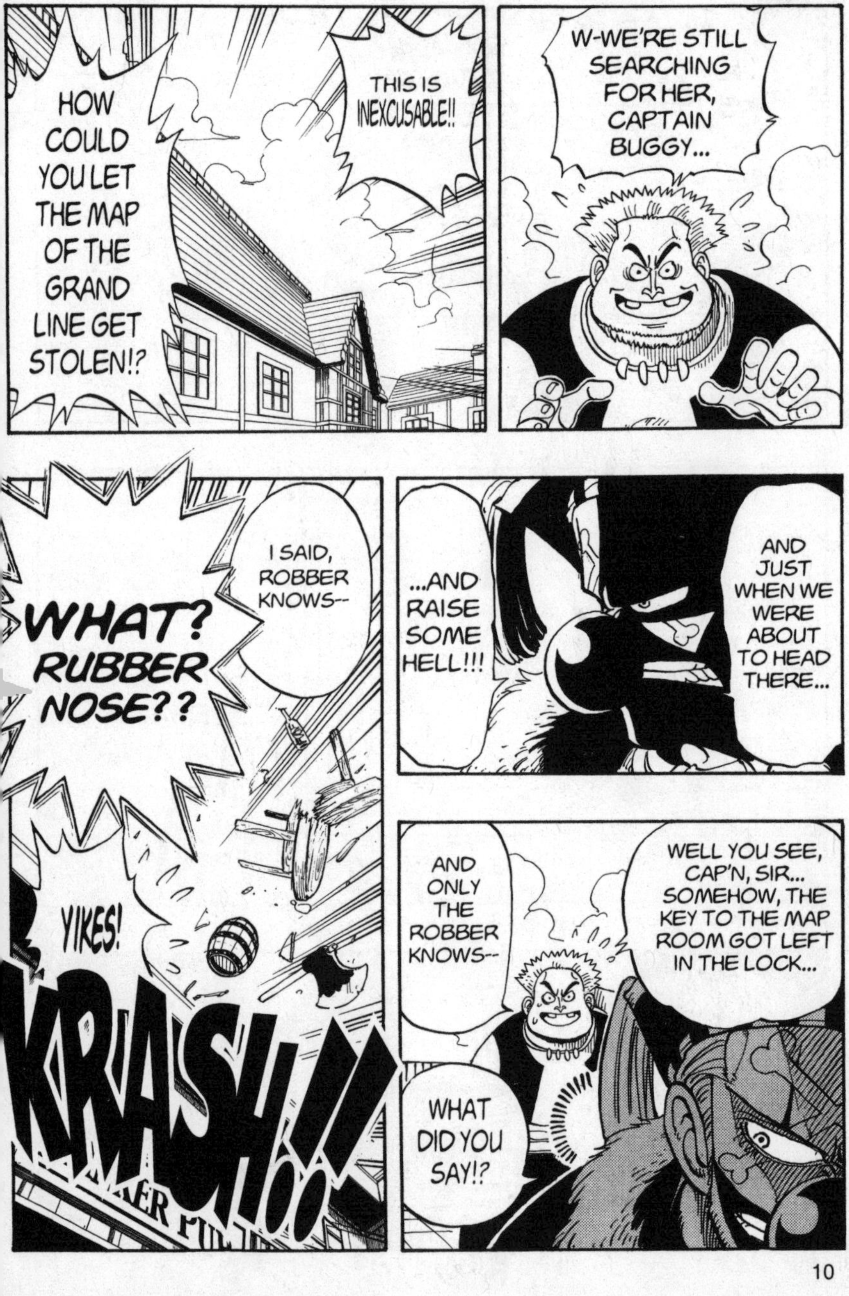

W-WE'RE STILL SEARCHING FOR HER, CAPTAIN BUGGY...
THIS IS INEXCUSABLE!!
HOW COULD YOU LET THE MAP OF THE GRAND LINE GET STOLEN!?
AND JUST WHEN WE WERE ABOUT TO HEAD THERE...
...AND RAISE SOME HELL!!!
WELL YOU SEE, CAP'N, SIR... SOMEHOW, THE KEY TO THE MAP ROOM GOT LEFT IN THE LOCK...
AND ONLY THE ROBBER KNOWS--
WHAT DID YOU SAY!?
I SAID, ROBBER KNOWS--
WHAT? RUBBER NOSE??
YIKES!
KRASH!!

READ THIS WAY

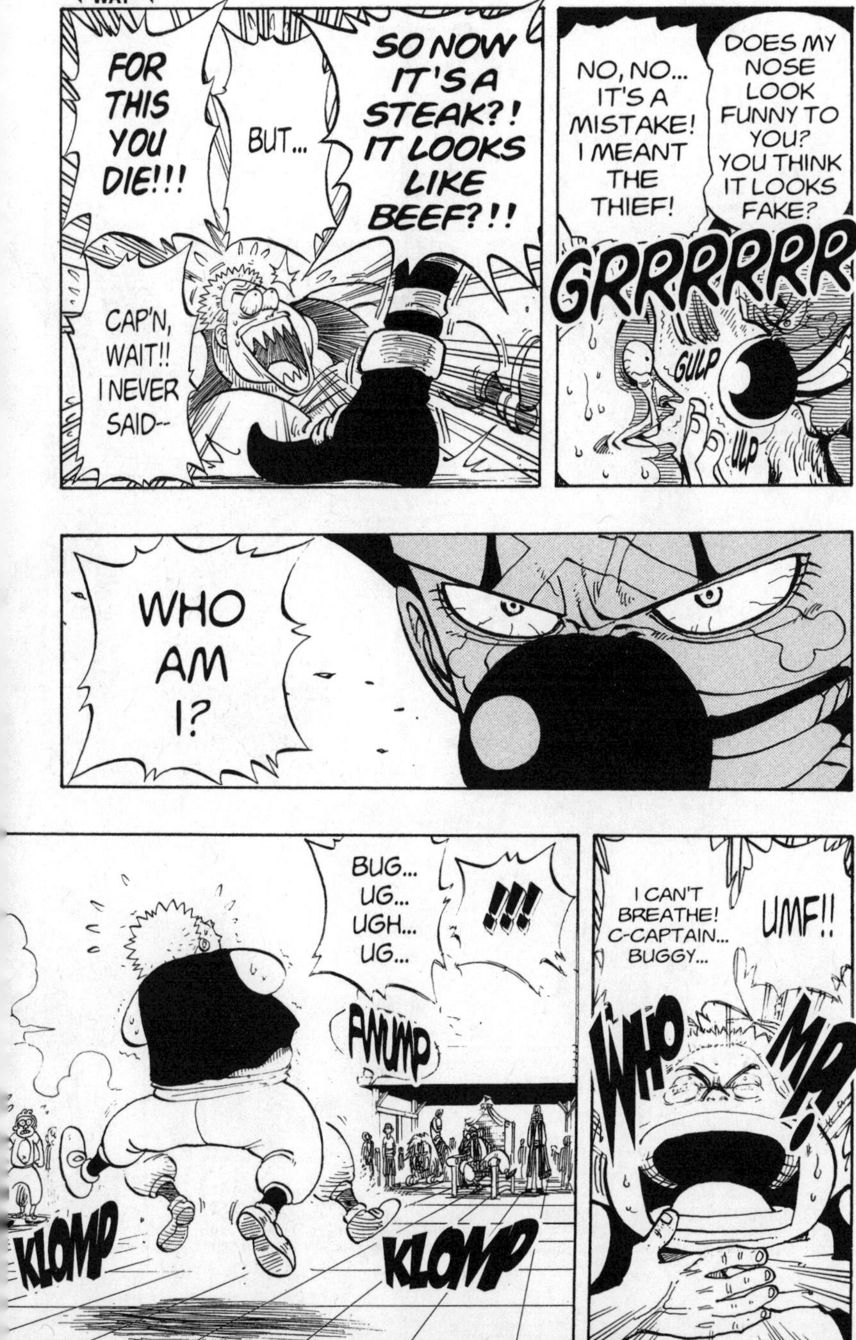
DOES MY NOSE LOOK FUNNY TO YOU? YOU THINK IT LOOKS FAKE?
NO, NO... IT'S A MISTAKE! I MEANT THE THIEF!
GRRRRRR
GULP
ULP
SO NOW IT'S A STEAK?! IT LOOKS LIKE BEEF?!!
BUT...
FOR THIS YOU DIE!!!
CAP'N, WAIT!! I NEVER SAID--
WHO AM I?
UMF!!
I CAN'T BREATHE! C-CAPTAIN... BUGGY...
WHOMP
!!!
BUG... UG... UGH... UG...
FWUMP
KLOMP
KLOMP

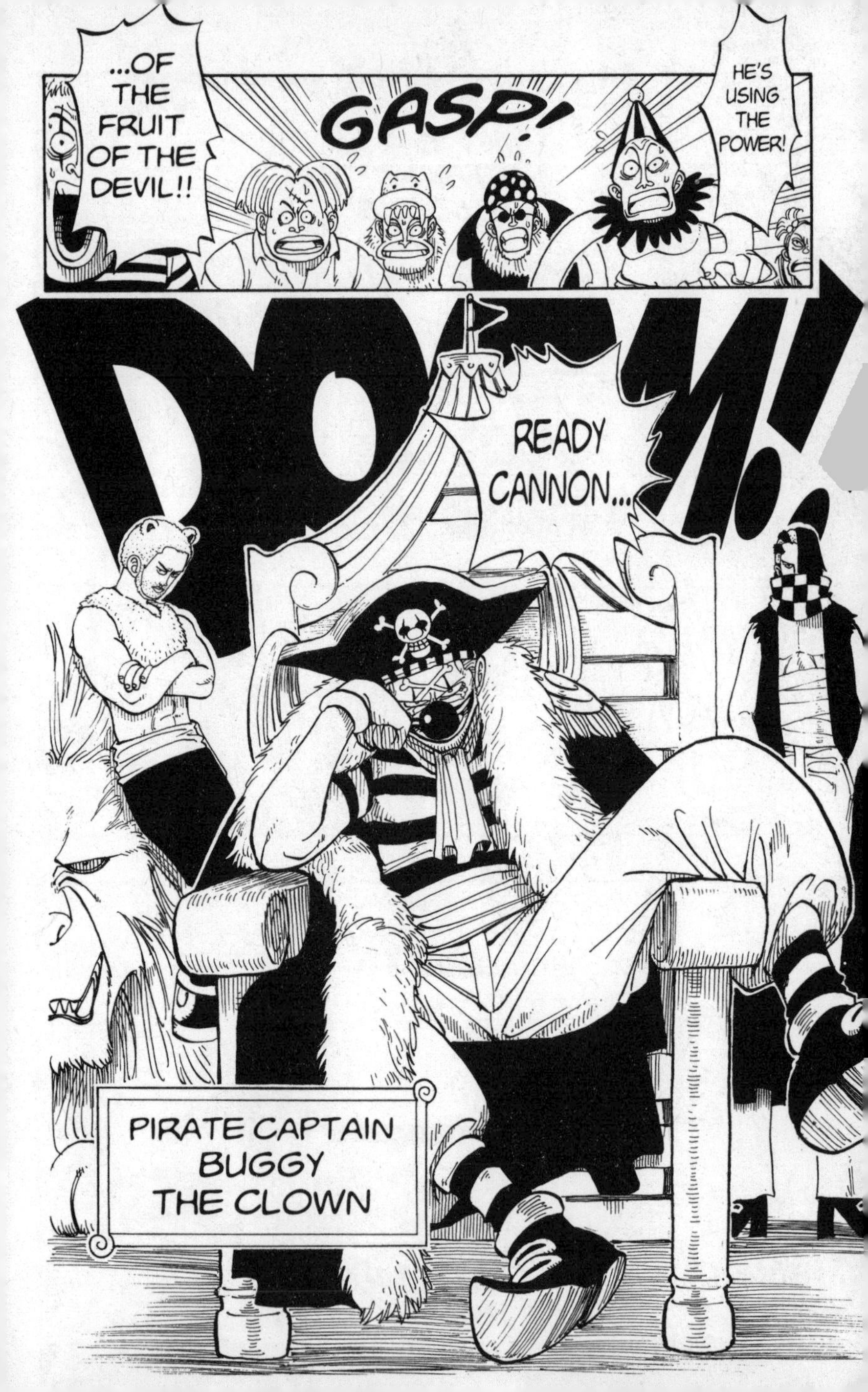
HE'S USING THE POWER!
GASP!
...OF THE FRUIT OF THE DEVIL!!
READY CANNON...
PIRATE CAPTAIN BUGGY THE CLOWN

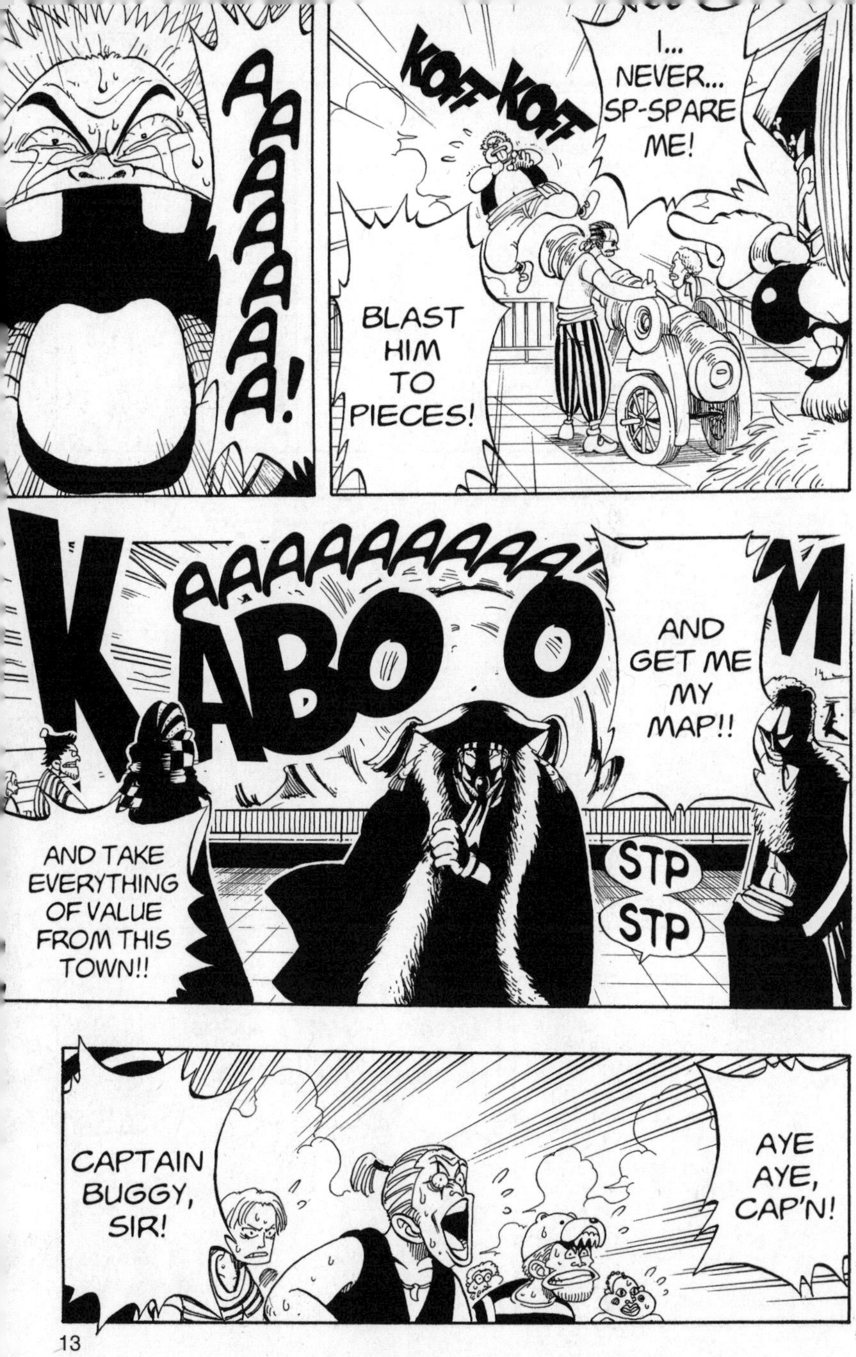
I... NEVER... SP-SPARE ME!
KOFF KOFF
BLAST HIM TO PIECES!
AAAAAAA!
KABOOM
AAAAAAAAA
AND GET ME MY MAP!!
STP
STP
AND TAKE EVERYTHING OF VALUE FROM THIS TOWN!!
AYE AYE, CAP'N!
CAPTAIN BUGGY, SIR!

READ THIS WAY

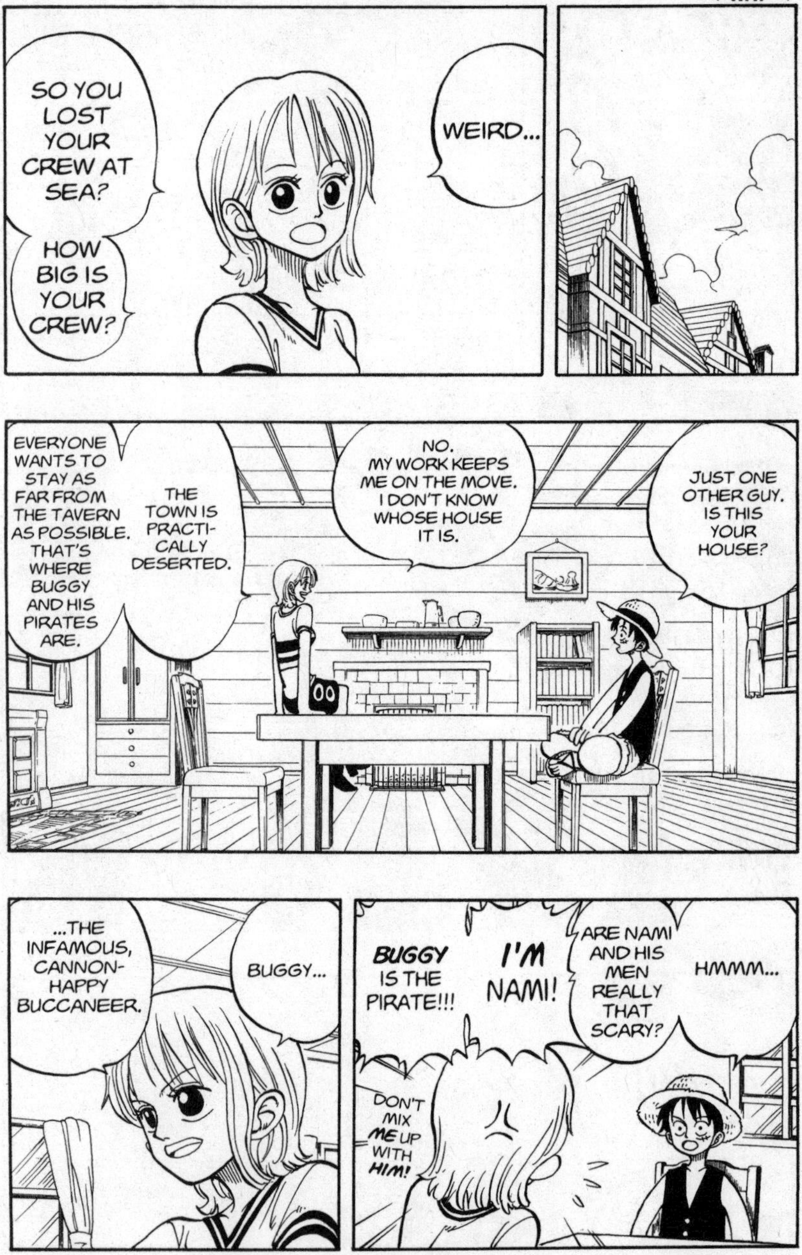

WEIRD...
SO YOU LOST YOUR CREW AT SEA?
HOW BIG IS YOUR CREW?
JUST ONE OTHER GUY. IS THIS YOUR HOUSE?
NO. MY WORK KEEPS ME ON THE MOVE. I DON'T KNOW WHOSE HOUSE IT IS.
THE TOWN IS PRACTICALLY DESERTED.
EVERYONE WANTS TO STAY AS FAR FROM THE TAVERN AS POSSIBLE. THAT'S WHERE BUGGY AND HIS PIRATES ARE.
HMMM...
ARE NAMI AND HIS MEN REALLY THAT SCARY?
I'M NAMI!
BUGGY IS THE PIRATE!!!
DON'T MIX ME UP WITH HIM!
BUGGY...
...THE INFAMOUS, CANNON-HAPPY BUCCANEER.

READ THIS WAY

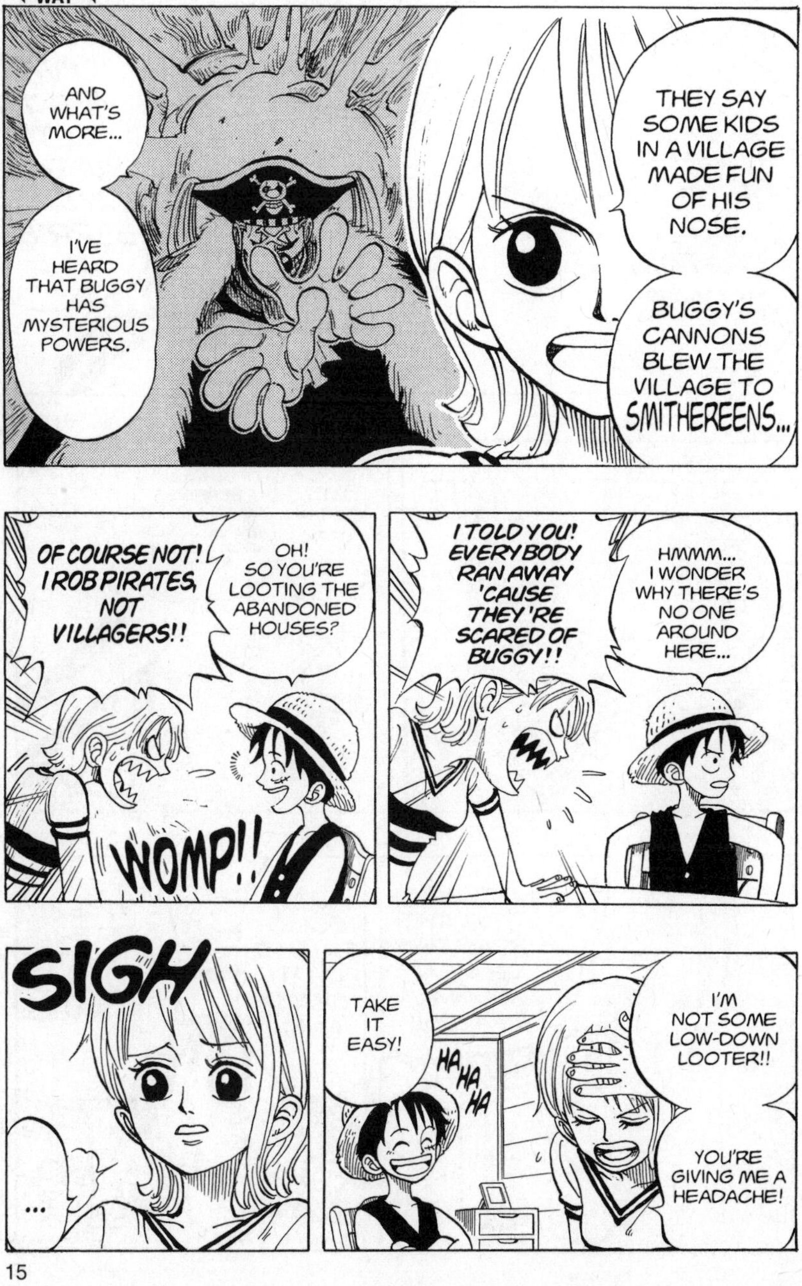
THEY SAY SOME KIDS IN A VILLAGE MADE FUN OF HIS NOSE.
BUGGY'S CANNONS BLEW THE VILLAGE TO SMITHEREENS...
AND WHAT'S MORE...
I'VE HEARD THAT BUGGY HAS MYSTERIOUS POWERS.
HMMM... I WONDER WHY THERE'S NO ONE AROUND HERE...
I TOLD YOU! EVERYBODY RAN AWAY 'CAUSE THEY'RE SCARED OF BUGGY!!
OH! SO YOU'RE LOOTING THE ABANDONED HOUSES?
OF COURSE NOT! I ROB PIRATES, NOT VILLAGERS!!
WOMP!!
I'M NOT SOME LOW-DOWN LOOTER!!
YOU'RE GIVING ME A HEADACHE!
TAKE IT EASY!
HA HA HA
SIGH
...

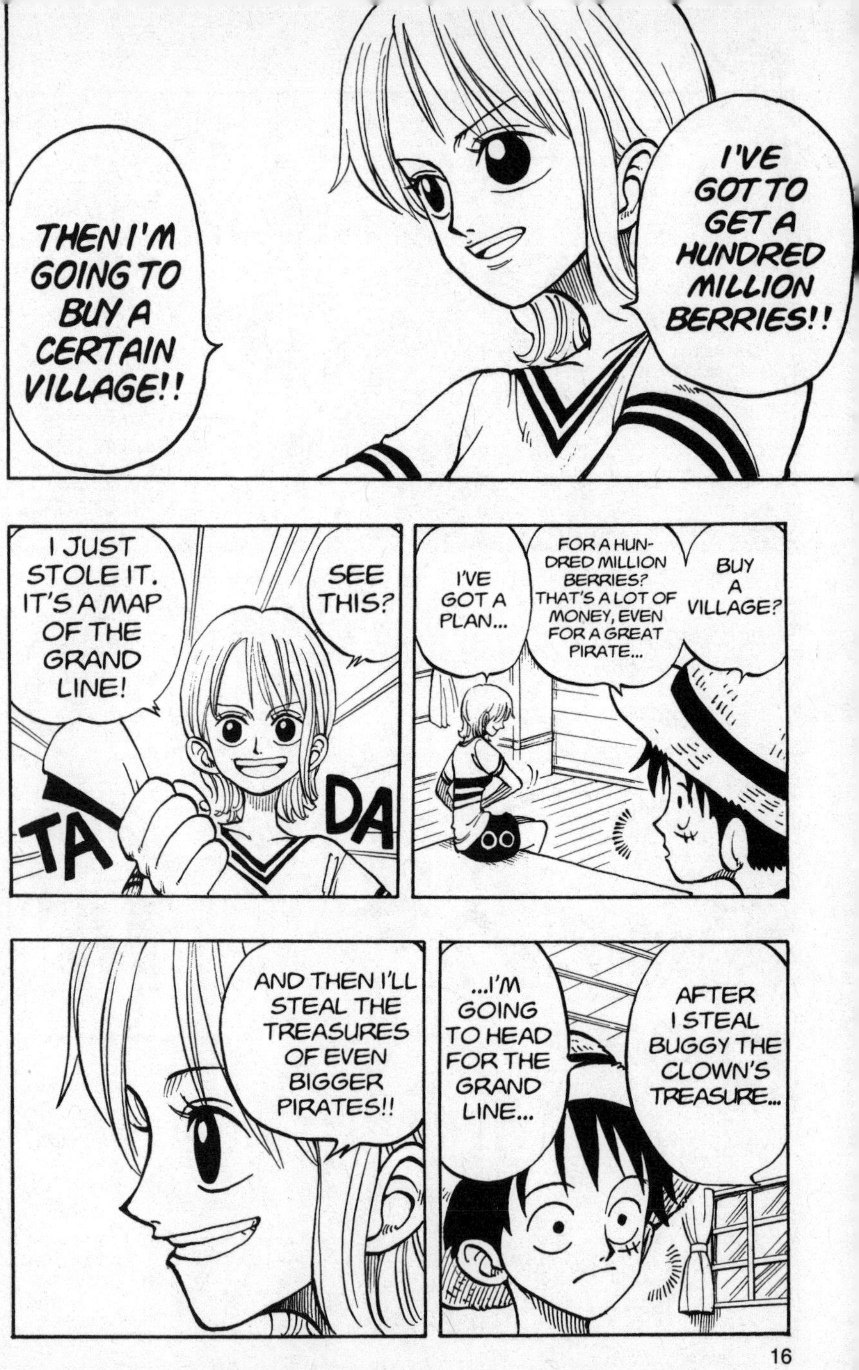
I'VE GOT TO GET A HUNDRED MILLION BERRIES!!
THEN I'M GOING TO BUY A CERTAIN VILLAGE!!
BUY A VILLAGE?
FOR A HUN-DRED MILLION BERRIES? THAT'S A LOT OF MONEY, EVEN FOR A GREAT PIRATE...
I'VE GOT A PLAN...
SEE THIS?
I JUST STOLE IT. IT'S A MAP OF THE GRAND LINE!
TA
DA
AFTER I STEAL BUGGY THE CLOWN'S TREASURE...
...I'M GOING TO HEAD FOR THE GRAND LINE...
AND THEN I'LL STEAL THE TREASURES OF EVEN BIGGER PIRATES!!

READ THIS WAY

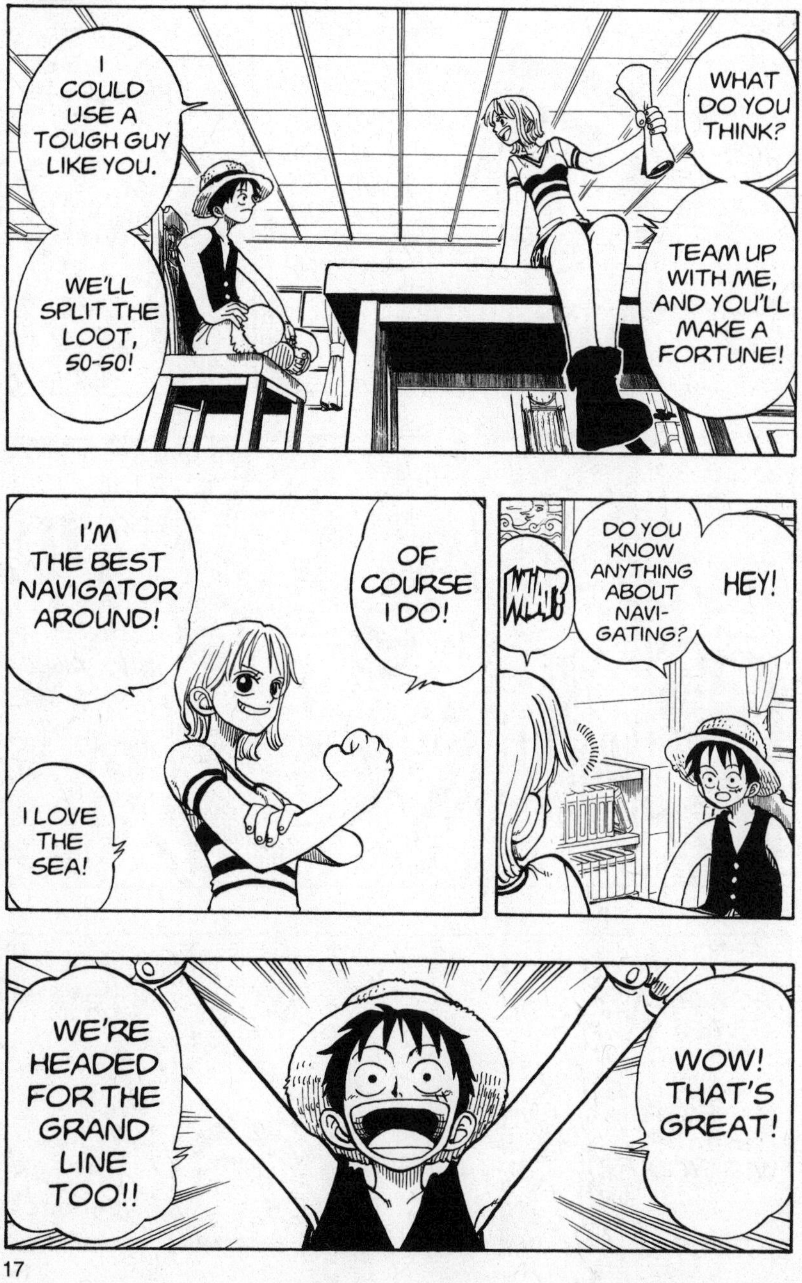
WHAT DO YOU THINK?
TEAM UP WITH ME, AND YOU'LL MAKE A FORTUNE!
I COULD USE A TOUGH GUY LIKE YOU.
WE'LL SPLIT THE LOOT, 50-50!
HEY!
DO YOU KNOW ANYTHING ABOUT NAVI-GATING?
WHAT?
OF COURSE I DO!
I'M THE BEST NAVIGATOR AROUND!
I LOVE THE SEA!
WOW! THAT'S GREAT!
WE'RE HEADED FOR THE GRAND LINE TOO!!

READ THIS WAY

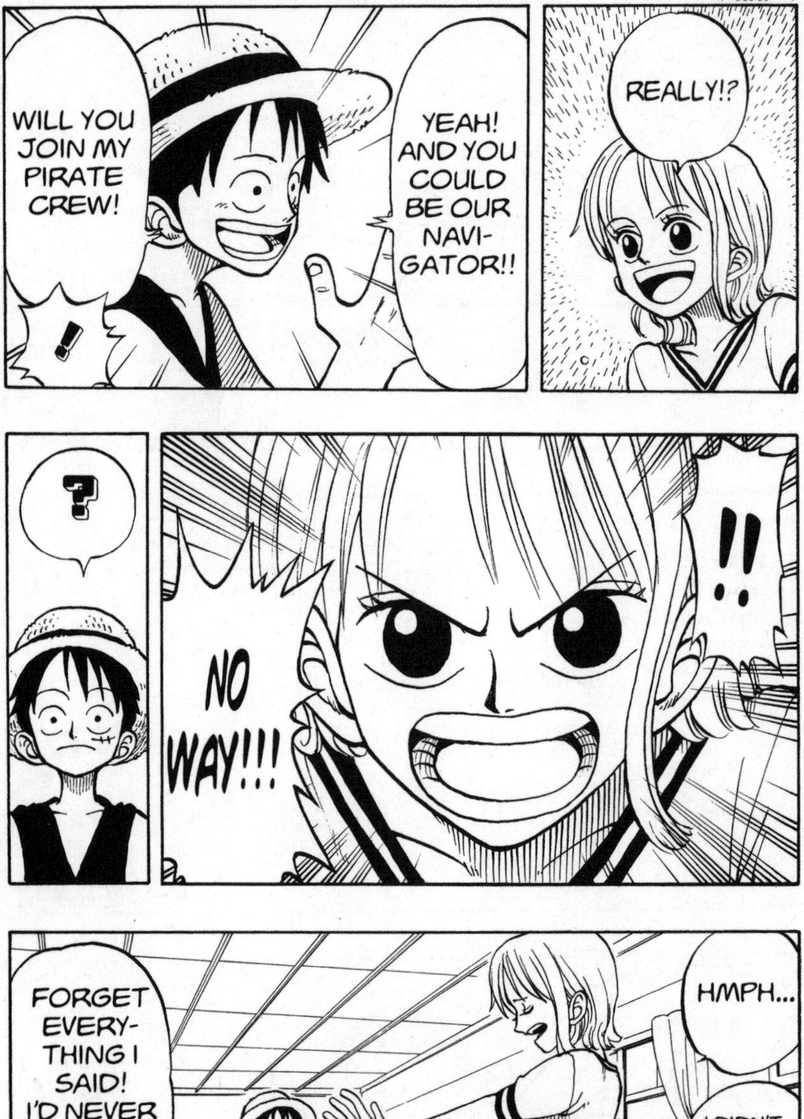
REALLY!?
YEAH! AND YOU COULD BE OUR NAVI-GATOR!!
WILL YOU JOIN MY PIRATE CREW!
!
!!
NO WAY!!!
?
HMPH...
I DIDN'T KNOW THAT YOU WERE A PIRATE!
FORGET EVERY-THING I SAID! I'D NEVER TEAM UP WITH YOU!

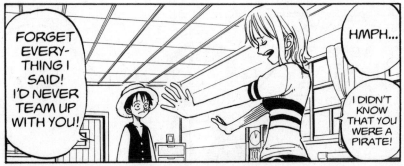

READ THIS WAY

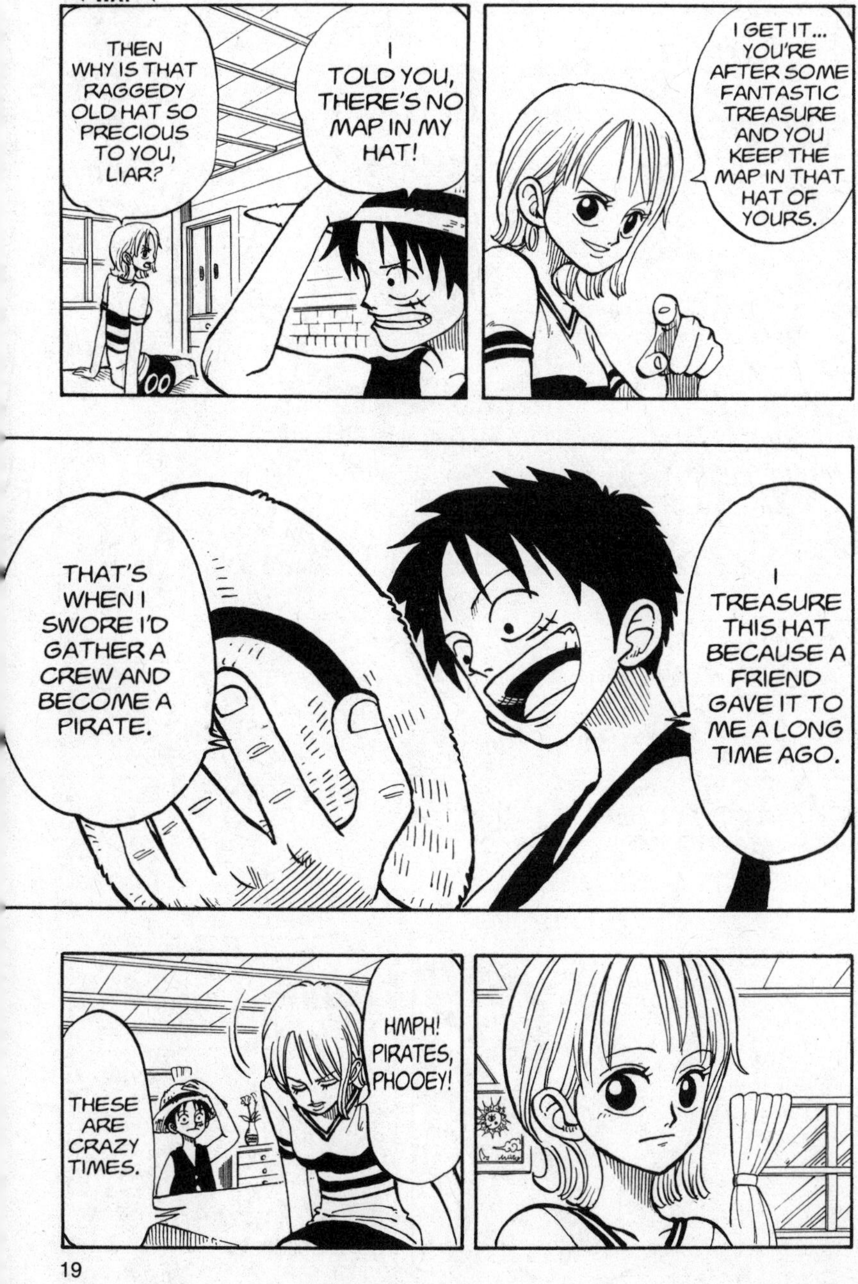
I GET IT... YOU'RE AFTER SOME FANTASTIC TREASURE AND YOU KEEP THE MAP IN THAT HAT OF YOURS.
I TOLD YOU, THERE'S NO MAP IN MY HAT!
THEN WHY IS THAT RAGGEDY OLD HAT SO PRECIOUS TO YOU, LIAR?
I TREASURE THIS HAT BECAUSE A FRIEND GAVE IT TO ME A LONG TIME AGO.
THAT'S WHEN I SWORE I'D GATHER A CREW AND BECOME A PIRATE.
HMPH! PIRATES, PHOOEY!
THESE ARE CRAZY TIMES.

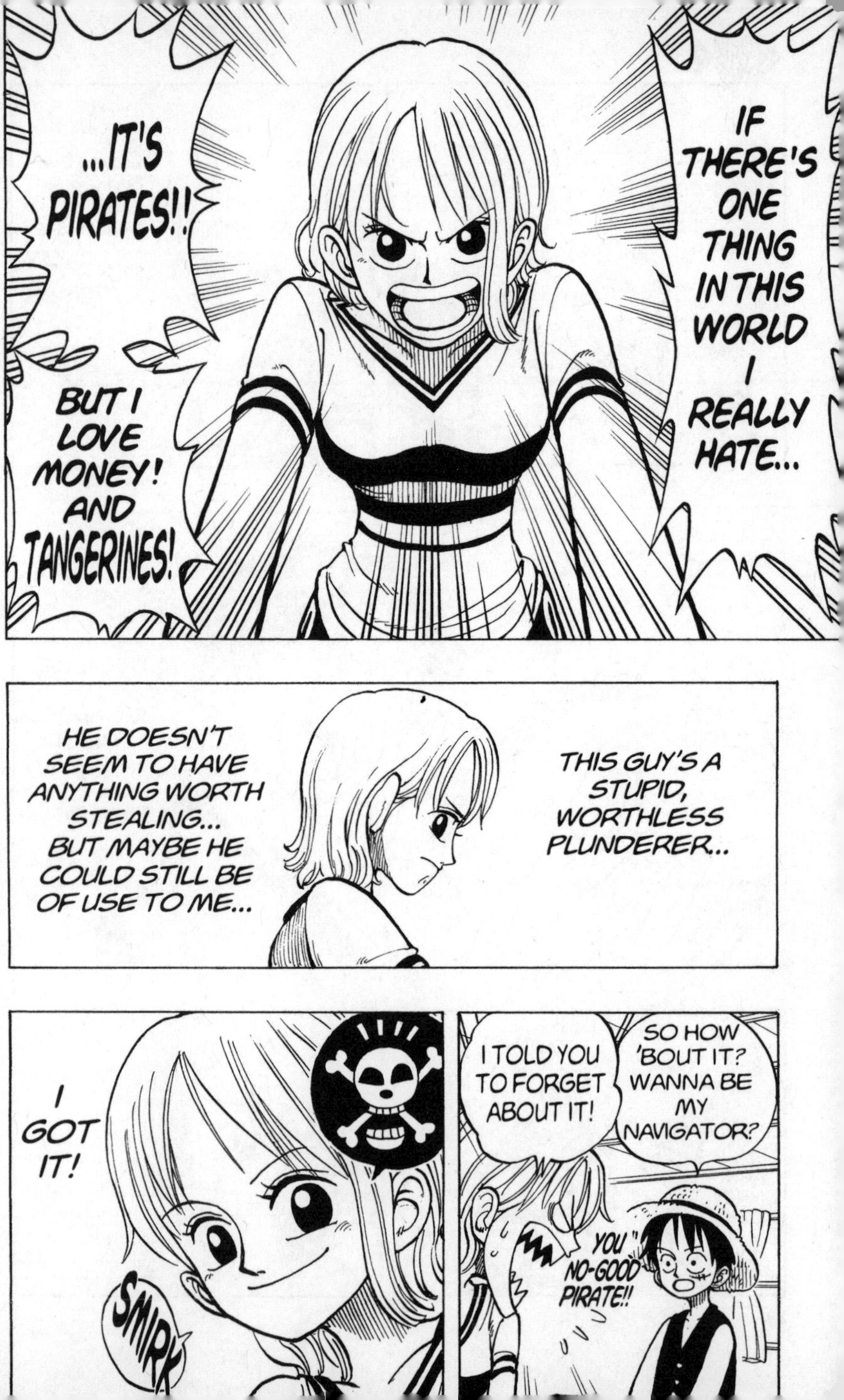
IF THERE'S ONE THING IN THIS WORLD I REALLY HATE...
...IT'S PIRATES!!
BUT I LOVE MONEY! AND TANGERINES!
THIS GUY'S A STUPID, WORTHLESS PLUNDERER...
HE DOESN'T SEEM TO HAVE ANYTHING WORTH STEALING... BUT MAYBE HE COULD STILL BE OF USE TO ME...
SO HOW 'BOUT IT? WANNA BE MY NAVIGATOR?
I TOLD YOU TO FORGET ABOUT IT!
YOU NO-GOOD PIRATE!!
I GOT IT!
SMIRK

READ THIS WAY

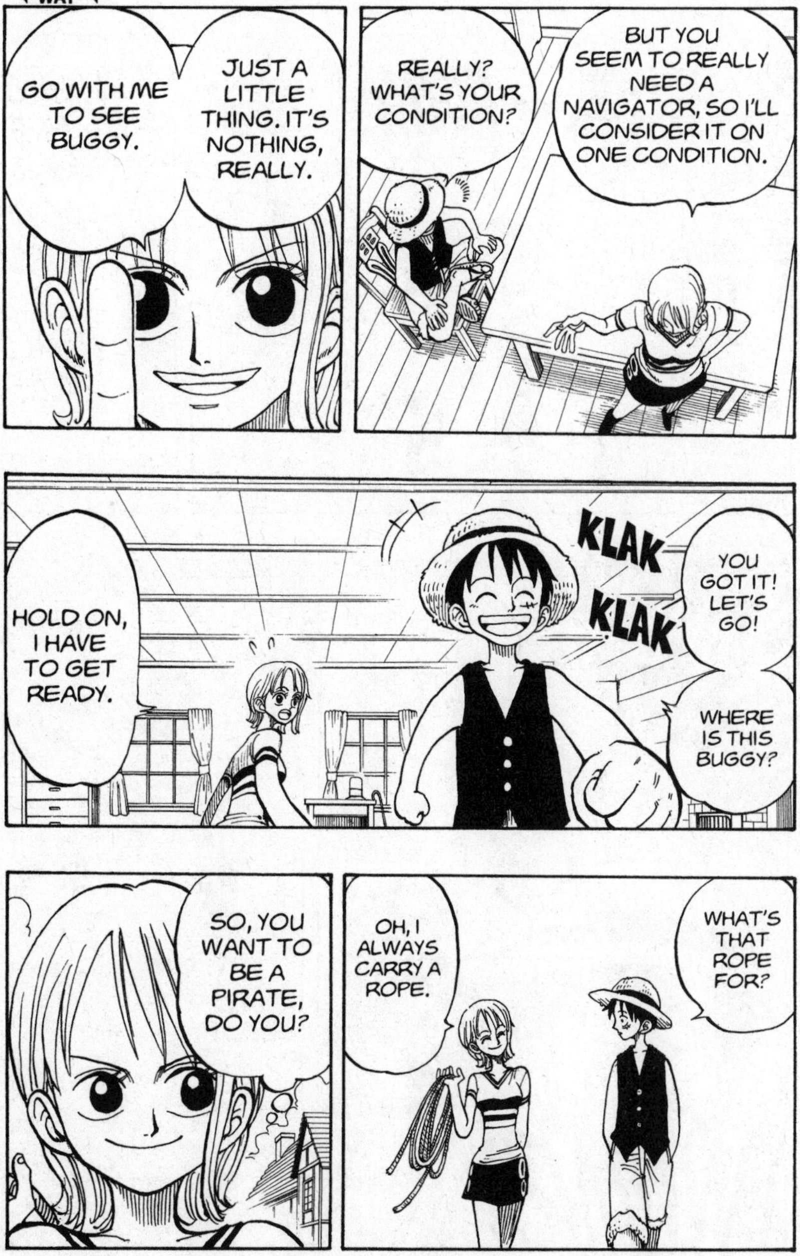
BUT YOU SEEM TO REALLY NEED A NAVIGATOR, SO I'LL CONSIDER IT ON ONE CONDITION.
REALLY? WHAT'S YOUR CONDITION?
JUST A LITTLE THING. IT'S NOTHING, REALLY.
GO WITH ME TO SEE BUGGY.
YOU GOT IT! LET'S GO!
WHERE IS THIS BUGGY?
KLAK
KLAK
HOLD ON, I HAVE TO GET READY.
WHAT'S THAT ROPE FOR?
OH, I ALWAYS CARRY A ROPE.
SO, YOU WANT TO BE A PIRATE, DO YOU?

READ THIS WAY

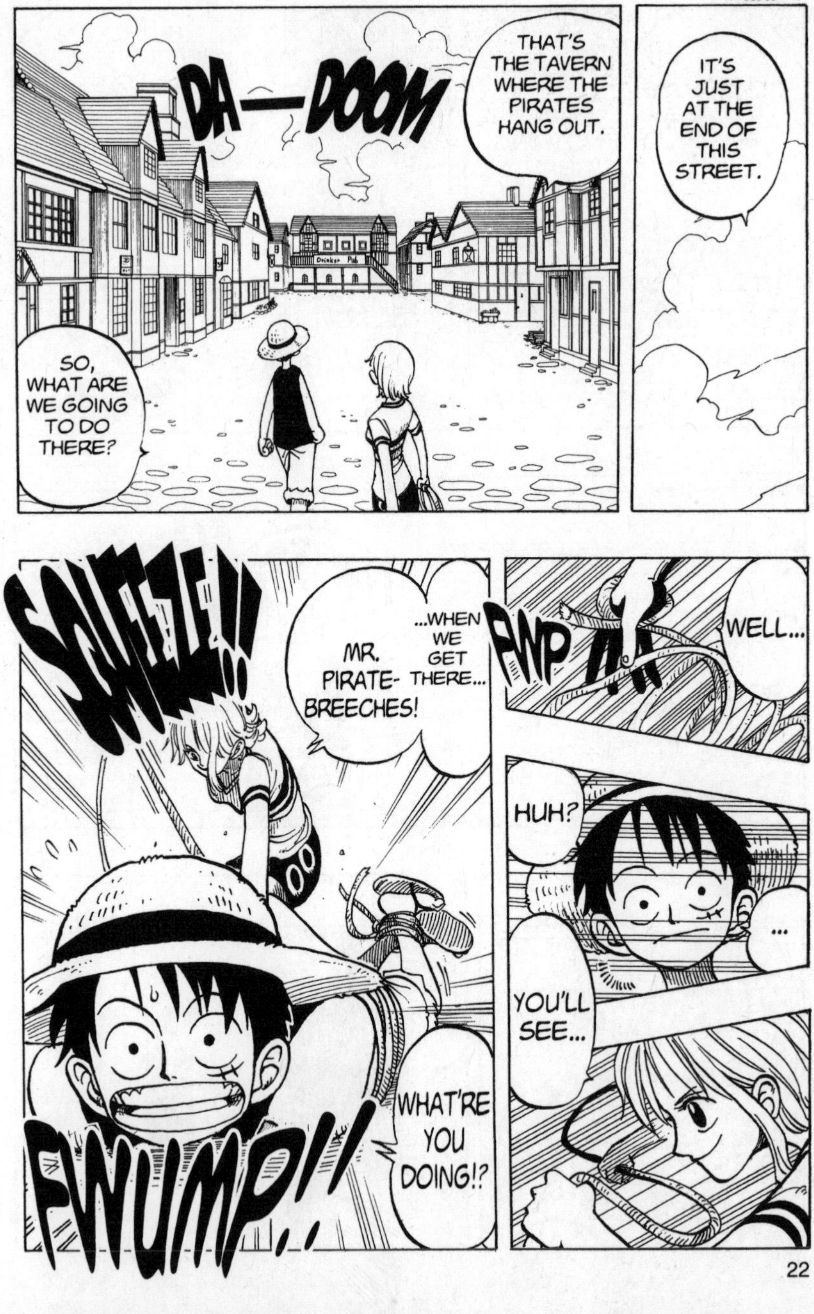
IT'S JUST AT THE END OF THIS STREET.
THAT'S THE TAVERN WHERE THE PIRATES HANG OUT.
DA—DOOM
Drinker Pub
SO, WHAT ARE WE GOING TO DO THERE?
WELL...
HUH?
...
YOU'LL SEE...
...WHEN WE GET THERE...
MR. PIRATE-BREECHES!
SQUEEZE!!
WHAT'RE YOU DOING!?
FWUMP!!

READ THIS WAY

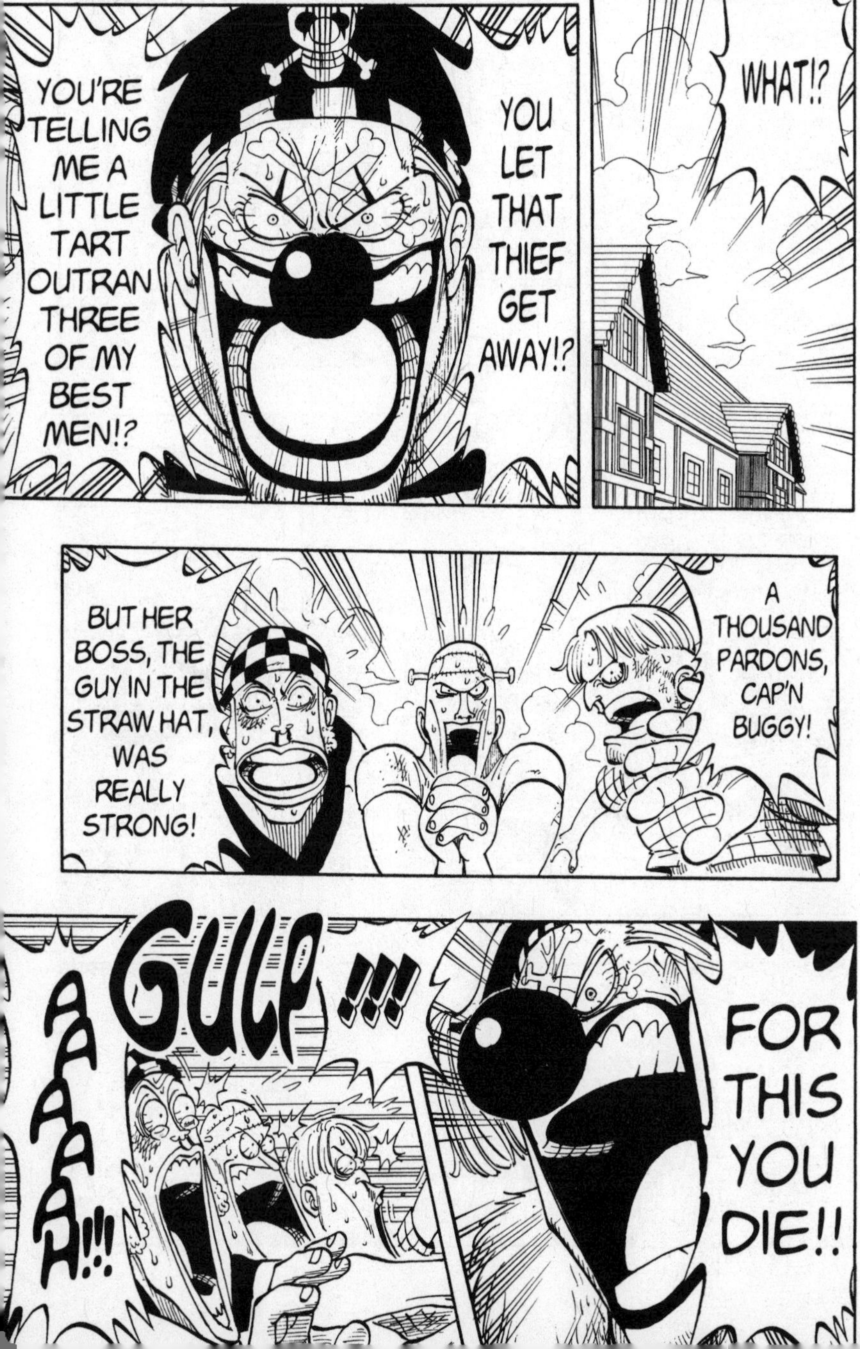
WHAT!?
YOU LET THAT THIEF GET AWAY!?
YOU'RE TELLING ME A LITTLE TART OUTRAN THREE OF MY BEST MEN!?
A THOUSAND PARDONS, CAP'N BUGGY!
BUT HER BOSS, THE GUY IN THE STRAW HAT, WAS REALLY STRONG!
FOR THIS YOU DIE!!
GULP!!!
AAAAAH!!!

READ THIS WAY

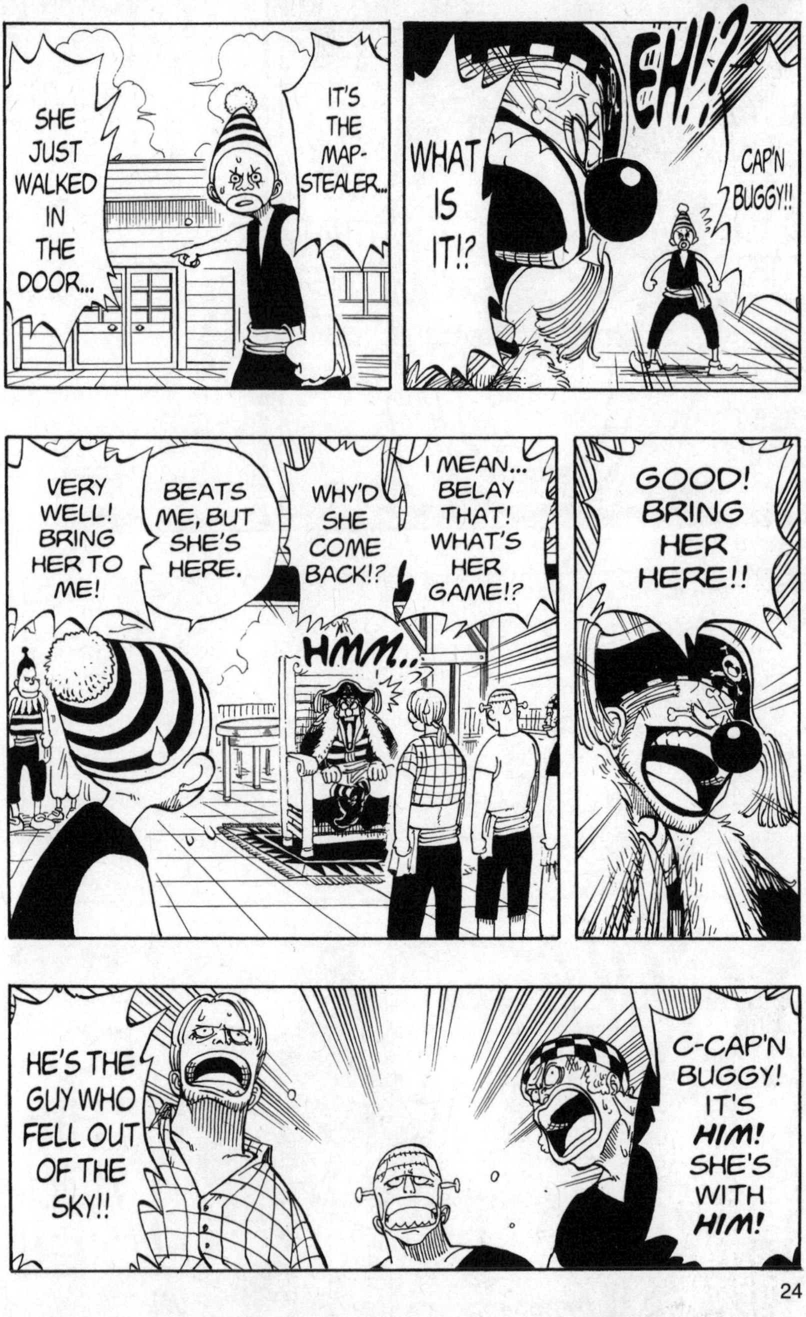
EH!?
CAP'N BUGGY!!
WHAT IS IT!?
IT'S THE MAP-STEALER...
SHE JUST WALKED IN THE DOOR...
GOOD! BRING HER HERE!!
I MEAN... BELAY THAT! WHAT'S HER GAME!?
WHY'D SHE COME BACK!?
HMM..
BEATS ME, BUT SHE'S HERE.
VERY WELL! BRING HER TO ME!
C-CAP'N BUGGY! IT'S *HIM!* SHE'S WITH *HIM!*
HE'S THE GUY WHO FELL OUT OF THE SKY!!

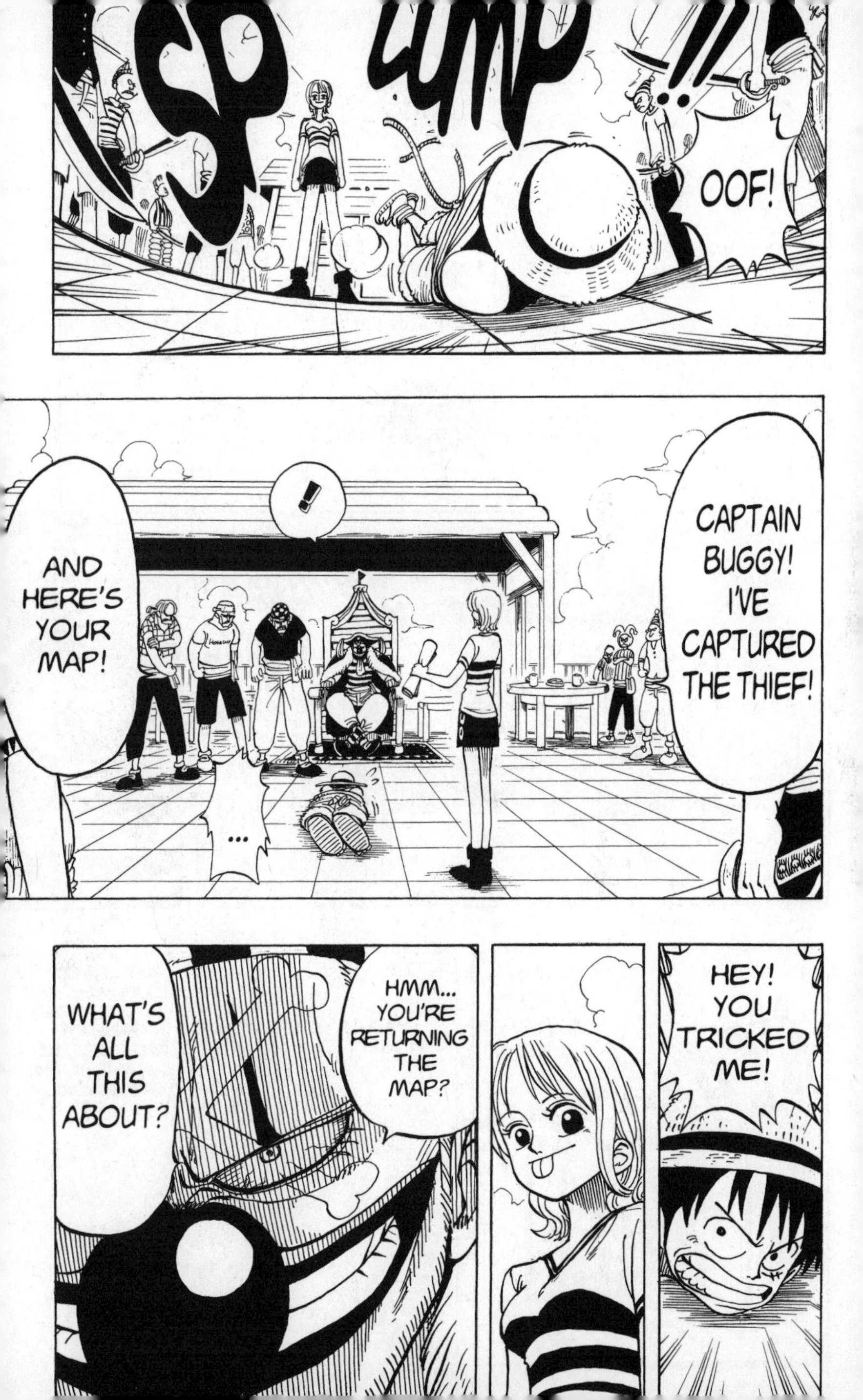
OOF!
CAPTAIN BUGGY! I'VE CAPTURED THE THIEF!
!
AND HERE'S YOUR MAP!
...
HEY! YOU TRICKED ME!
HMM... YOU'RE RETURNING THE MAP?
WHAT'S ALL THIS ABOUT?

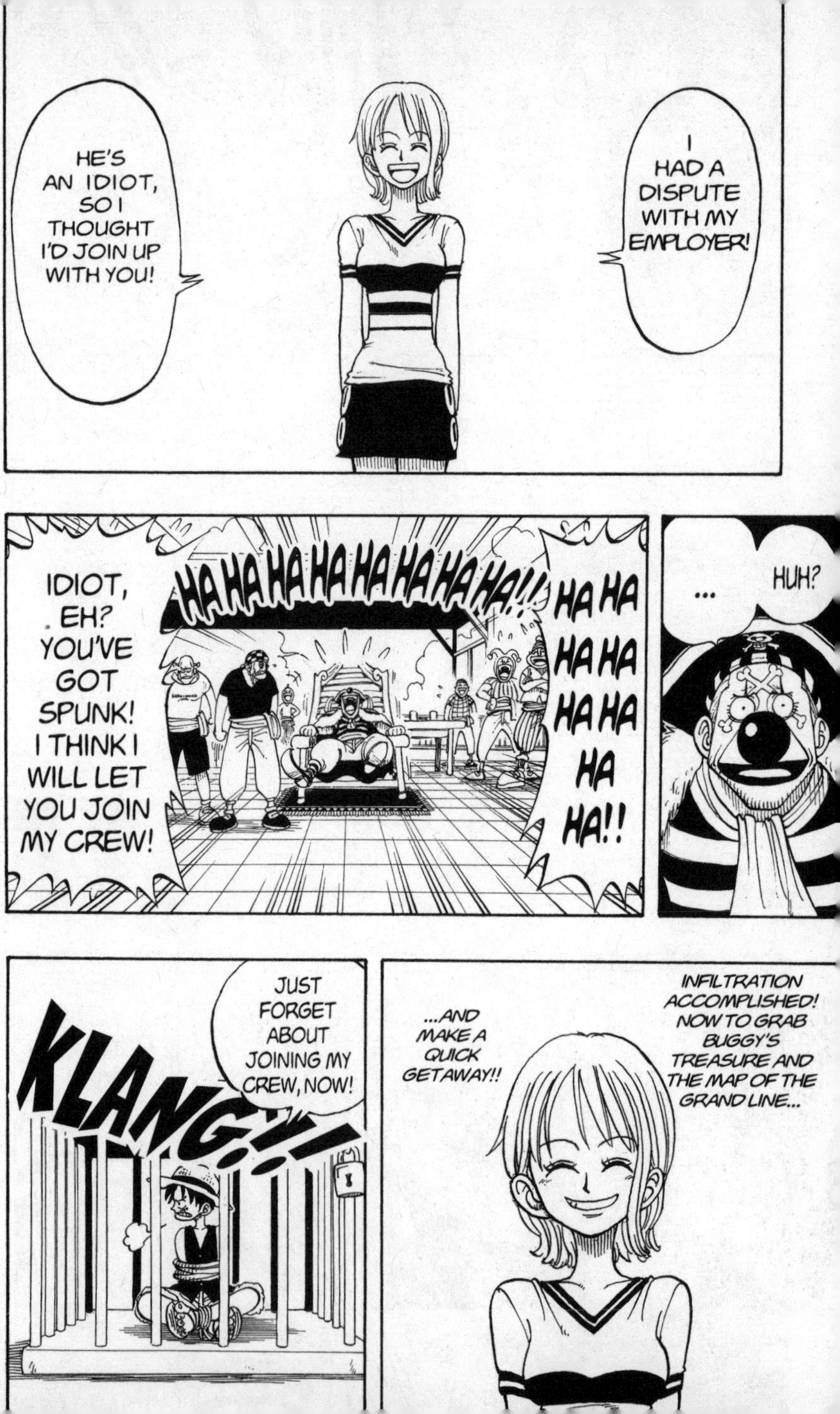
I HAD A DISPUTE WITH MY EMPLOYER!
HE'S AN IDIOT, SO I THOUGHT I'D JOIN UP WITH YOU!
HUH?
...
HA HA HA HA HA HA HA HA HA!!
HAHAHAHAHAHAHAHAHA!!
IDIOT, EH? YOU'VE GOT SPUNK! I THINK I WILL LET YOU JOIN MY CREW!
INFILTRATION ACCOMPLISHED! NOW TO GRAB BUGGY'S TREASURE AND THE MAP OF THE GRAND LINE...
...AND MAKE A QUICK GETAWAY!!
JUST FORGET ABOUT JOINING MY CREW, NOW!
KLANG!!

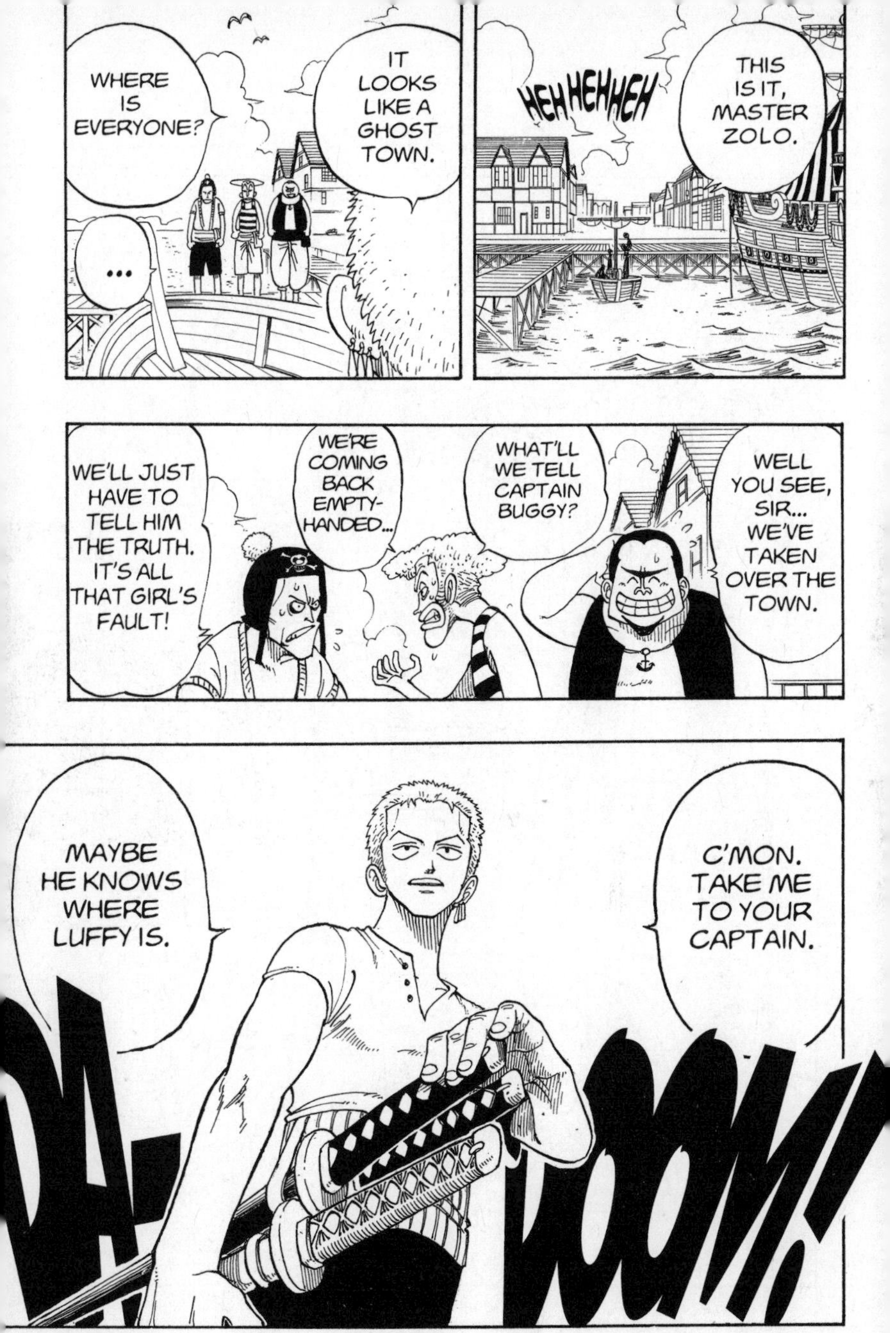
HEH HEHHEH
THIS IS IT, MASTER ZOLO.
IT LOOKS LIKE A GHOST TOWN.
WHERE IS EVERYONE?
...
WELL YOU SEE, SIR... WE'VE TAKEN OVER THE TOWN.
WHAT'LL WE TELL CAPTAIN BUGGY?
WE'RE COMING BACK EMPTY-HANDED...
WE'LL JUST HAVE TO TELL HIM THE TRUTH. IT'S ALL THAT GIRL'S FAULT!
C'MON. TAKE ME TO YOUR CAPTAIN.
MAYBE HE KNOWS WHERE LUFFY IS.
DA-DOOM!!

One Piece Rough Sketch!

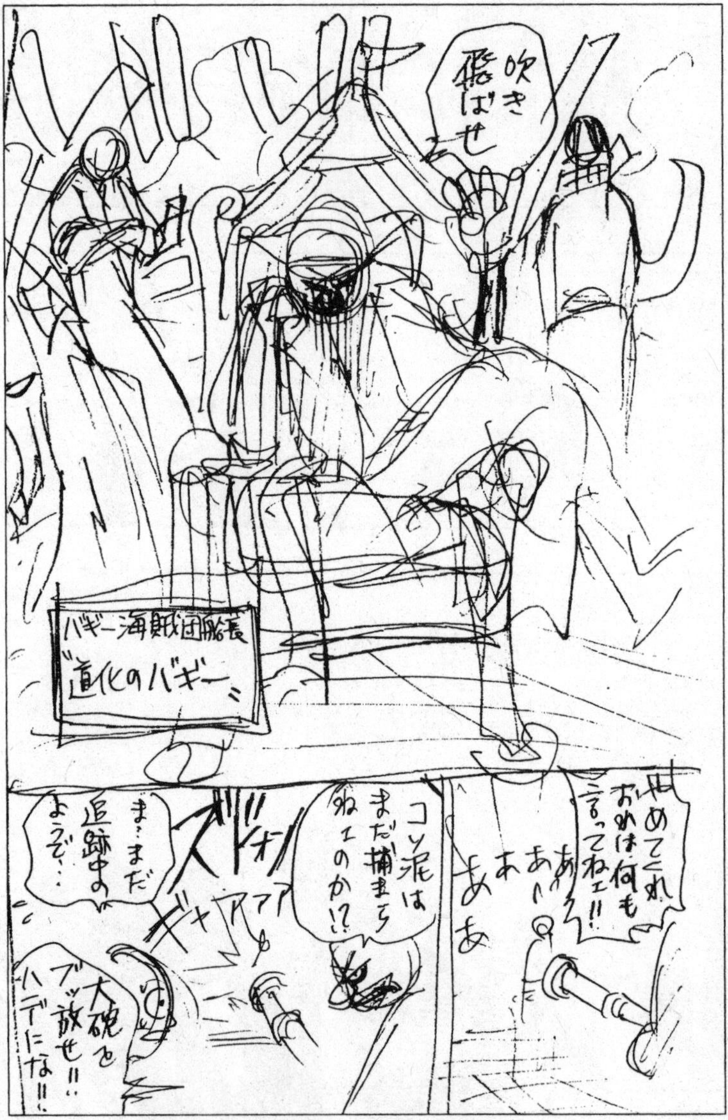
吹き飛ばせ
バギー海賊団船長
道化のバギー
やめてくれ おれは何も言ってねェ!!
あああああ
コソ泥はまだ捕まらねェのか!?
ま…まだ追跡中のようで…
ズドォン
ギャアアア
大砲をブッ放せ!! ハデにな!!

Chapter 10:
INCIDENT AT THE TAVERN

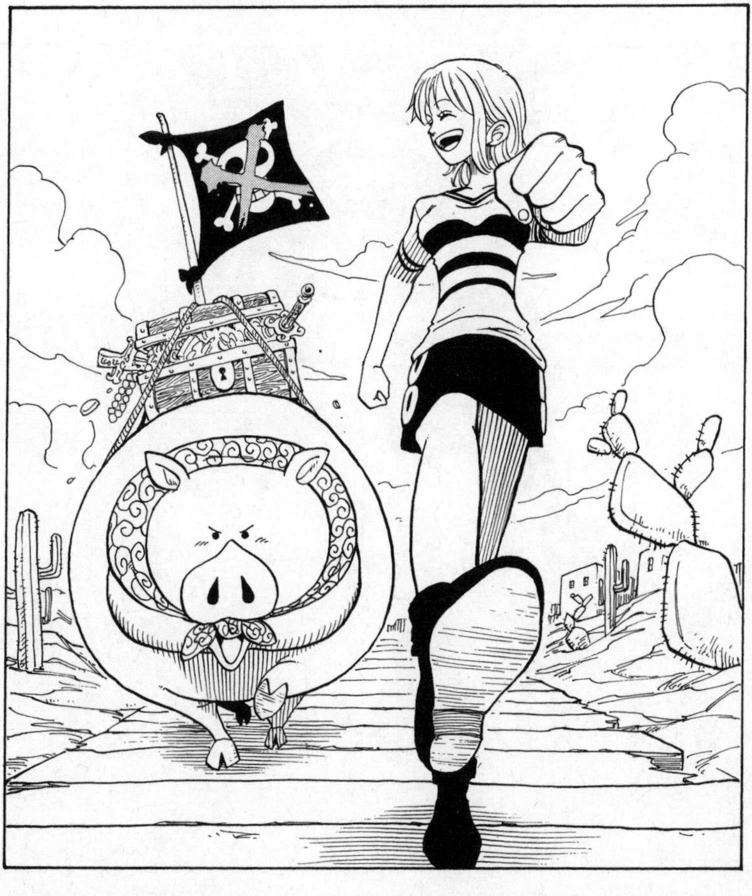

READ THIS WAY

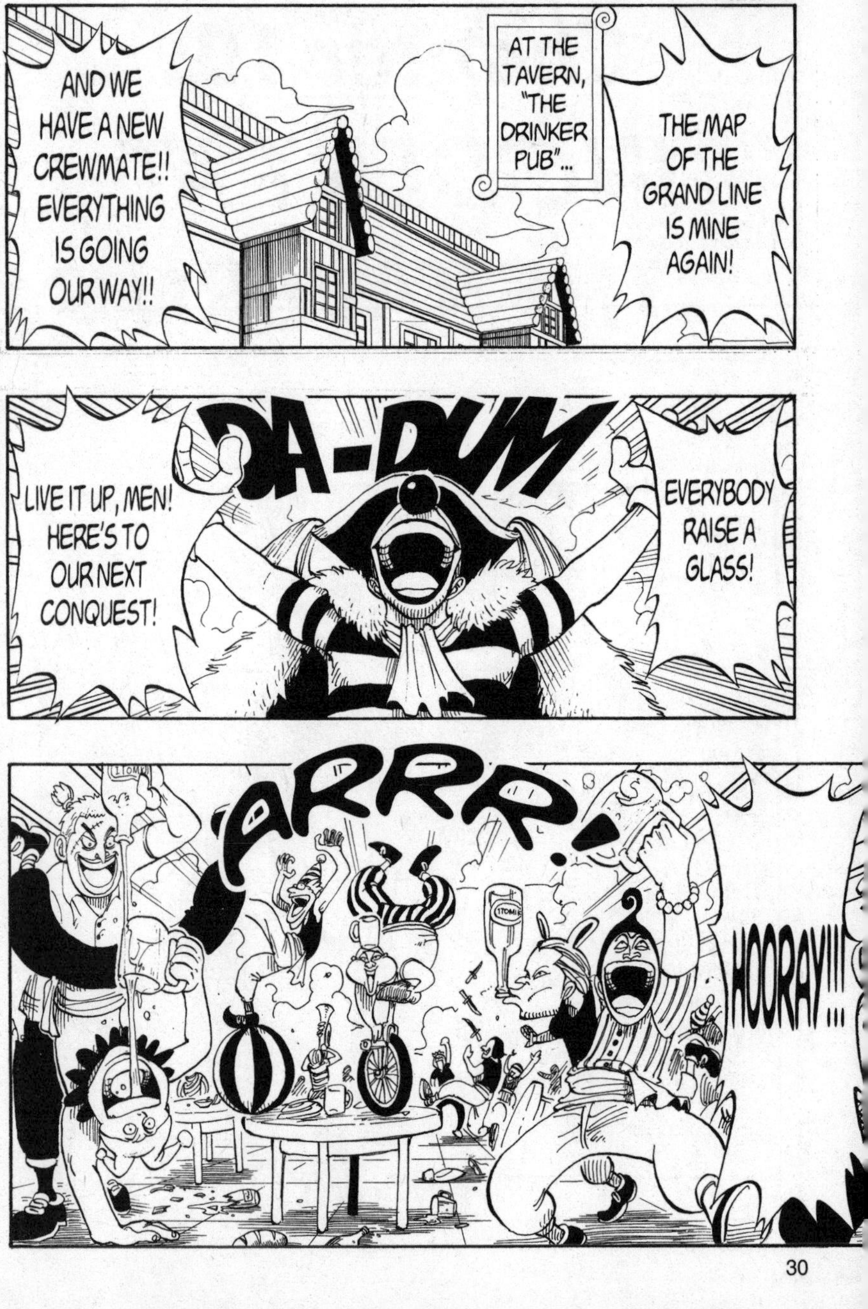
THE MAP OF THE GRAND LINE IS MINE AGAIN!
AT THE TAVERN, "THE DRINKER PUB"...
AND WE HAVE A NEW CREWMATE!! EVERYTHING IS GOING OUR WAY!!
EVERYBODY RAISE A GLASS!
DA-DUM
LIVE IT UP, MEN! HERE'S TO OUR NEXT CONQUEST!
HOORAY!!!
ARRR!

READ THIS WAY

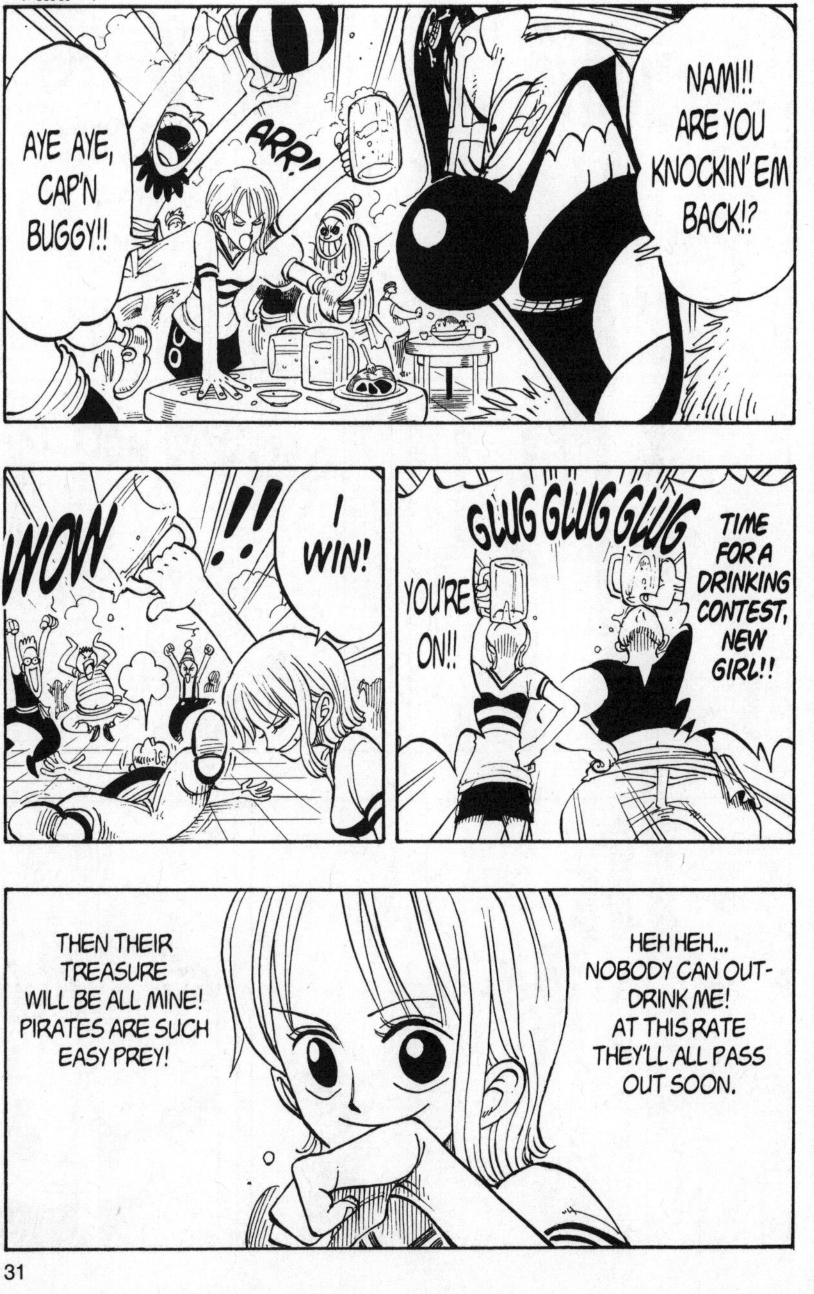

NAMI!! ARE YOU KNOCKIN' EM BACK!?
ARR!
AYE AYE, CAP'N BUGGY!!
TIME FOR A DRINKING CONTEST, NEW GIRL!!
GLUG GLUG GLUG
YOU'RE ON!!
I WIN!
!!
WOW
HEH HEH... NOBODY CAN OUT-DRINK ME! AT THIS RATE THEY'LL ALL PASS OUT SOON.
THEN THEIR TREASURE WILL BE ALL MINE! PIRATES ARE SUCH EASY PREY!

READ THIS WAY

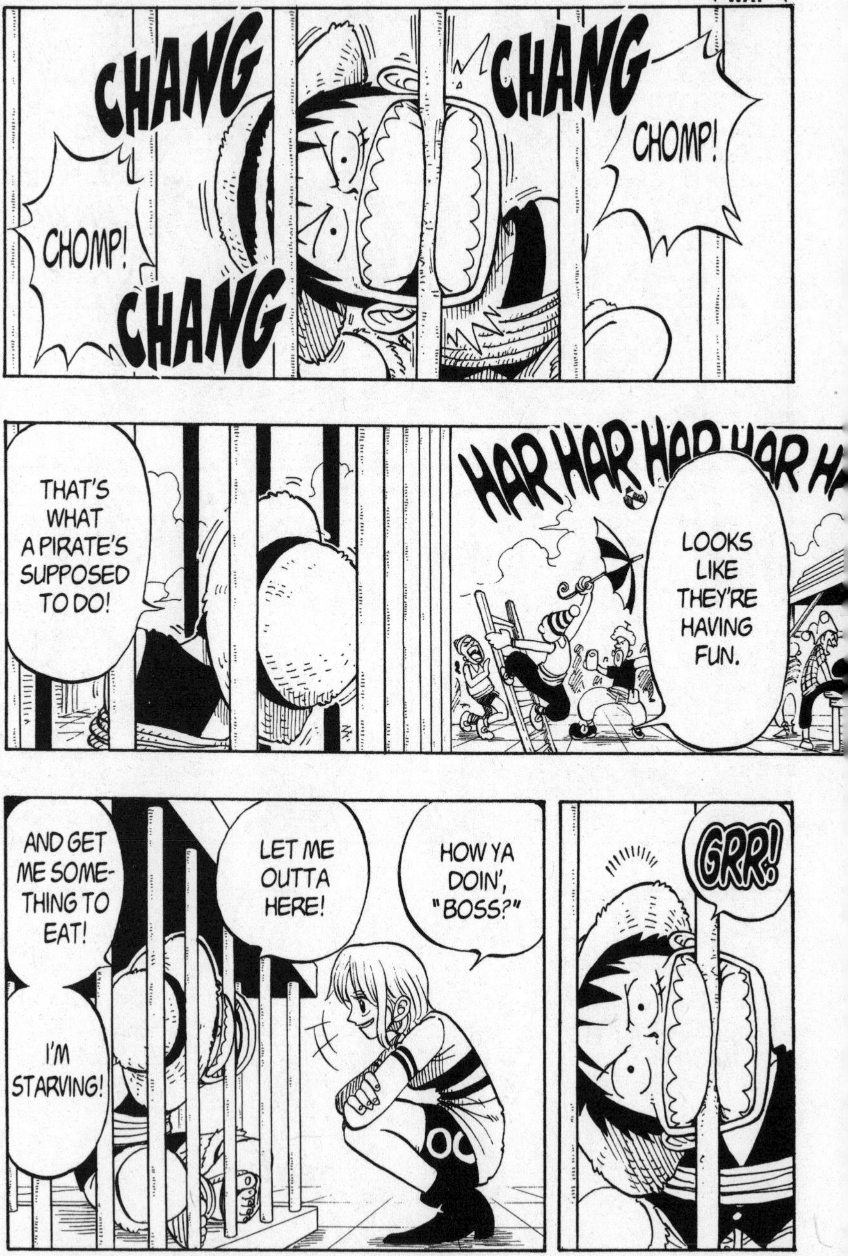
CHANG
CHOMP!
CHANG
CHOMP!
CHANG
HAR HAR HAR HAR
LOOKS LIKE THEY'RE HAVING FUN.
THAT'S WHAT A PIRATE'S SUPPOSED TO DO!
GRR!
HOW YA DOIN', "BOSS?"
LET ME OUTTA HERE!
AND GET ME SOME-THING TO EAT!
I'M STARVING!

READ THIS WAY

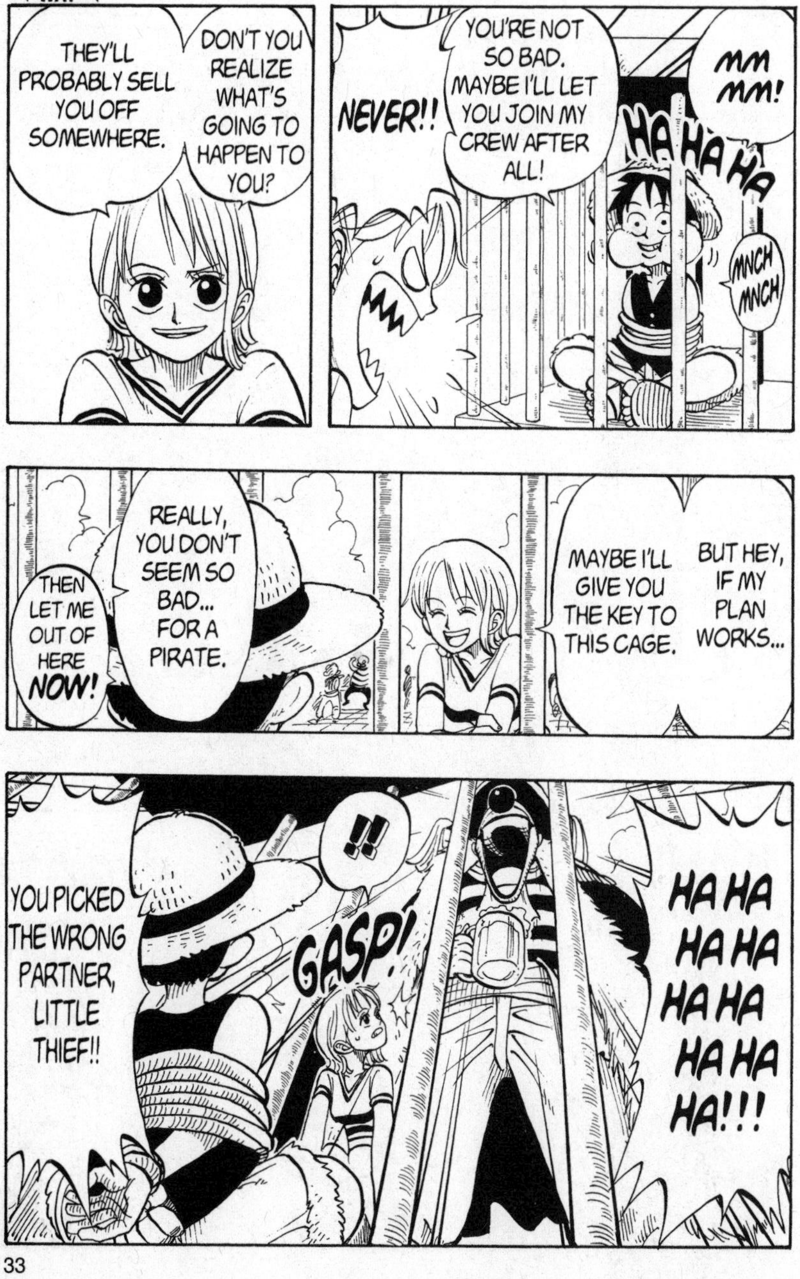
MM MM!
YOU'RE NOT SO BAD. MAYBE I'LL LET YOU JOIN MY CREW AFTER ALL!
HA HA HA
NEVER!!
MNCH MNCH
DON'T YOU REALIZE WHAT'S GOING TO HAPPEN TO YOU?
THEY'LL PROBABLY SELL YOU OFF SOMEWHERE.
BUT HEY, IF MY PLAN WORKS...
MAYBE I'LL GIVE YOU THE KEY TO THIS CAGE.
REALLY, YOU DON'T SEEM SO BAD... FOR A PIRATE.
THEN LET ME OUT OF HERE NOW!
HA HA HA HA HA HA HA HA HA!!!
!!
GASP!
YOU PICKED THE WRONG PARTNER, LITTLE THIEF!!

READ THIS WAY

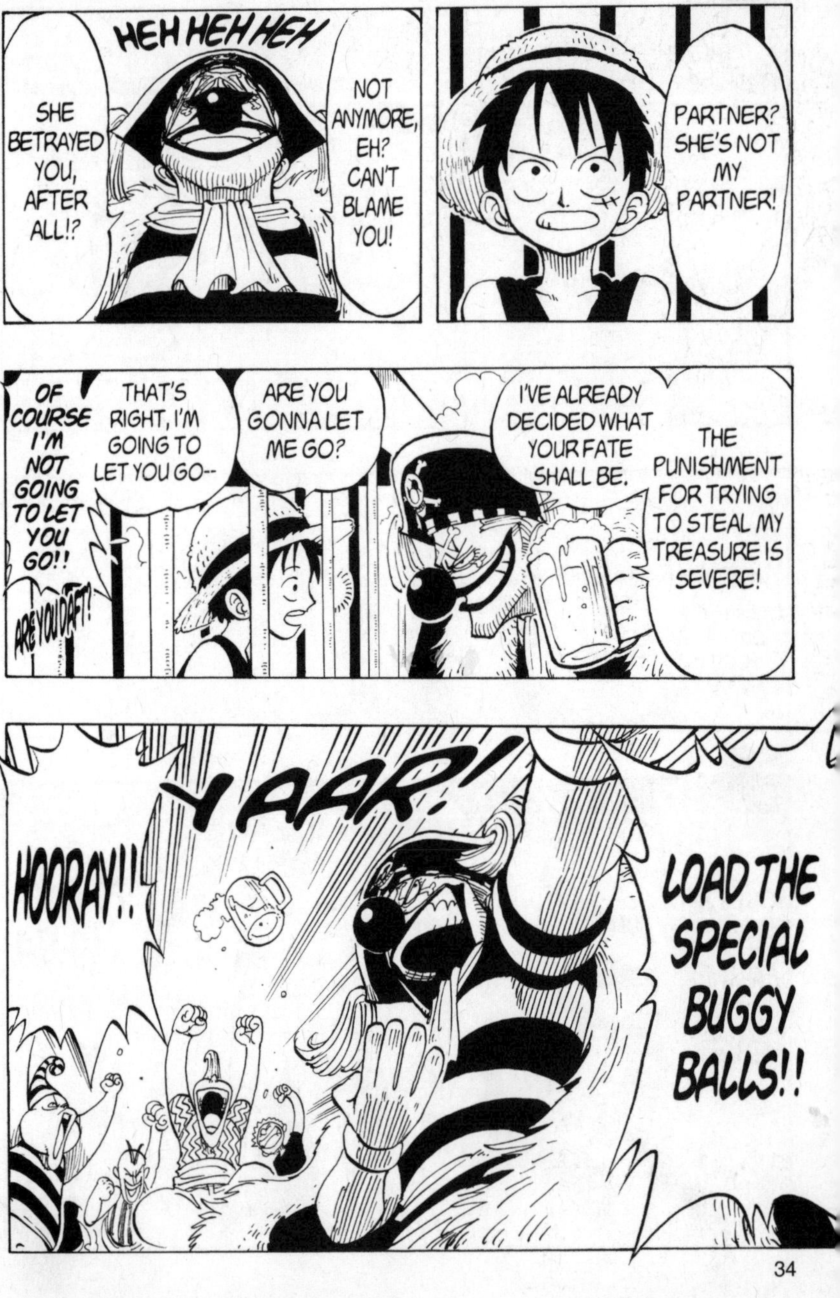
PARTNER? SHE'S NOT MY PARTNER!
HEH HEH HEH
NOT ANYMORE, EH? CAN'T BLAME YOU!
SHE BETRAYED YOU, AFTER ALL!?
THE PUNISHMENT FOR TRYING TO STEAL MY TREASURE IS SEVERE!
I'VE ALREADY DECIDED WHAT YOUR FATE SHALL BE.
ARE YOU GONNA LET ME GO?
THAT'S RIGHT, I'M GOING TO LET YOU GO--
OF COURSE I'M NOT GOING TO LET YOU GO!!
ARE YOU DAFT!
LOAD THE SPECIAL BUGGY BALLS!!
YAAR!
HOORAY!!

READ THIS WAY

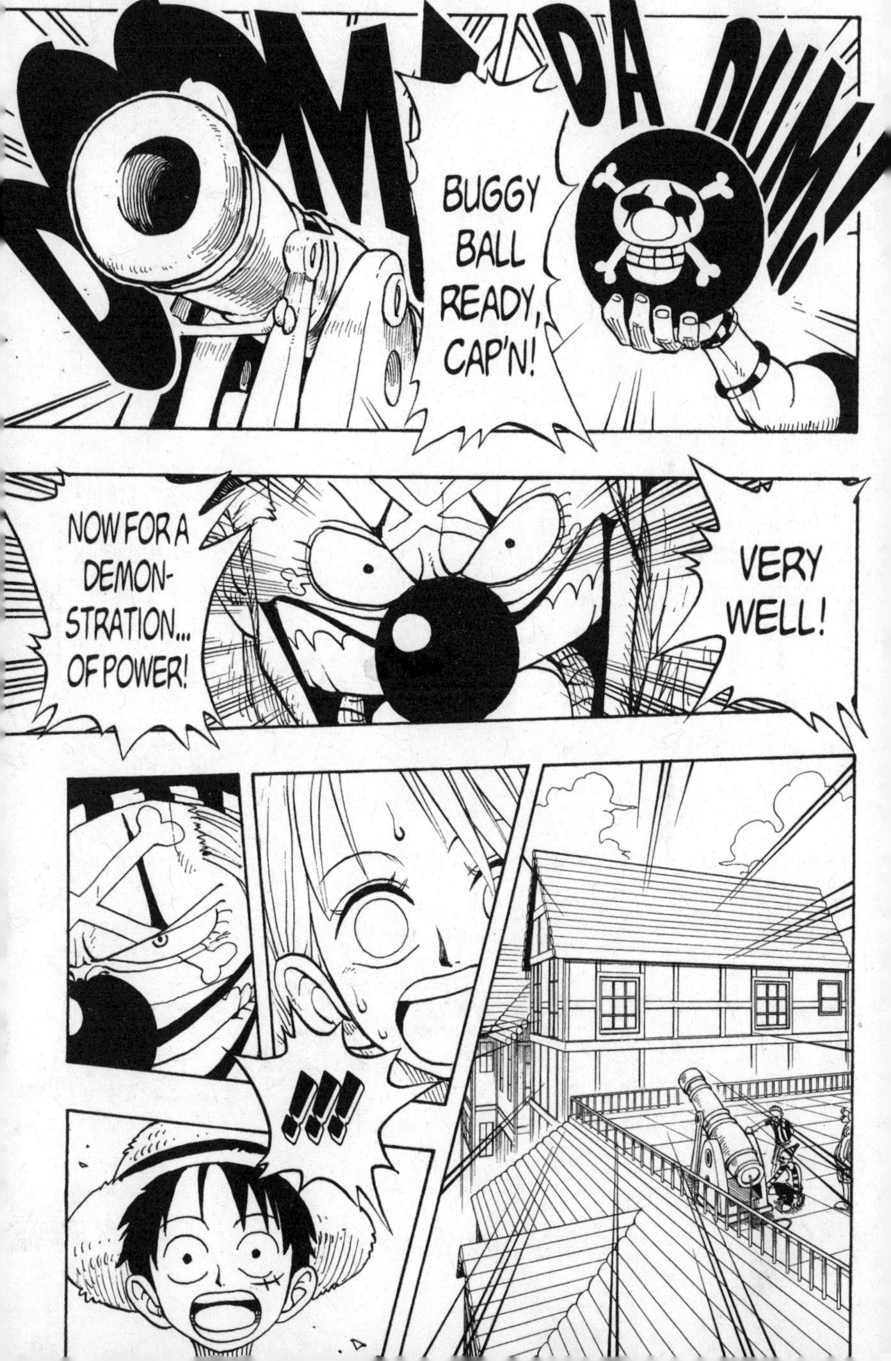
DA DUM!!
BUGGY BALL READY, CAP'N!
BOOM
VERY WELL!
NOW FOR A DEMON-STRATION... OF POWER!
!!!

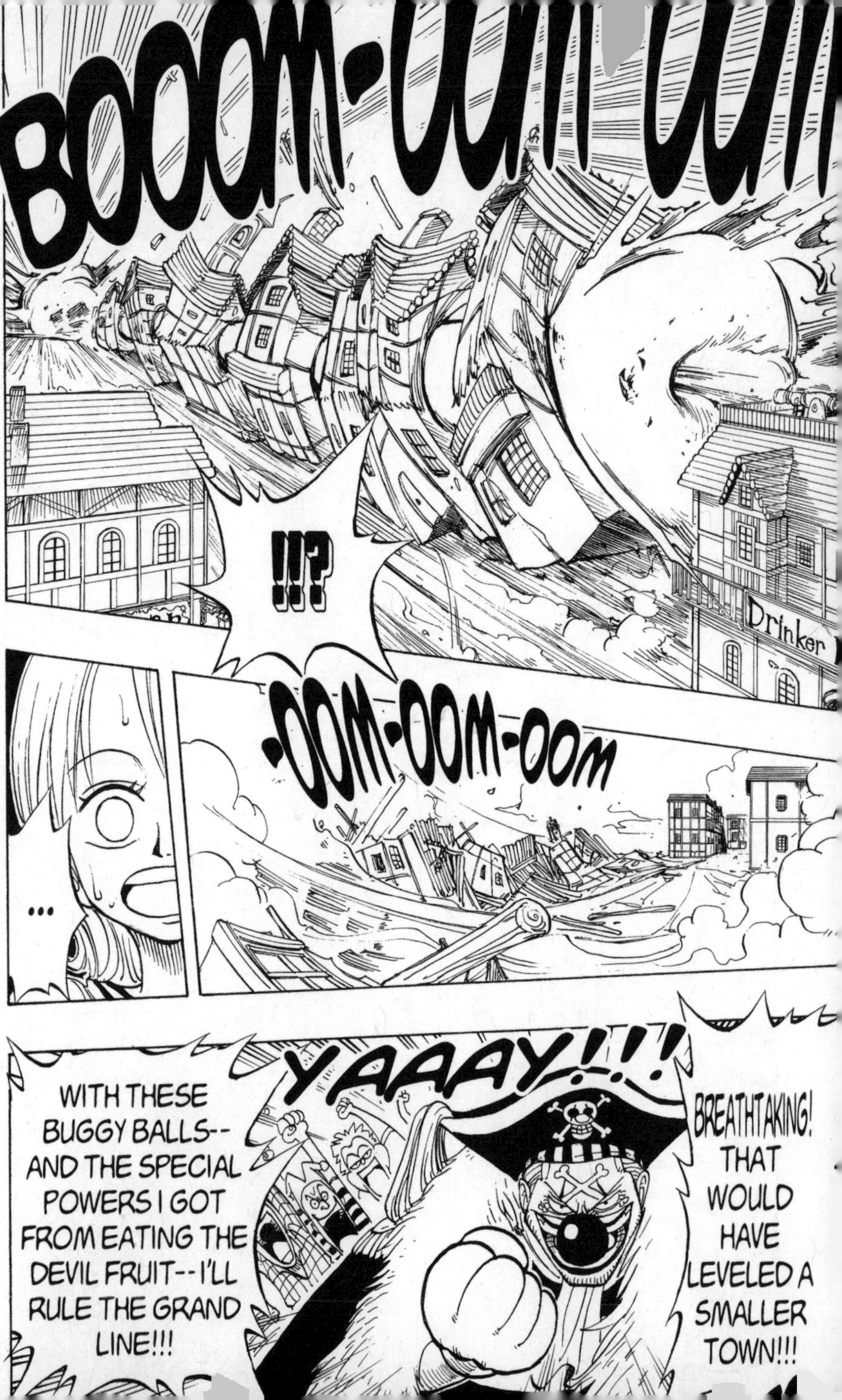
BOOM-UUM-UUM
!!?
Drinker
-OOM-OOM-OOM
...
YAAAY!!!
BREATHTAKING! THAT WOULD HAVE LEVELED A SMALLER TOWN!!!
WITH THESE BUGGY BALLS-- AND THE SPECIAL POWERS I GOT FROM EATING THE DEVIL FRUIT--I'LL RULE THE GRAND LINE!!!

READ THIS WAY

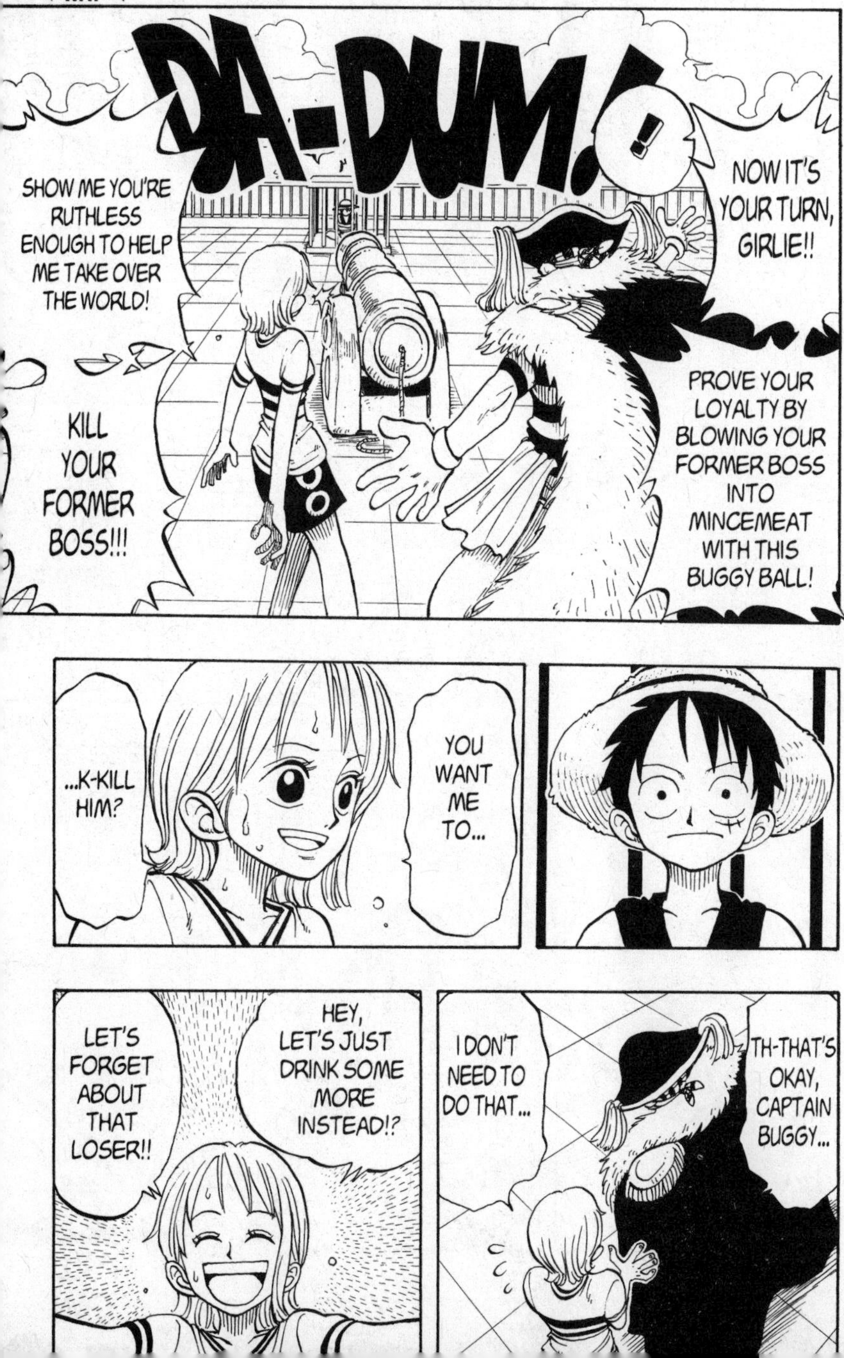
DA-DUM!
NOW IT'S YOUR TURN, GIRLIE!!
PROVE YOUR LOYALTY BY BLOWING YOUR FORMER BOSS INTO MINCEMEAT WITH THIS BUGGY BALL!
SHOW ME YOU'RE RUTHLESS ENOUGH TO HELP ME TAKE OVER THE WORLD!
KILL YOUR FORMER BOSS!!!
YOU WANT ME TO...
...K-KILL HIM?
TH-THAT'S OKAY, CAPTAIN BUGGY...
I DON'T NEED TO DO THAT...
HEY, LET'S JUST DRINK SOME MORE INSTEAD!?
LET'S FORGET ABOUT THAT LOSER!!

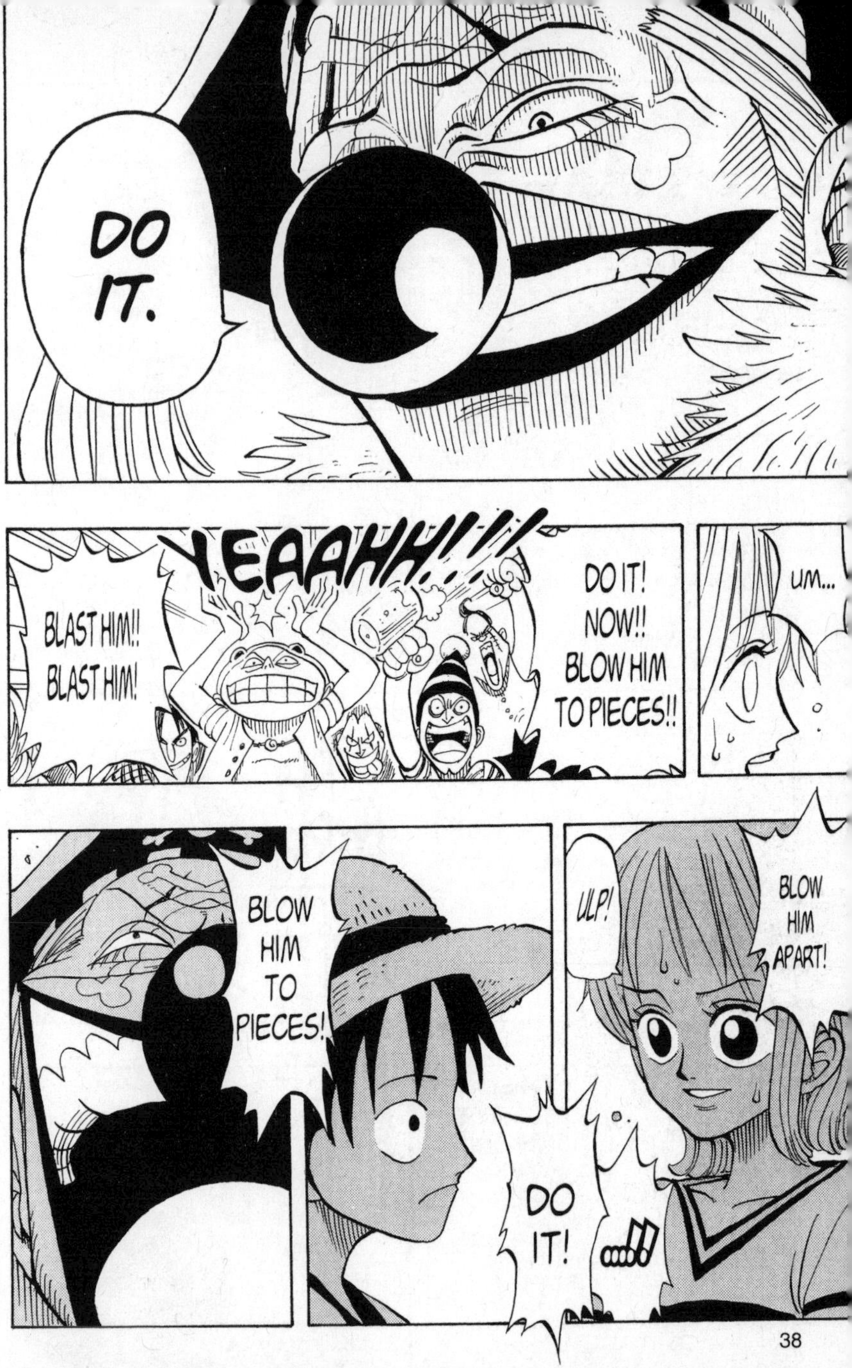
DO IT.
UM...
DO IT! NOW!! BLOW HIM TO PIECES!!
YEAAHH!!!!
BLAST HIM!! BLAST HIM!
BLOW HIM APART!
ULP!
...!!
DO IT!
BLOW HIM TO PIECES!

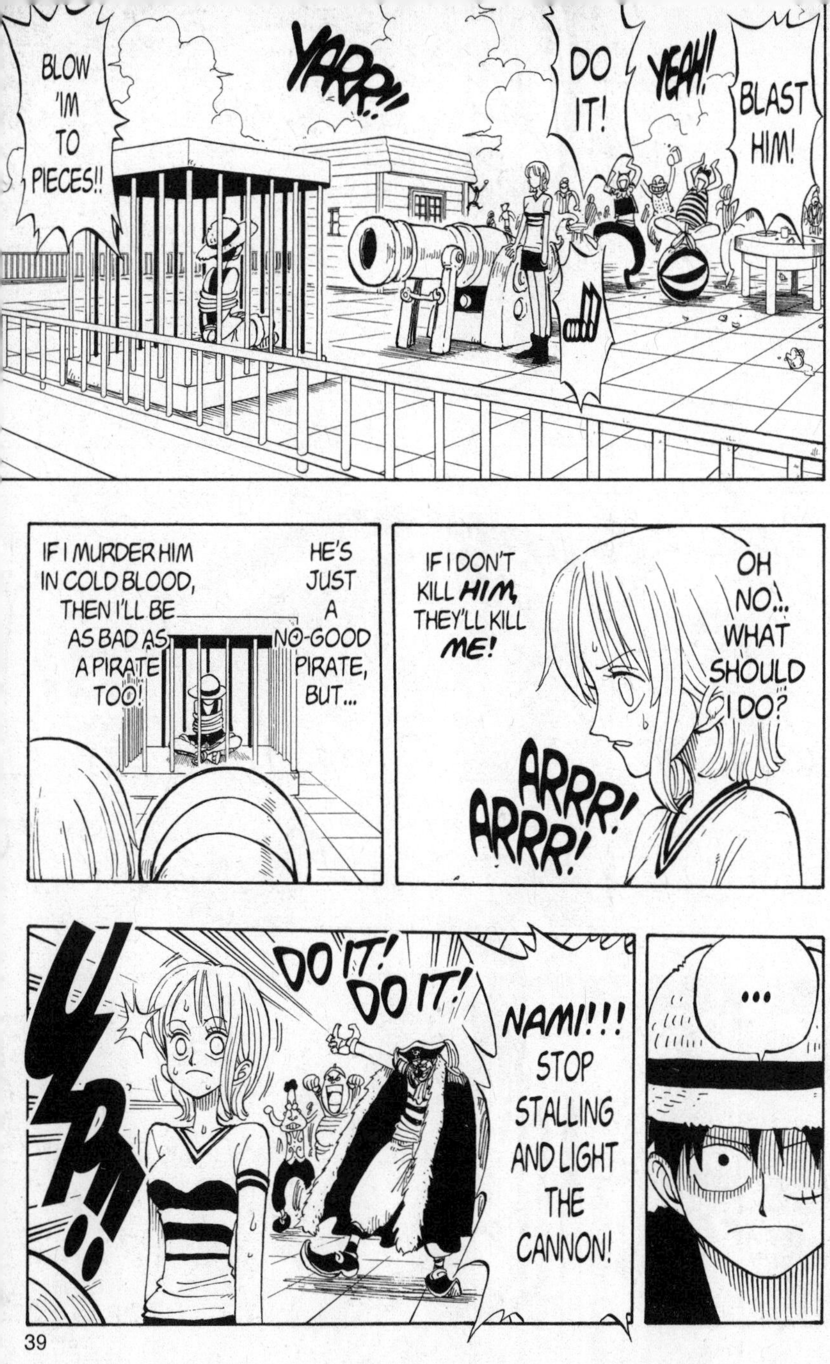
BLAST HIM!
YEAH!
DO IT!
YARR?!!
BLOW 'IM TO PIECES!!
OH NO... WHAT SHOULD I DO?
IF I DON'T KILL HIM, THEY'LL KILL ME!
ARRR! ARRR!
HE'S JUST A NO-GOOD PIRATE, BUT...
IF I MURDER HIM IN COLD BLOOD, THEN I'LL BE AS BAD AS A PIRATE TOO!
...
NAMI!!! STOP STALLING AND LIGHT THE CANNON!
DO IT! DO IT!

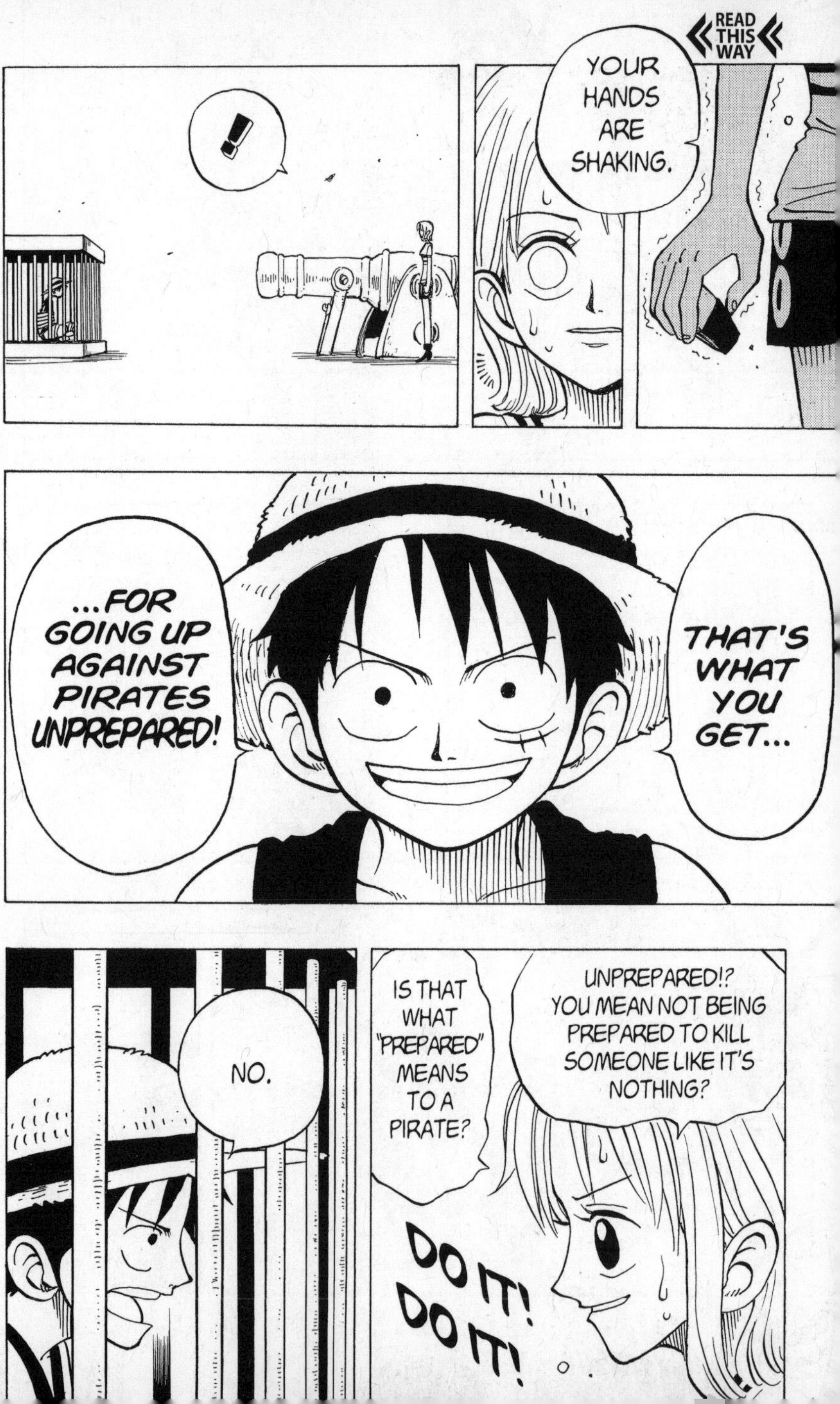
READ THIS WAY
YOUR HANDS ARE SHAKING.
!
THAT'S WHAT YOU GET...
...FOR GOING UP AGAINST PIRATES UNPREPARED!
UNPREPARED!? YOU MEAN NOT BEING PREPARED TO KILL SOMEONE LIKE IT'S NOTHING?
IS THAT WHAT "PREPARED" MEANS TO A PIRATE?
DO IT! DO IT!
NO.

READ THIS WAY

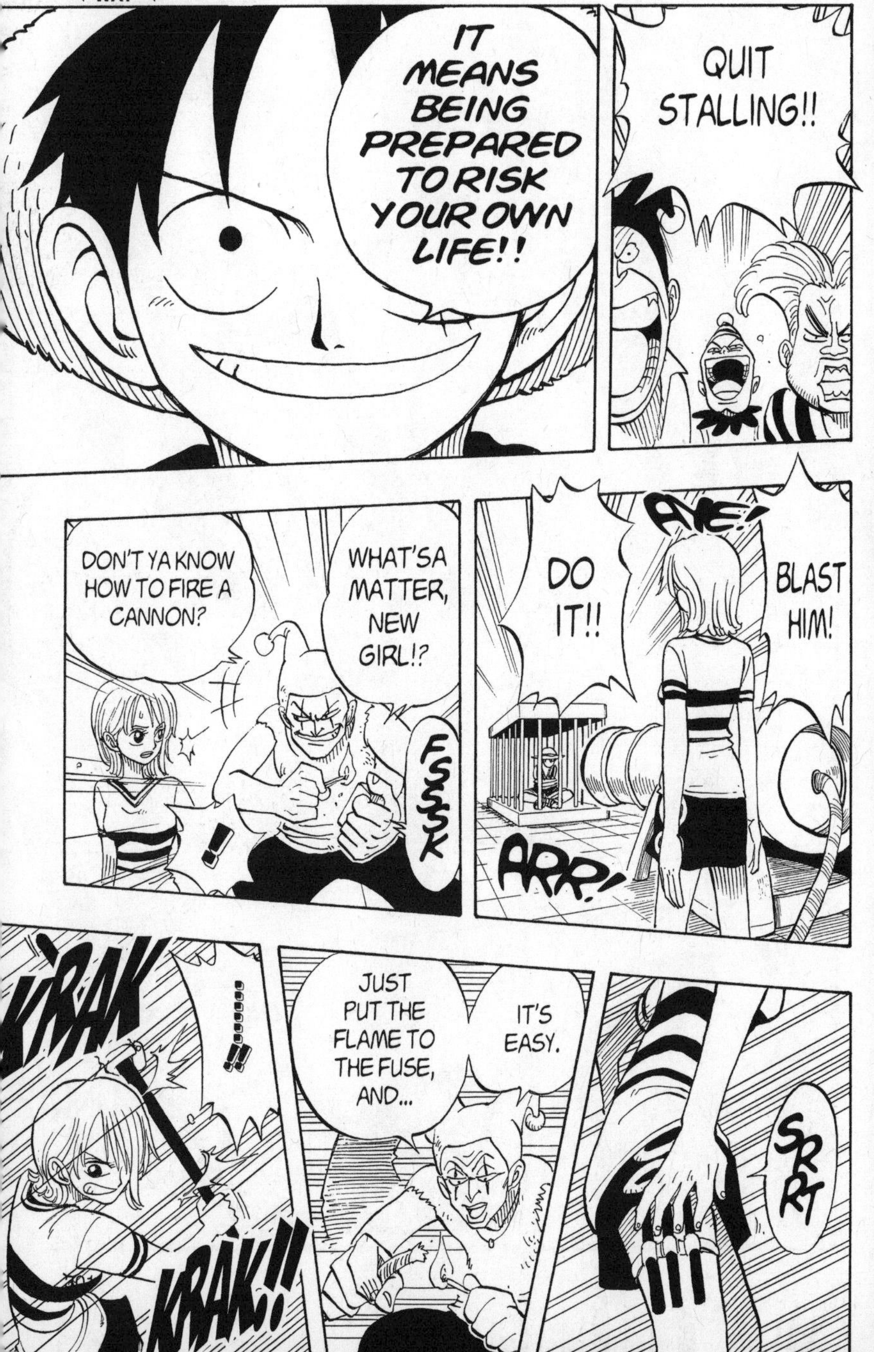
QUIT STALLING!!
IT MEANS BEING PREPARED TO RISK YOUR OWN LIFE!!
AYE!
BLAST HIM!
DO IT!!
ARR!
WHAT'SA MATTER, NEW GIRL!?
DON'T YA KNOW HOW TO FIRE A CANNON?
FSSSK
!
SRRT
IT'S EASY.
JUST PUT THE FLAME TO THE FUSE, AND...
......!!
KRAK
KRAK!!

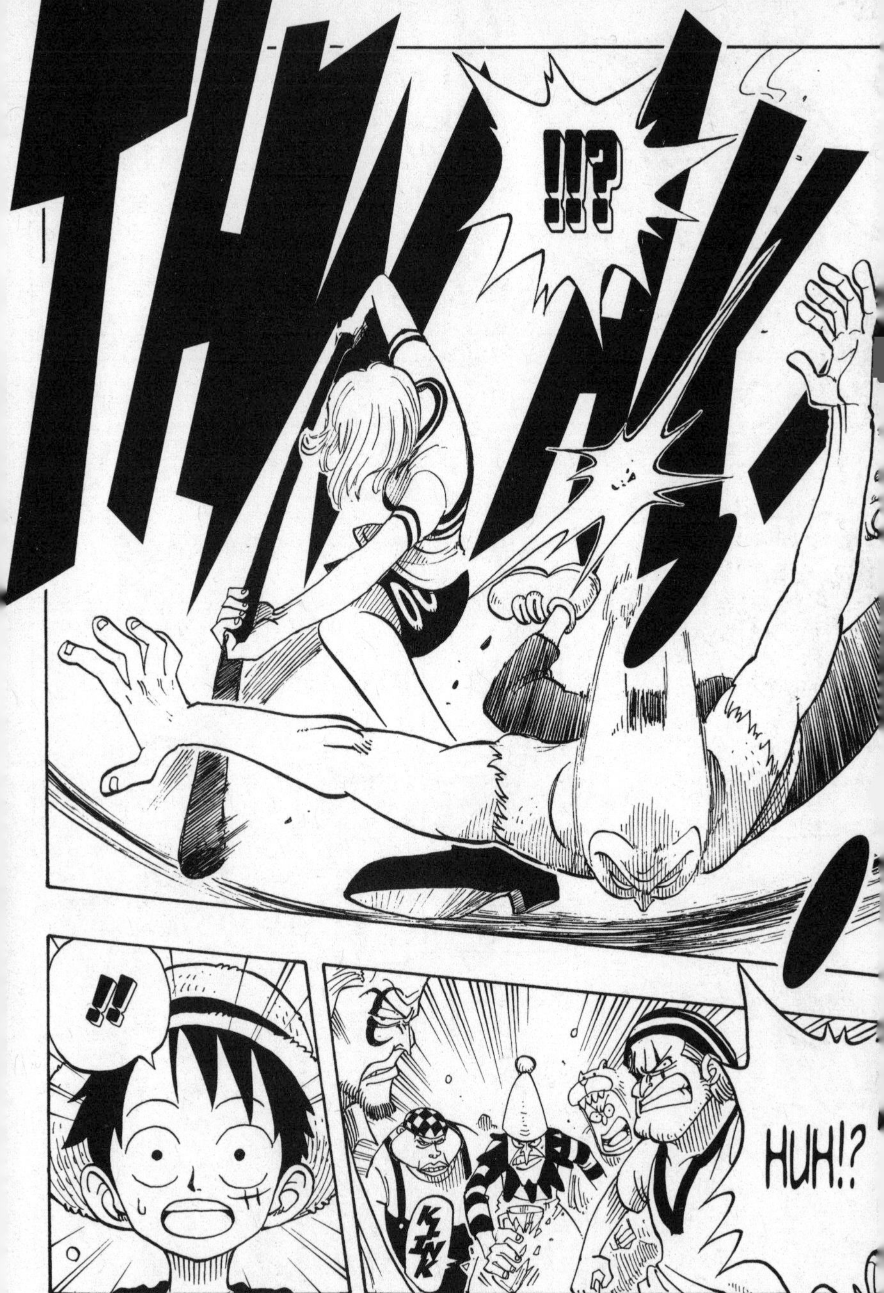
THWACK
!!?
HUH!?
KLINK
!!

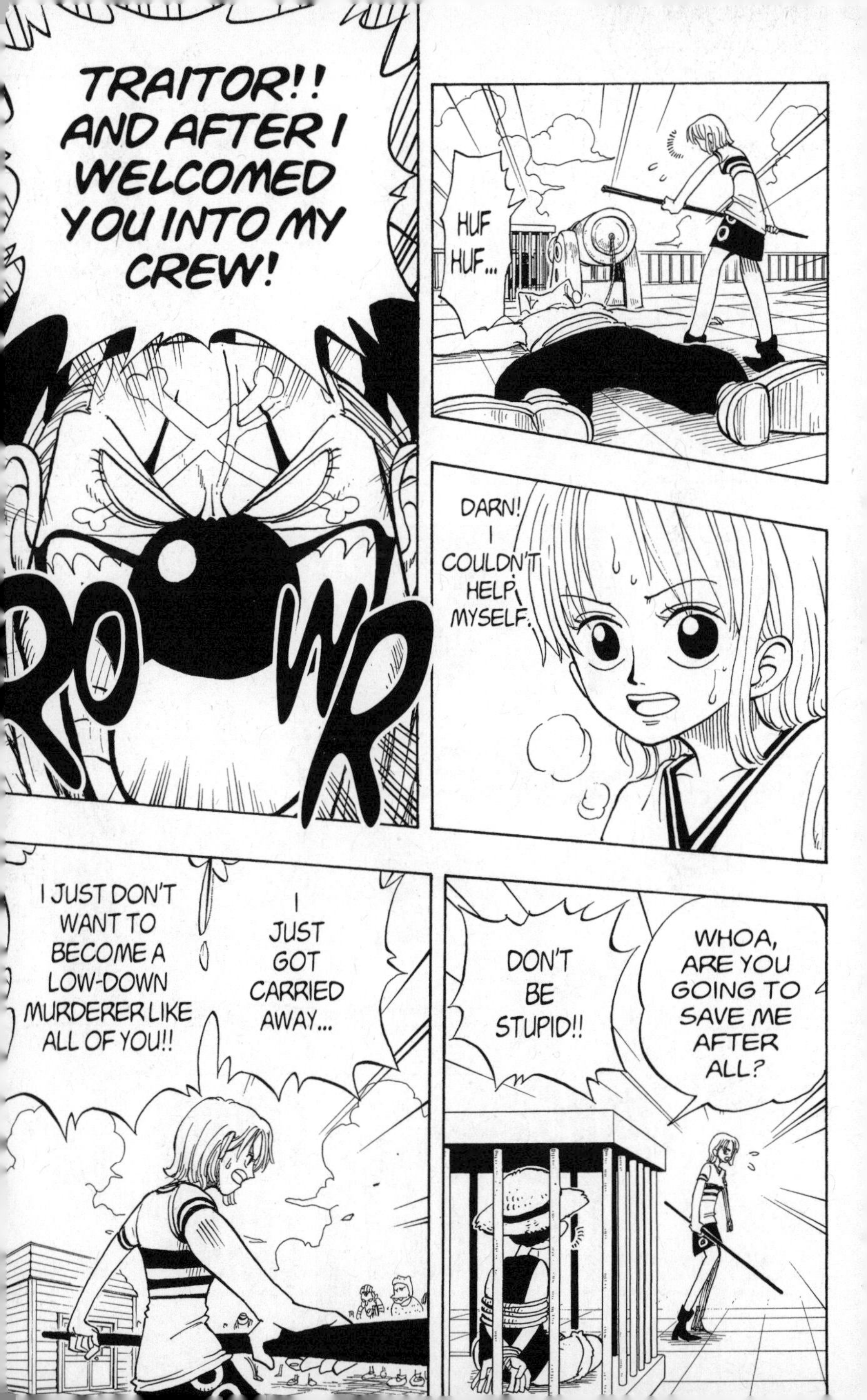
HUF HUF...
DARN! I COULDN'T HELP MYSELF.
TRAITOR!! AND AFTER I WELCOMED YOU INTO MY CREW!
ROWR
WHOA, ARE YOU GOING TO SAVE ME AFTER ALL?
DON'T BE STUPID!!
I JUST GOT CARRIED AWAY...
I JUST DON'T WANT TO BECOME A LOW-DOWN MURDERER LIKE ALL OF YOU!!

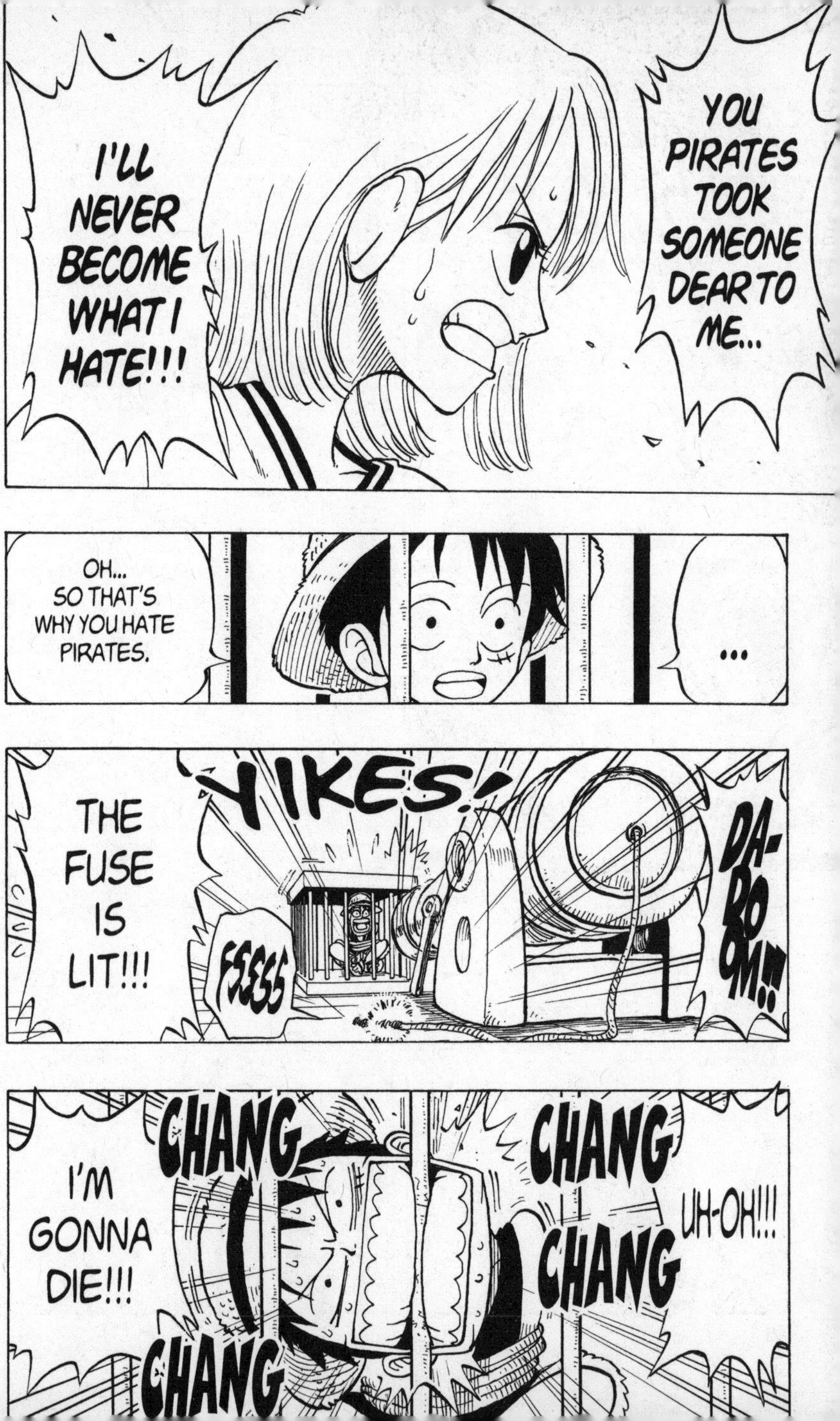
YOU PIRATES TOOK SOMEONE DEAR TO ME...
I'LL NEVER BECOME WHAT I HATE!!!
...
OH... SO THAT'S WHY YOU HATE PIRATES.
DA-BOOM!!
YIKES!
FSSSS
THE FUSE IS LIT!!!
CHANG
UH-OH!!!
CHANG
CHANG
I'M GONNA DIE!!!
CHANG

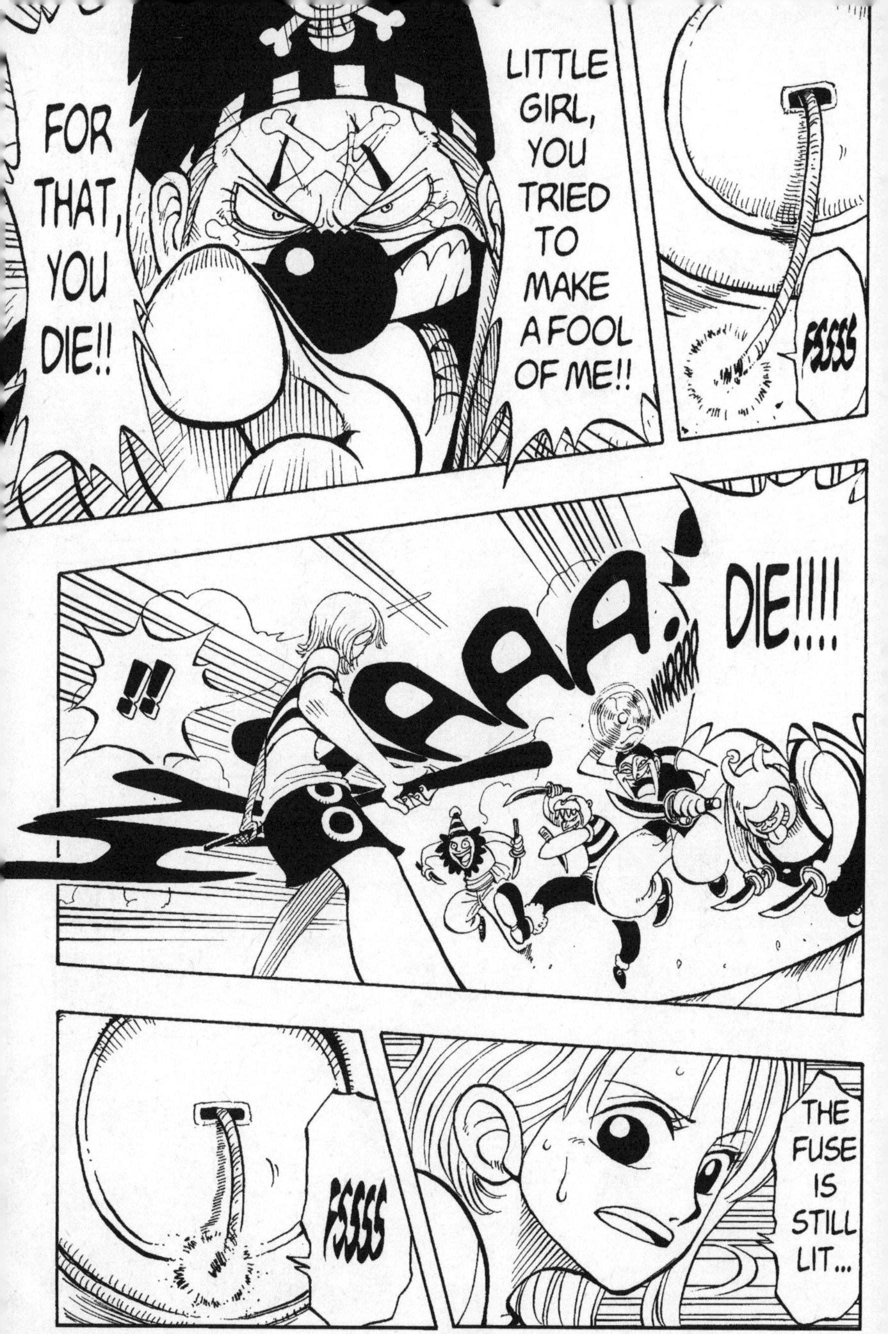
FSSSS
LITTLE GIRL, YOU TRIED TO MAKE A FOOL OF ME!!
FOR THAT, YOU DIE!!
DIE!!!!
AAA
WHRRRR
!!
THE FUSE IS STILL LIT...
FSSSSS

READ THIS WAY

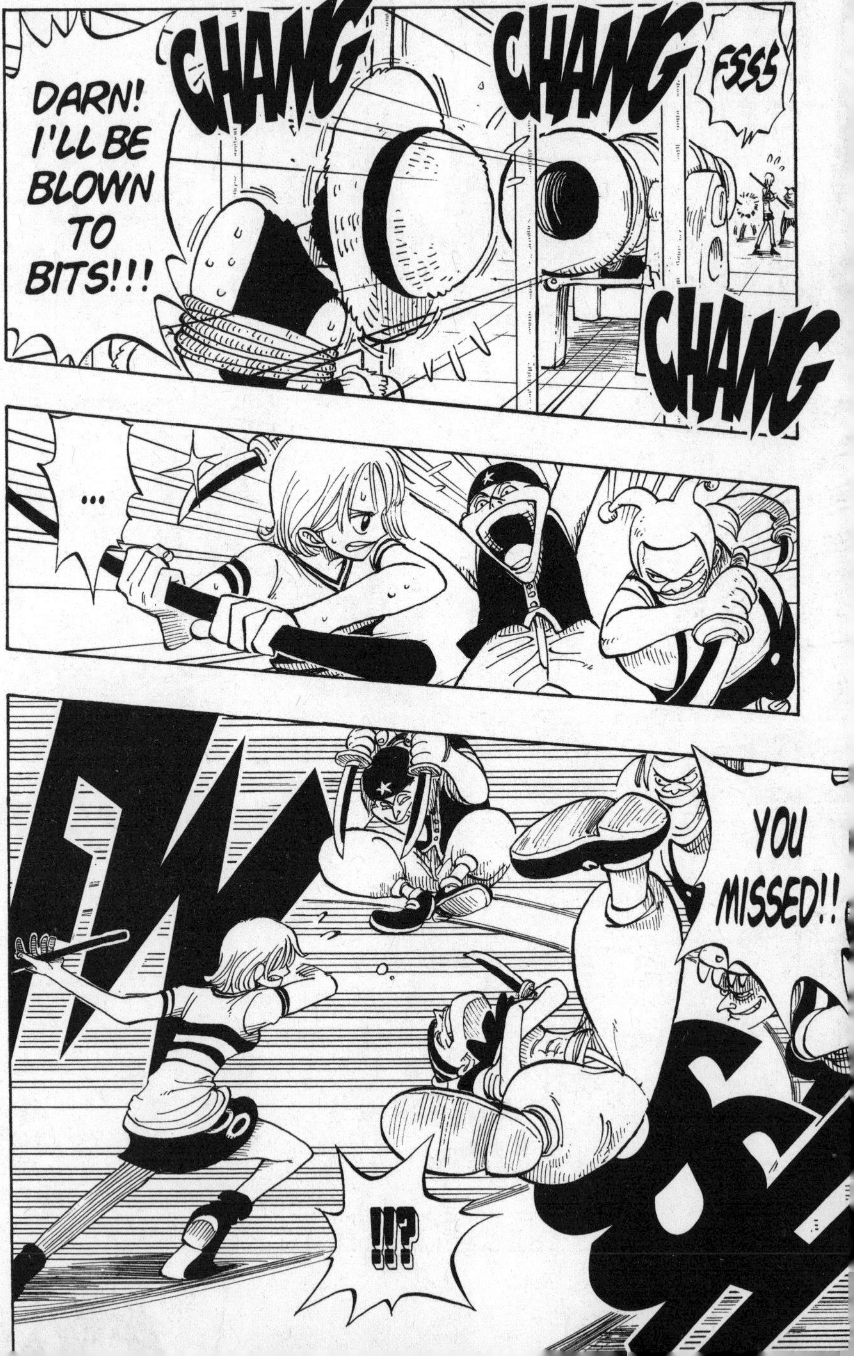
FSSS
CHANG
CHANG
DARN! I'LL BE BLOWN TO BITS!!!
CHANG
...
YOU MISSED!!
!!?

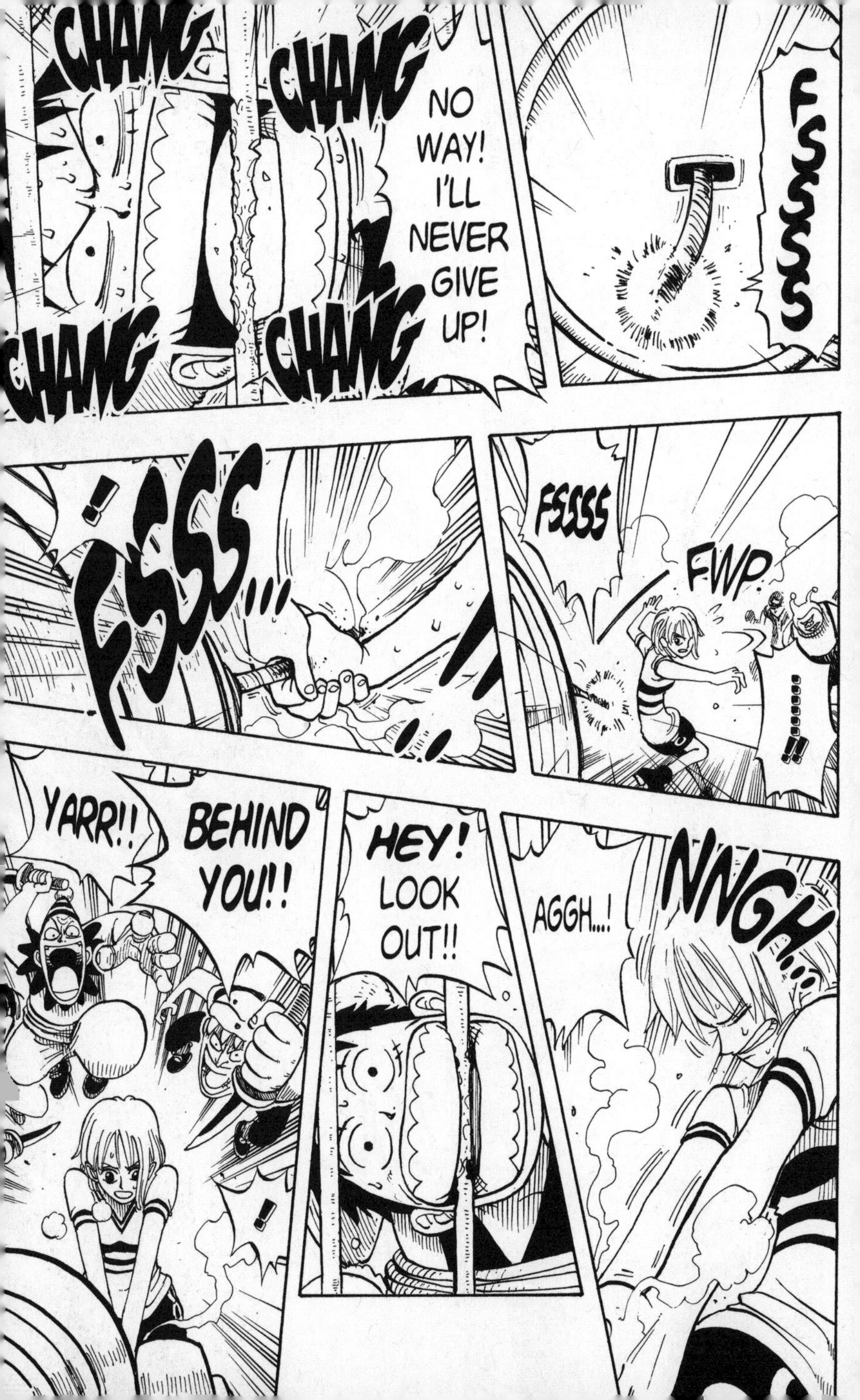
FSSSSS
CHANG
NO WAY! I'LL NEVER GIVE UP!
CHANG
CHANG
CHANG
FSSSS
FWP
FSSS...
NNGH...
AGGH...!
HEY! LOOK OUT!!
BEHIND YOU!!
YARR!!

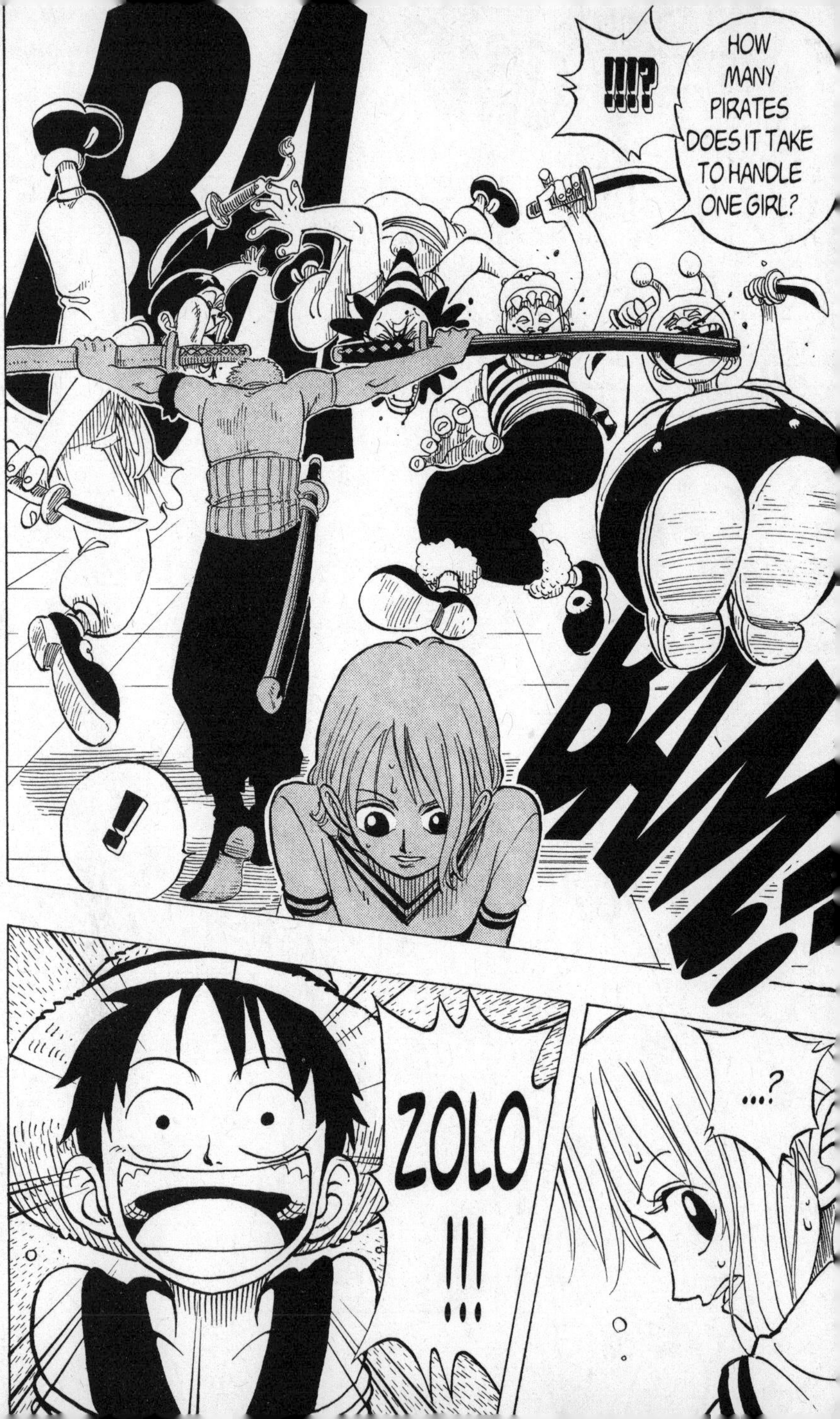
HOW MANY PIRATES DOES IT TAKE TO HANDLE ONE GIRL?
!!!?
BA
BAM
!
...?
ZOLO!!!

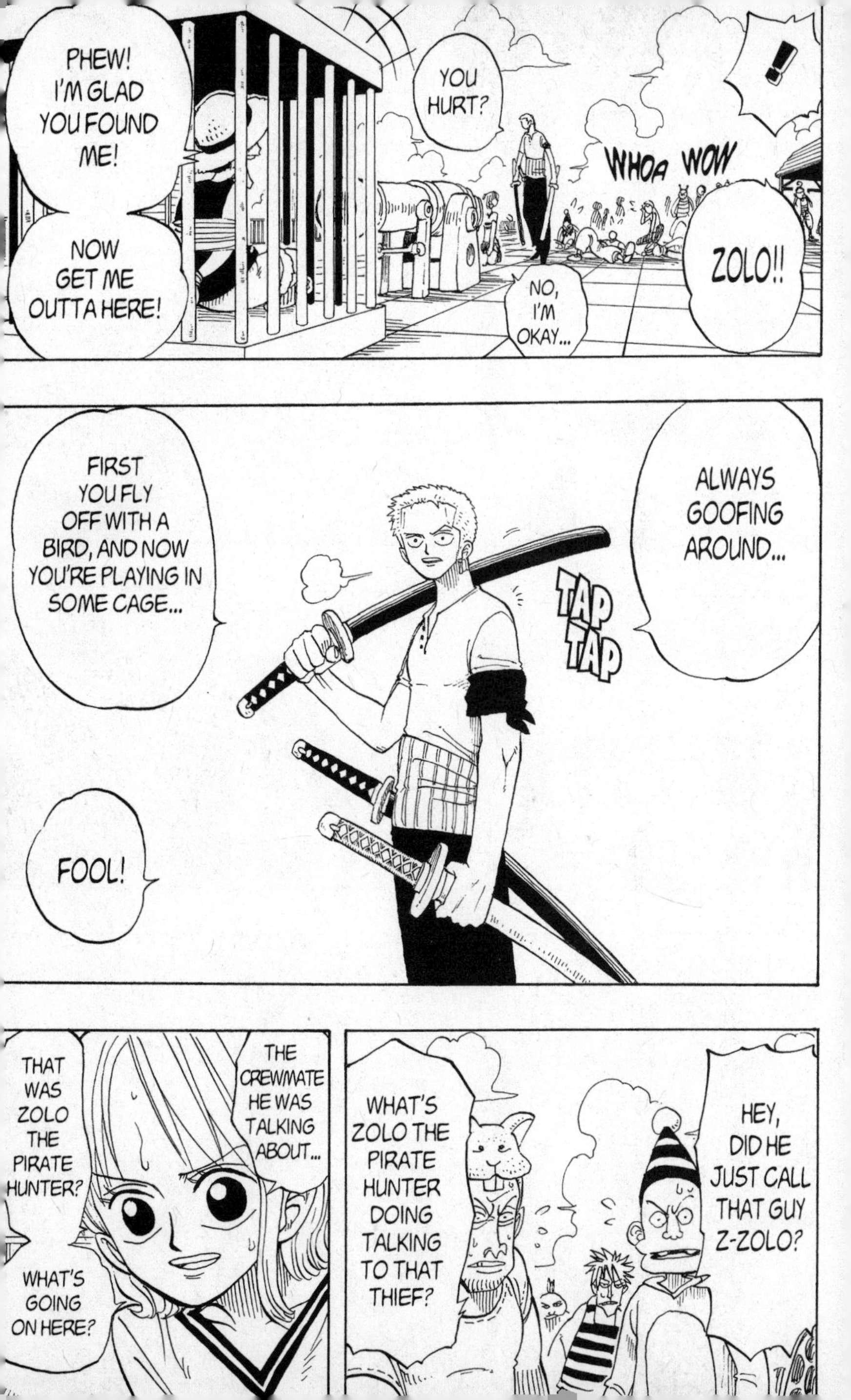
!
WHOA WOW
ZOLO!!
YOU HURT?
NO, I'M OKAY...
PHEW! I'M GLAD YOU FOUND ME!
NOW GET ME OUTTA HERE!
ALWAYS GOOFING AROUND...
TAP TAP
FIRST YOU FLY OFF WITH A BIRD, AND NOW YOU'RE PLAYING IN SOME CAGE...
FOOL!
HEY, DID HE JUST CALL THAT GUY Z-ZOLO?
WHAT'S ZOLO THE PIRATE HUNTER DOING TALKING TO THAT THIEF?
THE CREWMATE HE WAS TALKING ABOUT...
THAT WAS ZOLO THE PIRATE HUNTER?
WHAT'S GOING ON HERE?

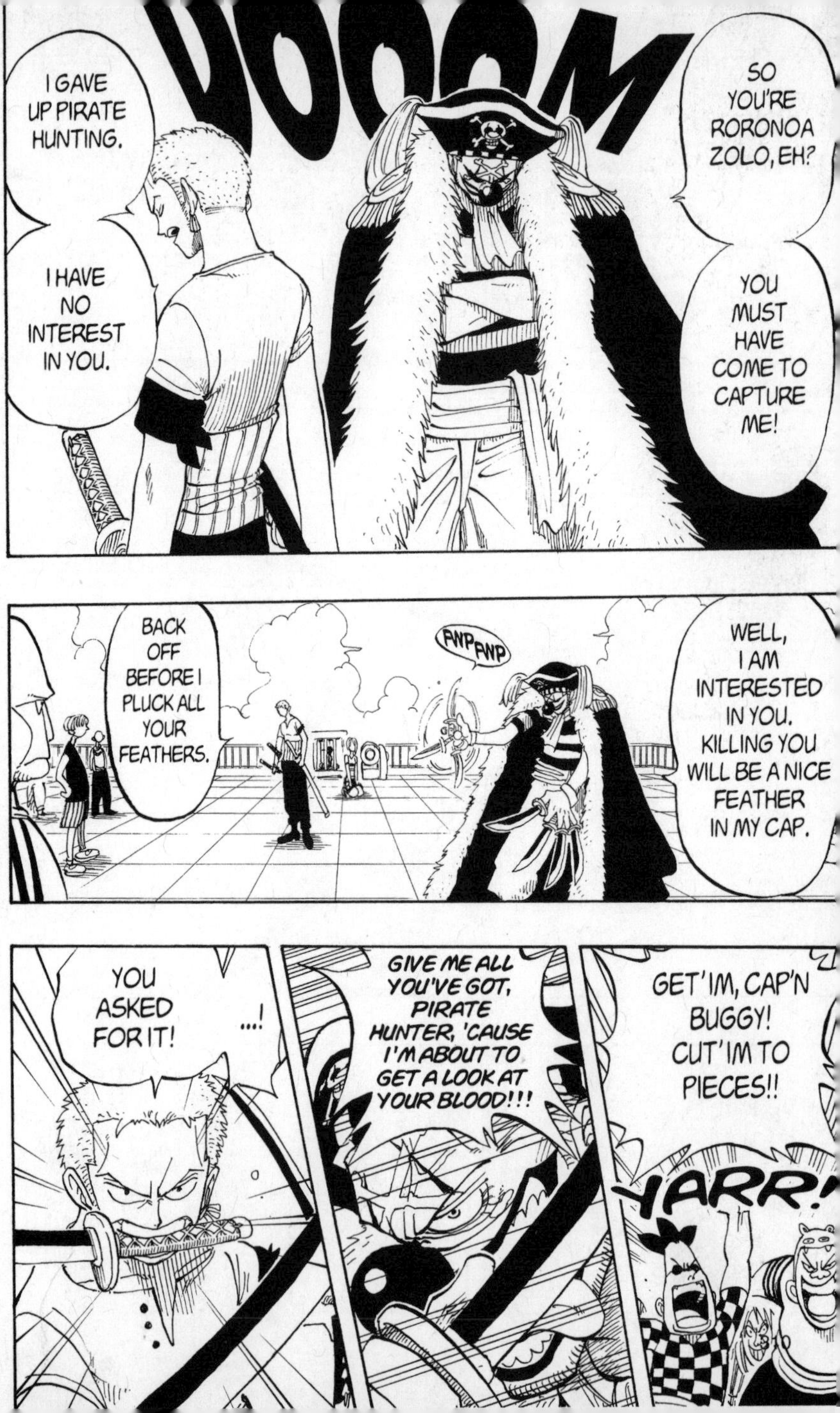
SO YOU'RE RORONOA ZOLO, EH?
YOU MUST HAVE COME TO CAPTURE ME!
VOOOM
I GAVE UP PIRATE HUNTING.
I HAVE NO INTEREST IN YOU.
WELL, I AM INTERESTED IN YOU. KILLING YOU WILL BE A NICE FEATHER IN MY CAP.
FWP FWP
BACK OFF BEFORE I PLUCK ALL YOUR FEATHERS.
GET'IM, CAP'N BUGGY! CUT'IM TO PIECES!!
YARR!
GIVE ME ALL YOU'VE GOT, PIRATE HUNTER, 'CAUSE I'M ABOUT TO GET A LOOK AT YOUR BLOOD!!!
...!
YOU ASKED FOR IT!

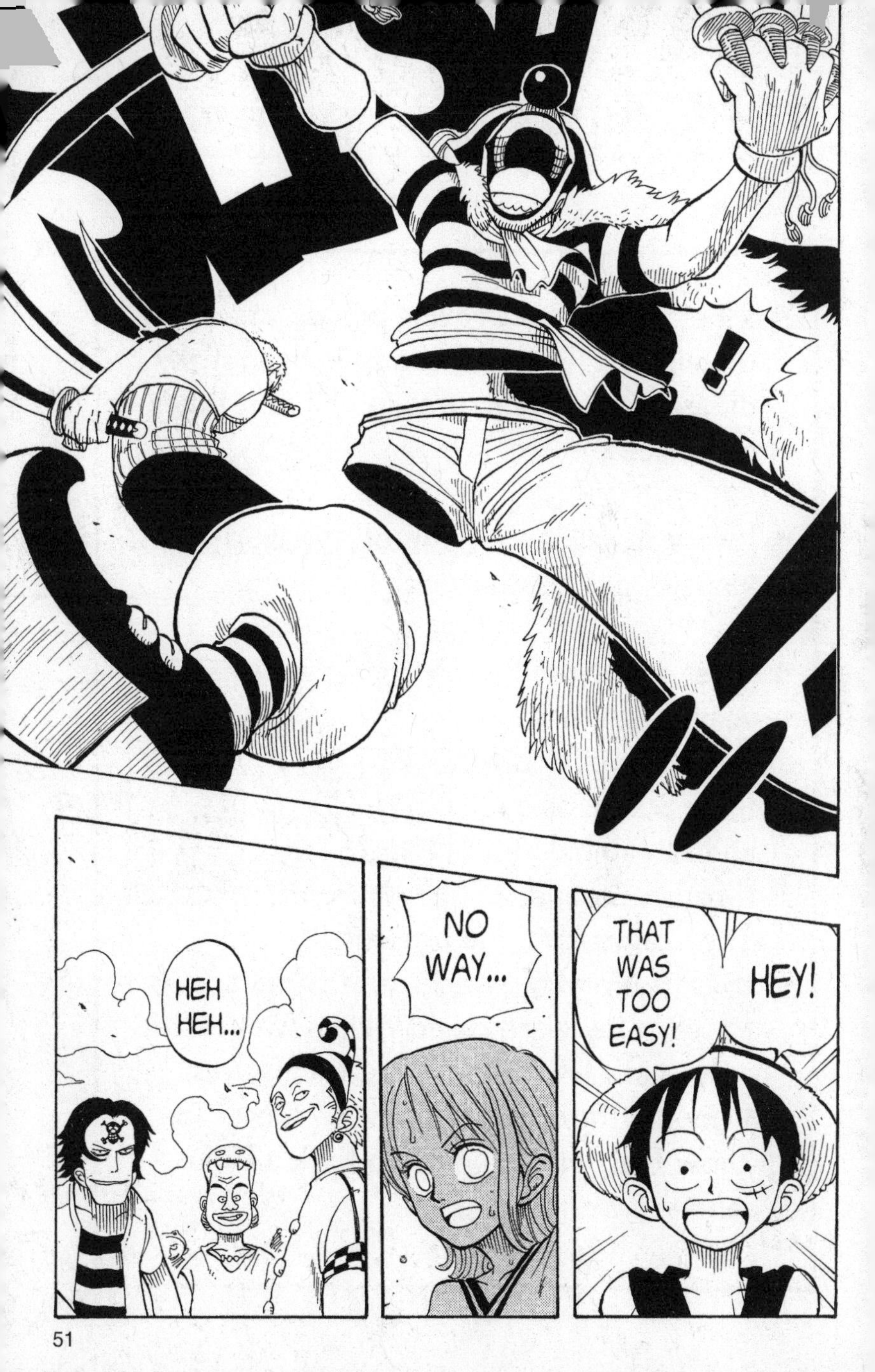
!
HEY!
THAT WAS TOO EASY!
NO WAY...
HEH HEH...

VIKINGS, PART 1

- All pirates are sea-roving plunderers, but throughout history there have been many different kinds of pirates in different times and places.

- I want to talk about one of my favorite kinds of pirates: the Vikings.

- Over a thousand years ago, Viking raiders swept down from Scandinavia and ran amok through Europe. They came from the present-day countries of Norway, Sweden and Denmark. As to why they were called Vikings, well, that's easy: that's what they called themselves. Why did they call themselves Vikings? To know that, we'd have to go back a thousand years and ask them.

<EUROPE>
SCANDINAVIA
AROUND HERE
ENGLAND

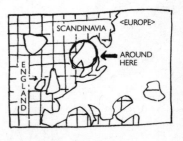

Chapter 11:
FLIGHT

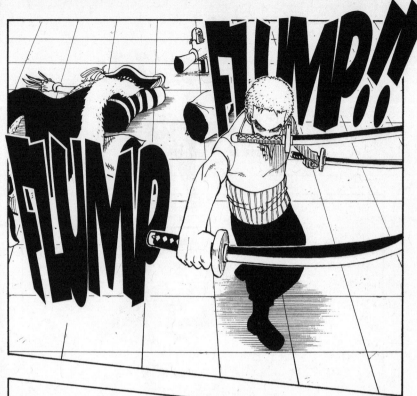

FLUMP!!!

FLUMP

HEH HEH HEH...

THAT WAS ALMOST DISAP- POINTING...

HMPH!

....?

54

READ THIS WAY

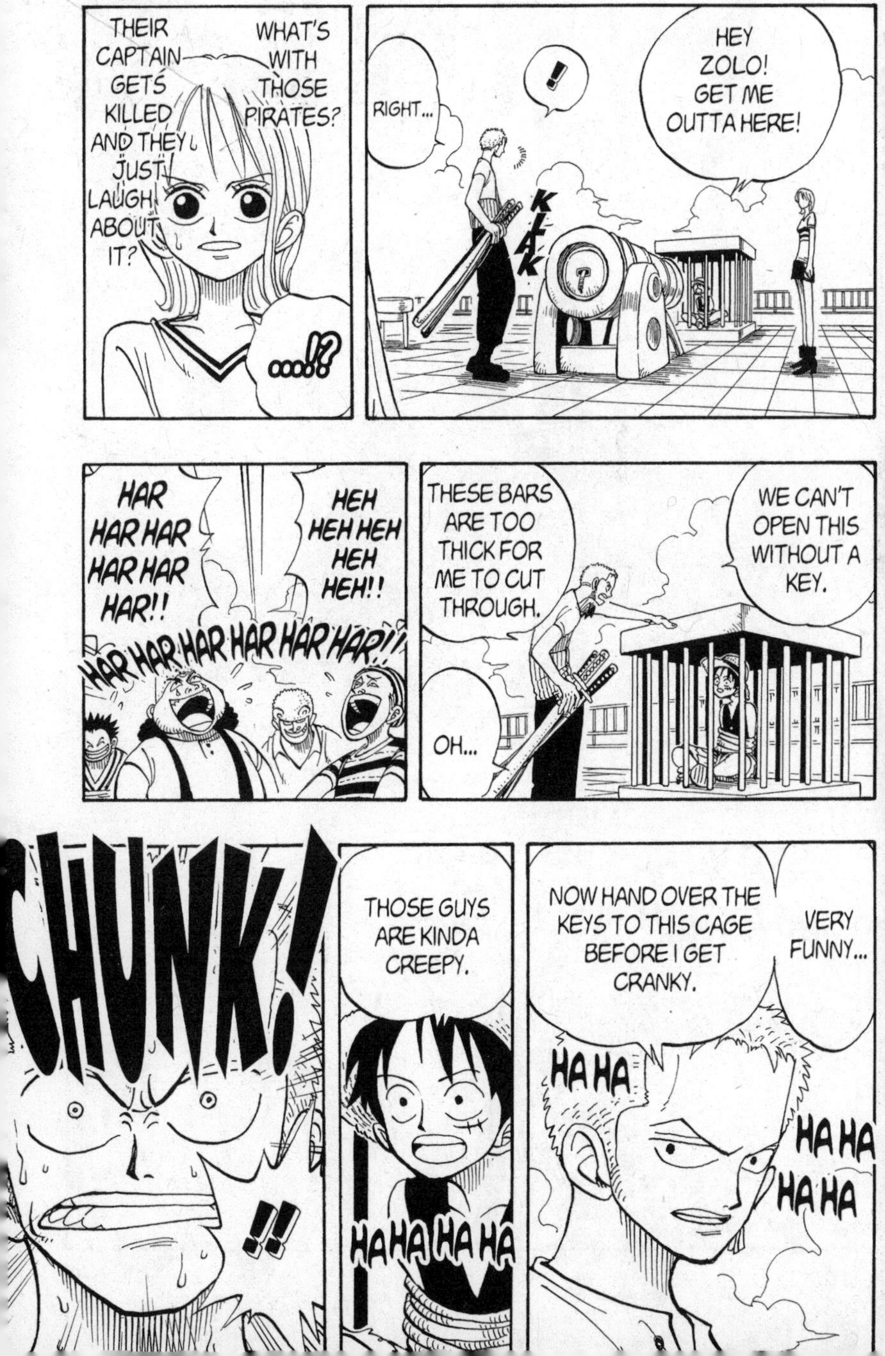
HEY ZOLO! GET ME OUTTA HERE!
!
KLAK
RIGHT...
WHAT'S WITH THOSE PIRATES?
THEIR CAPTAIN GETS KILLED AND THEY JUST LAUGH ABOUT IT?
ooo!!?
WE CAN'T OPEN THIS WITHOUT A KEY.
THESE BARS ARE TOO THICK FOR ME TO CUT THROUGH.
OH...
HEH HEH HEH HEH HEH!!
HAR HAR HAR HAR HAR HAR!!
HAR HAR HAR HAR HAR HAR!!
VERY FUNNY...
NOW HAND OVER THE KEYS TO THIS CAGE BEFORE I GET CRANKY.
HA HA
HA HA HA HA
THOSE GUYS ARE KINDA CREEPY.
HA HA HA HA
CHUNK!
!!

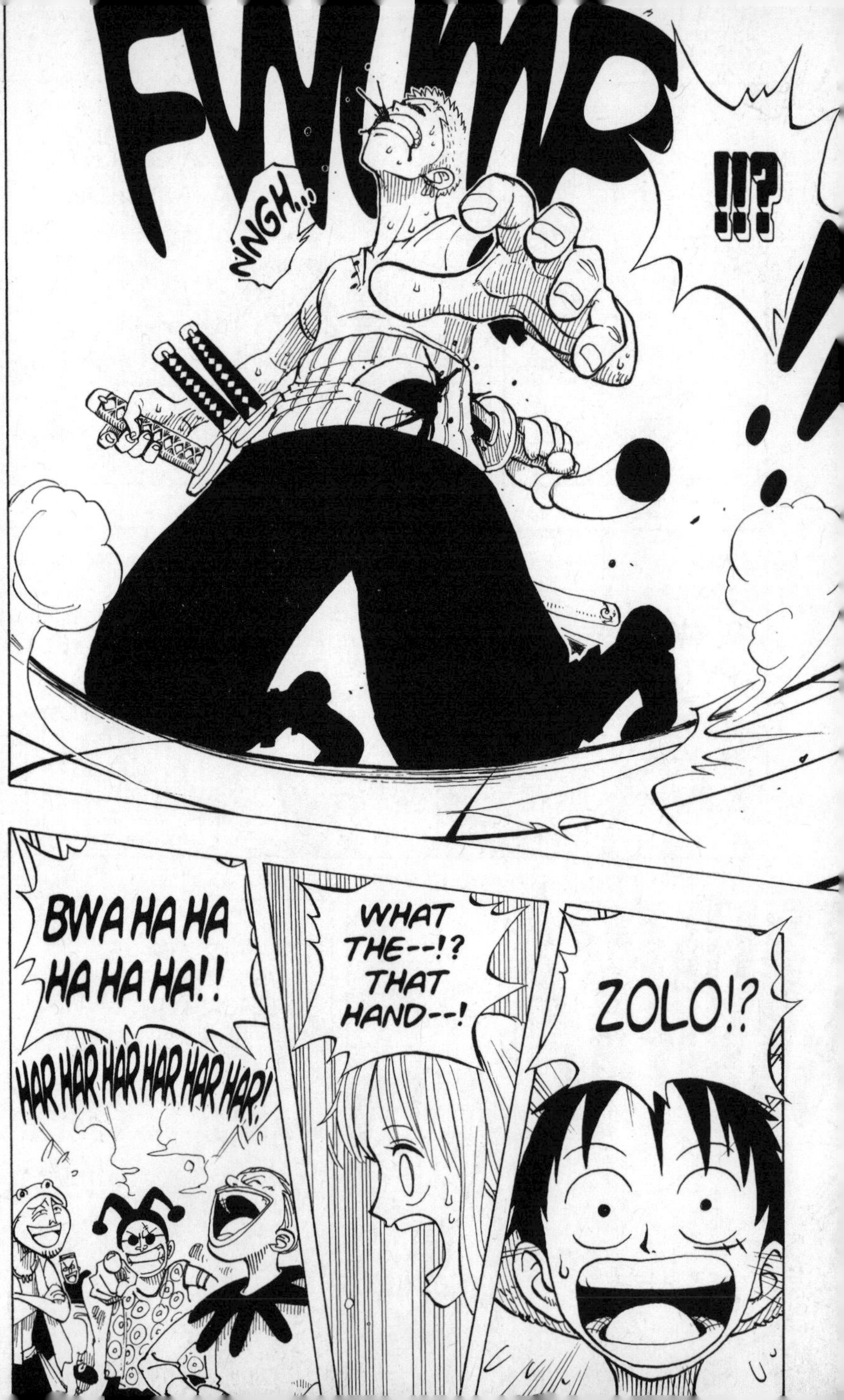
!!?
FWUMP
NNGH..
ZOLO!?
WHAT THE--!? THAT HAND--!
BWA HA HA HA HA HA!!
HAR HAR HAR HAR HAR HAR!

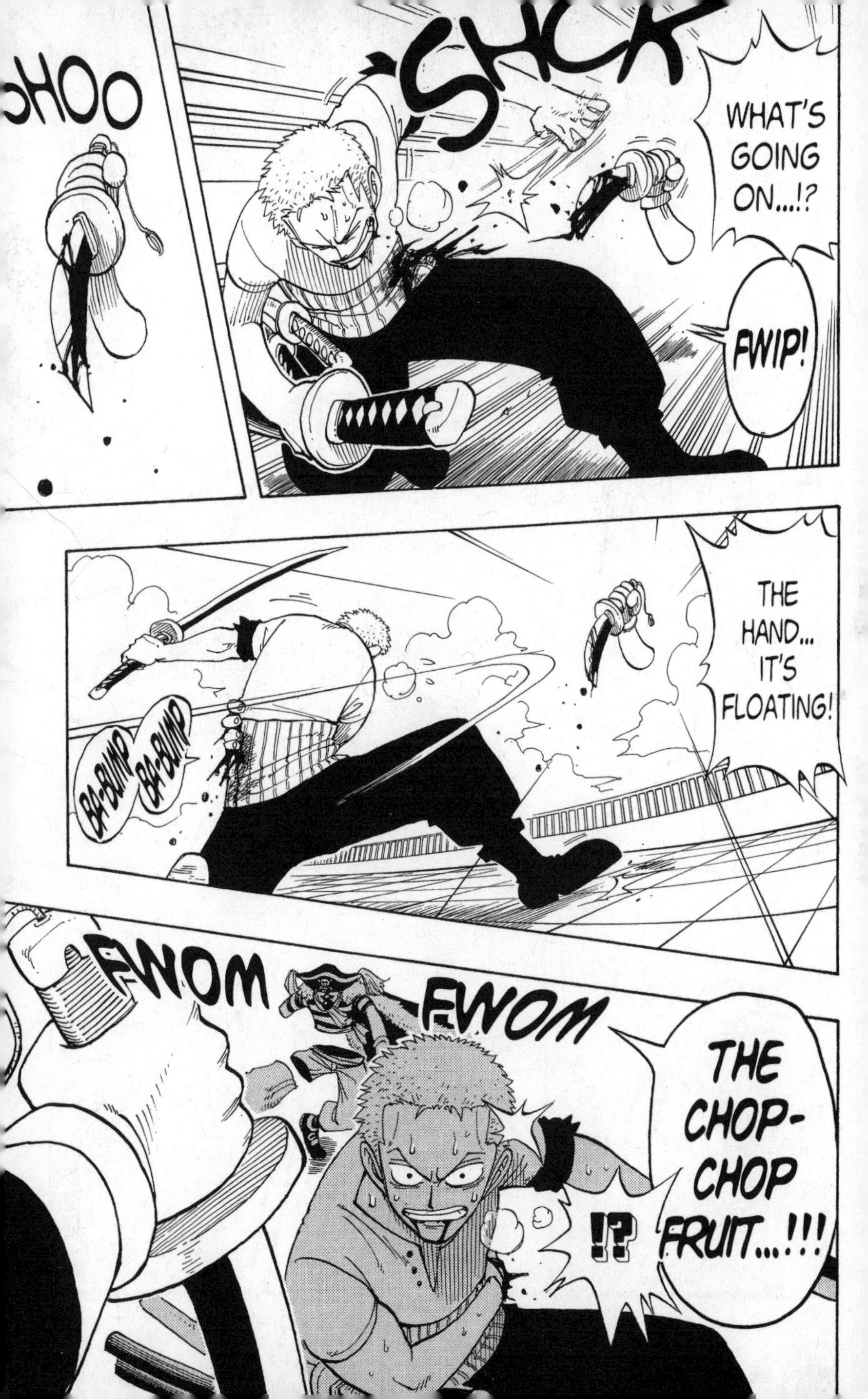
SHCK
WHAT'S GOING ON...!?
FWIP!
SHOO
THE HAND... IT'S FLOATING!
BA-BUMP
BA-BUMP
FWOM
FWOM
THE CHOP-CHOP FRUIT...!!!
!?

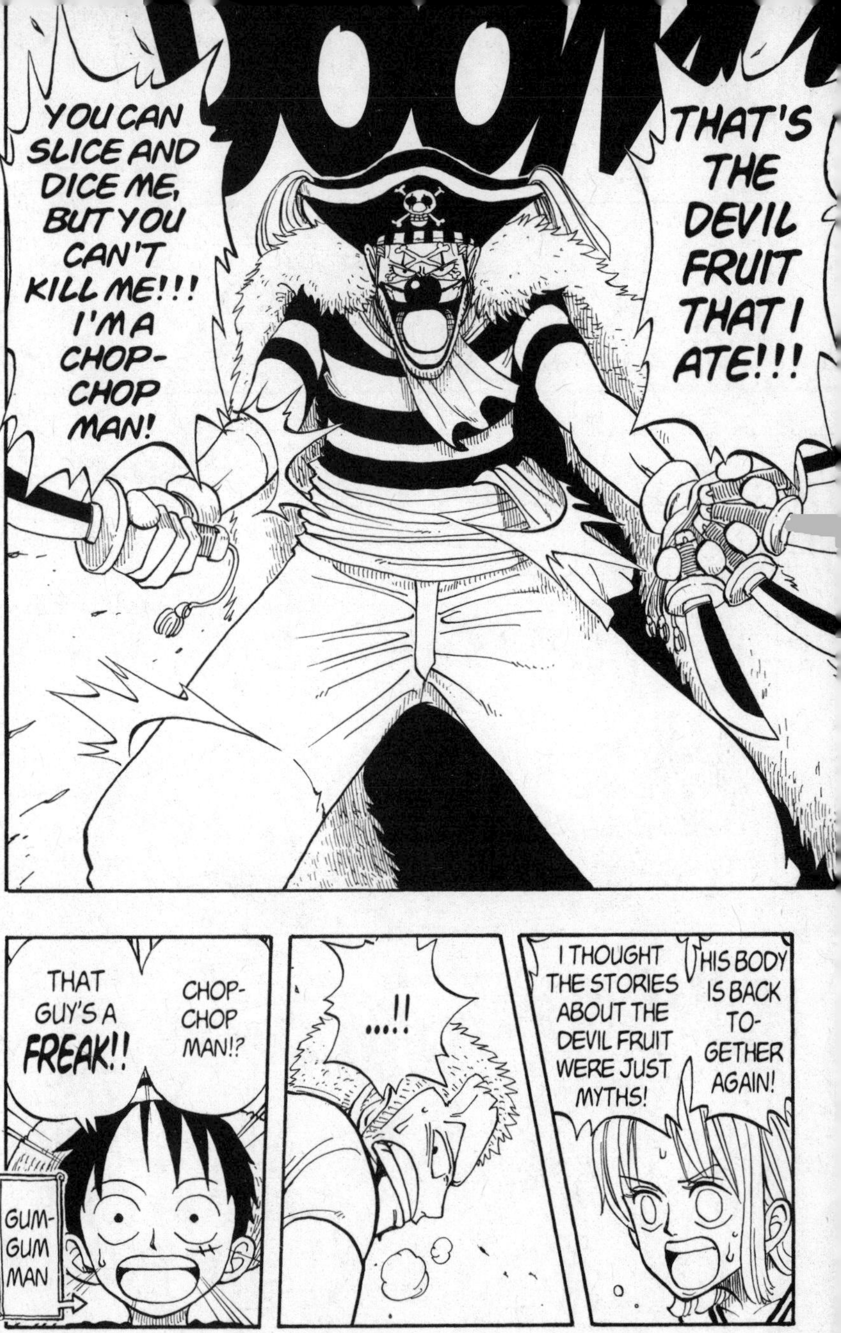
THAT'S THE DEVIL FRUIT THAT I ATE!!!
YOU CAN SLICE AND DICE ME, BUT YOU CAN'T KILL ME!!! I'M A CHOP-CHOP MAN!
HIS BODY IS BACK TO-GETHER AGAIN!
I THOUGHT THE STORIES ABOUT THE DEVIL FRUIT WERE JUST MYTHS!
....!!
CHOP-CHOP MAN!?
THAT GUY'S A FREAK!!
GUM-GUM MAN

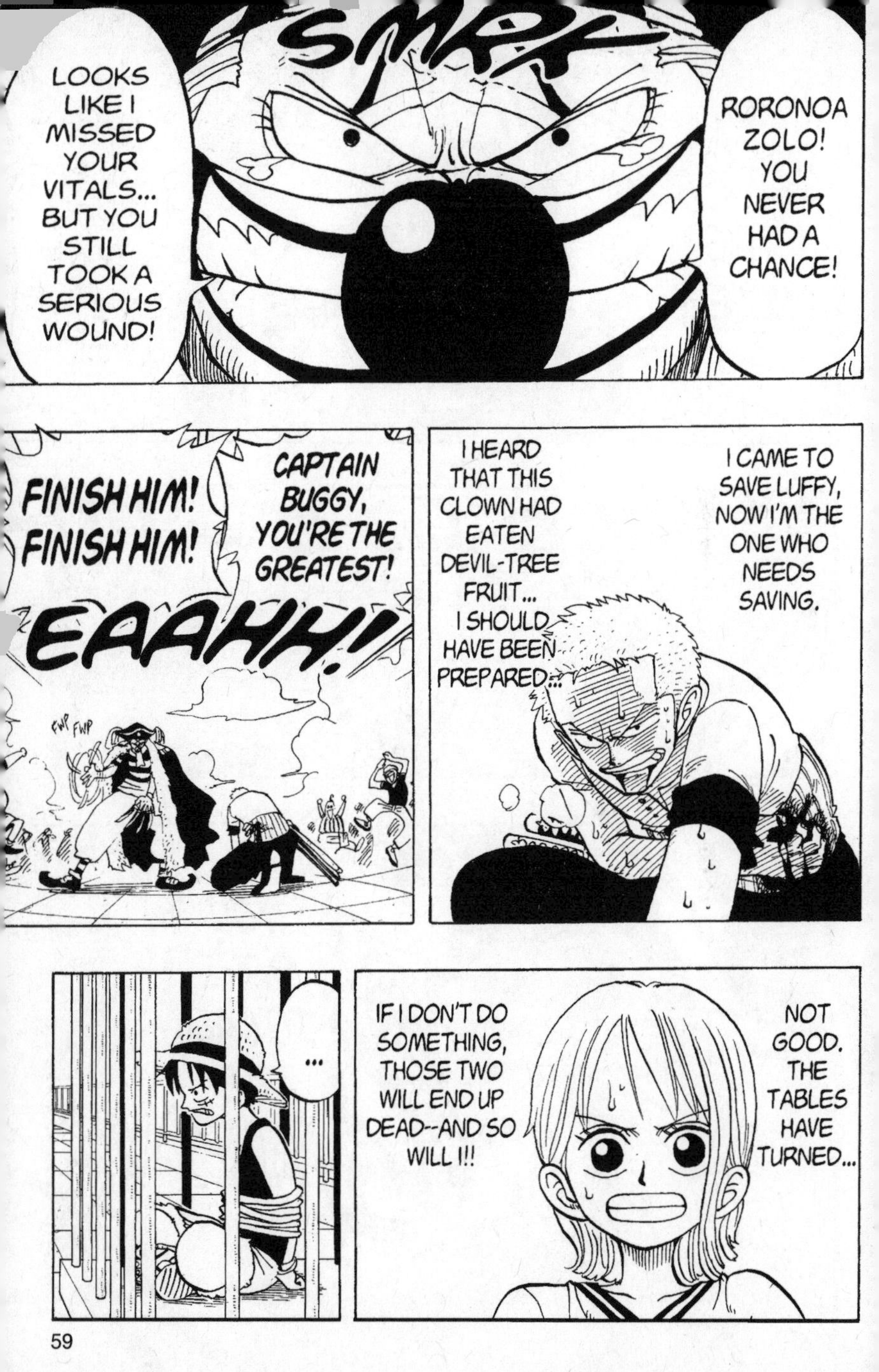
SMAK
RORONOA ZOLO! YOU NEVER HAD A CHANCE!
LOOKS LIKE I MISSED YOUR VITALS... BUT YOU STILL TOOK A SERIOUS WOUND!
I CAME TO SAVE LUFFY, NOW I'M THE ONE WHO NEEDS SAVING.
I HEARD THAT THIS CLOWN HAD EATEN DEVIL-TREE FRUIT... I SHOULD HAVE BEEN PREPARED...
CAPTAIN BUGGY, YOU'RE THE GREATEST!
FINISH HIM! FINISH HIM!
EAAHH!!
FWP FWP
NOT GOOD. THE TABLES HAVE TURNED...
IF I DON'T DO SOMETHING, THOSE TWO WILL END UP DEAD--AND SO WILL I!!!
...

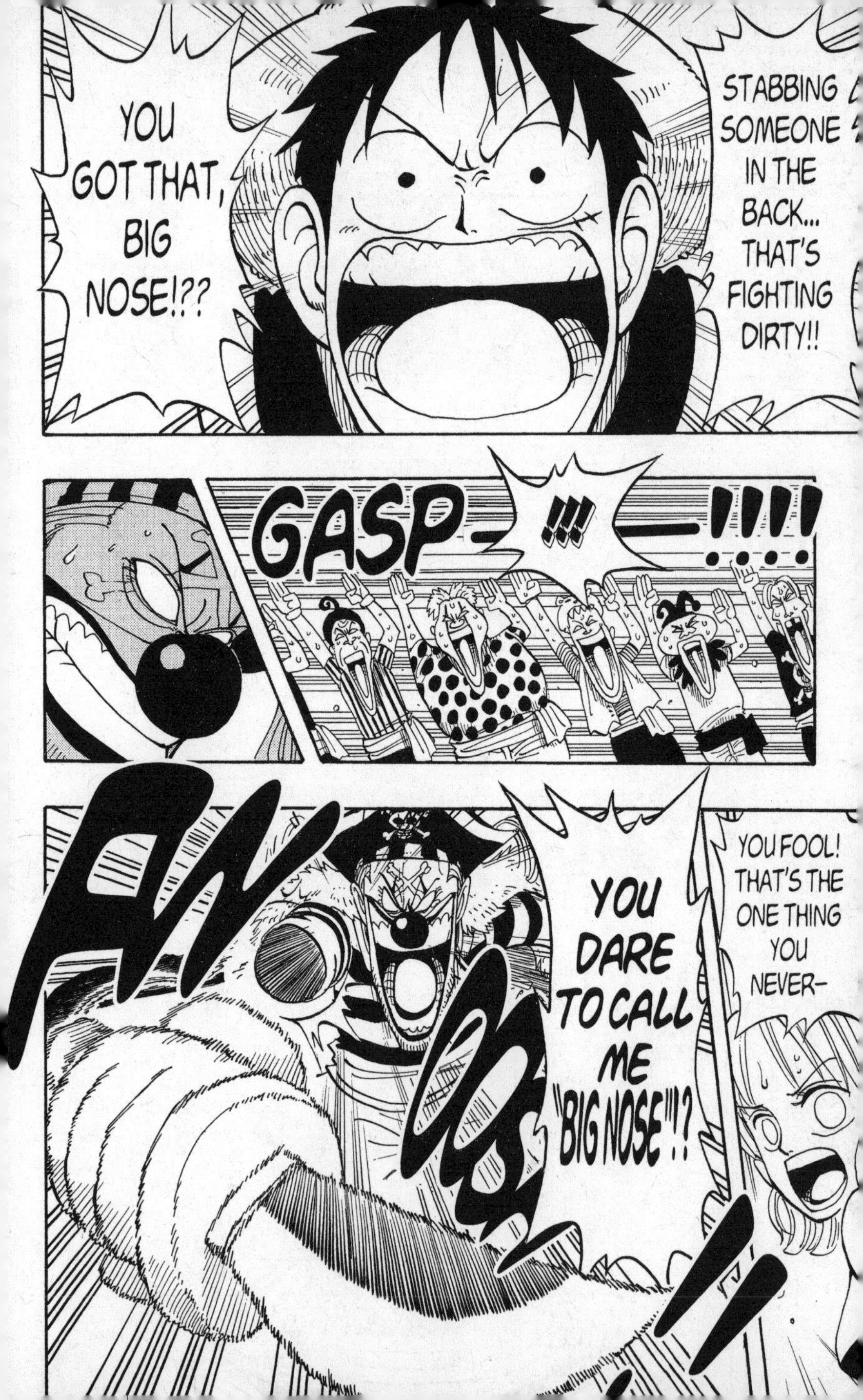
STABBING SOMEONE IN THE BACK... THAT'S FIGHTING DIRTY!!
YOU GOT THAT, BIG NOSE!??
GASP—!!! —!!!!
YOU FOOL! THAT'S THE ONE THING YOU NEVER-
YOU DARE TO CALL ME "BIG NOSE"!?

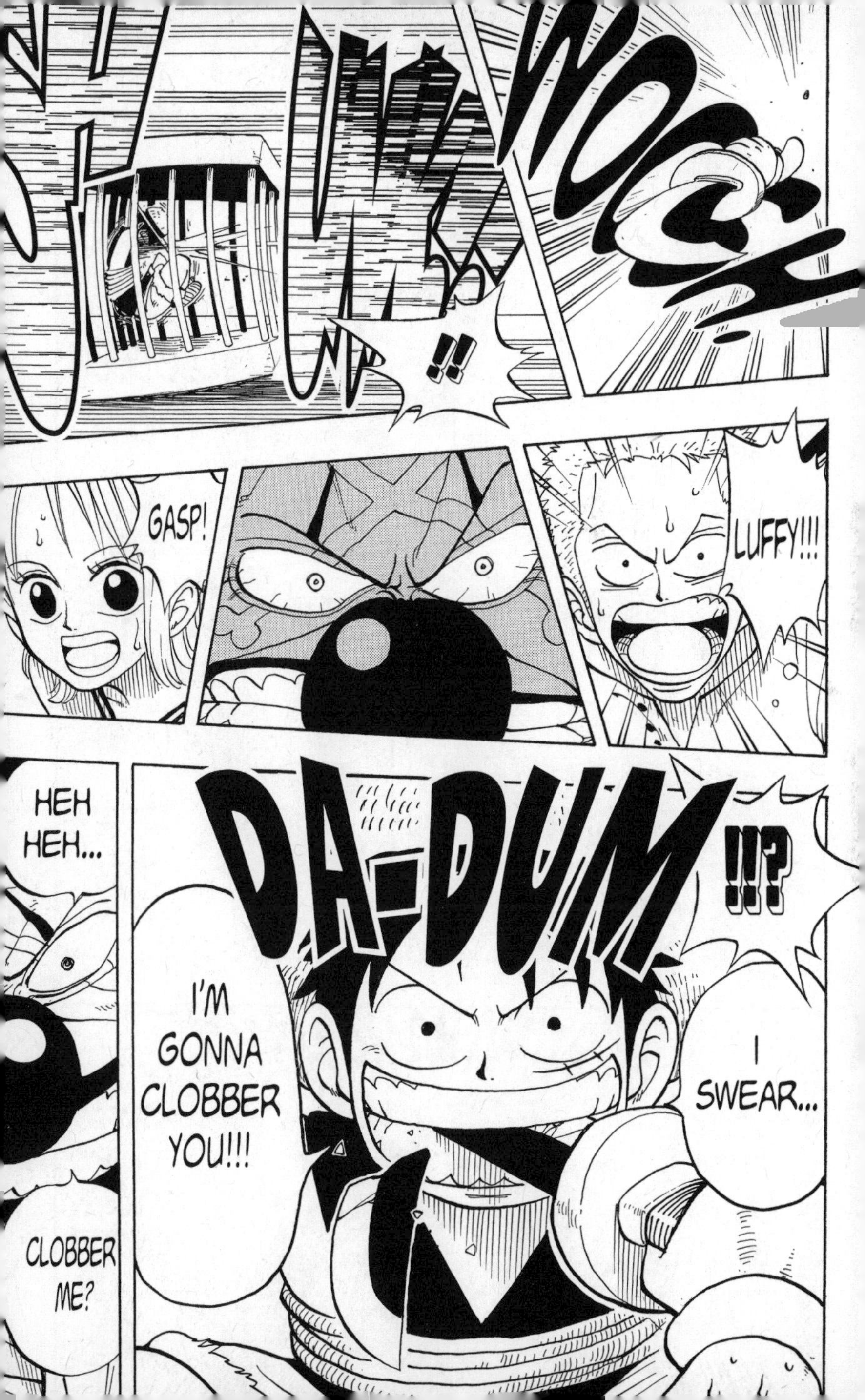
WOOSH
!!
LUFFY!!!
GASP!
DA-DUM!!?
I SWEAR...
I'M GONNA CLOBBER YOU!!!
HEH HEH...
CLOBBER ME?

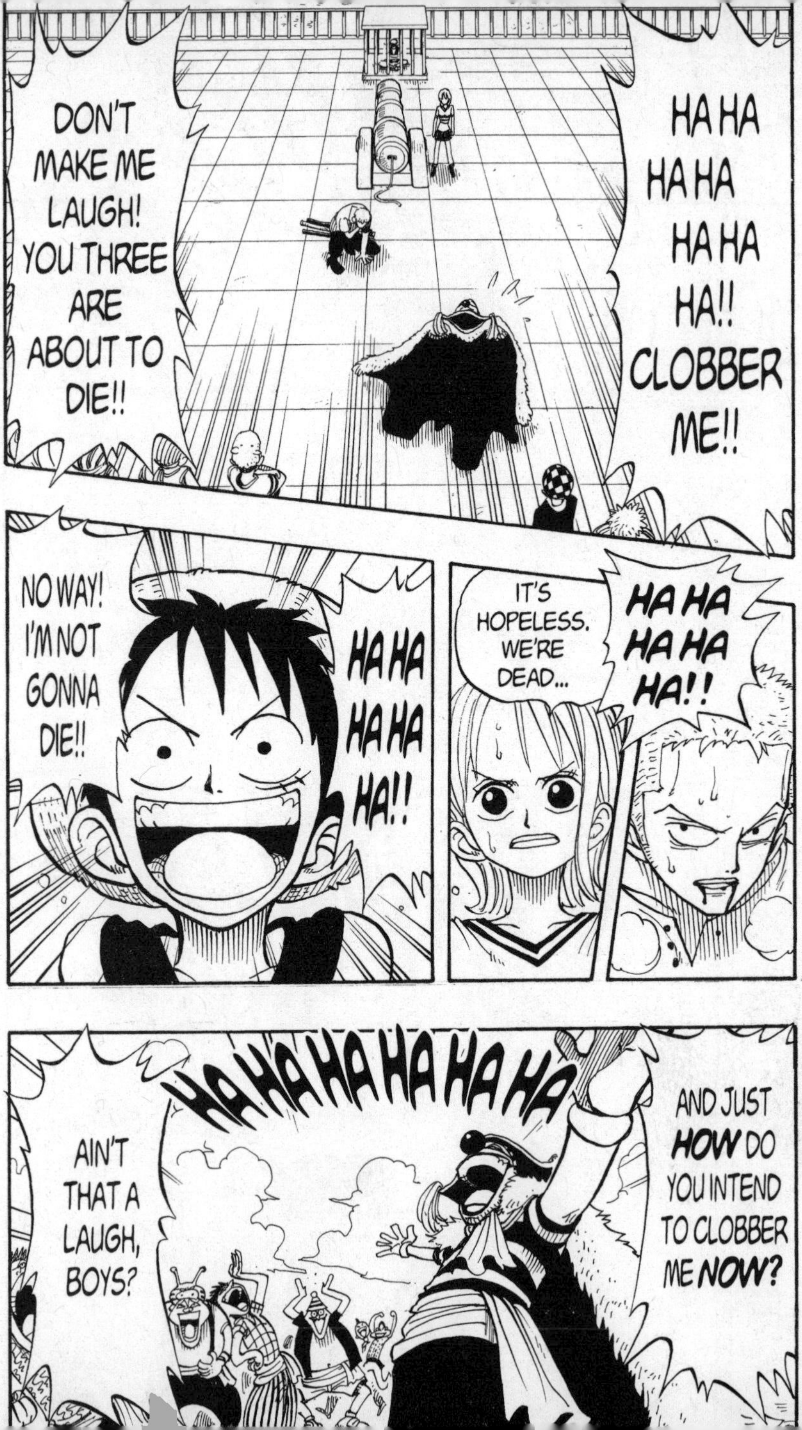
HA HA HA HA HA HA HA!! CLOBBER ME!!
DON'T MAKE ME LAUGH! YOU THREE ARE ABOUT TO DIE!!
HA HA HA HA HA!!
IT'S HOPELESS. WE'RE DEAD...
HA HA HA HA HA!!
NO WAY! I'M NOT GONNA DIE!!
AND JUST HOW DO YOU INTEND TO CLOBBER ME NOW?
HA HA HA HA HA HA HA HA
AIN'T THAT A LAUGH, BOYS?

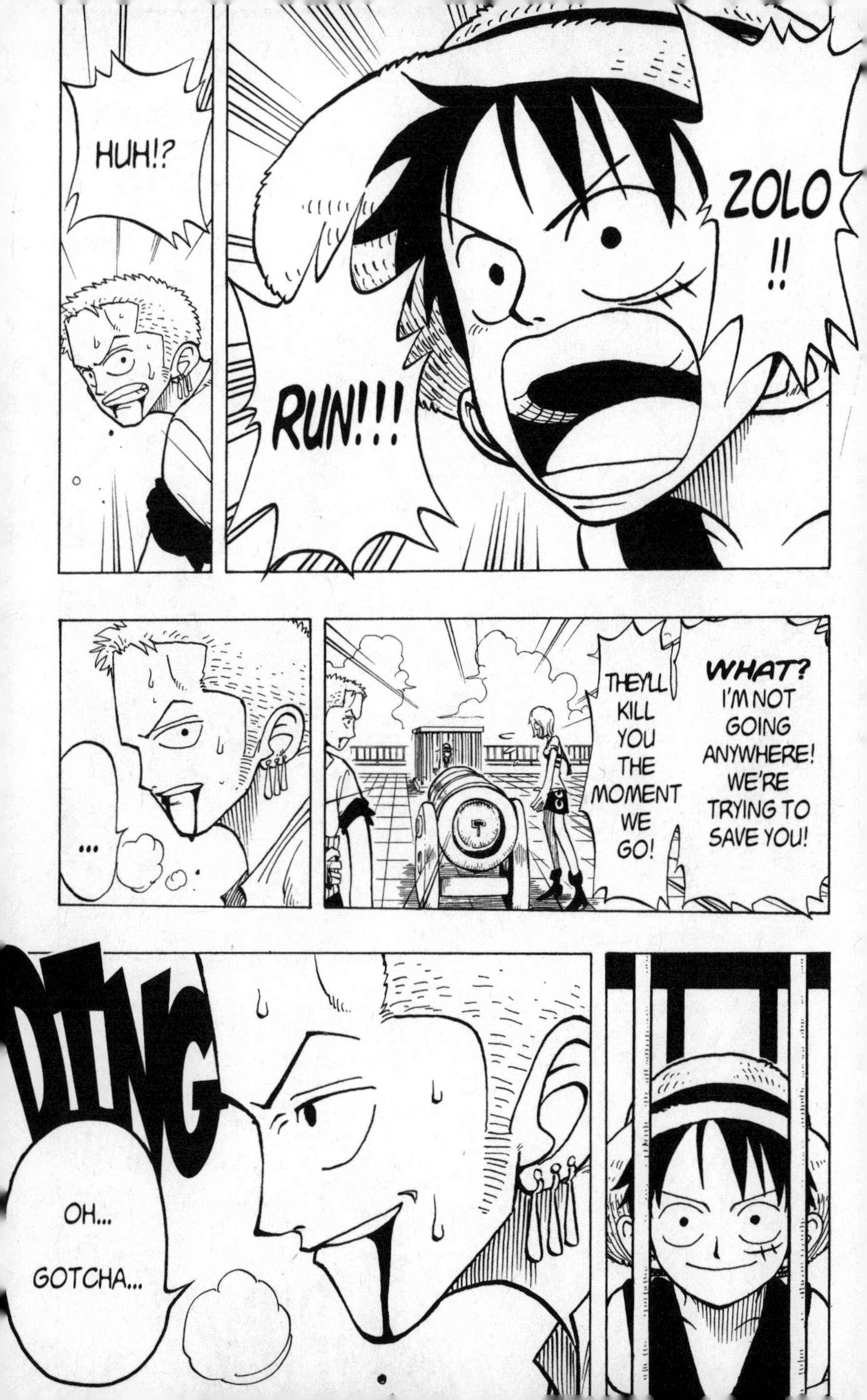
ZOLO !!
RUN!!!
HUH!?
WHAT? I'M NOT GOING ANYWHERE! WE'RE TRYING TO SAVE YOU!
THEY'LL KILL YOU THE MOMENT WE GO!
...
DING
OH... GOTCHA...

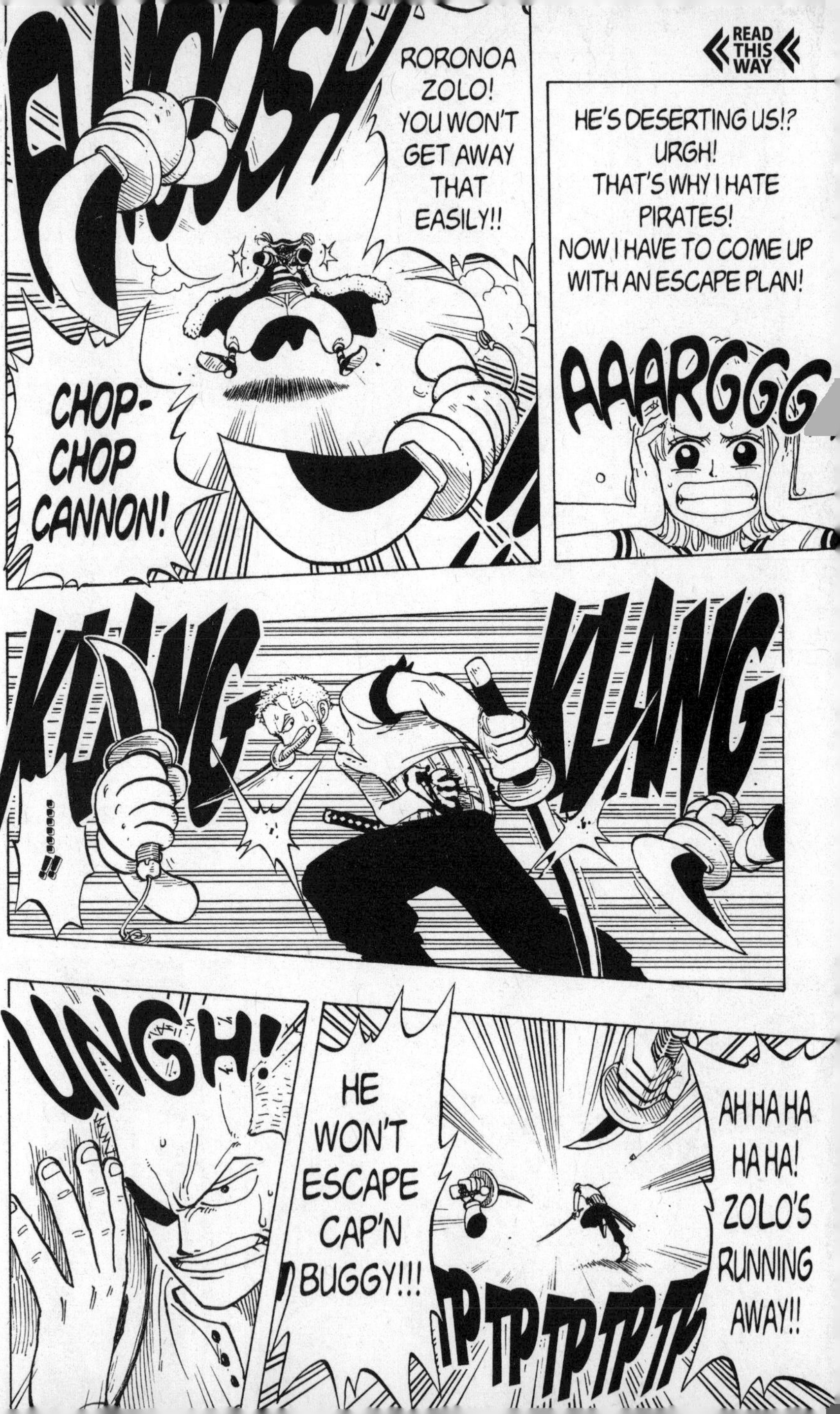
READ THIS WAY
HE'S DESERTING US!? URGH! THAT'S WHY I HATE PIRATES! NOW I HAVE TO COME UP WITH AN ESCAPE PLAN!
AAARGGG
FWOOSH
RORONOA ZOLO! YOU WON'T GET AWAY THAT EASILY!!
CHOP-CHOP CANNON!
KLANG
KLANG
AH HA HA HA HA! ZOLO'S RUNNING AWAY!!
TP TP TP TP TP
HE WON'T ESCAPE CAP'N BUGGY!!!
UNGH!

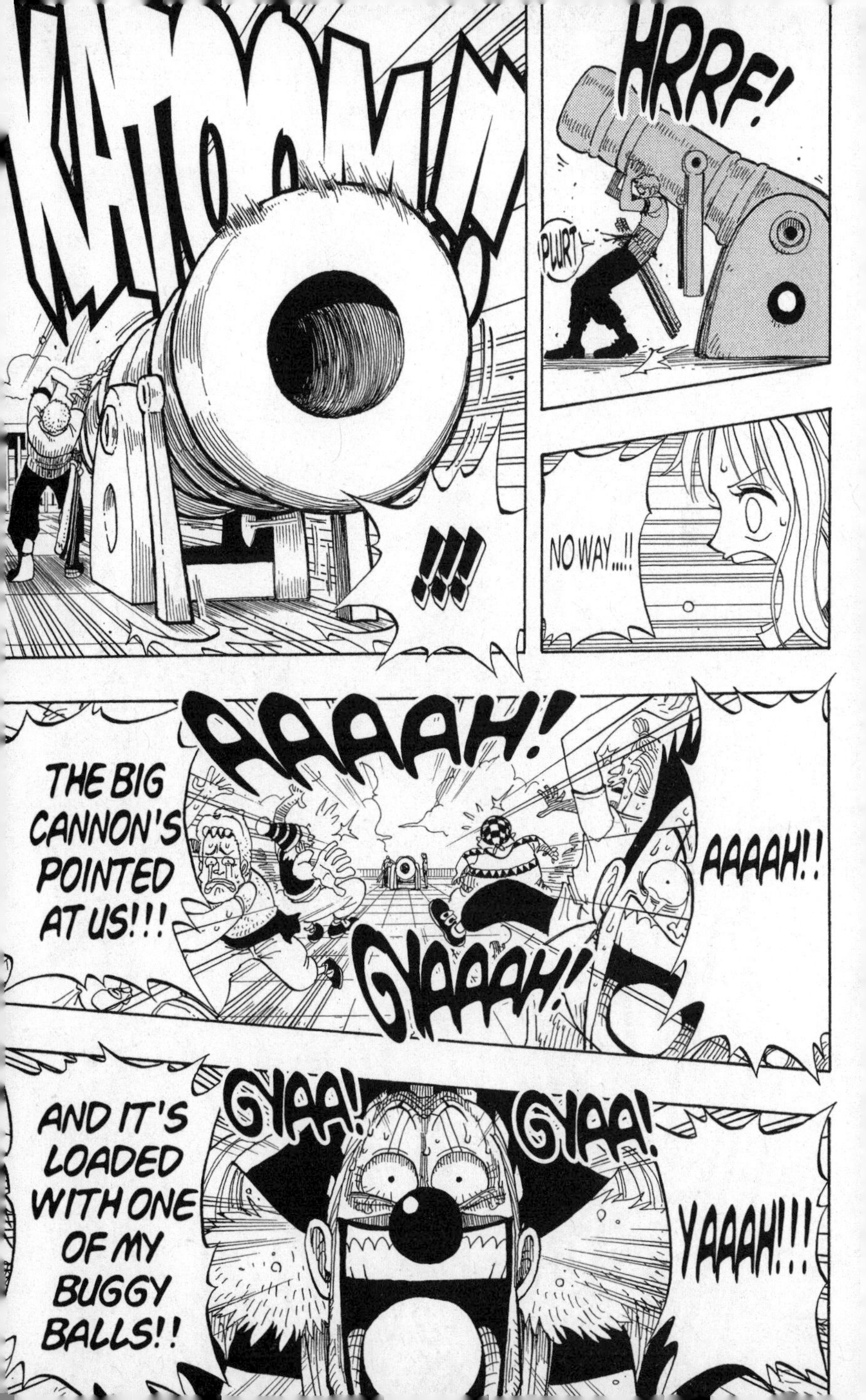
HRRF!
PWURT
NO WAY...!!
!!!
AAAAH!!
AAAAH!
GYAAAH!
THE BIG CANNON'S POINTED AT US!!!
YAAAH!!!
GYAA!
GYAA!
AND IT'S LOADED WITH ONE OF MY BUGGY BALLS!!

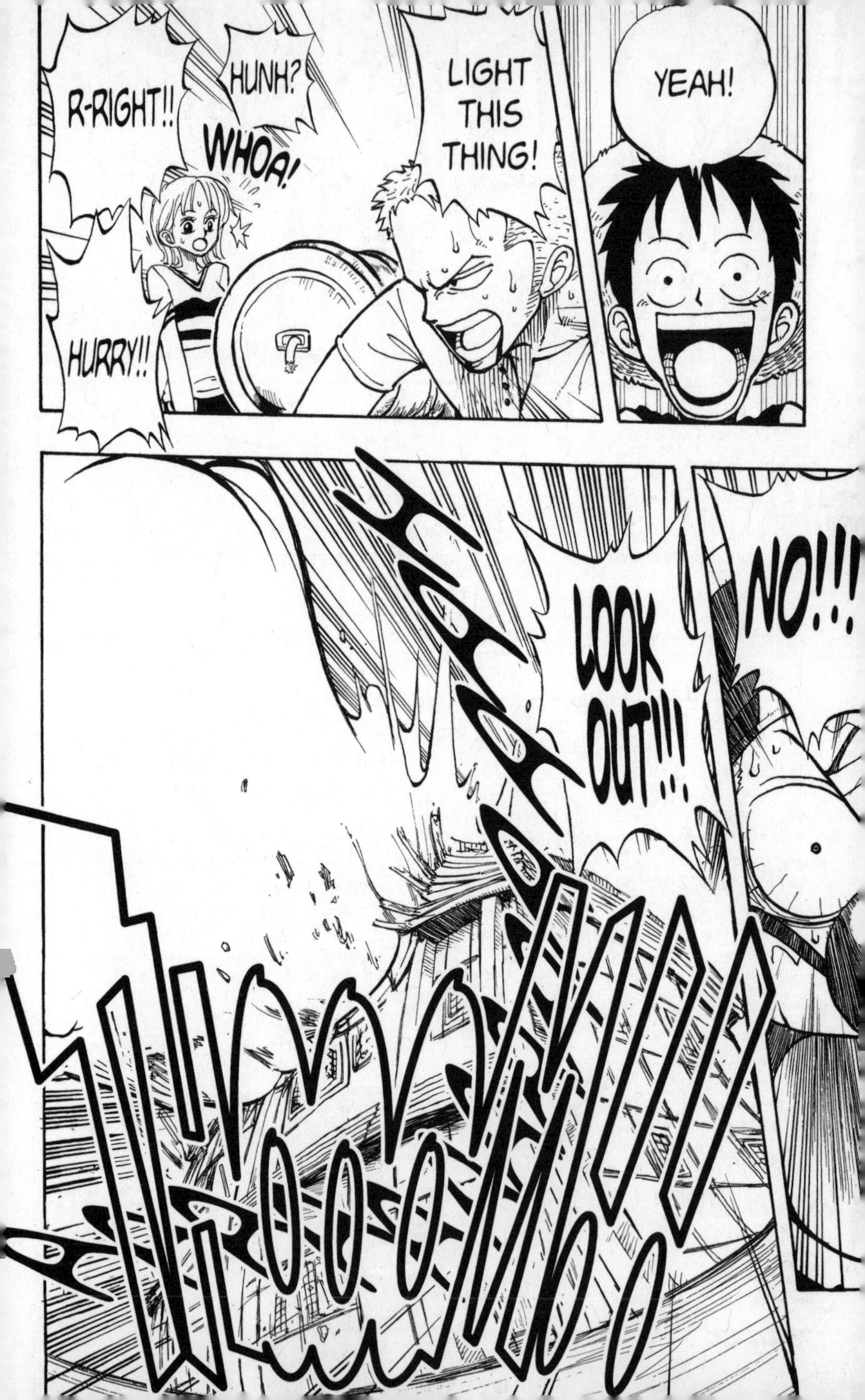
YEAH!
LIGHT THIS THING!
HUNH?
WHOA!
R-RIGHT!!
HURRY!!
NO!!!
LOOK OUT!!!

READ THIS WAY

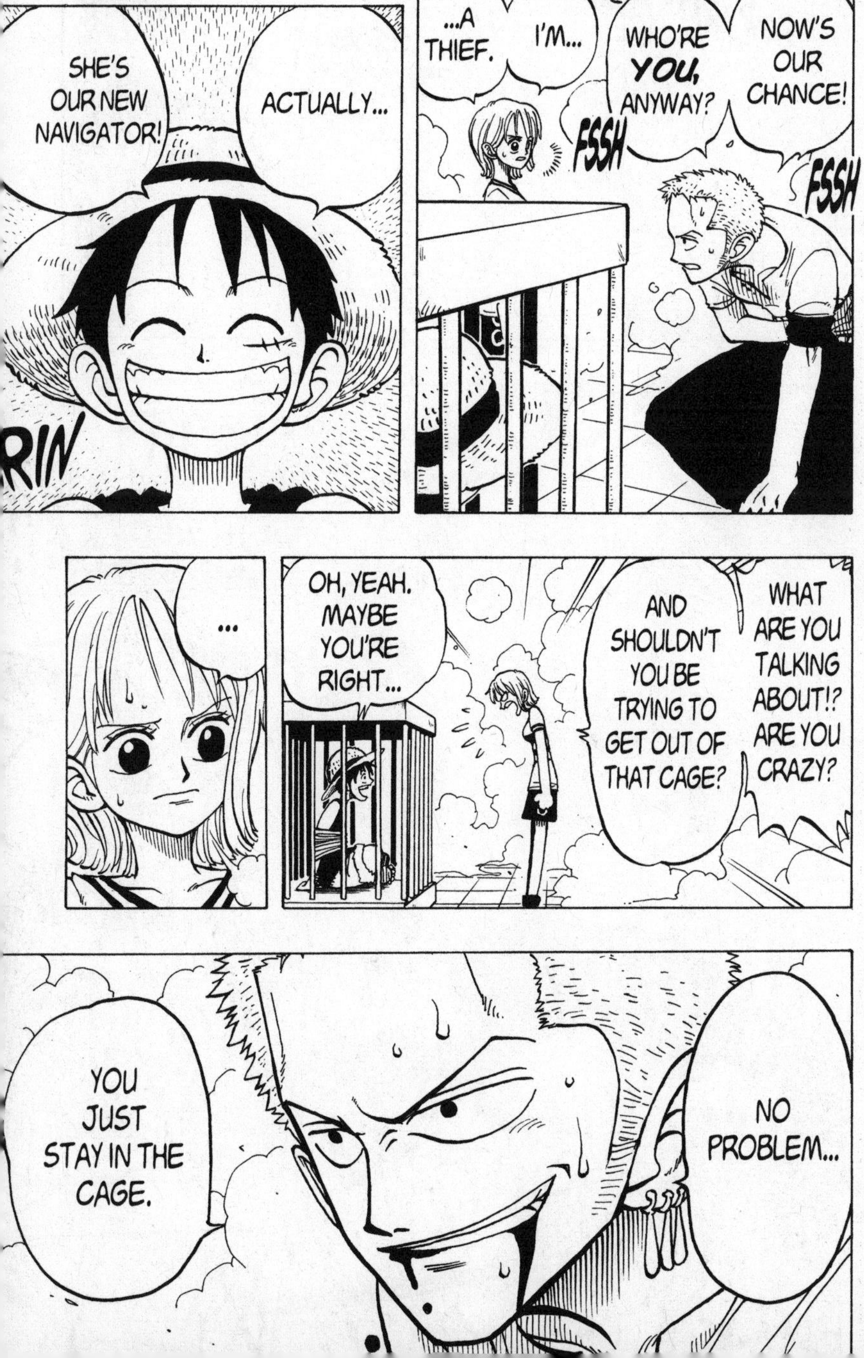
NOW'S OUR CHANCE!
FSSH
WHO'RE YOU, ANYWAY?
FSSH
I'M...
...A THIEF.
FSSH
ACTUALLY...
SHE'S OUR NEW NAVIGATOR!
RIN
WHAT ARE YOU TALKING ABOUT!? ARE YOU CRAZY?
AND SHOULDN'T YOU BE TRYING TO GET OUT OF THAT CAGE?
OH, YEAH. MAYBE YOU'RE RIGHT...
...
NO PROBLEM...
YOU JUST STAY IN THE CAGE.

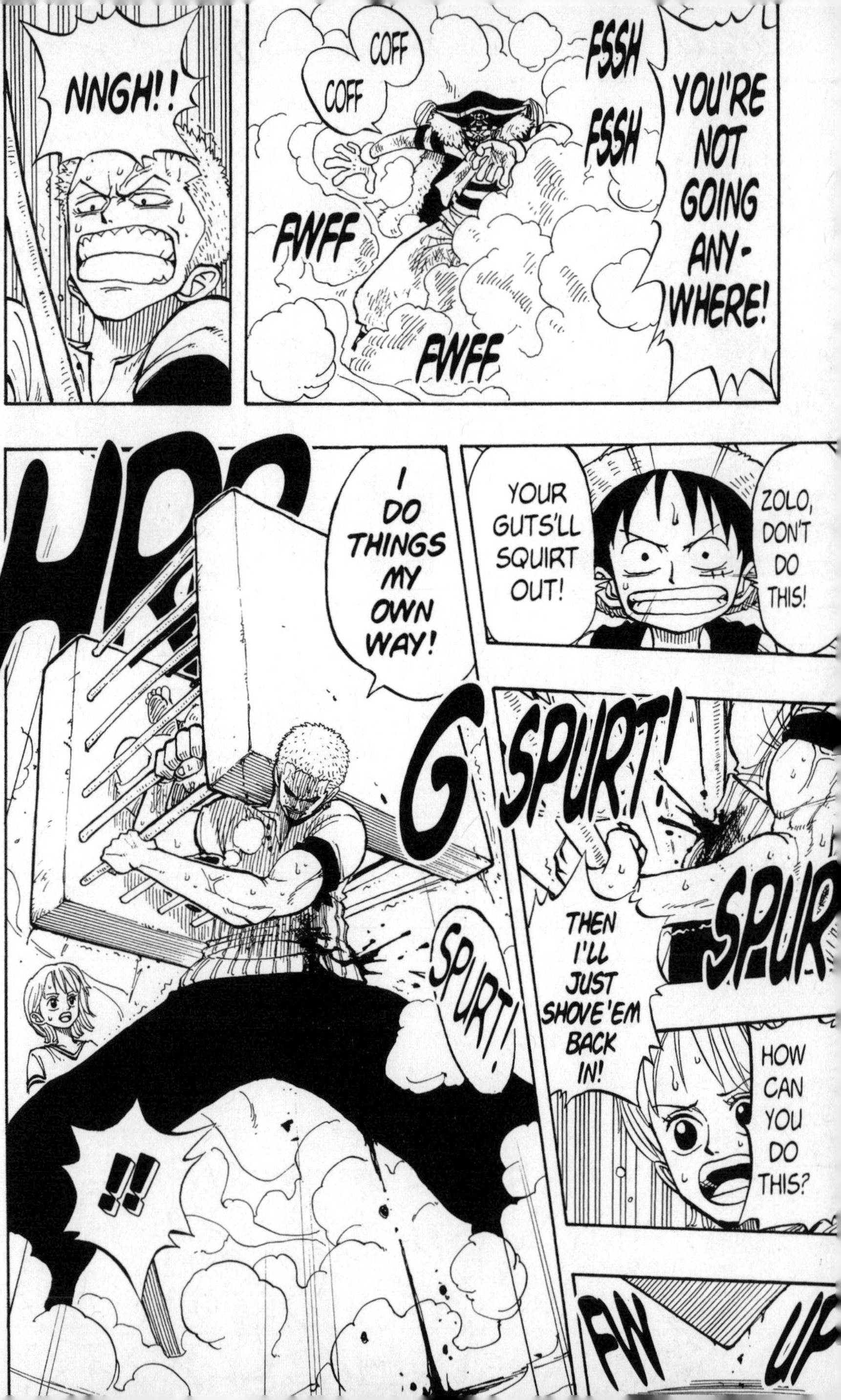
YOU'RE NOT GOING ANY-WHERE!
FSSH
FSSH
COFF
COFF
FWFF
FWFF
NNGH!!
ZOLO, DON'T DO THIS!
YOUR GUTS'LL SQUIRT OUT!
SPURT!
SPUR
HOW CAN YOU DO THIS?
THEN I'LL JUST SHOVE 'EM BACK IN!
FW
UP
I DO THINGS MY OWN WAY!
G
SPURT!
!!

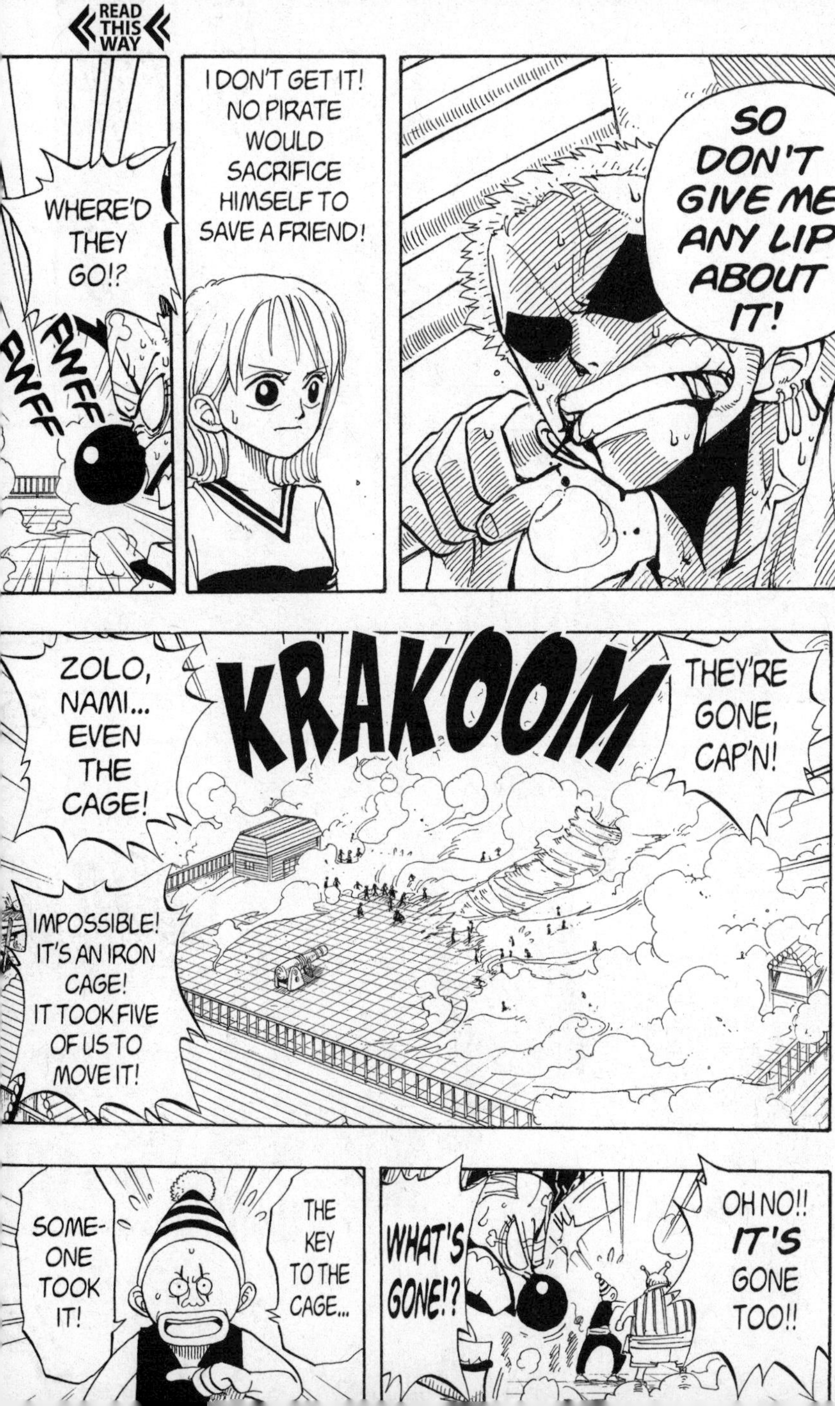
READ THIS WAY
SO DON'T GIVE ME ANY LIP ABOUT IT!
I DON'T GET IT! NO PIRATE WOULD SACRIFICE HIMSELF TO SAVE A FRIEND!
WHERE'D THEY GO!?
FWFF FWFF
THEY'RE GONE, CAP'N!
KRAKOOM
ZOLO, NAMI... EVEN THE CAGE!
IMPOSSIBLE! IT'S AN IRON CAGE! IT TOOK FIVE OF US TO MOVE IT!
OH NO!! IT'S GONE TOO!!
WHAT'S GONE!?
THE KEY TO THE CAGE...
SOME-ONE TOOK IT!

READ THIS WAY

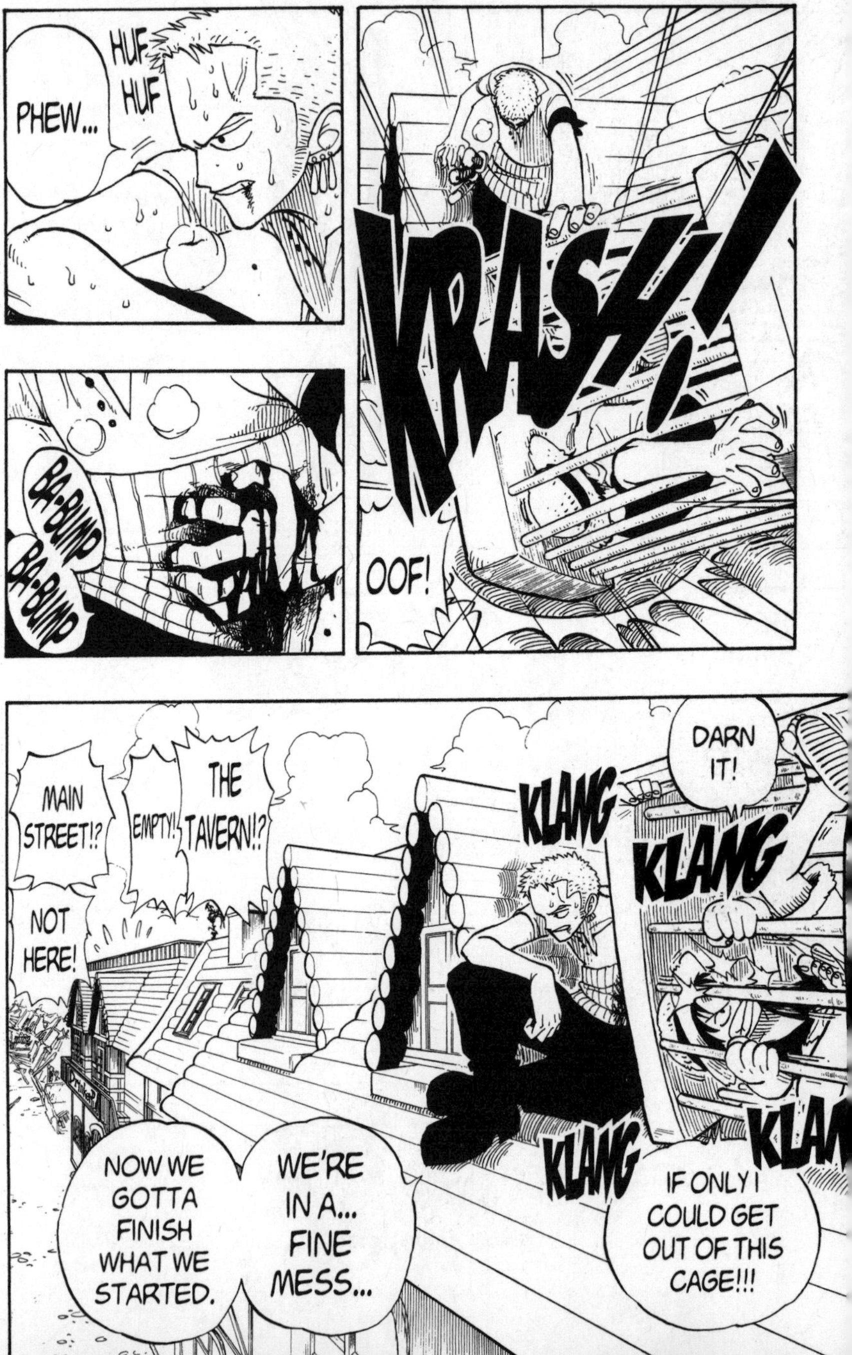
KRASH!
OOF!
HUF HUF
PHEW...
BA-BUMP BA-BUMP
DARN IT!
KLANG
KLANG
IF ONLY I COULD GET OUT OF THIS CAGE!!!
KLAN
KLANG
THE TAVERN!?
EMPTY!
MAIN STREET!?
NOT HERE!
WE'RE IN A... FINE MESS...
NOW WE GOTTA FINISH WHAT WE STARTED.

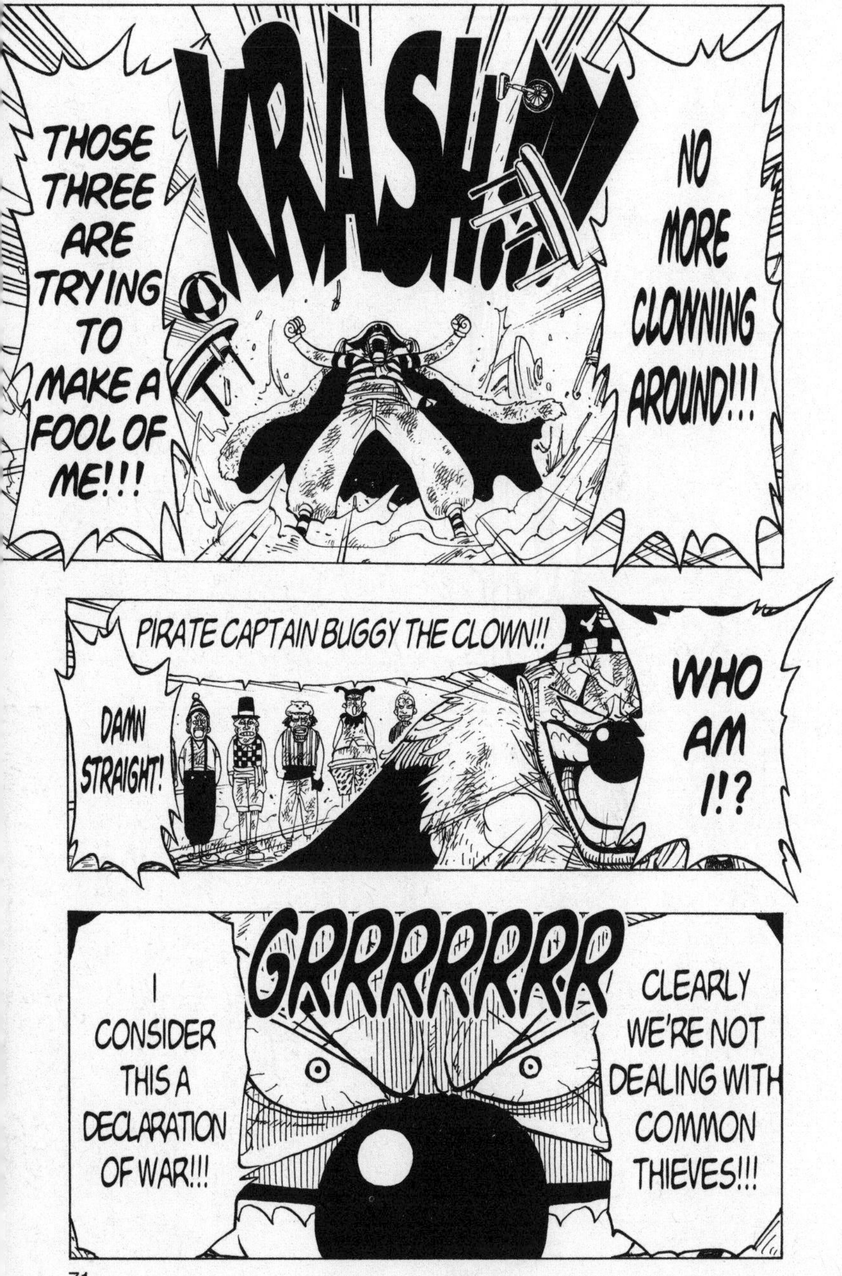
KRASH!!
NO MORE CLOWNING AROUND!!!
THOSE THREE ARE TRYING TO MAKE A FOOL OF ME!!!
WHO AM I!?
PIRATE CAPTAIN BUGGY THE CLOWN!!
DAMN STRAIGHT!
GRRRRRRR
CLEARLY WE'RE NOT DEALING WITH COMMON THIEVES!!!
I CONSIDER THIS A DECLARATION OF WAR!!!

One Piece Rough Sketch!

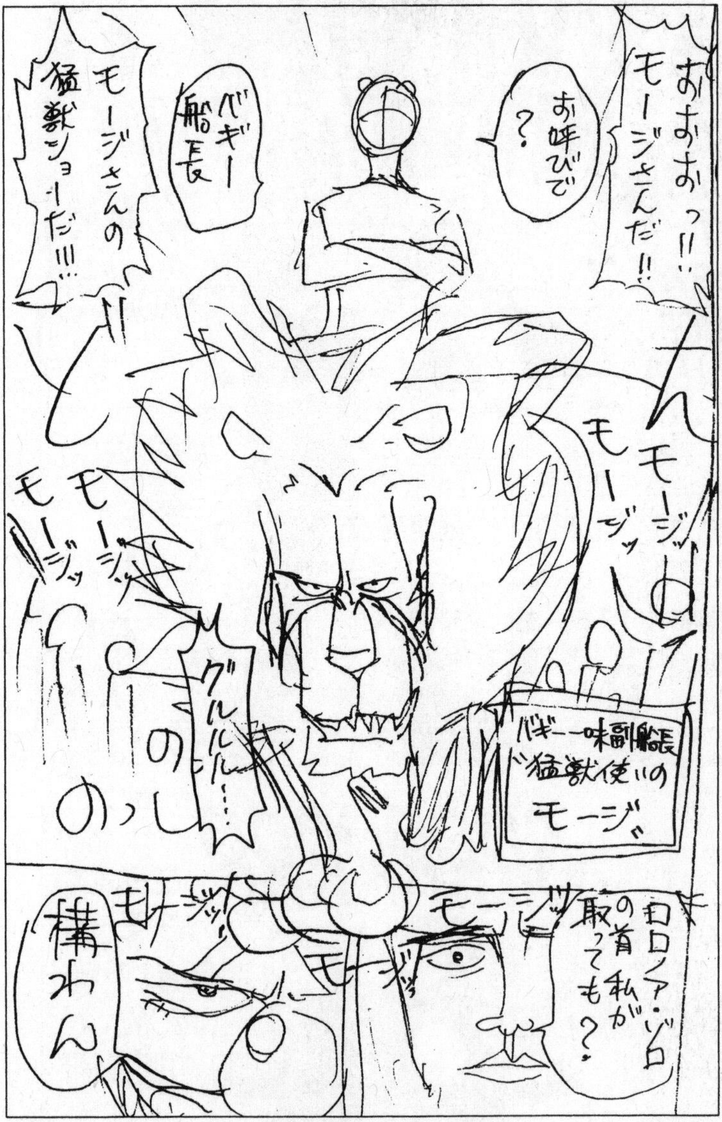

おおおっ!! モージさんだ!!
お呼びで?
バギー船長
モージさんの猛獣ショーだ!!!
モージッ モージッ
モージッ モージッ
グルルル…
のっしのっし
バギー一味副船長 猛獣使いのモージ
ロロノア・ゾロの首 私が取っても?
構わん

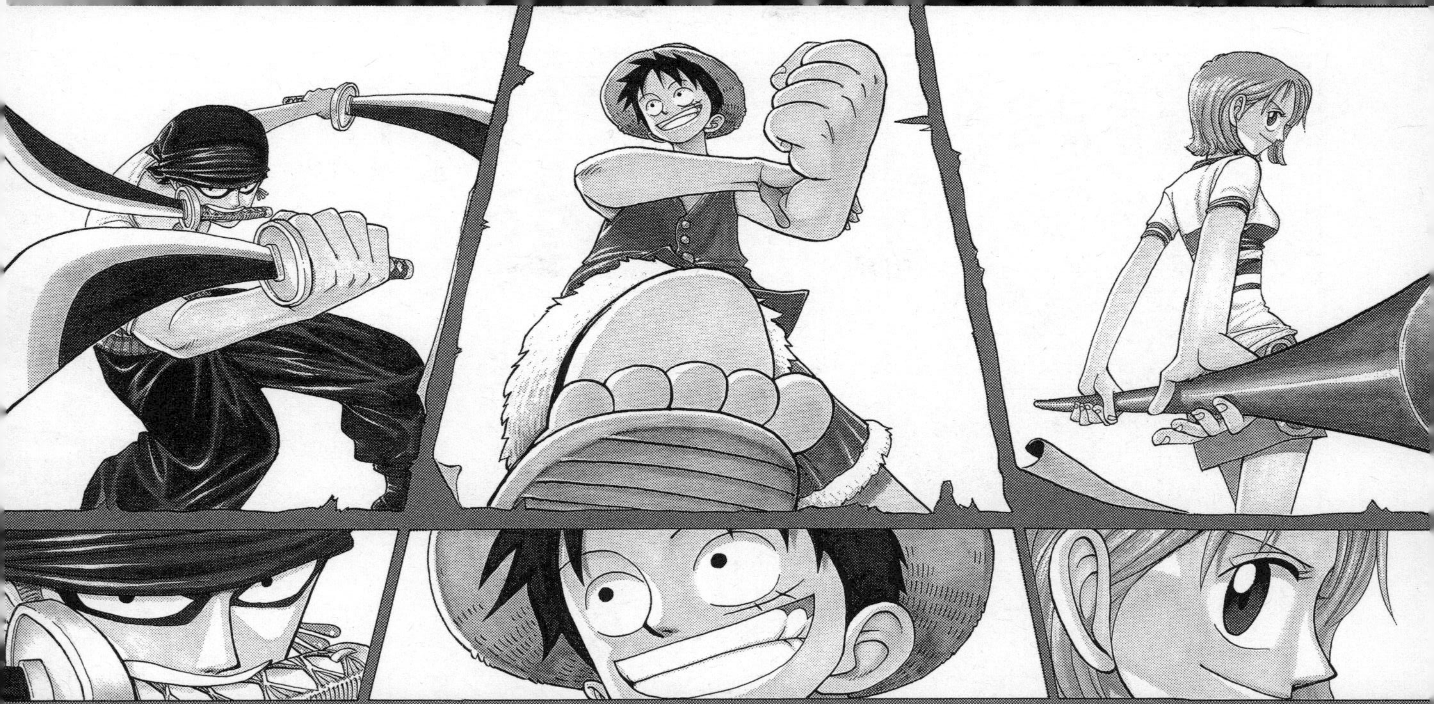

Chapter 12: DOG

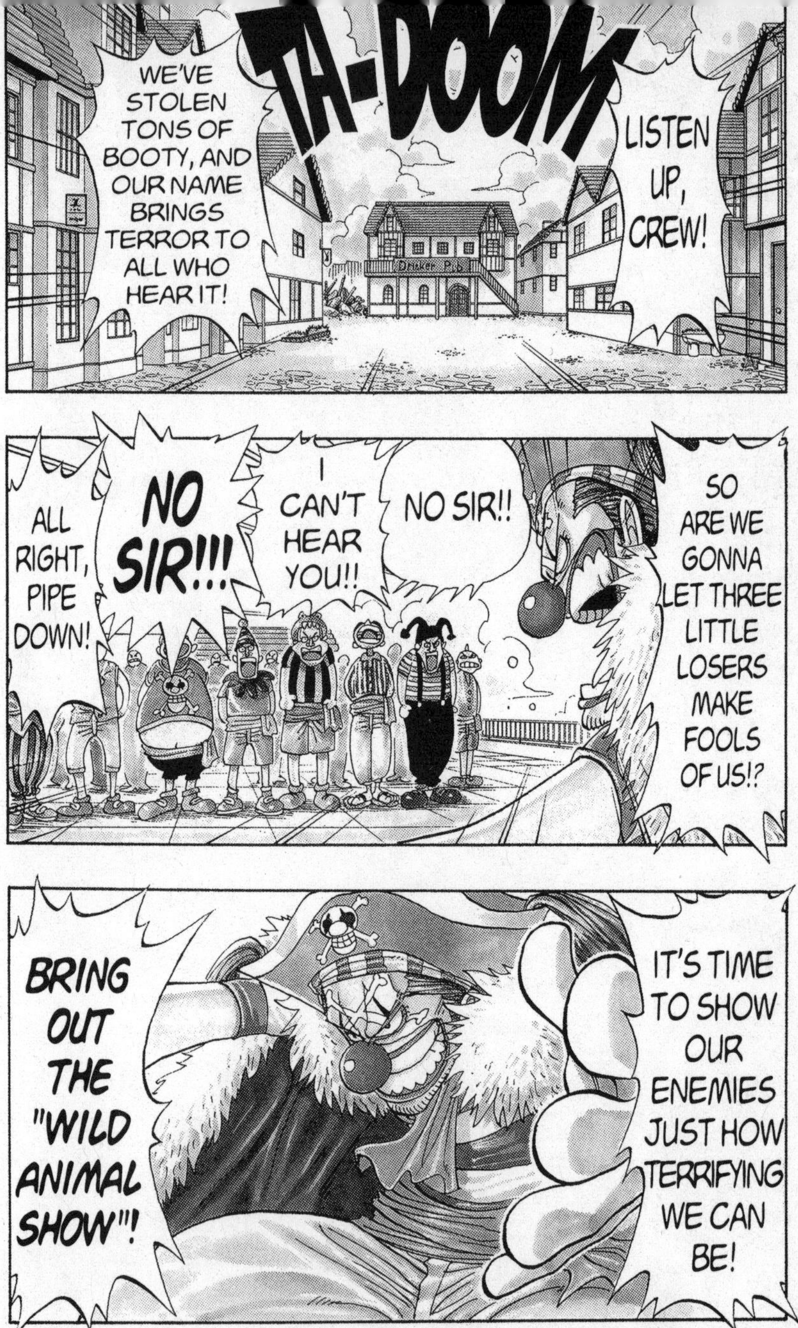
LISTEN UP, CREW!
TA-DOOM
WE'VE STOLEN TONS OF BOOTY, AND OUR NAME BRINGS TERROR TO ALL WHO HEAR IT!
SO ARE WE GONNA LET THREE LITTLE LOSERS MAKE FOOLS OF US!?
NO SIR!!
I CAN'T HEAR YOU!!
NO SIR!!!
ALL RIGHT, PIPE DOWN!
IT'S TIME TO SHOW OUR ENEMIES JUST HOW TERRIFYING WE CAN BE!
BRING OUT THE "WILD ANIMAL SHOW"!

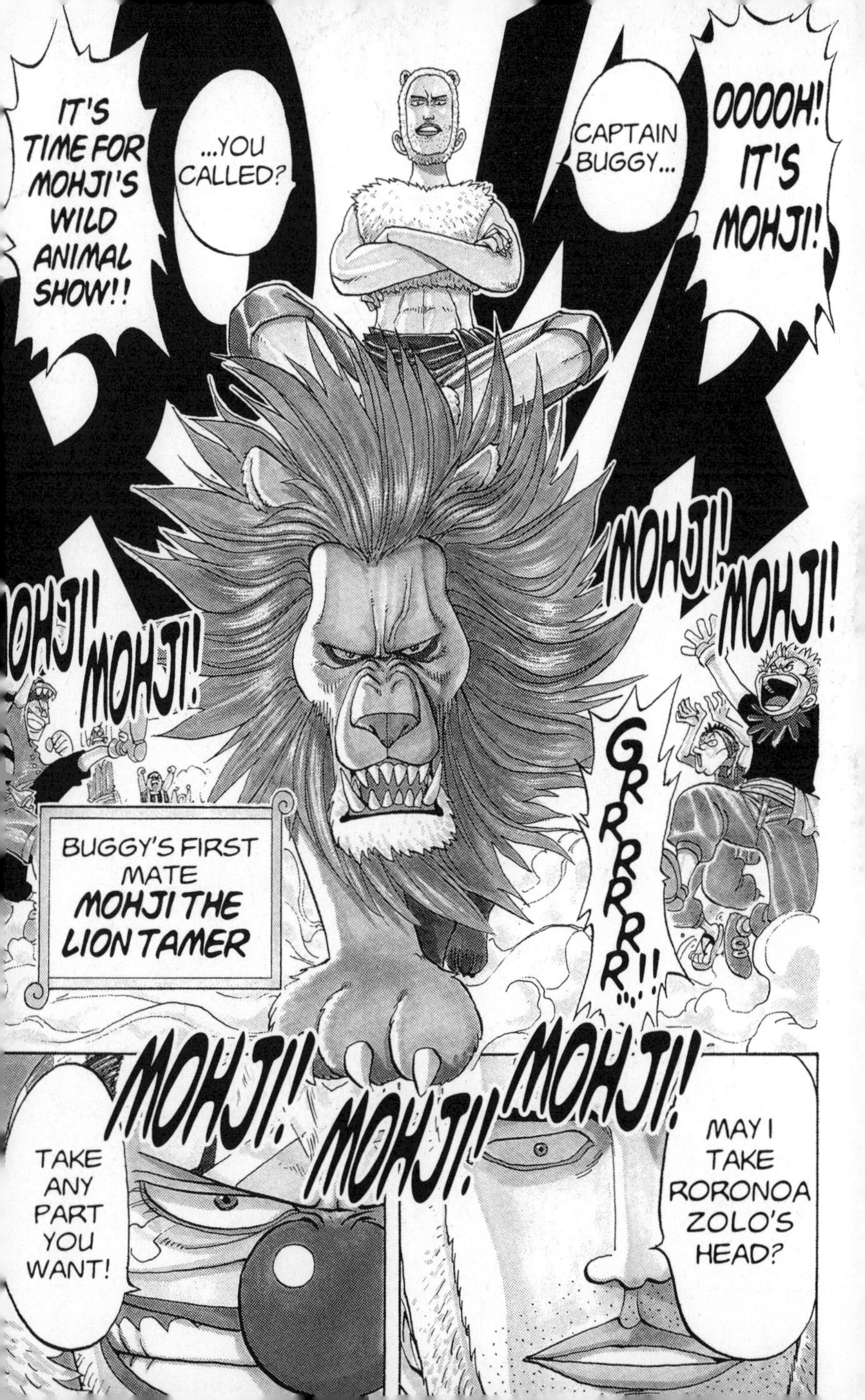
OOOOH! IT'S MOHJI!
CAPTAIN BUGGY...
...YOU CALLED?
IT'S TIME FOR MOHJI'S WILD ANIMAL SHOW!!
MOHJI! MOHJI!
GRRRRR...!!
OHJI! MOHJI!
BUGGY'S FIRST MATE MOHJI THE LION TAMER
MAY I TAKE RORONOA ZOLO'S HEAD?
MOHJI! MOHJI! MOHJI!
TAKE ANY PART YOU WANT!

READ THIS WAY

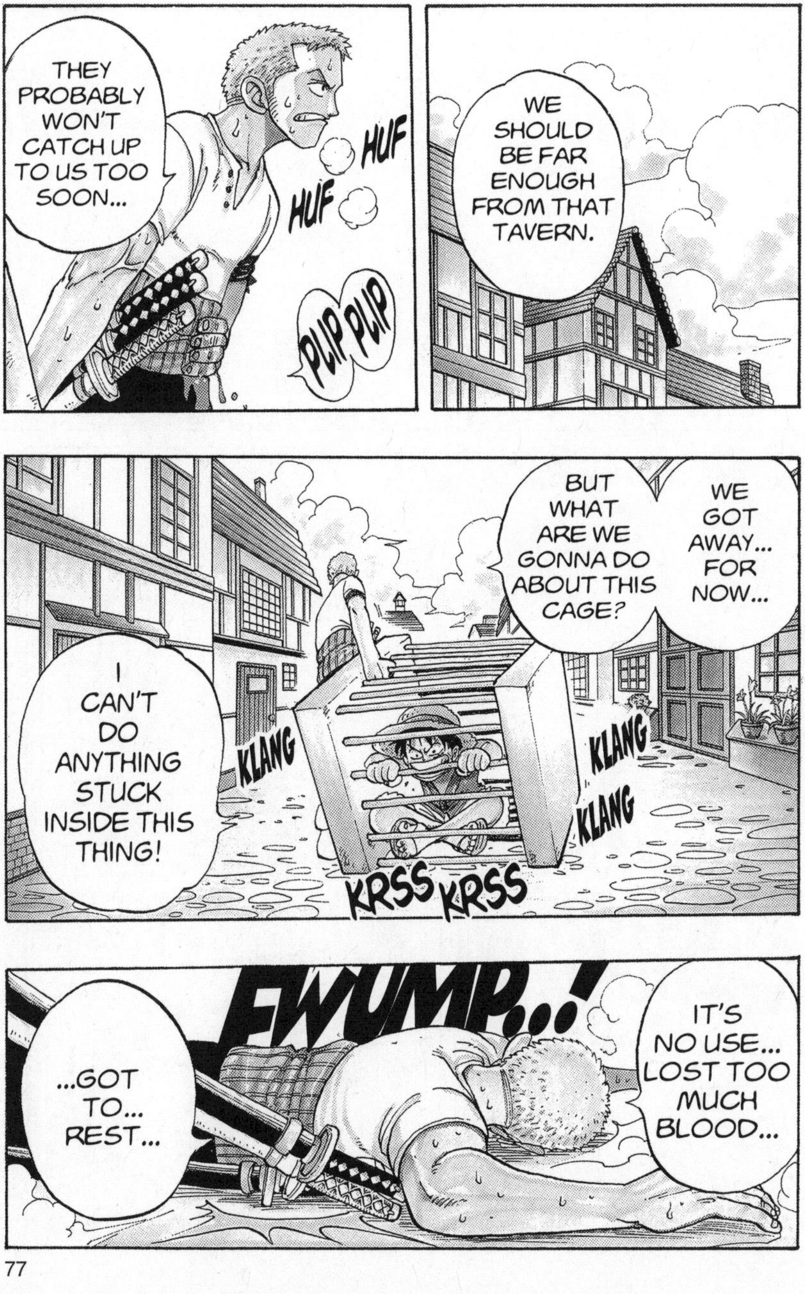
WE SHOULD BE FAR ENOUGH FROM THAT TAVERN.
THEY PROBABLY WON'T CATCH UP TO US TOO SOON...
HUF
HUF
PLIP PLIP
WE GOT AWAY... FOR NOW...
BUT WHAT ARE WE GONNA DO ABOUT THIS CAGE?
KLANG
KLANG
I CAN'T DO ANYTHING STUCK INSIDE THIS THING!
KLANG
KRSS KRSS
FWUMP...!
IT'S NO USE... LOST TOO MUCH BLOOD...
...GOT TO... REST...

READ THIS WAY

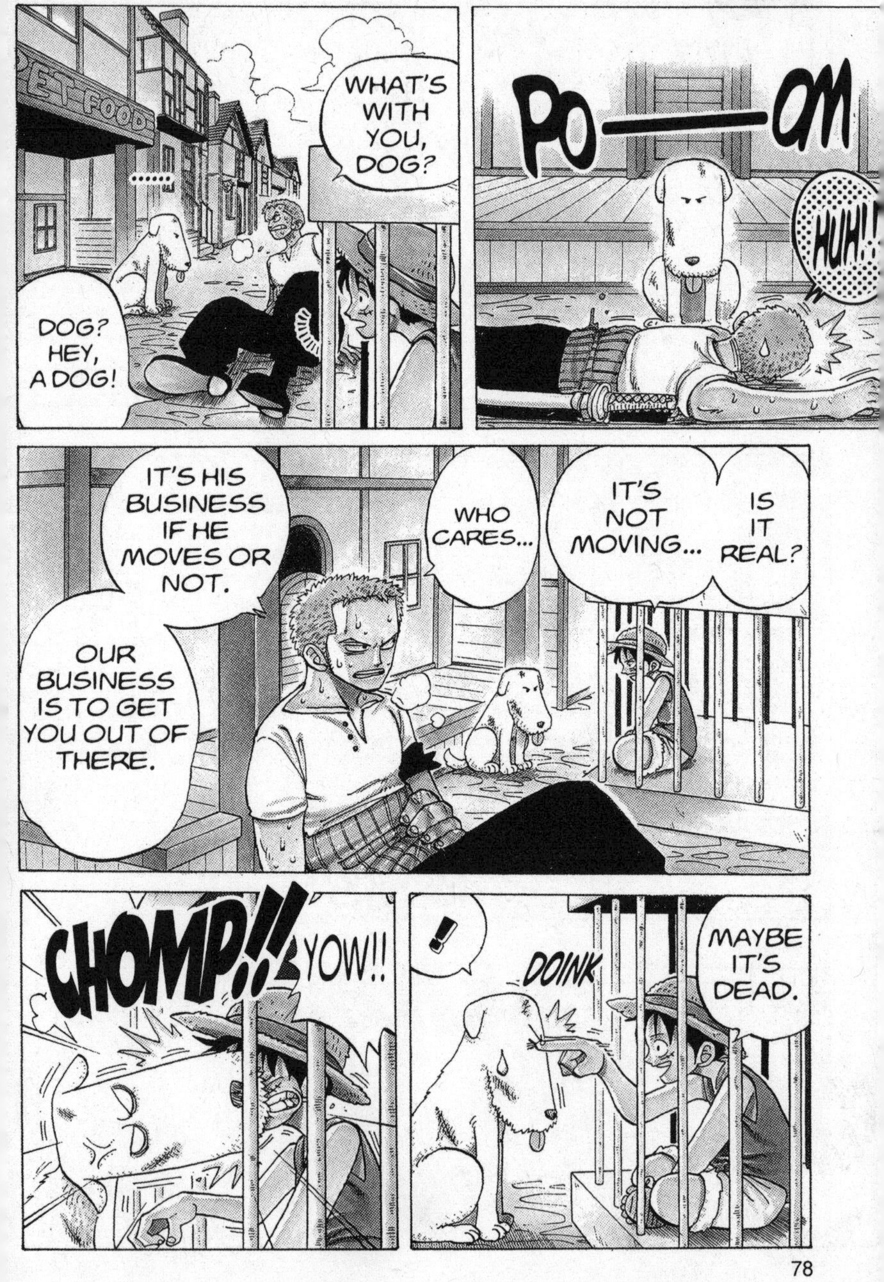
PO——OM
HUH!!
WHAT'S WITH YOU, DOG?
......
DOG? HEY, A DOG!
IS IT REAL?
IT'S NOT MOVING...
WHO CARES...
IT'S HIS BUSINESS IF HE MOVES OR NOT.
OUR BUSINESS IS TO GET YOU OUT OF THERE.
MAYBE IT'S DEAD.
DOINK
!
YOW!!
CHOMP!!

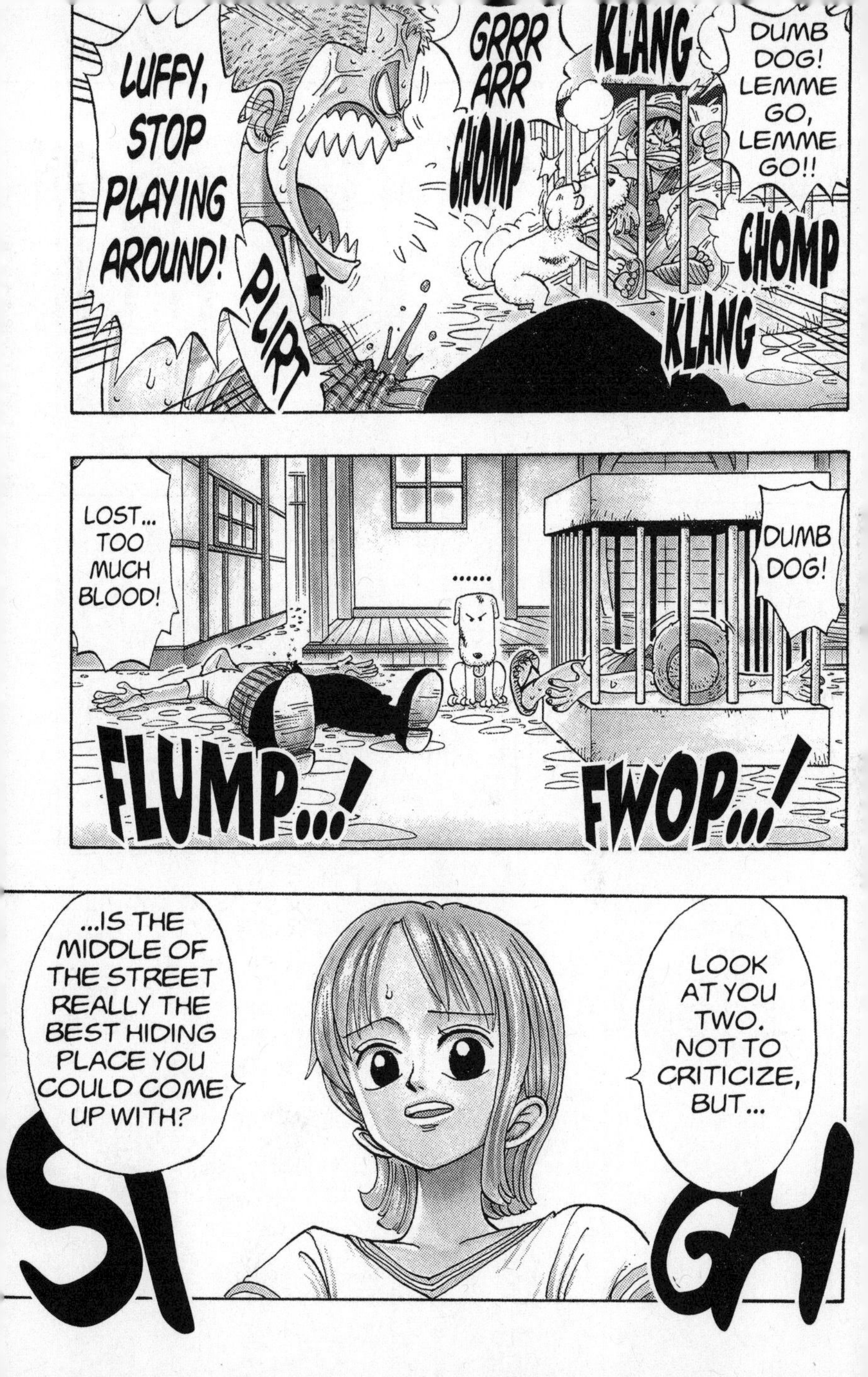
DUMB DOG! LEMME GO, LEMME GO!!
KLANG
GRRR ARR
CHOMP
CHOMP
KLANG
LUFFY, STOP PLAYING AROUND!
PURT
DUMB DOG!
......
LOST... TOO MUCH BLOOD!
FWOP...!
FLUMP...!
LOOK AT YOU TWO. NOT TO CRITICIZE, BUT...
...IS THE MIDDLE OF THE STREET REALLY THE BEST HIDING PLACE YOU COULD COME UP WITH?
SIGH

READ THIS WAY

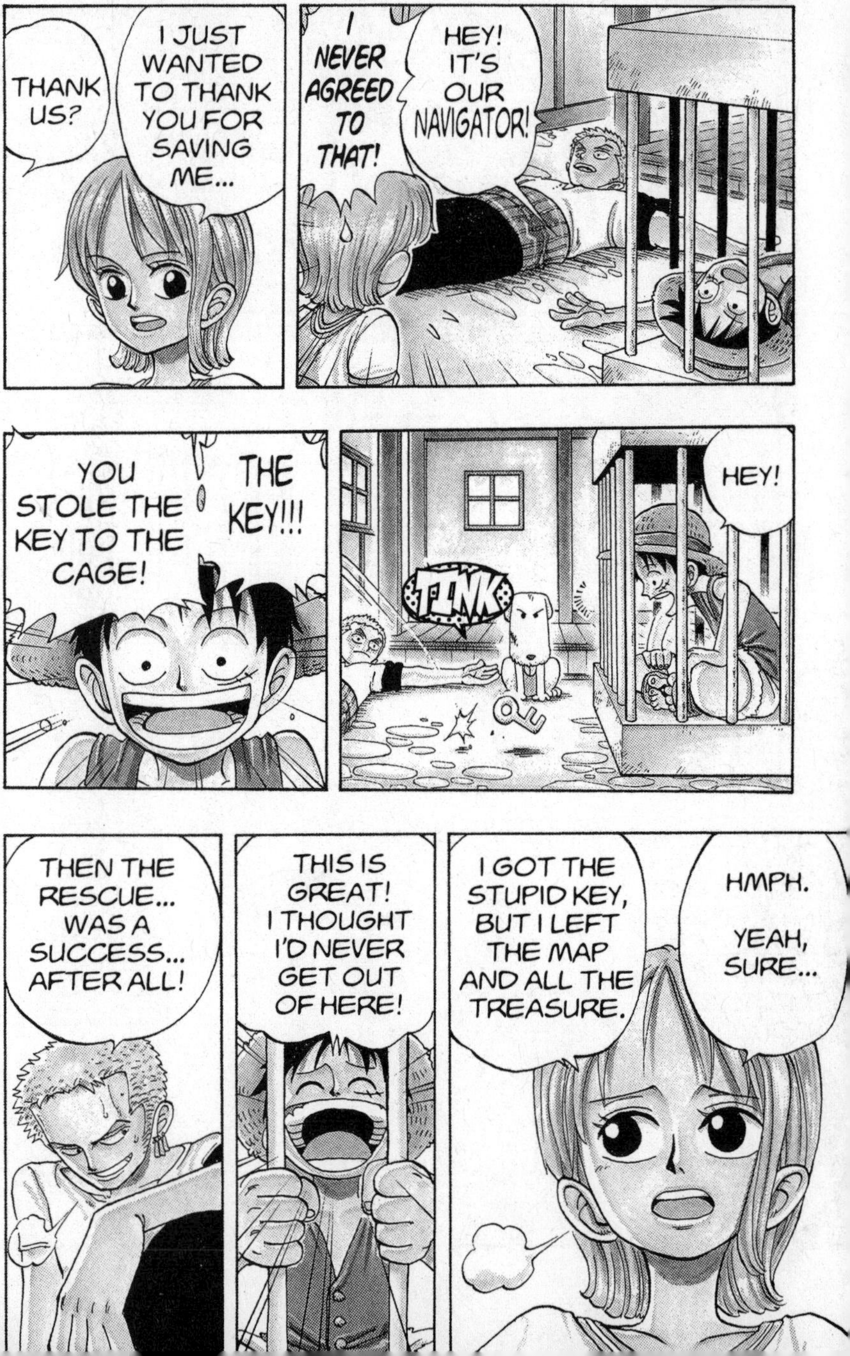
HEY! IT'S OUR NAVIGATOR!
I NEVER AGREED TO THAT!
I JUST WANTED TO THANK YOU FOR SAVING ME...
THANK US?
HEY!
TINK
THE KEY!!!
YOU STOLE THE KEY TO THE CAGE!
HMPH.
YEAH, SURE...
I GOT THE STUPID KEY, BUT I LEFT THE MAP AND ALL THE TREASURE.
THIS IS GREAT! I THOUGHT I'D NEVER GET OUT OF HERE!
THEN THE RESCUE... WAS A SUCCESS... AFTER ALL!

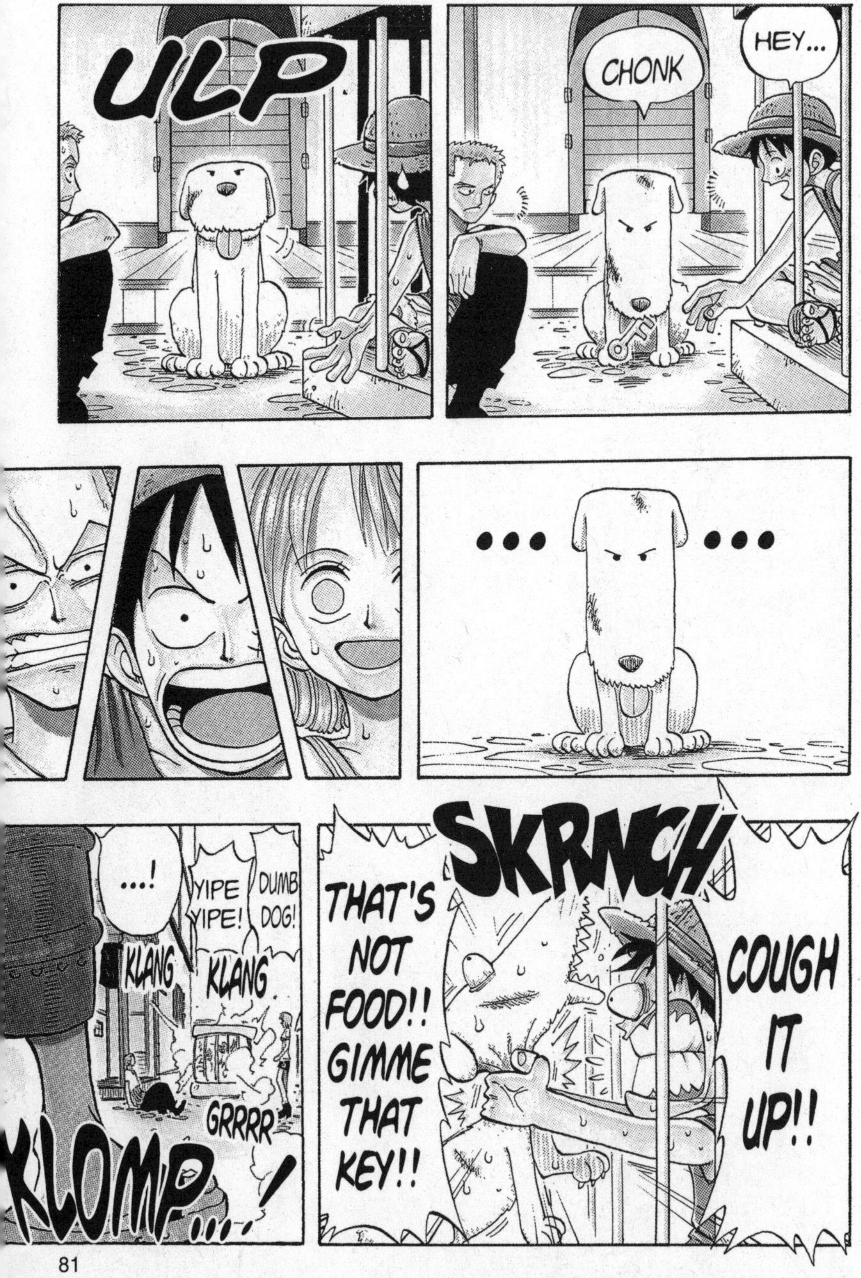
HEY...
CHONK
ULP
• • •   • • •
SKRNCH
COUGH IT UP!!
THAT'S NOT FOOD!! GIMME THAT KEY!!
DUMB DOG!
YIPE YIPE!
...!
KLANG
KLANG
GRRRR
KLOMP...!

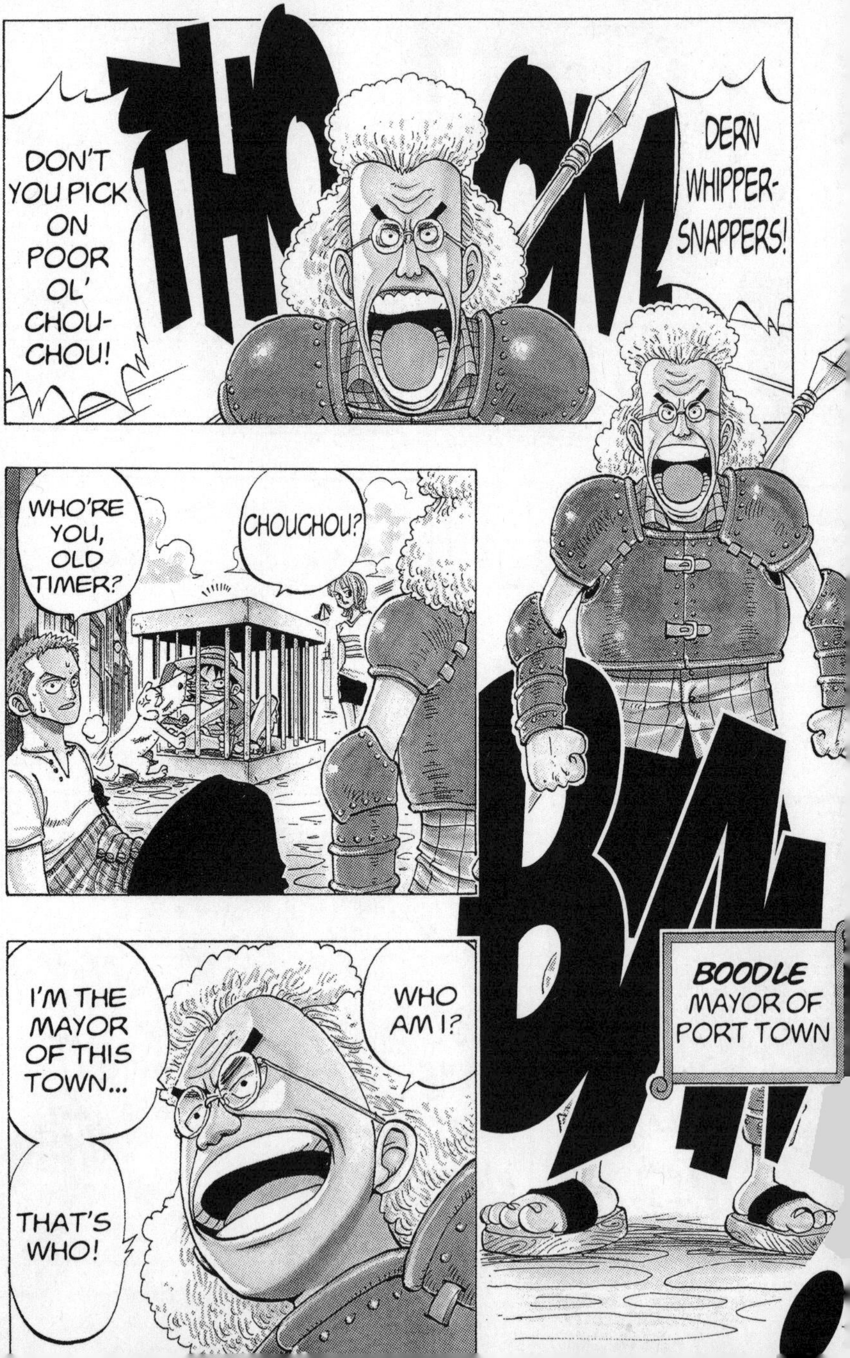
DERN WHIPPER-SNAPPERS!
THOOM
DON'T YOU PICK ON POOR OL' CHOU-CHOU!
BAM
BOODLE
MAYOR OF PORT TOWN
CHOUCHOU?
WHO'RE YOU, OLD TIMER?
WHO AM I?
I'M THE MAYOR OF THIS TOWN...
THAT'S WHO!

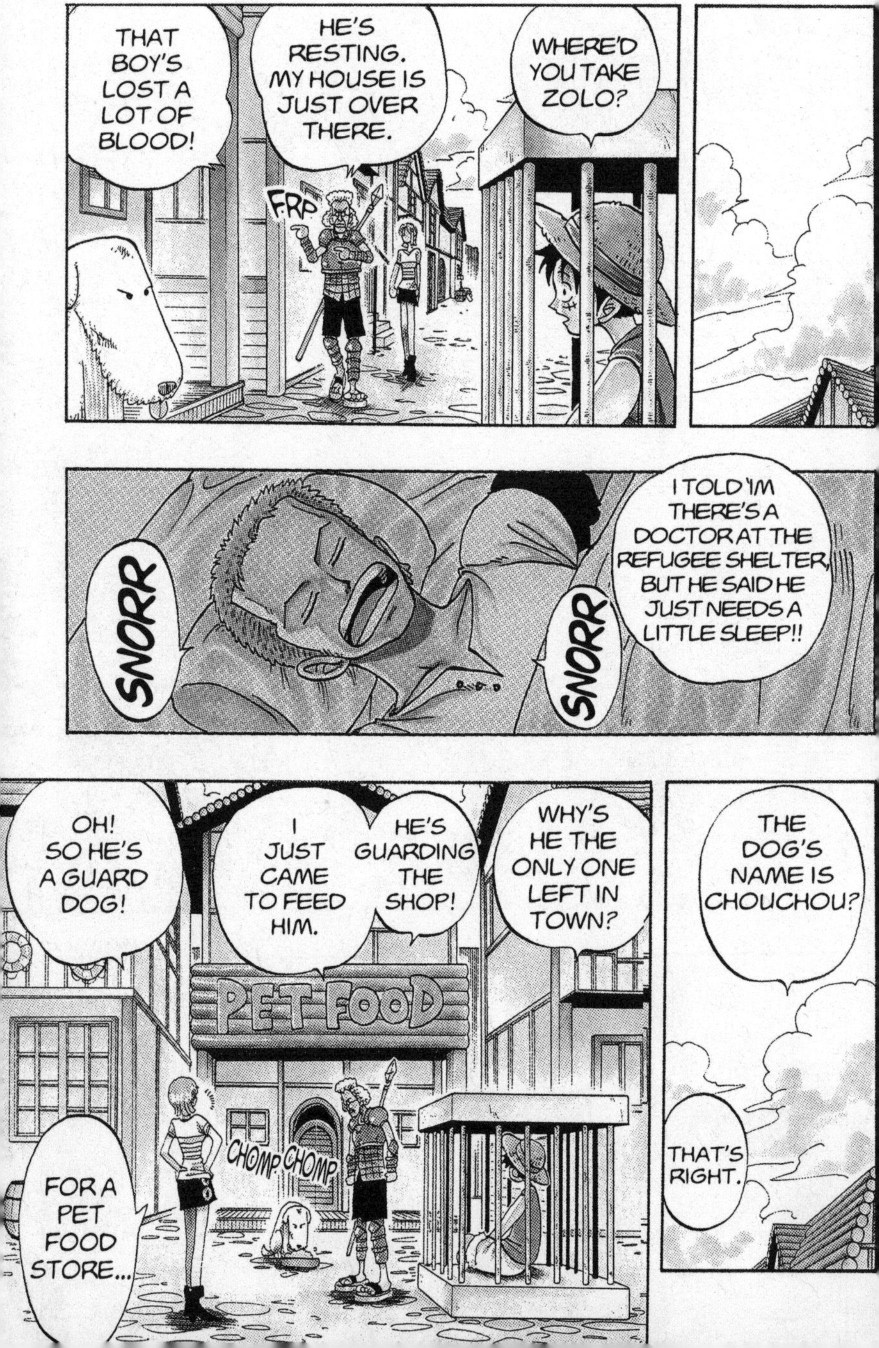
WHERE'D YOU TAKE ZOLO?
HE'S RESTING. MY HOUSE IS JUST OVER THERE.
FRP
THAT BOY'S LOST A LOT OF BLOOD!
I TOLD 'IM THERE'S A DOCTOR AT THE REFUGEE SHELTER, BUT HE SAID HE JUST NEEDS A LITTLE SLEEP!!
SNORR
SNORR
THE DOG'S NAME IS CHOUCHOU?
THAT'S RIGHT.
WHY'S HE THE ONLY ONE LEFT IN TOWN?
HE'S GUARDING THE SHOP!
I JUST CAME TO FEED HIM.
OH! SO HE'S A GUARD DOG!
PET FOOD
CHOMP CHOMP
FOR A PET FOOD STORE...

READ THIS WAY

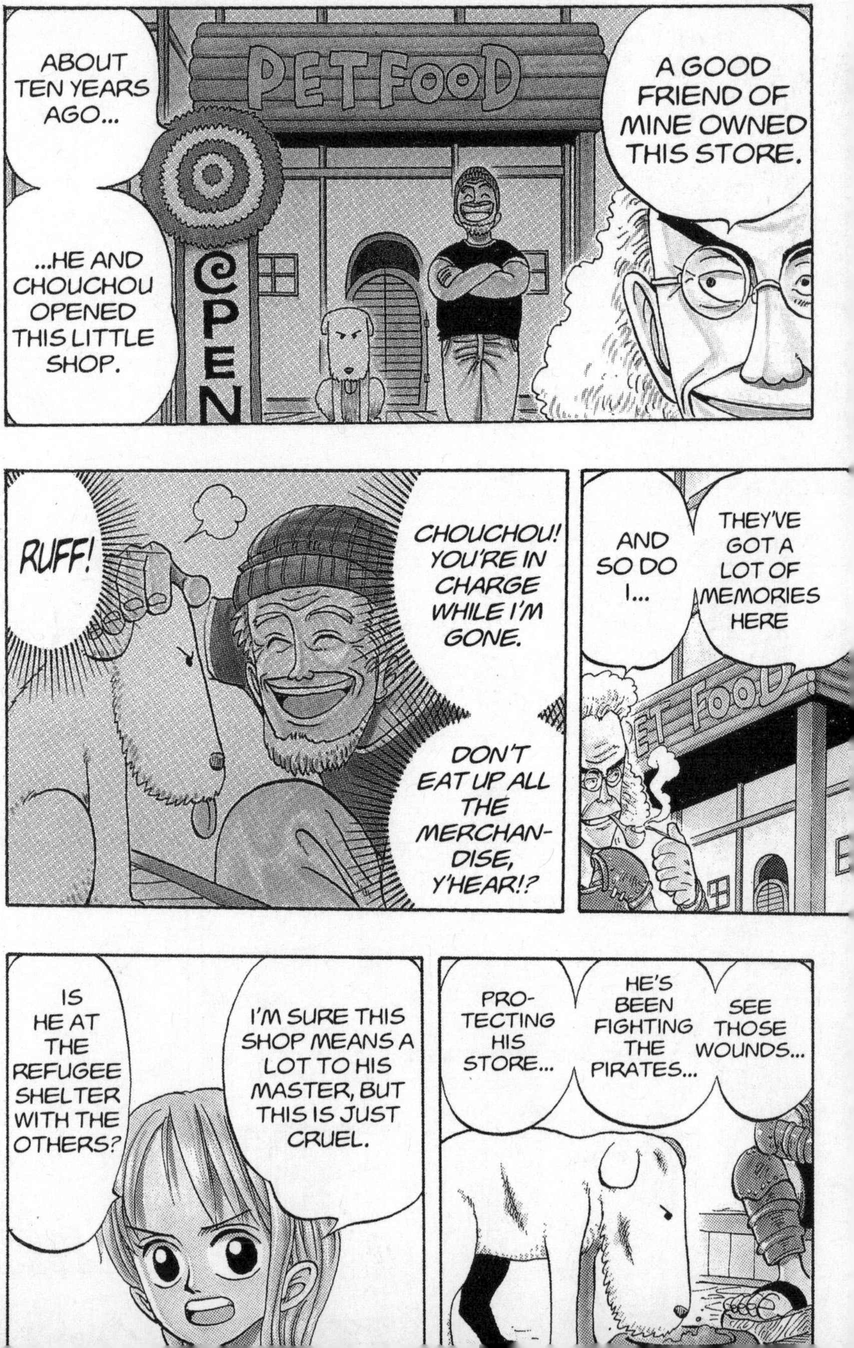
A GOOD FRIEND OF MINE OWNED THIS STORE.
PET FOOD
OPEN
ABOUT TEN YEARS AGO...
...HE AND CHOUCHOU OPENED THIS LITTLE SHOP.
THEY'VE GOT A LOT OF MEMORIES HERE
AND SO DO I...
PET FOOD
CHOUCHOU! YOU'RE IN CHARGE WHILE I'M GONE.
DON'T EAT UP ALL THE MERCHANDISE, Y'HEAR!?
RUFF!
SEE THOSE WOUNDS...
HE'S BEEN FIGHTING THE PIRATES...
PRO-TECTING HIS STORE...
I'M SURE THIS SHOP MEANS A LOT TO HIS MASTER, BUT THIS IS JUST CRUEL.
IS HE AT THE REFUGEE SHELTER WITH THE OTHERS?

READ THIS WAY

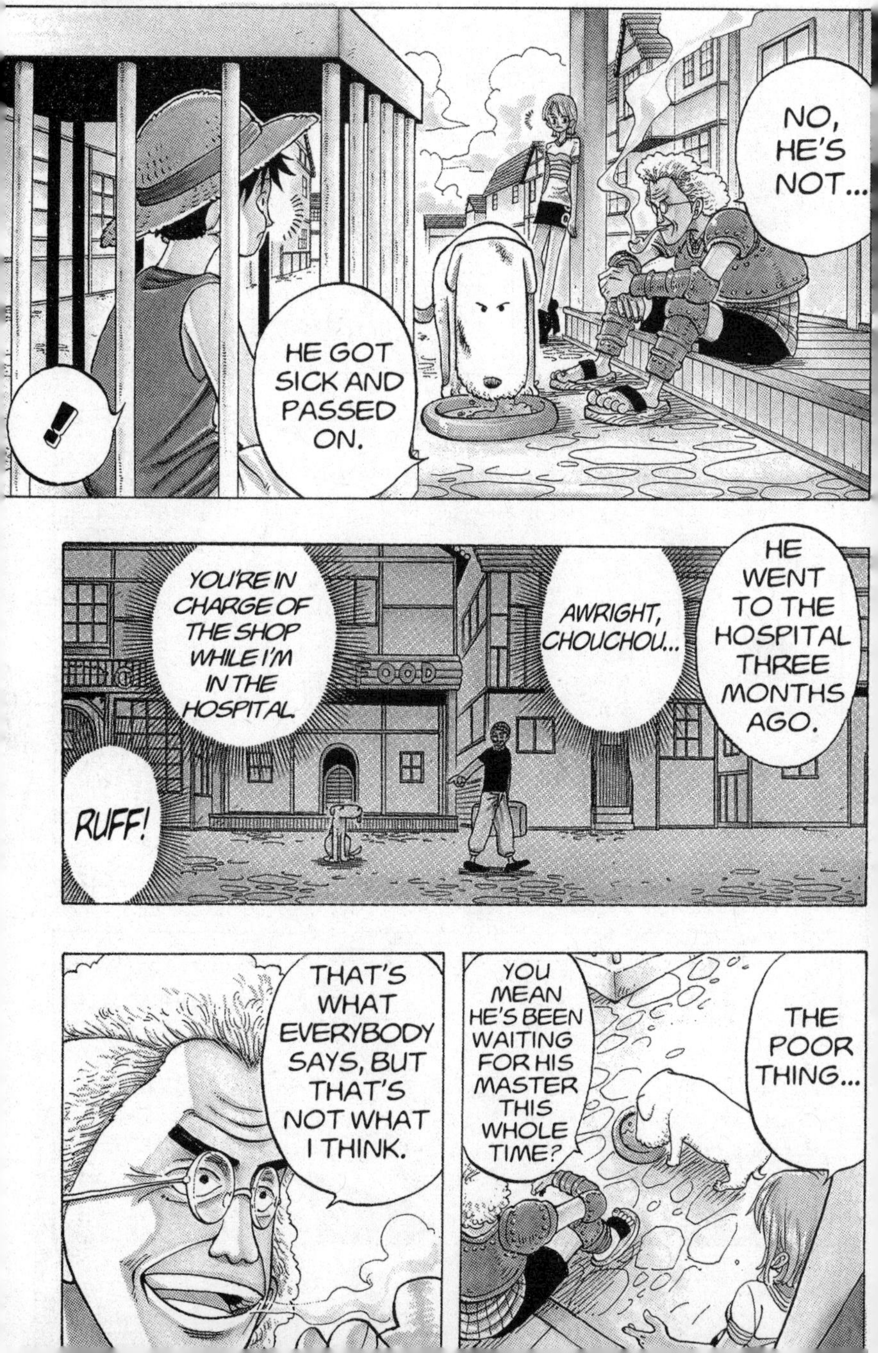

NO, HE'S NOT...
HE GOT SICK AND PASSED ON.
!
HE WENT TO THE HOSPITAL THREE MONTHS AGO.
AWRIGHT, CHOUCHOU...
YOU'RE IN CHARGE OF THE SHOP WHILE I'M IN THE HOSPITAL.
RUFF!
FOOD
THE POOR THING...
YOU MEAN HE'S BEEN WAITING FOR HIS MASTER THIS WHOLE TIME?
THAT'S WHAT EVERYBODY SAYS, BUT THAT'S NOT WHAT I THINK.

READ THIS WAY

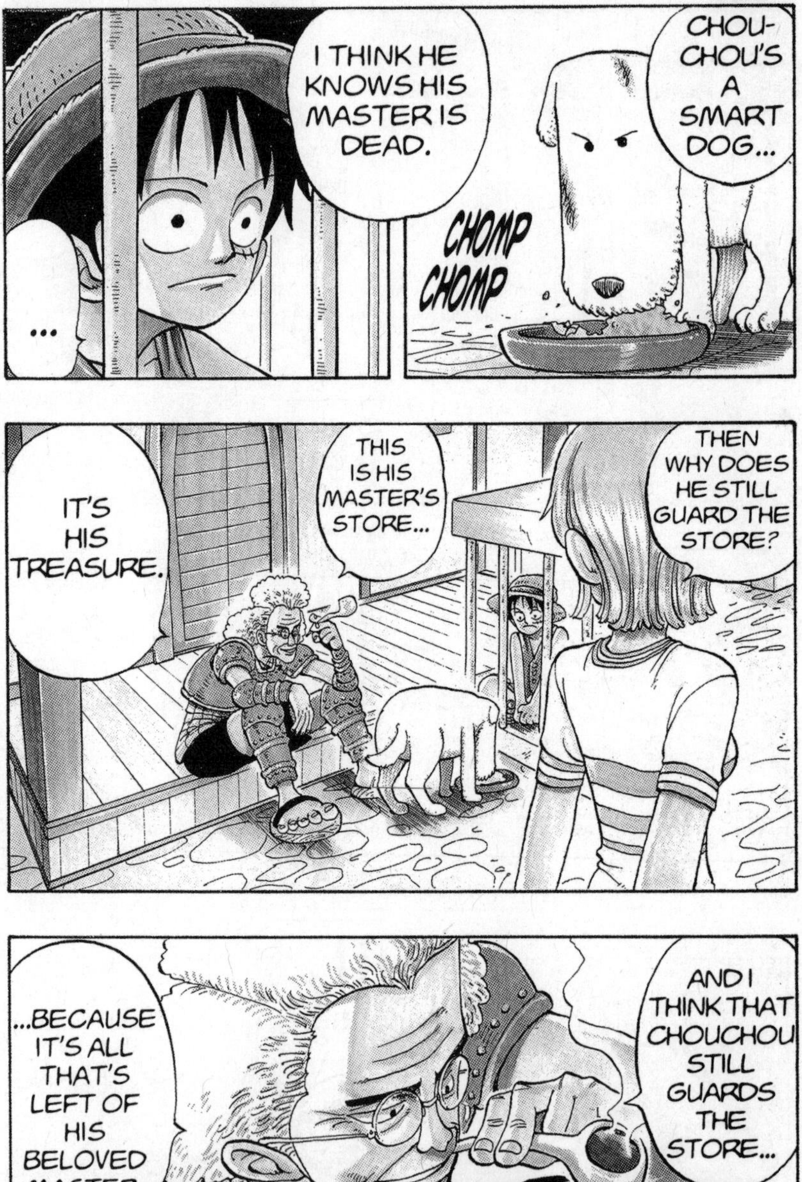
CHOU-CHOU'S A SMART DOG...
CHOMP CHOMP
I THINK HE KNOWS HIS MASTER IS DEAD.
...
THEN WHY DOES HE STILL GUARD THE STORE?
THIS IS HIS MASTER'S STORE...
IT'S HIS TREASURE.
AND I THINK THAT CHOUCHOU STILL GUARDS THE STORE...
...BECAUSE IT'S ALL THAT'S LEFT OF HIS BELOVED MASTER.

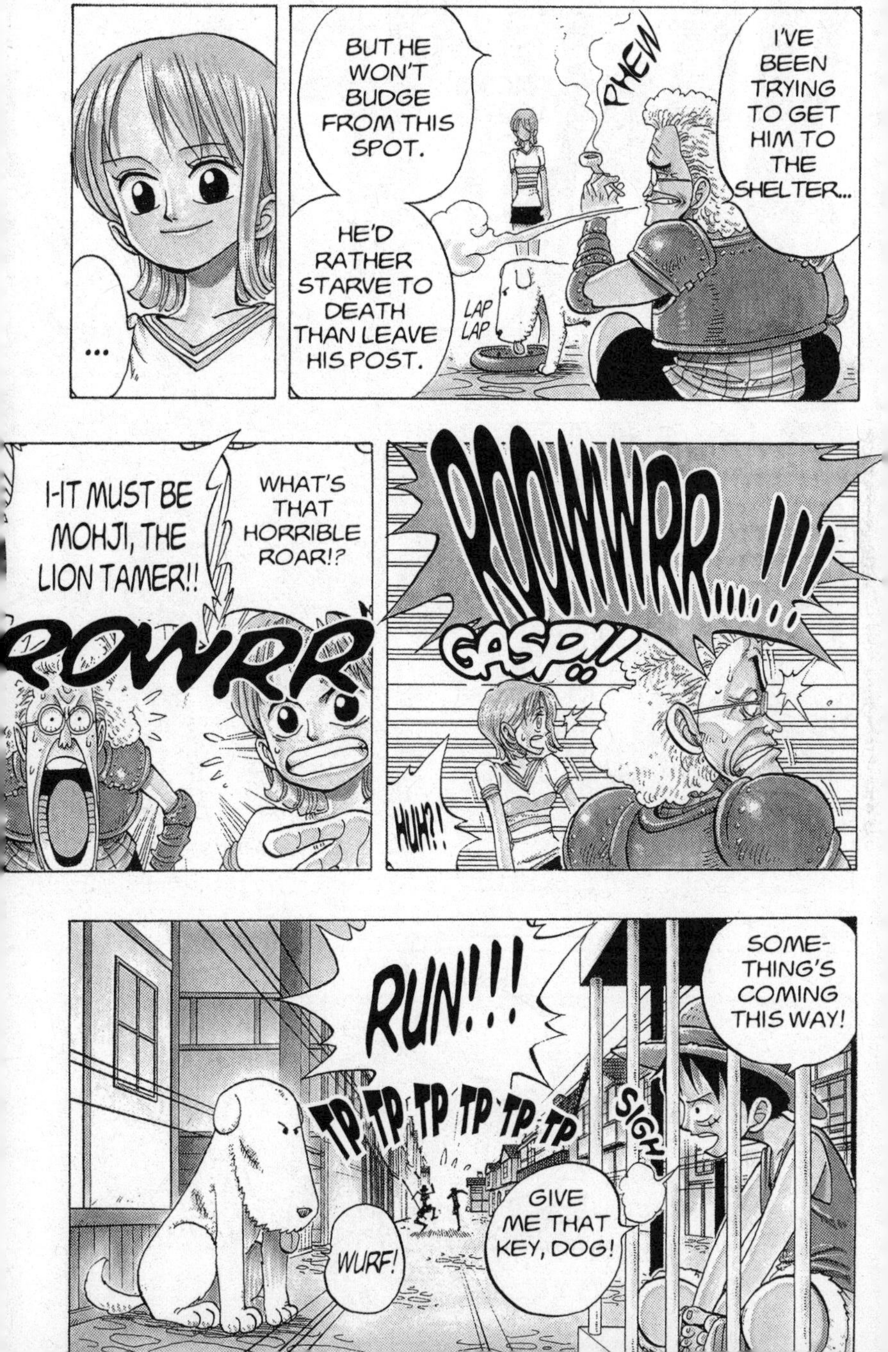
I'VE BEEN TRYING TO GET HIM TO THE SHELTER...
PHEW
BUT HE WON'T BUDGE FROM THIS SPOT.
HE'D RATHER STARVE TO DEATH THAN LEAVE HIS POST.
LAP LAP
...
ROOWWRR...!!!
GASP!!
HUH?!
WHAT'S THAT HORRIBLE ROAR!?
I-IT MUST BE MOHJI, THE LION TAMER!!
ROWRR
SOME-THING'S COMING THIS WAY!
RUN!!!
SIGH
TP TP TP TP TP TP
GIVE ME THAT KEY, DOG!
WURF!

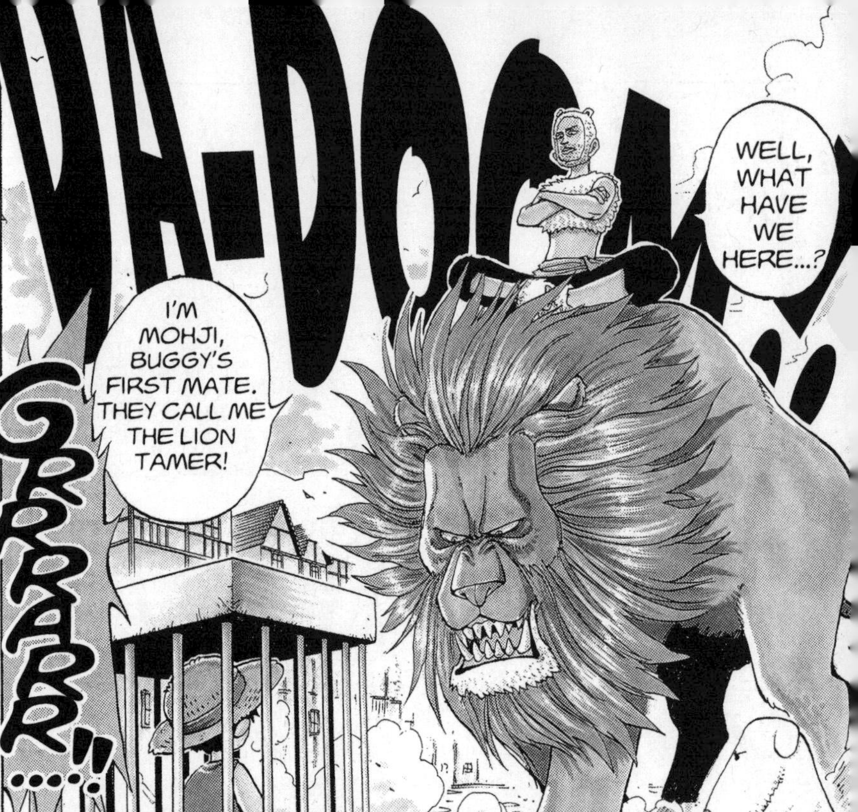
KA-DOOM
WELL, WHAT HAVE WE HERE...?
I'M MOHJI, BUGGY'S FIRST MATE. THEY CALL ME THE LION TAMER!
GRRRARR...!!

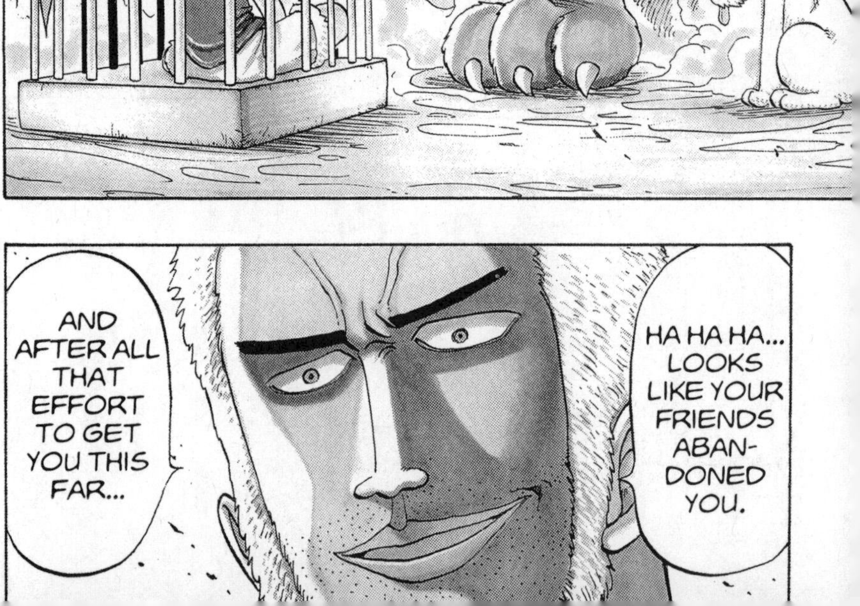
HA HA HA... LOOKS LIKE YOUR FRIENDS ABAN-DONED YOU.
AND AFTER ALL THAT EFFORT TO GET YOU THIS FAR...

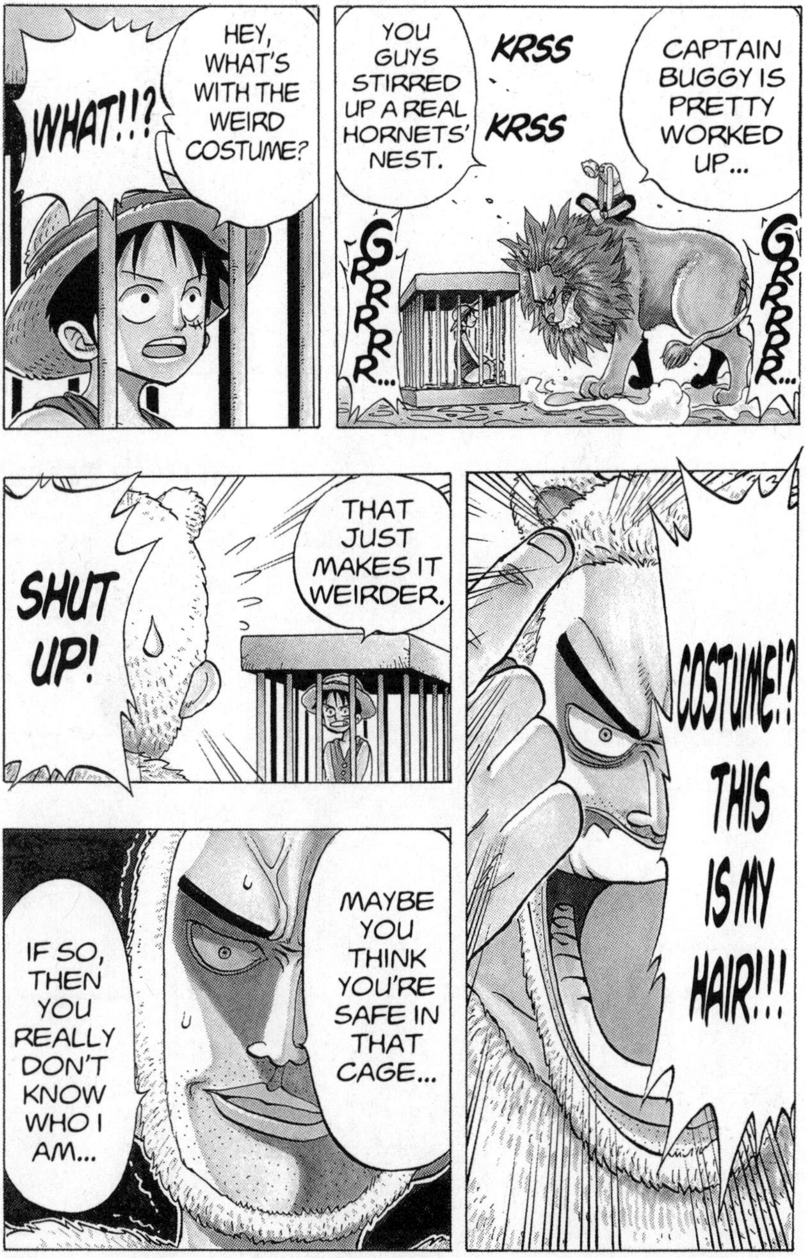
CAPTAIN BUGGY IS PRETTY WORKED UP...
KRSS
KRSS
YOU GUYS STIRRED UP A REAL HORNETS' NEST.
GRRRRR...
GRRRR...
HEY, WHAT'S WITH THE WEIRD COSTUME?
WHAT!!?
COSTUME!? THIS IS MY HAIR!!!
THAT JUST MAKES IT WEIRDER.
SHUT UP!
MAYBE YOU THINK YOU'RE SAFE IN THAT CAGE...
IF SO, THEN YOU REALLY DON'T KNOW WHO I AM...

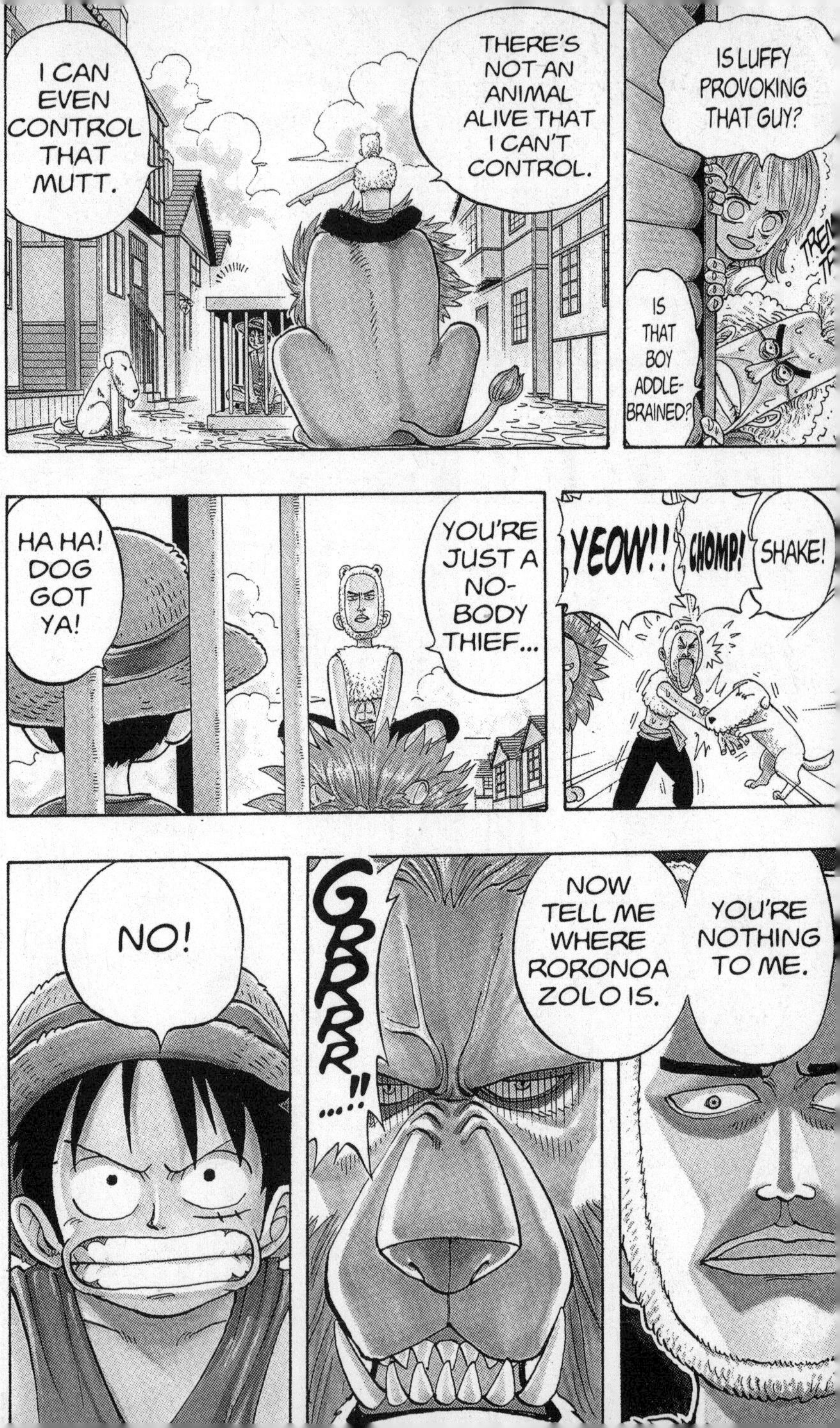

IS LUFFY PROVOKING THAT GUY?
IS THAT BOY ADDLE-BRAINED?
THERE'S NOT AN ANIMAL ALIVE THAT I CAN'T CONTROL.
I CAN EVEN CONTROL THAT MUTT.
SHAKE!
CHOMP!
YEOW!!
YOU'RE JUST A NO-BODY THIEF...
HA HA! DOG GOT YA!
YOU'RE NOTHING TO ME.
NOW TELL ME WHERE RORONOA ZOLO IS.
GRRRR!!
...!!
NO!

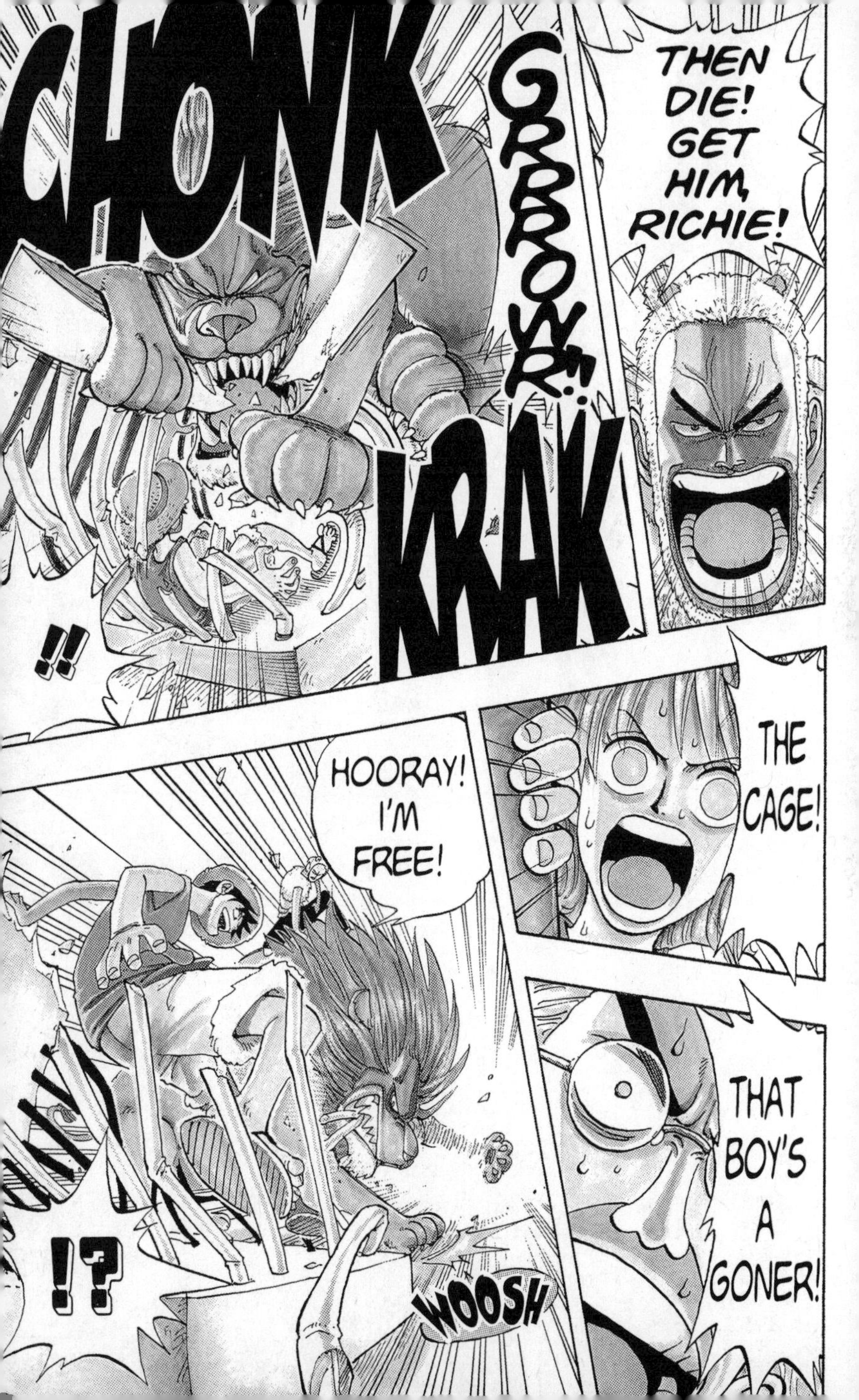
THEN DIE! GET HIM, RICHIE!
CHONK
GRRROWR!!
KRAK
!!
THE CAGE!
THAT BOY'S A GONER!
HOORAY! I'M FREE!
!?
WOOSH

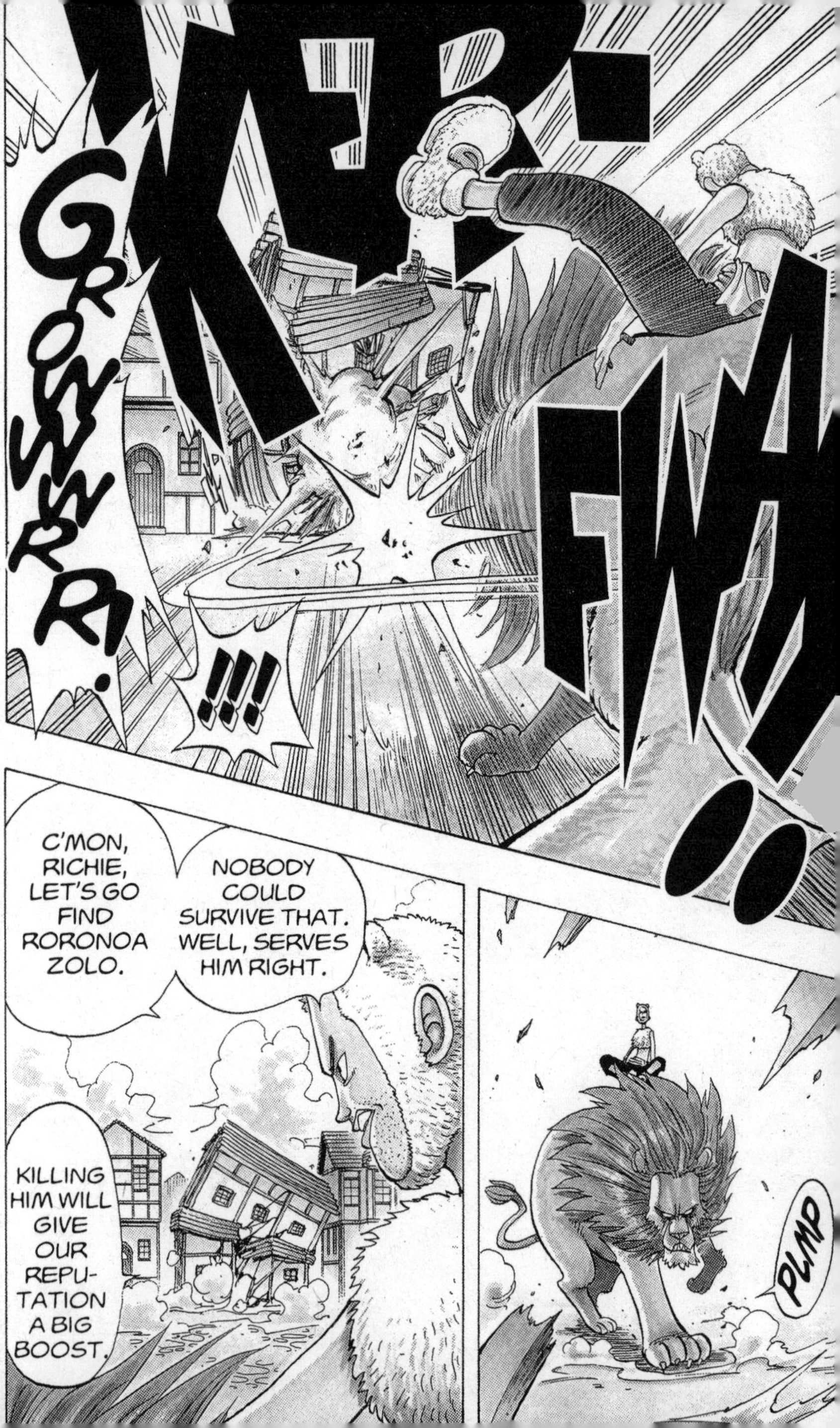
GROWWRR!
!!!!
PLMP
NOBODY COULD SURVIVE THAT. WELL, SERVES HIM RIGHT.
C'MON, RICHIE, LET'S GO FIND RORONOA ZOLO.
KILLING HIM WILL GIVE OUR REPU-TATION A BIG BOOST.

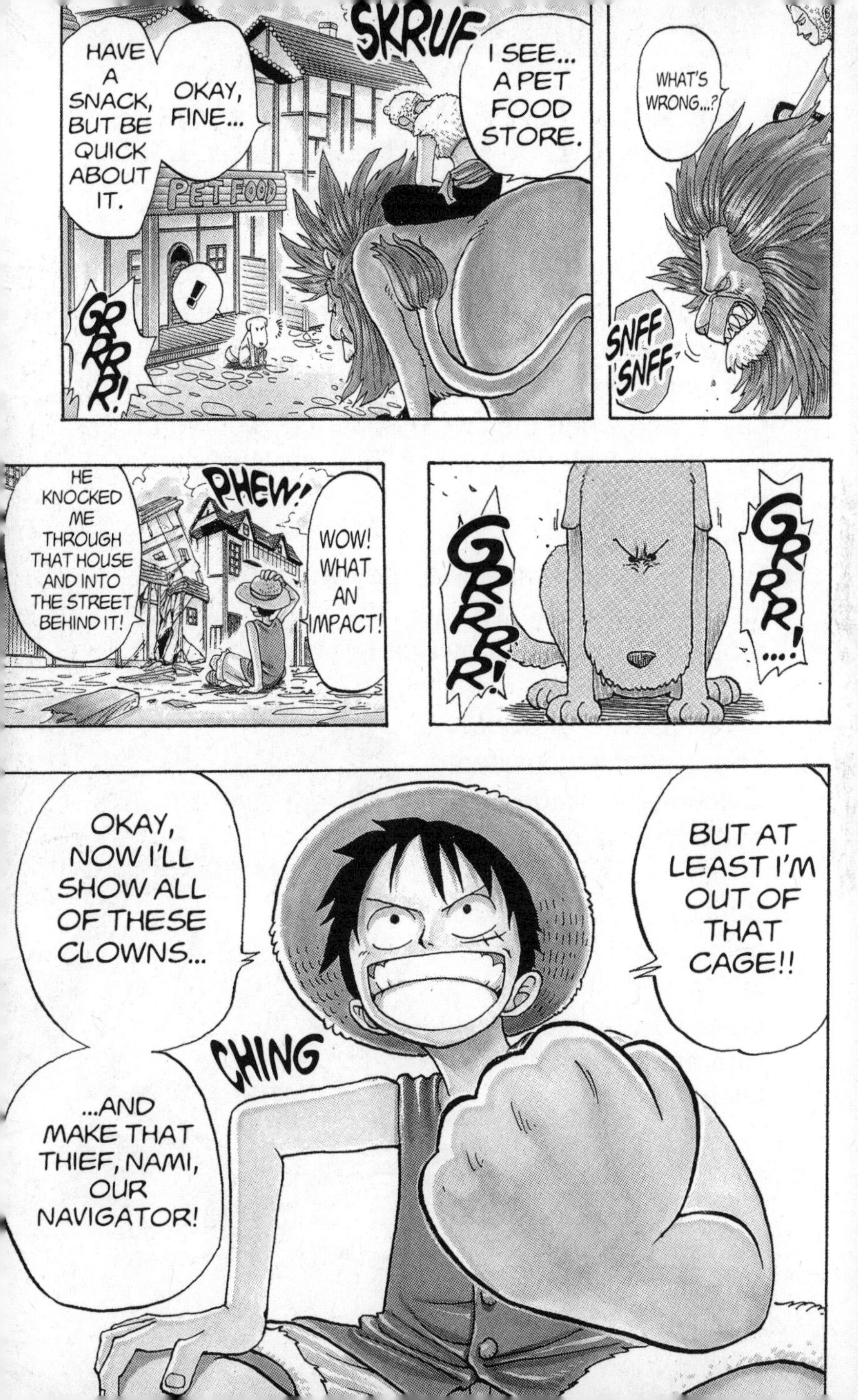
WHAT'S WRONG...?
SNFF SNFF
SKRUF
I SEE... A PET FOOD STORE.
OKAY, FINE...
HAVE A SNACK, BUT BE QUICK ABOUT IT.
PET FOOD
!
GRRRR!
GRRR...!
GRRRR!
PHEW!
WOW! WHAT AN IMPACT!
HE KNOCKED ME THROUGH THAT HOUSE AND INTO THE STREET BEHIND IT!
BUT AT LEAST I'M OUT OF THAT CAGE!!
OKAY, NOW I'LL SHOW ALL OF THESE CLOWNS...
CHING
...AND MAKE THAT THIEF, NAMI, OUR NAVIGATOR!

VIKINGS, PART 2

- These guys were really scary. How scary were they? Well, they'd sweep out of an inlet, attack ships or villages, and slaughter everyone, even the local priests. They stole food and anything of value, and when they were done they set fire to everything they didn't want. They were unbelievable villians.

- But from their perspective, they were just trying to make a living. They brought the spoils of their piracy home to better their villages. This was “men's work.” These people considered a lifetime of pillage and battle to be a good career.

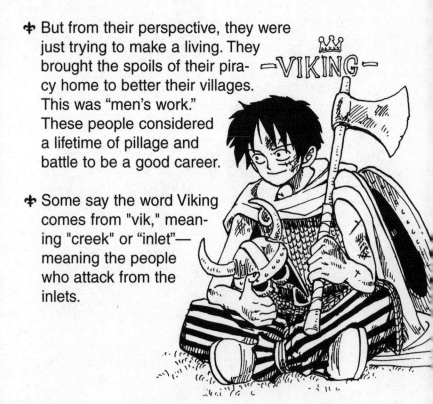

- Some say the word Viking comes from "vik," meaning "creek" or “inlet”—meaning the people who attack from the inlets.

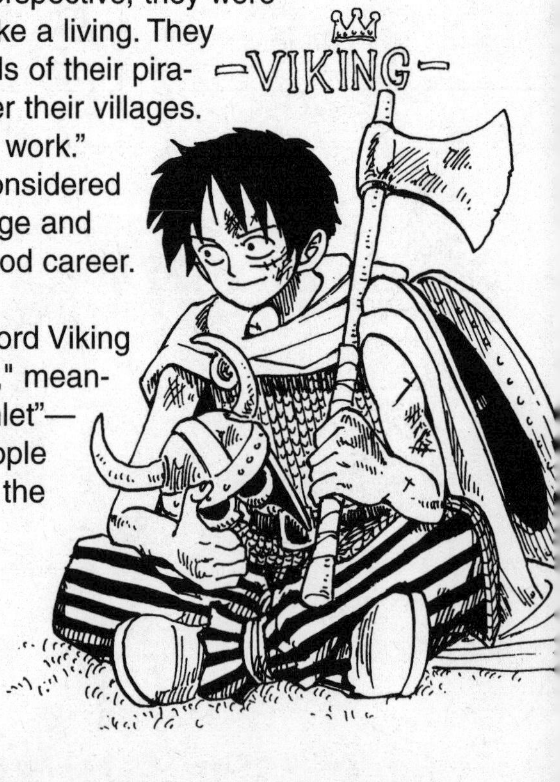

-VIKING-

Chapter 13:
TREASURE

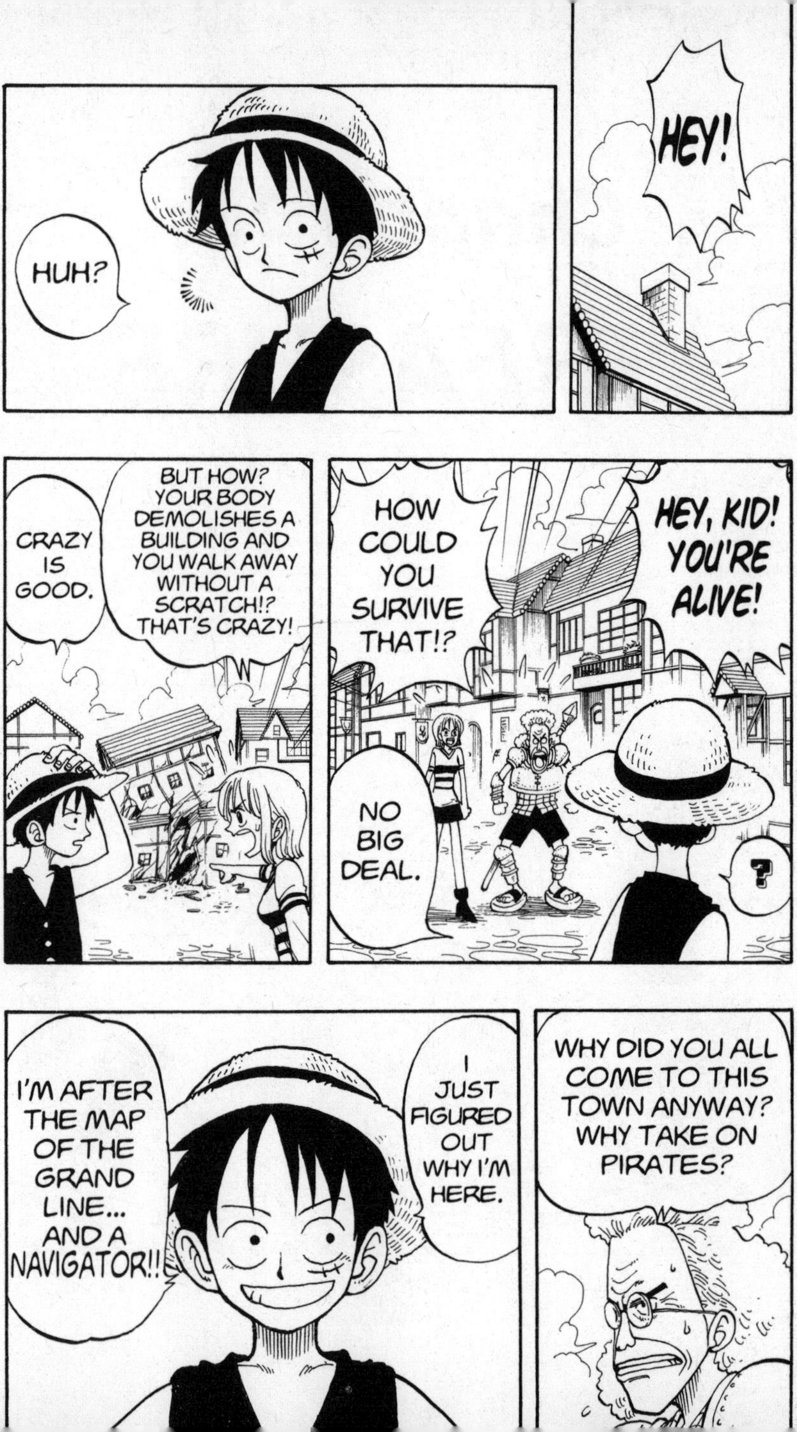

HEY!
HUH?
HEY, KID! YOU'RE ALIVE!
?
HOW COULD YOU SURVIVE THAT!?
NO BIG DEAL.
BUT HOW? YOUR BODY DEMOLISHES A BUILDING AND YOU WALK AWAY WITHOUT A SCRATCH!? THAT'S CRAZY!
CRAZY IS GOOD.
WHY DID YOU ALL COME TO THIS TOWN ANYWAY? WHY TAKE ON PIRATES?
I JUST FIGURED OUT WHY I'M HERE.
I'M AFTER THE MAP OF THE GRAND LINE... AND A NAVIGATOR!!

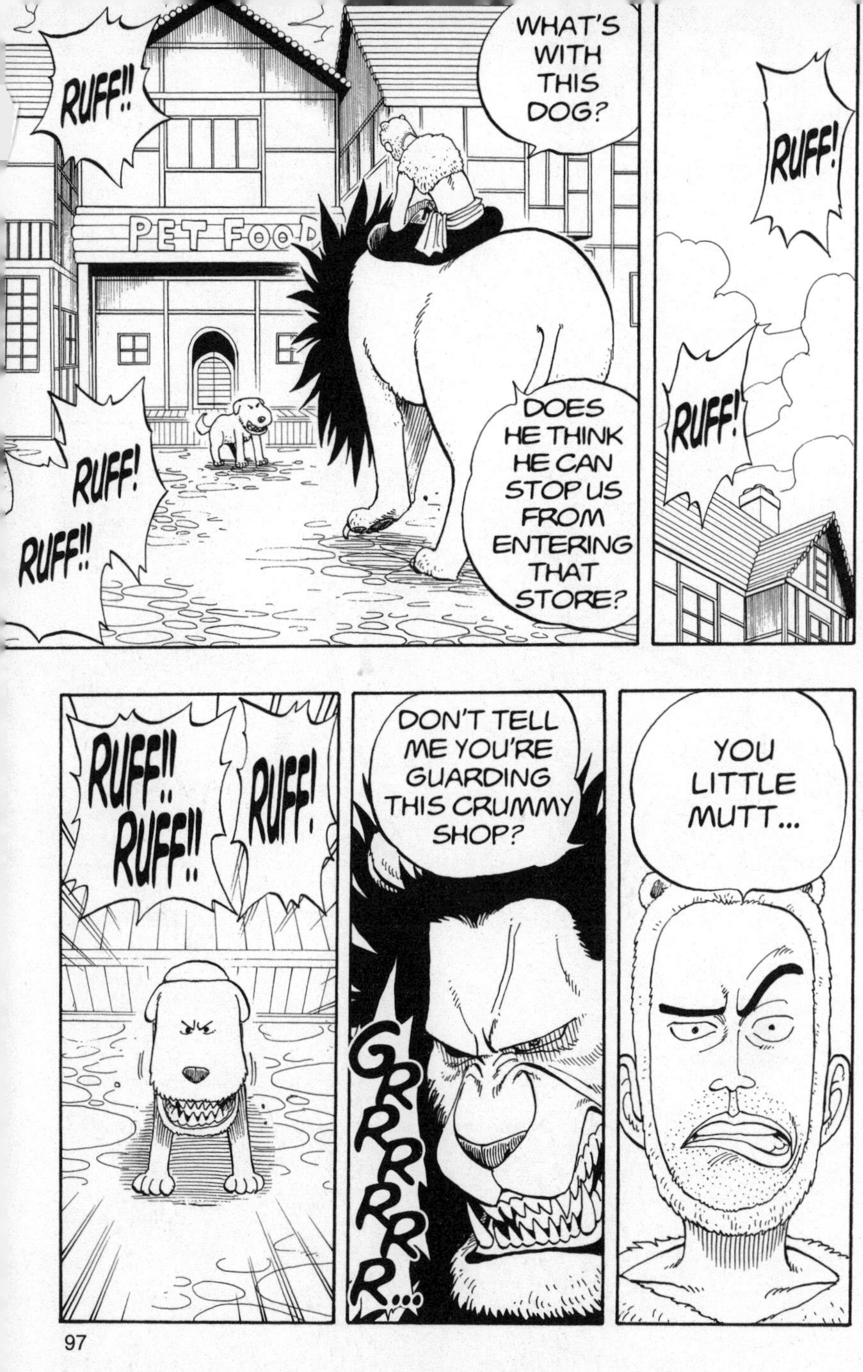
RUFF!
RUFF!
WHAT'S WITH THIS DOG?
RUFF!!
DOES HE THINK HE CAN STOP US FROM ENTERING THAT STORE?
RUFF!
RUFF!!
PET FOOD
YOU LITTLE MUTT...
DON'T TELL ME YOU'RE GUARDING THIS CRUMMY SHOP?
GRRRRR...
RUFF!
RUFF!! RUFF!!

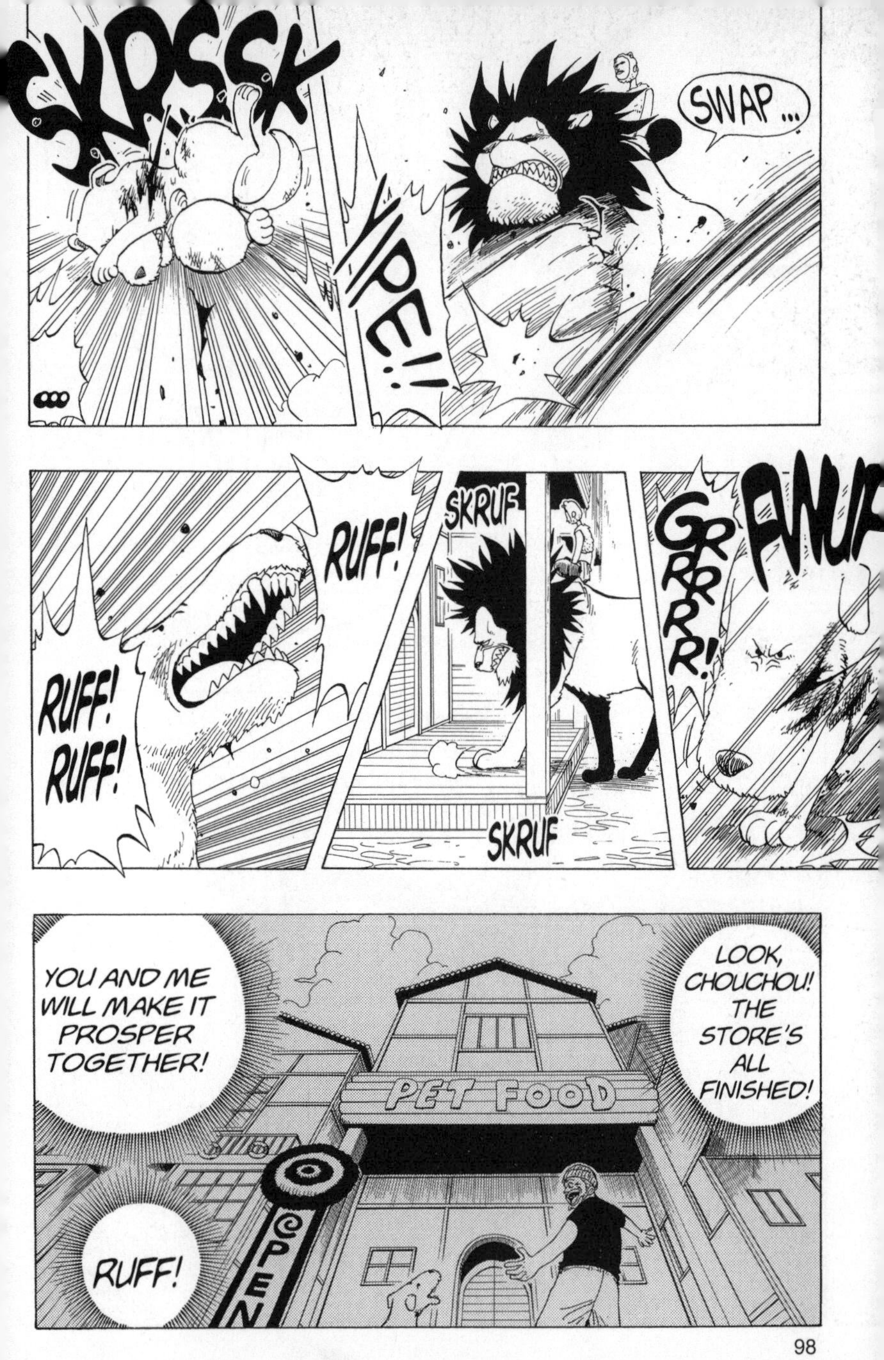
SWAP ...
YIPE!!
SKRSSK
GRRRRR!
ANUF
SKRUF
SKRUF
RUFF!
RUFF! RUFF!
LOOK, CHOUCHOU! THE STORE'S ALL FINISHED!
YOU AND ME WILL MAKE IT PROSPER TOGETHER!
RUFF!
PET FOOD
OPEN

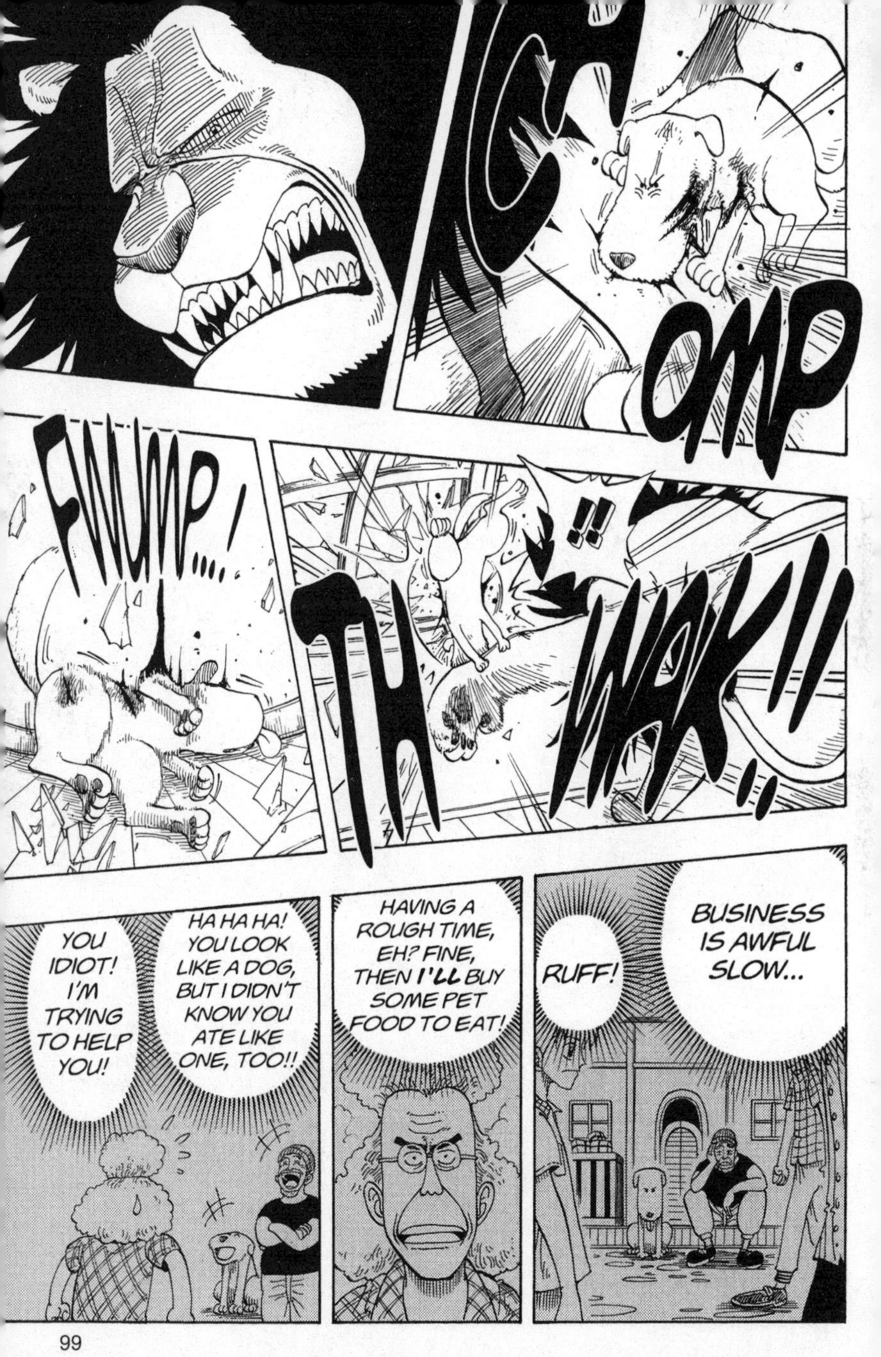
C OMP
!!
THWAK!!
FWUMP!....
BUSINESS IS AWFUL SLOW...
RUFF!
HAVING A ROUGH TIME, EH? FINE, THEN I'LL BUY SOME PET FOOD TO EAT!
HA HA HA! YOU LOOK LIKE A DOG, BUT I DIDN'T KNOW YOU ATE LIKE ONE, TOO!!
YOU IDIOT! I'M TRYING TO HELP YOU!

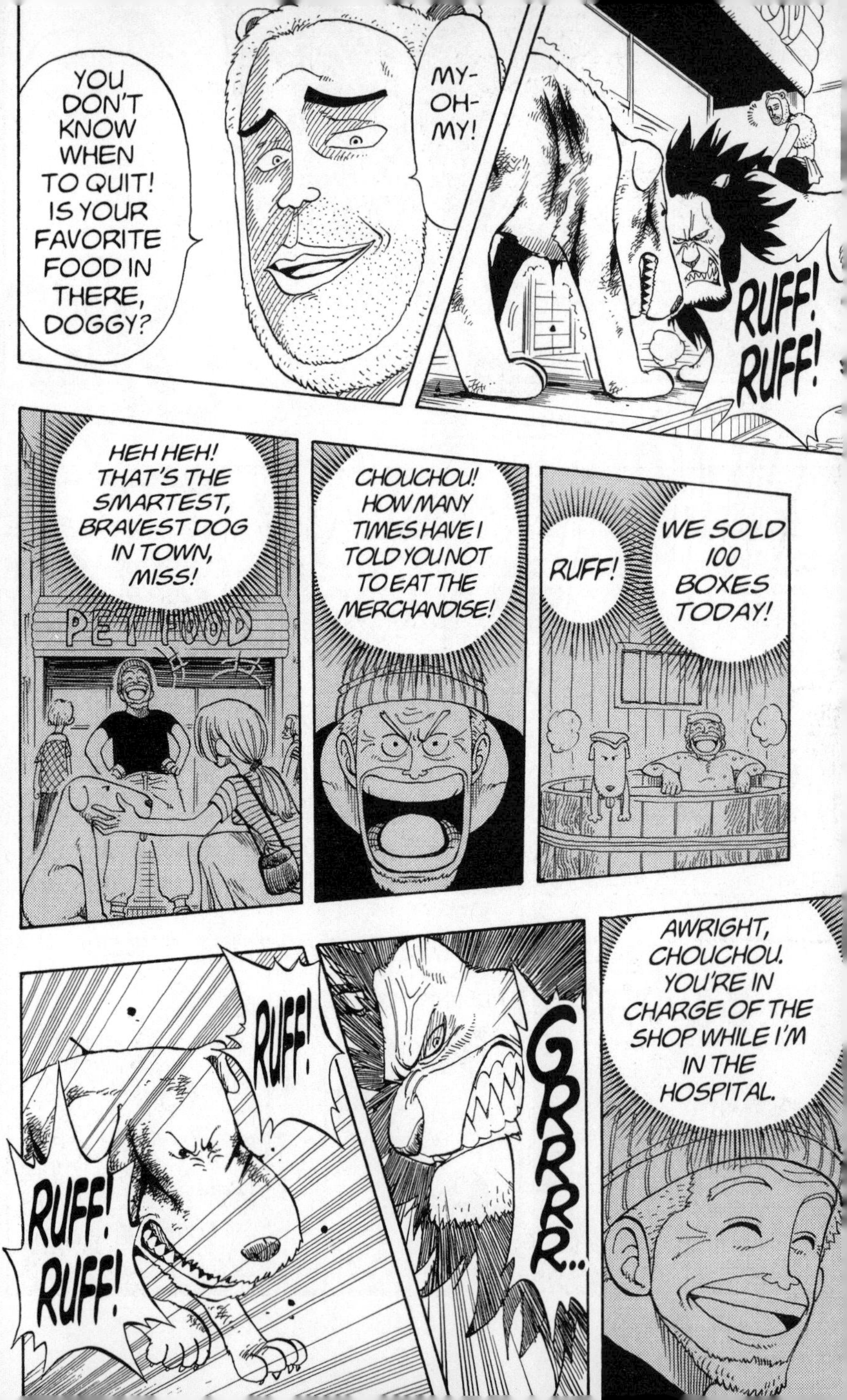
RUFF! RUFF!
MY-OH-MY!
YOU DON'T KNOW WHEN TO QUIT! IS YOUR FAVORITE FOOD IN THERE, DOGGY?
WE SOLD 100 BOXES TODAY!
RUFF!
CHOUCHOU! HOW MANY TIMES HAVE I TOLD YOU NOT TO EAT THE MERCHANDISE!
HEH HEH! THAT'S THE SMARTEST, BRAVEST DOG IN TOWN, MISS!
PET FOOD
AWRIGHT, CHOUCHOU. YOU'RE IN CHARGE OF THE SHOP WHILE I'M IN THE HOSPITAL.
GRRRR...
RUFF!
RUFF! RUFF!

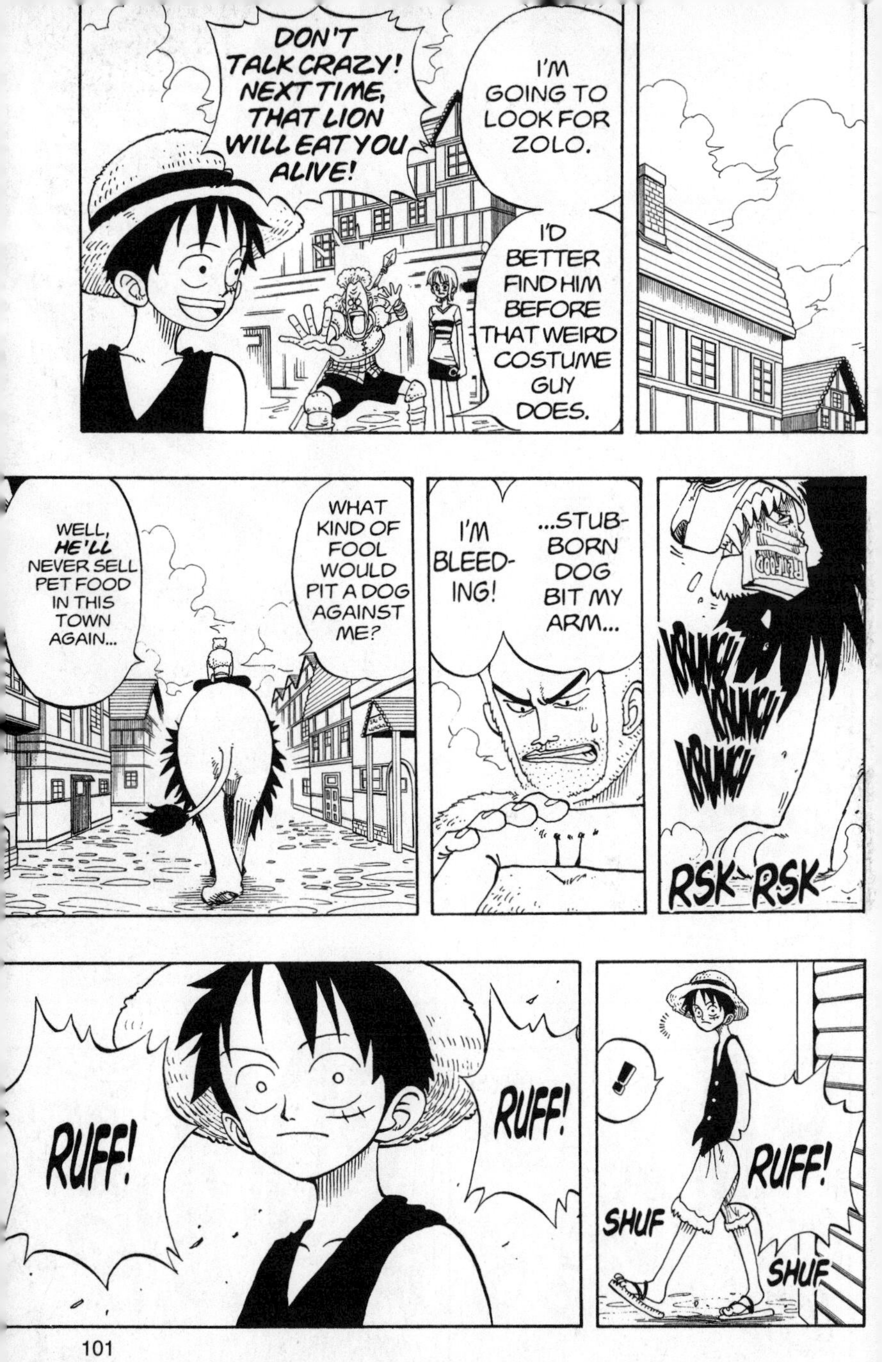
I'M GOING TO LOOK FOR ZOLO.
I'D BETTER FIND HIM BEFORE THAT WEIRD COSTUME GUY DOES.
DON'T TALK CRAZY! NEXT TIME, THAT LION WILL EAT YOU ALIVE!
PET FOOD
KRUNCH KRUNCH KRUNCH
RSK RSK
...STUB-BORN DOG BIT MY ARM...
I'M BLEED-ING!
WHAT KIND OF FOOL WOULD PIT A DOG AGAINST ME?
WELL, HE'LL NEVER SELL PET FOOD IN THIS TOWN AGAIN...
!
RUFF!
SHUF
SHUF
RUFF!
RUFF!

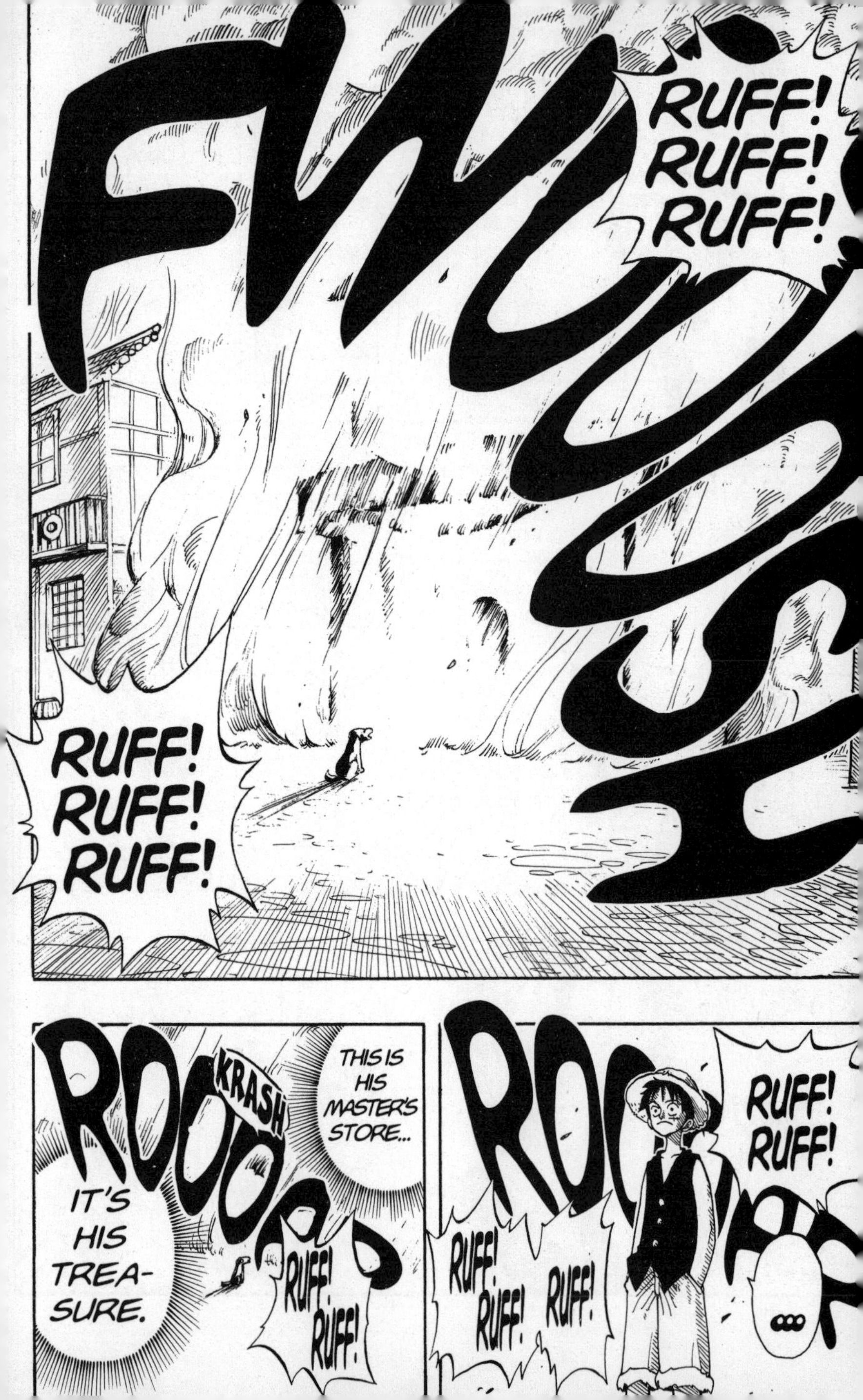
RUFF! RUFF! RUFF!
RUFF! RUFF! RUFF!
RUFF! RUFF!
RUFF! RUFF! RUFF!
...
KRASH
THIS IS HIS MASTER'S STORE...
IT'S HIS TREASURE.
RUFF! RUFF!

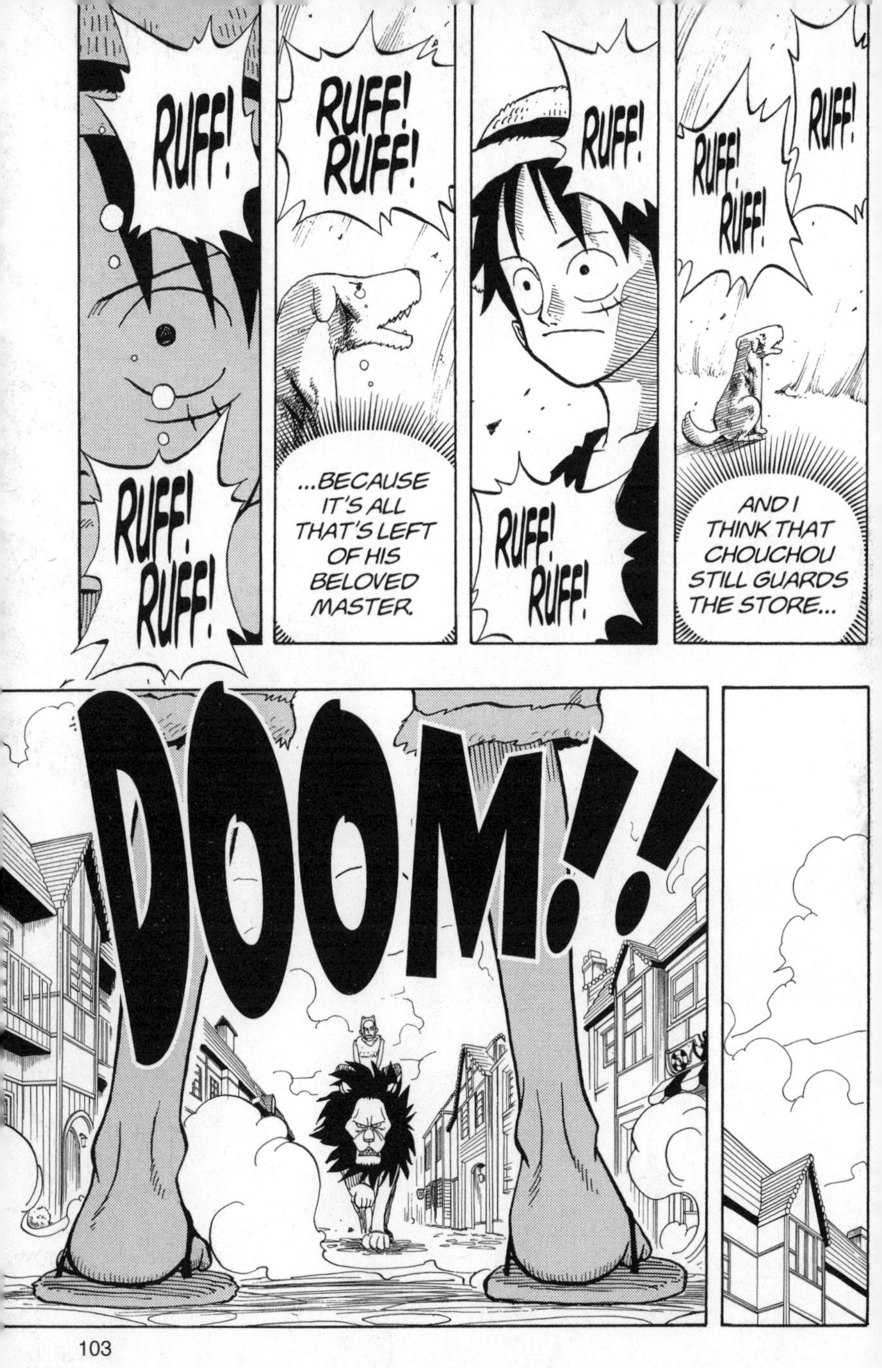
RUFF!
RUFF! RUFF!
AND I THINK THAT CHOUCHOU STILL GUARDS THE STORE...
RUFF!
RUFF! RUFF!
RUFF! RUFF!
...BECAUSE IT'S ALL THAT'S LEFT OF HIS BELOVED MASTER.
RUFF!
RUFF! RUFF!
DOOM!!

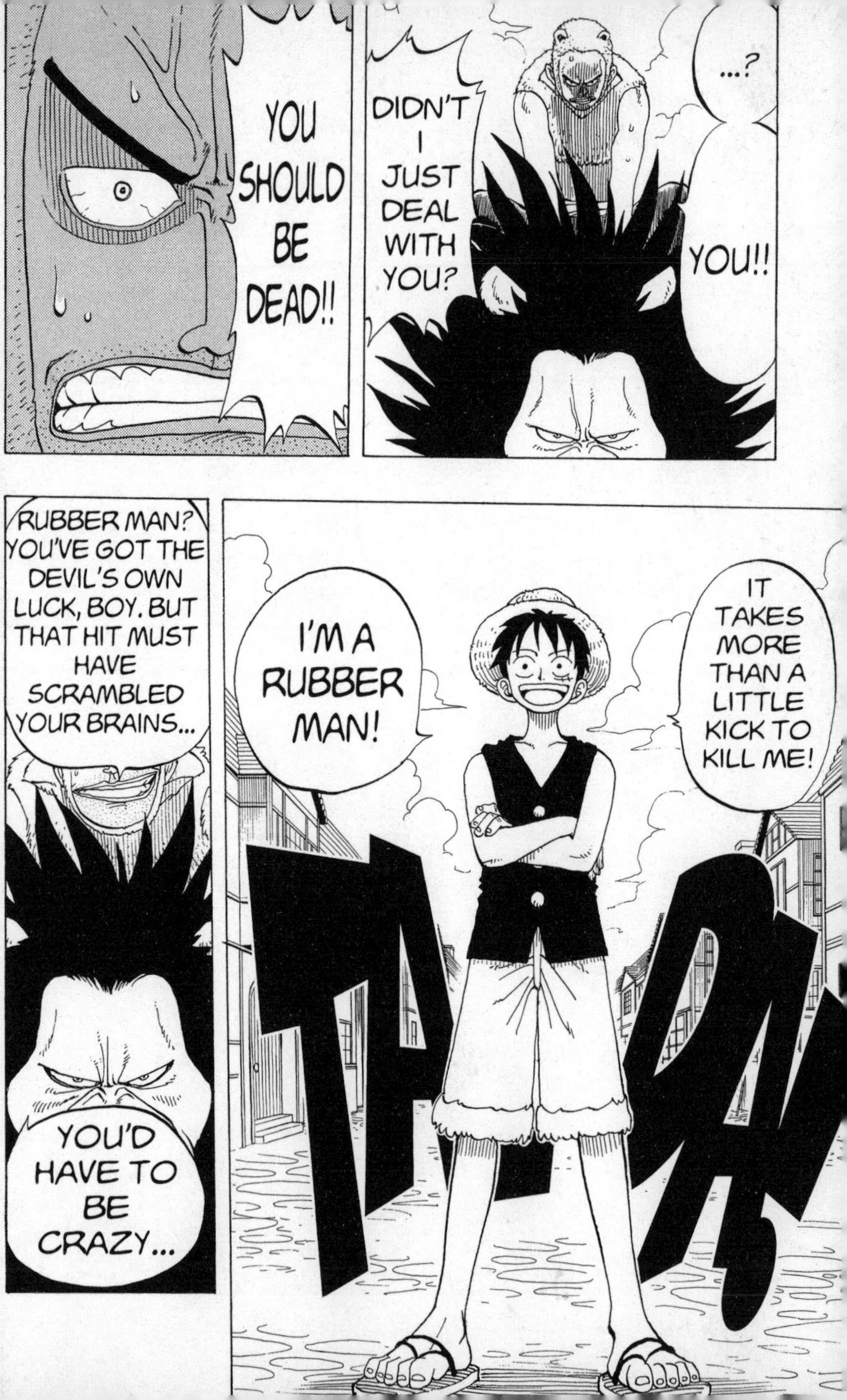
...?
YOU!!
DIDN'T I JUST DEAL WITH YOU?
YOU SHOULD BE DEAD!!
IT TAKES MORE THAN A LITTLE KICK TO KILL ME!
I'M A RUBBER MAN!
RUBBER MAN? YOU'VE GOT THE DEVIL'S OWN LUCK, BOY. BUT THAT HIT MUST HAVE SCRAMBLED YOUR BRAINS...
YOU'D HAVE TO BE CRAZY...

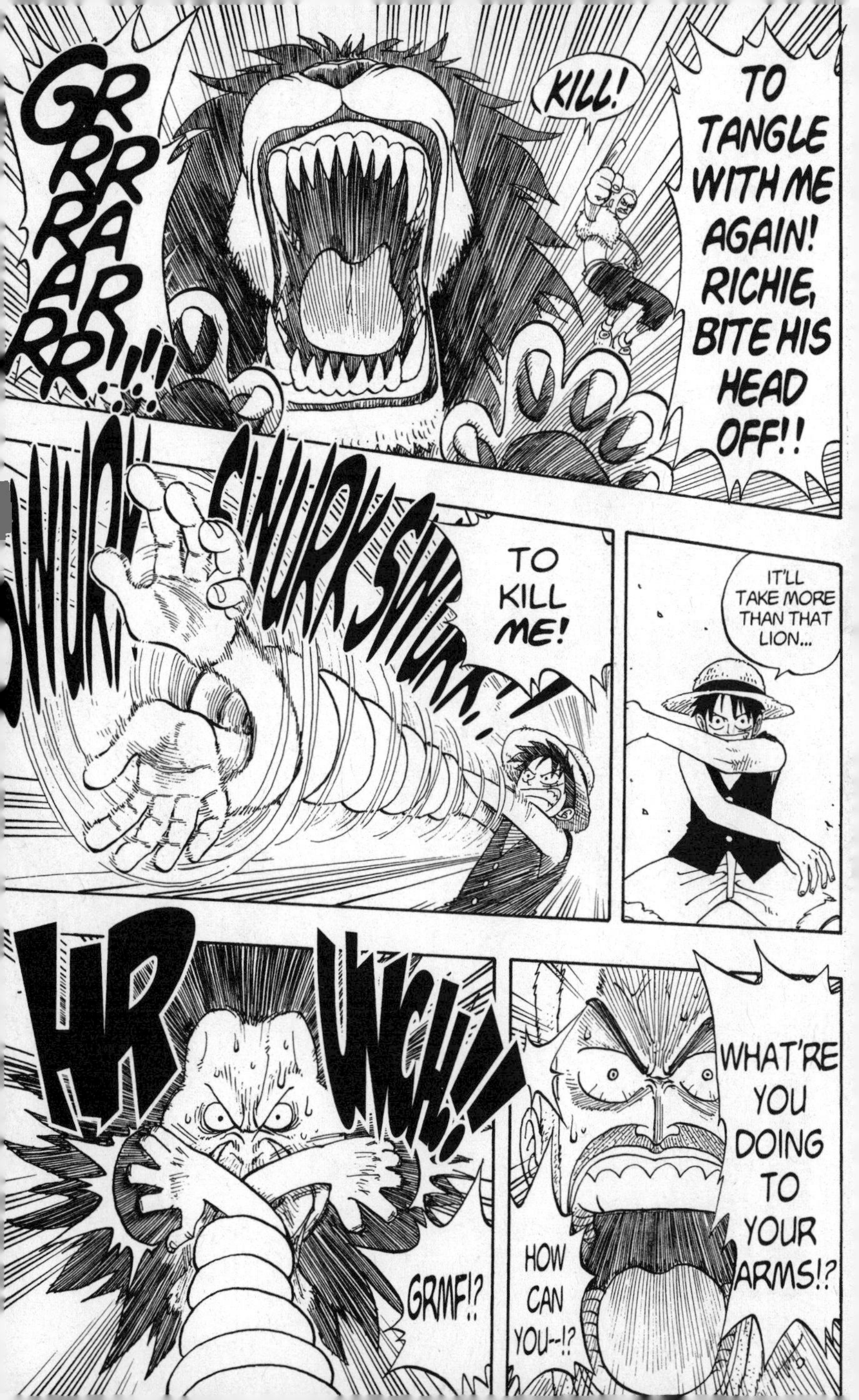
TO TANGLE WITH ME AGAIN! RICHIE, BITE HIS HEAD OFF!!
KILL!
GRRRARRARRR!!!
IT'LL TAKE MORE THAN THAT LION...
TO KILL ME!
SHWURK SHWURK!!
WHAT'RE YOU DOING TO YOUR ARMS!?
HOW CAN YOU--!?
HRUNCH!!
GRMF!?

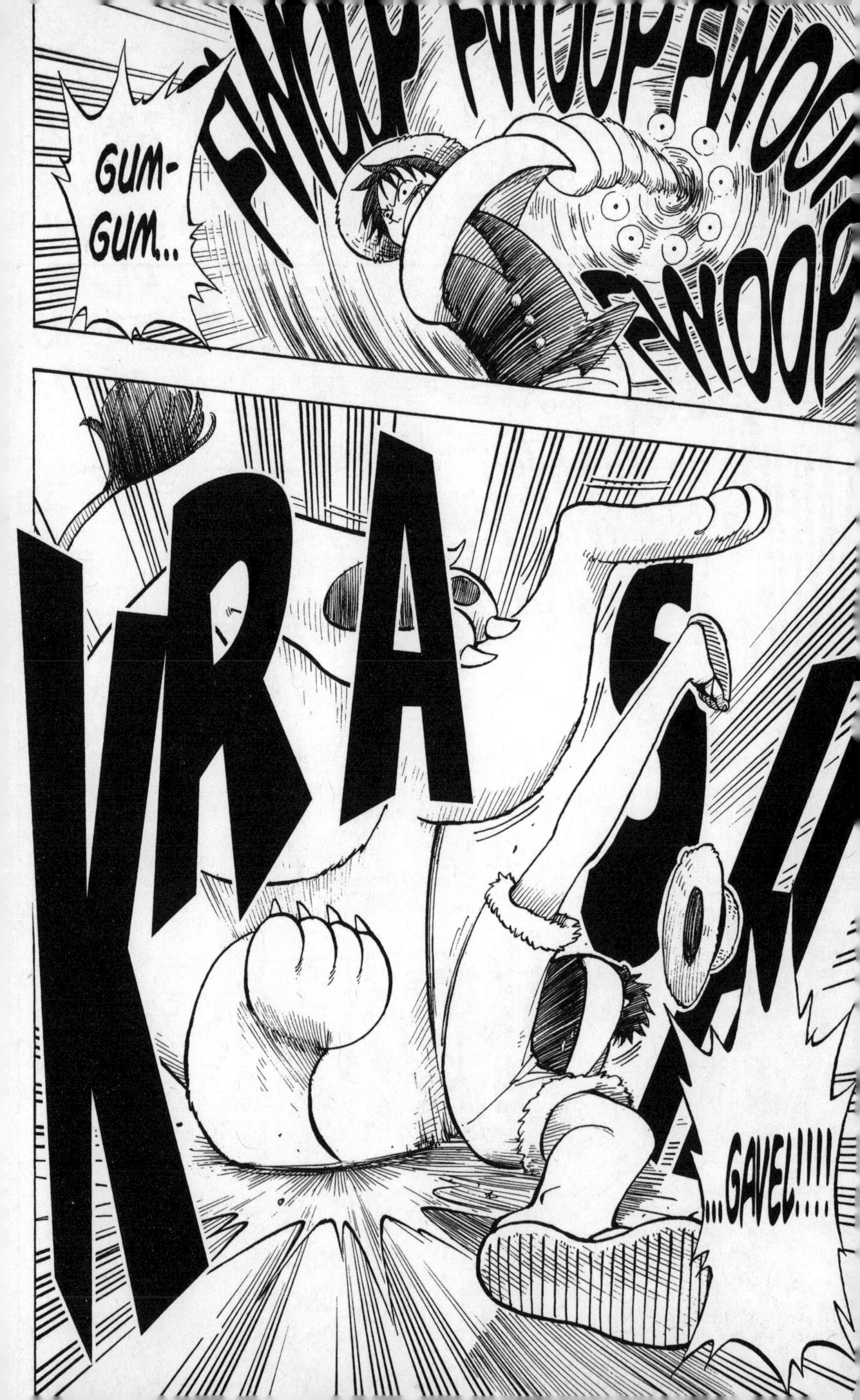
FWOOP FWOOP FWOOP
FWOOP
GUM-GUM...
KRASH
...GAVEL!!!!

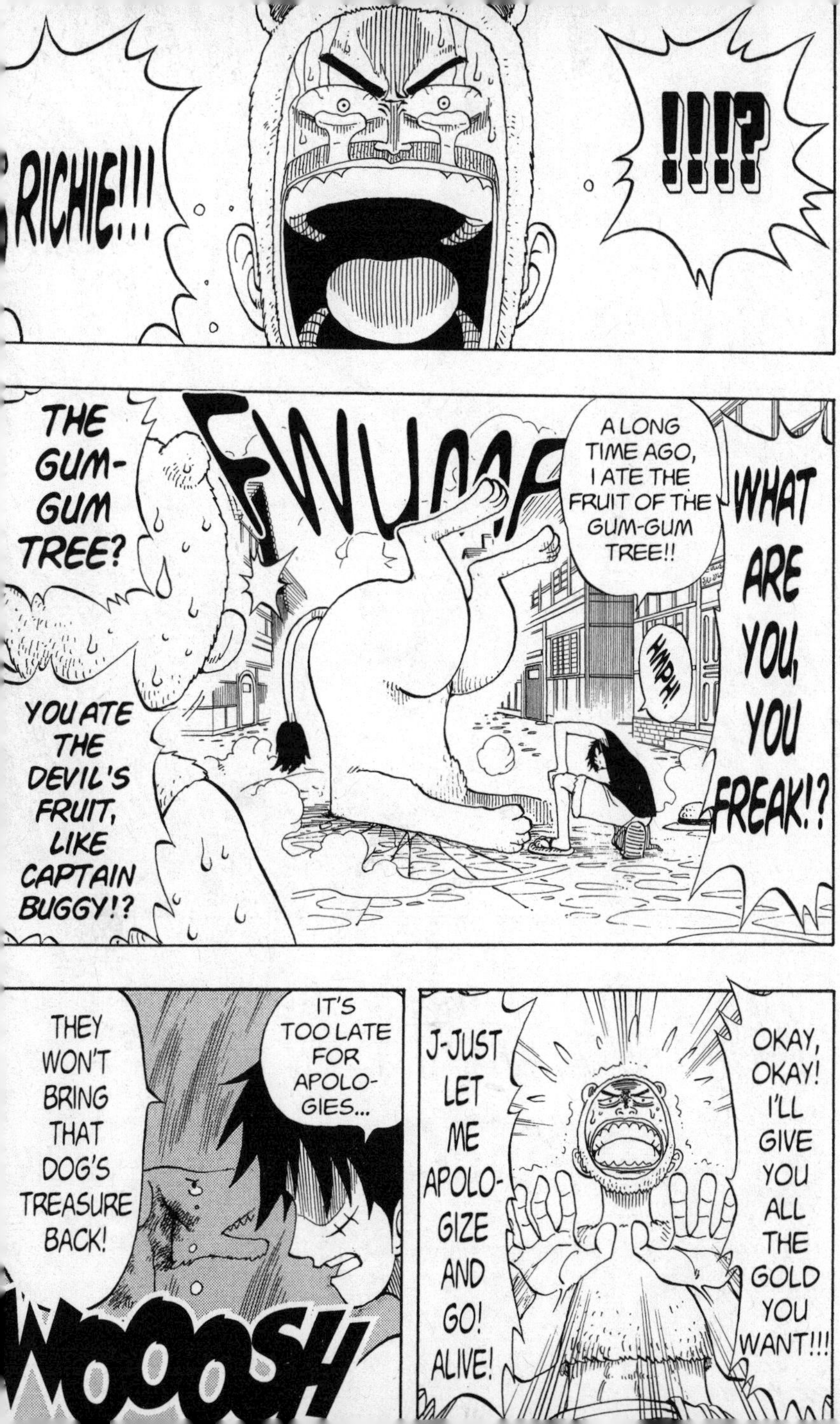
!!!?
RICHIE!!!
WHAT ARE YOU, YOU FREAK!?
A LONG TIME AGO, I ATE THE FRUIT OF THE GUM-GUM TREE!!
HMPH!
FWUMP
THE GUM-GUM TREE?
YOU ATE THE DEVIL'S FRUIT, LIKE CAPTAIN BUGGY!?
OKAY, OKAY! I'LL GIVE YOU ALL THE GOLD YOU WANT!!!
J-JUST LET ME APOLOGIZE AND GO! ALIVE!
IT'S TOO LATE FOR APOLOGIES...
THEY WON'T BRING THAT DOG'S TREASURE BACK!
WOOOSH

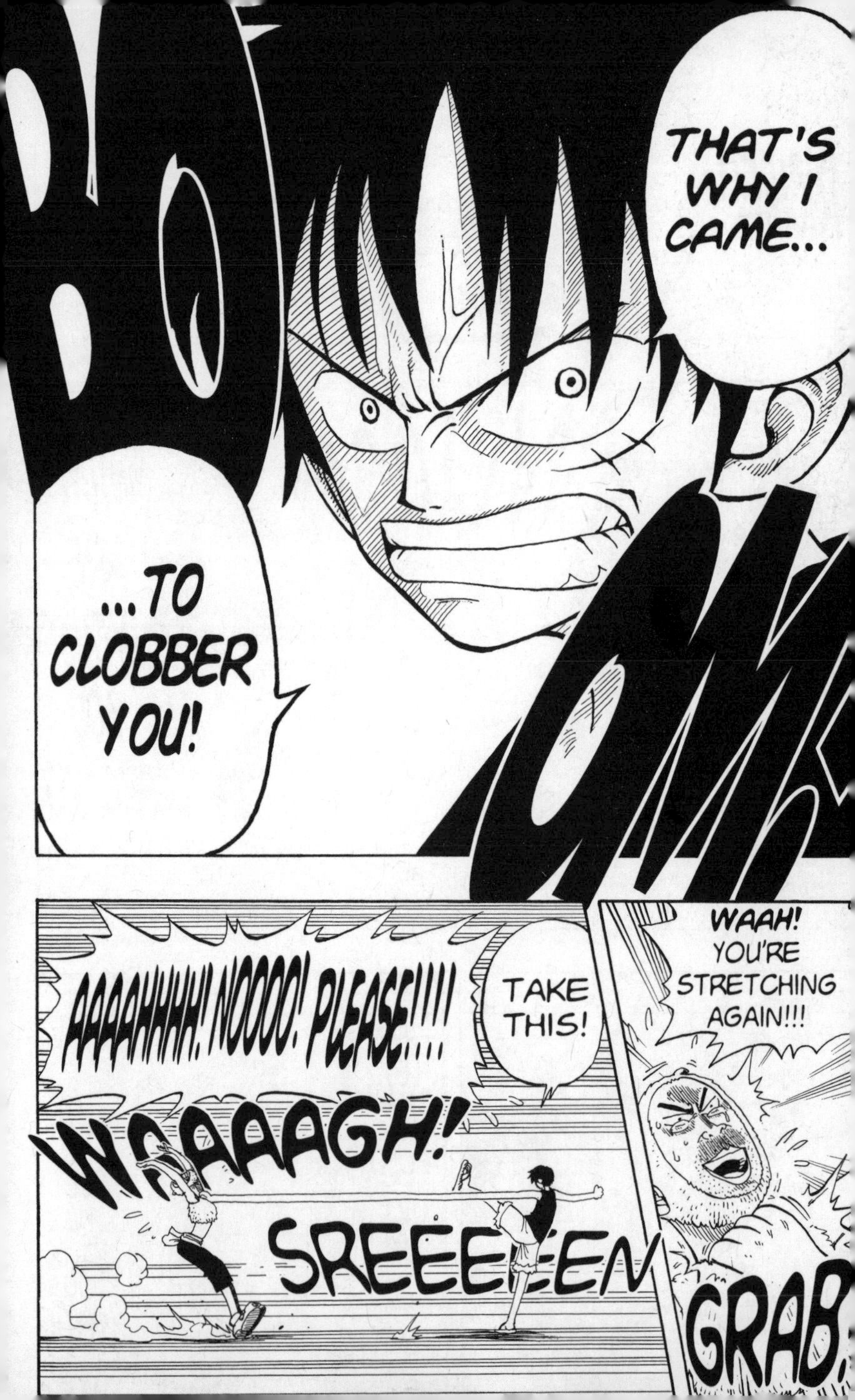
THAT'S WHY I CAME...
...TO CLOBBER YOU!
WAAH! YOU'RE STRETCHING AGAIN!!!
GRAB
TAKE THIS!
AAAAHHHH! NOOOO! PLEASE!!!!
WAAAAGH!
SREEEEEN

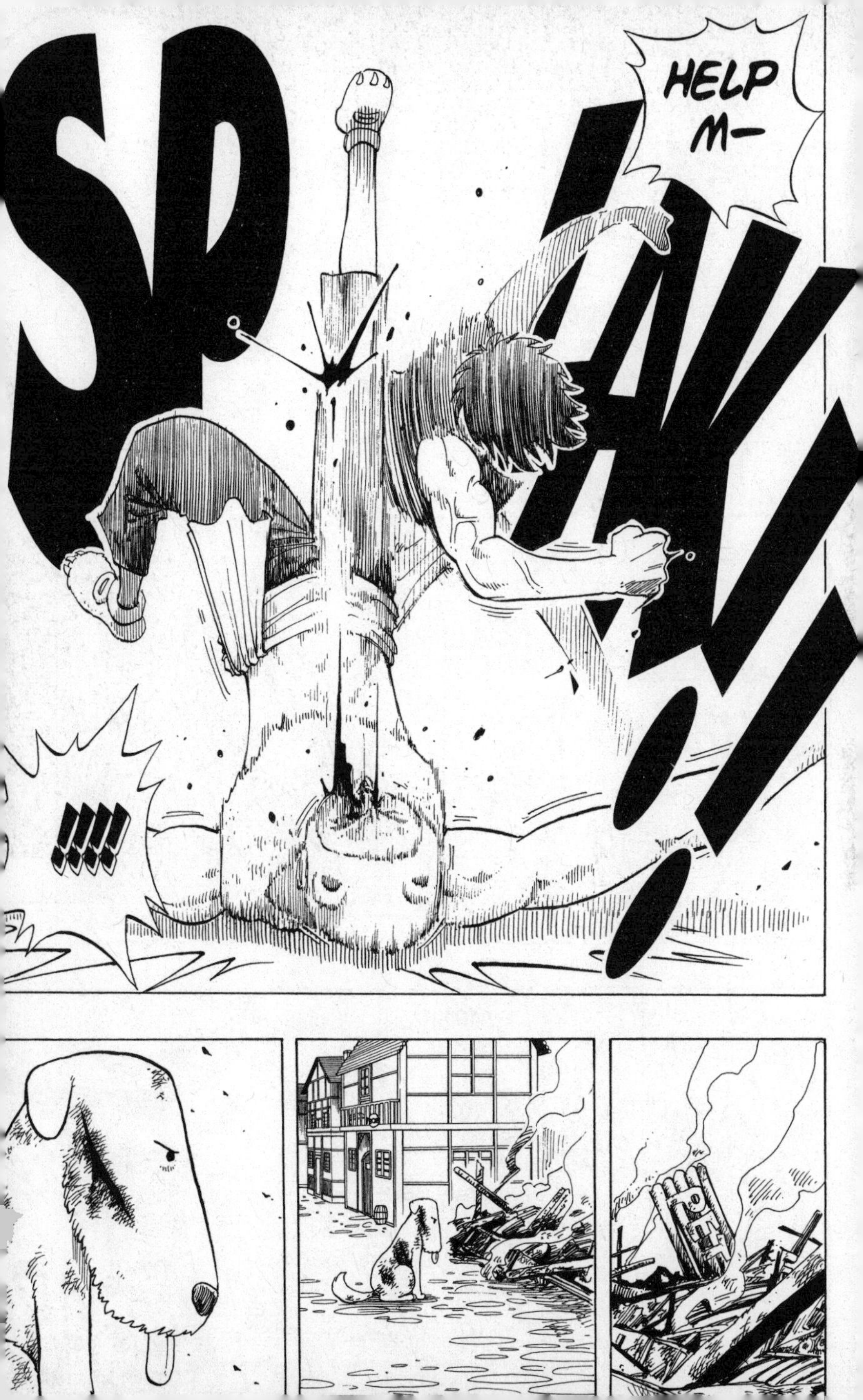
HELP M—
!!!!

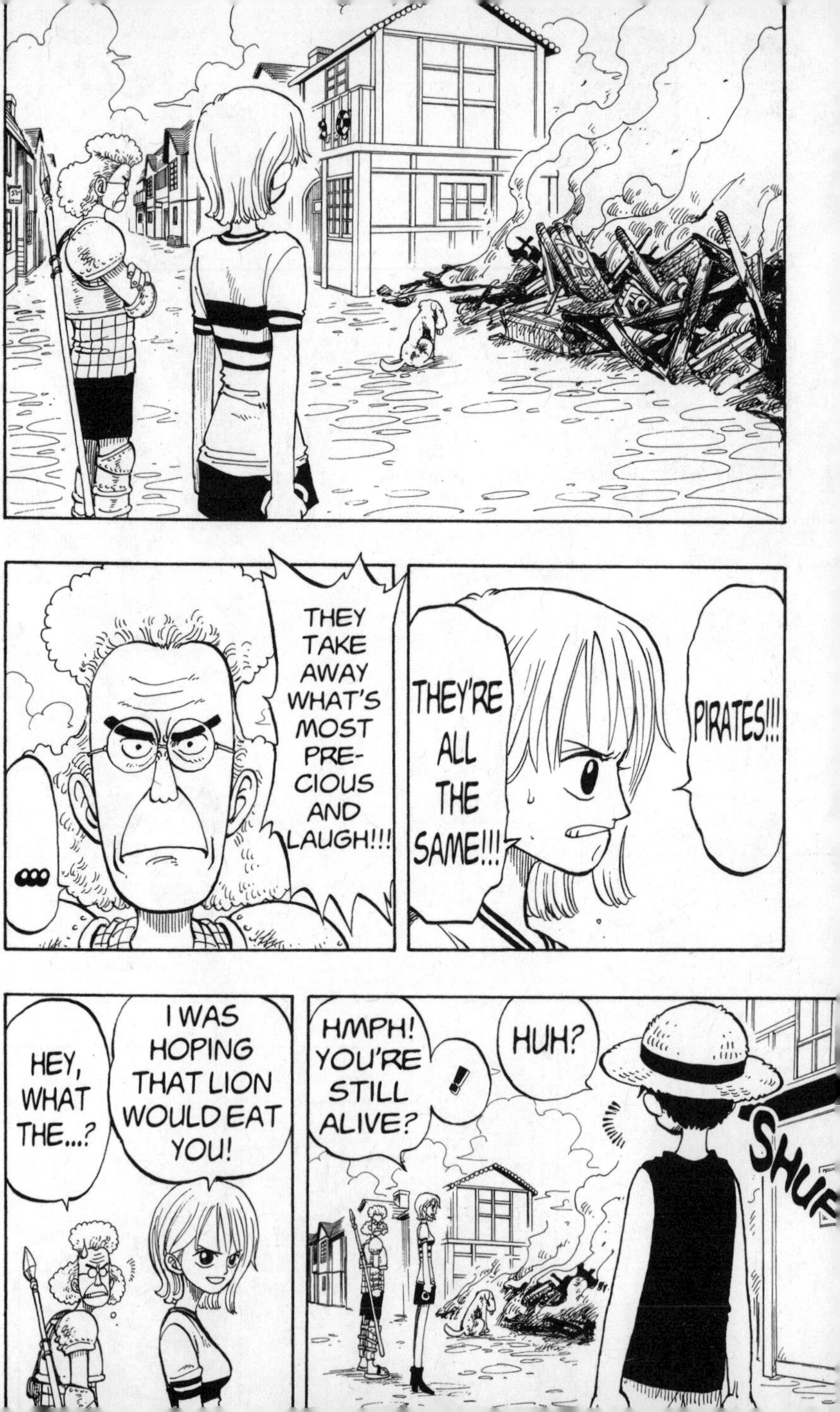
PIRATES!!!
THEY'RE ALL THE SAME!!!
THEY TAKE AWAY WHAT'S MOST PRE-CIOUS AND LAUGH!!!
...
HUH?
!
HMPH! YOU'RE STILL ALIVE?
SHUF
I WAS HOPING THAT LION WOULD EAT YOU!
HEY, WHAT THE...?

READ THIS WAY

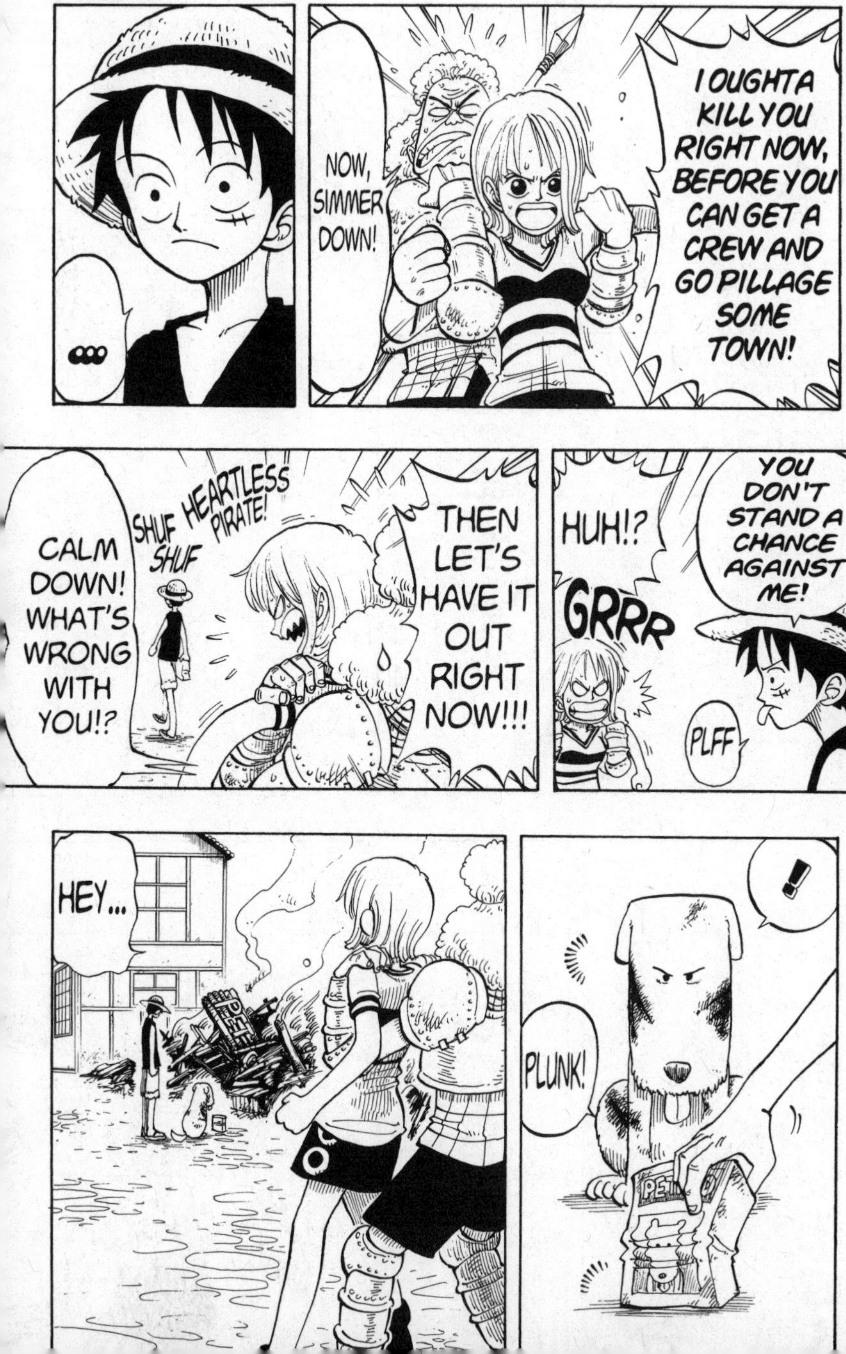
I OUGHTA KILL YOU RIGHT NOW, BEFORE YOU CAN GET A CREW AND GO PILLAGE SOME TOWN!
NOW, SIMMER DOWN!
...
YOU DON'T STAND A CHANCE AGAINST ME!
HUH!?
GRRR
PLFF
THEN LET'S HAVE IT OUT RIGHT NOW!!!
HEARTLESS PIRATE!
SHUF SHUF
CALM DOWN! WHAT'S WRONG WITH YOU!?
!
PLUNK!
HEY...

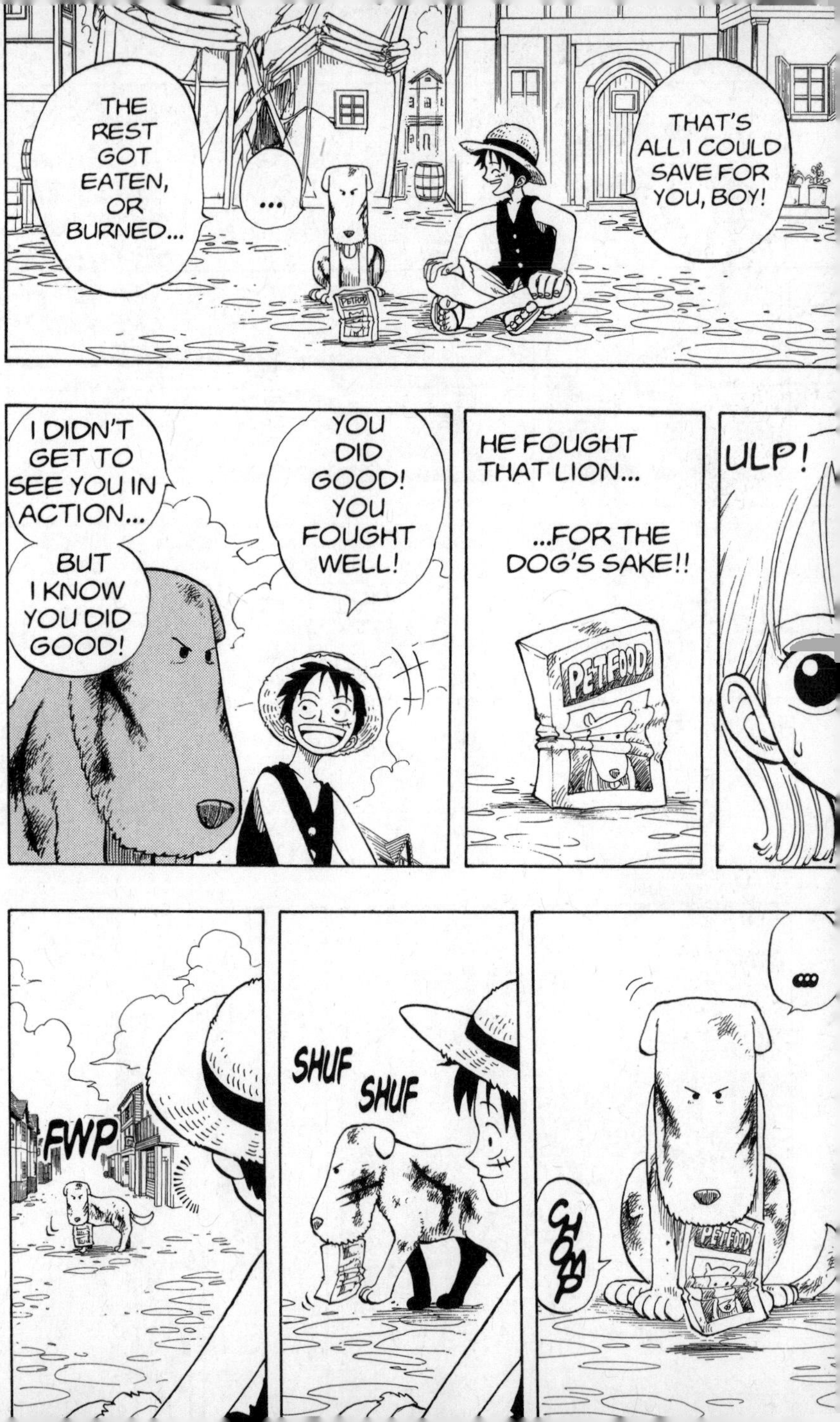
THAT'S ALL I COULD SAVE FOR YOU, BOY!
...
THE REST GOT EATEN, OR BURNED...
ULP!
HE FOUGHT THAT LION...
...FOR THE DOG'S SAKE!!
PETFOOD
YOU DID GOOD! YOU FOUGHT WELL!
I DIDN'T GET TO SEE YOU IN ACTION...
BUT I KNOW YOU DID GOOD!
...
CHOMP
PETFOOD
SHUF
SHUF
FWP

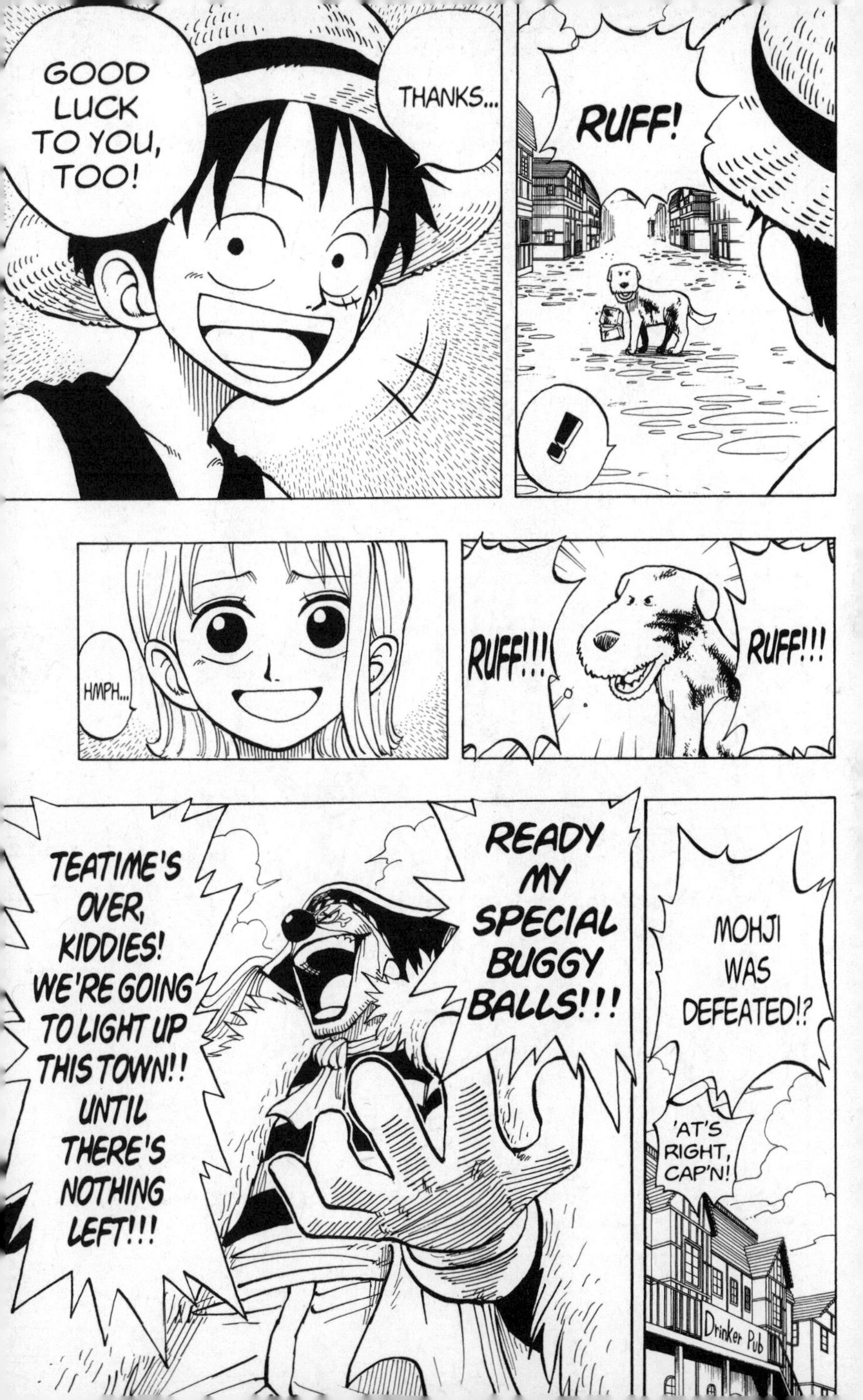
RUFF!
!
THANKS...
GOOD LUCK TO YOU, TOO!
RUFF!!!
RUFF!!!
HMPH...
MOHJI WAS DEFEATED!?
'AT'S RIGHT, CAP'N!
Drinker Pub
READY MY SPECIAL BUGGY BALLS!!!
TEATIME'S OVER, KIDDIES! WE'RE GOING TO LIGHT UP THIS TOWN!! UNTIL THERE'S NOTHING LEFT!!!

One Piece Rough Sketch!

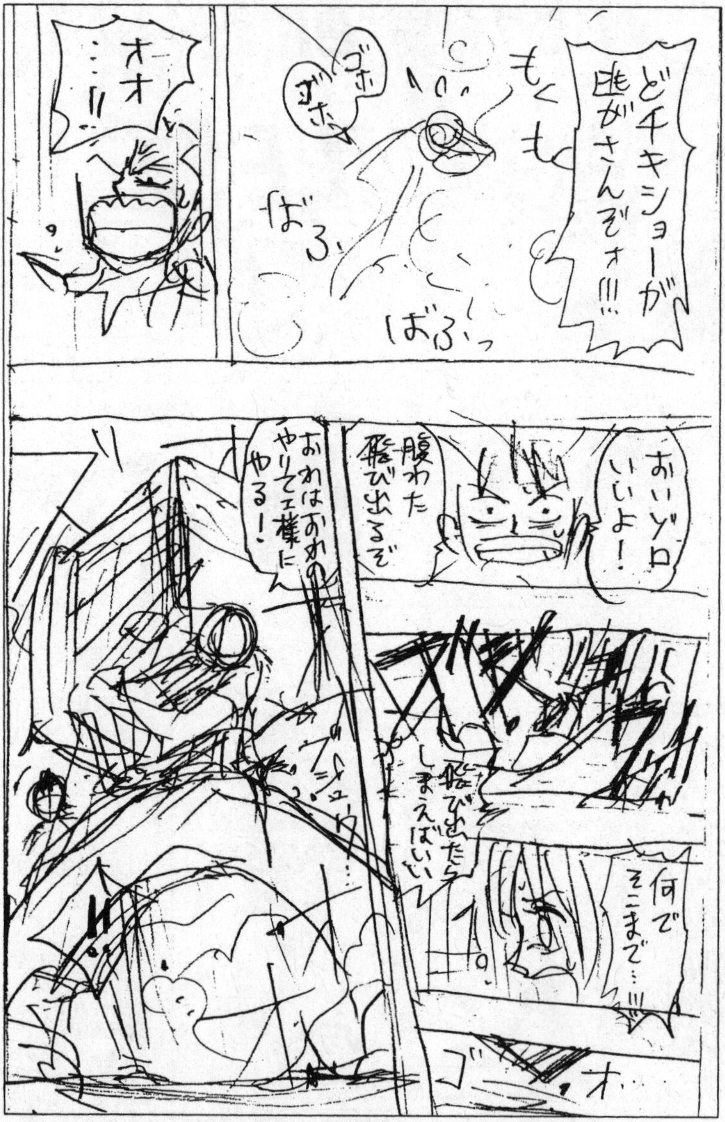
どチキショーが 逃がさんぞォ!!!
もくもく
ばふっ
ばふ
オオ…!!
おいゾロ いいよ！
腹わた 飛び出るぞ
おれはおれの やりてェ様に やる！
飛び出たら しまえばいい
何で そこまで…!!!
ゴ…オ…

Chapter 14: RECKLESS

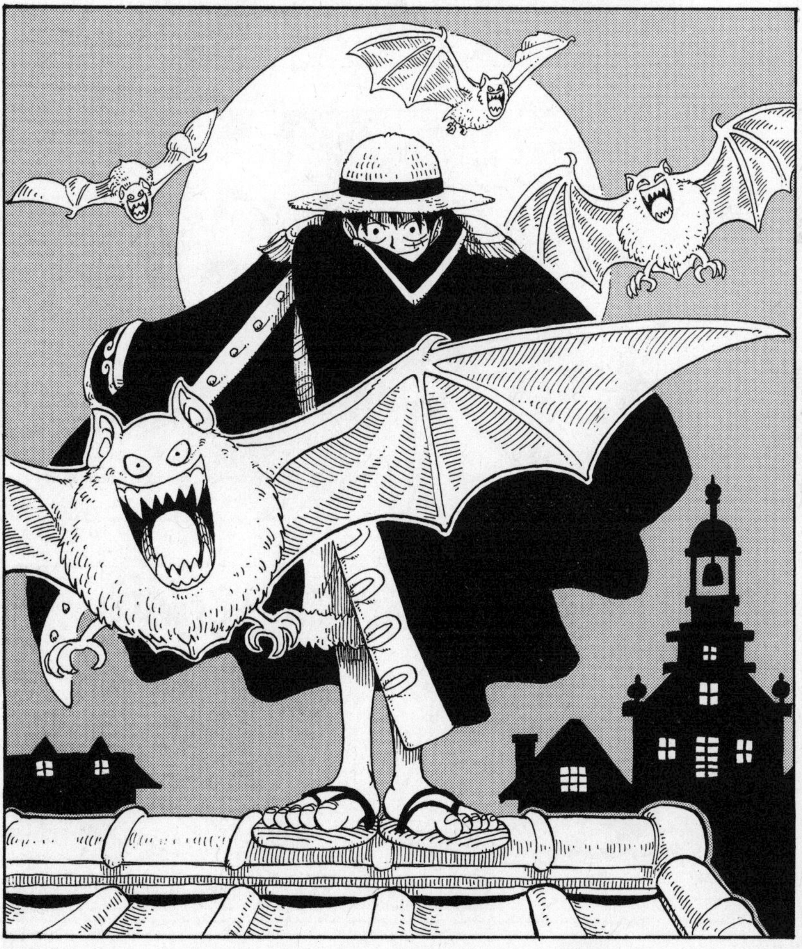

READ THIS WAY

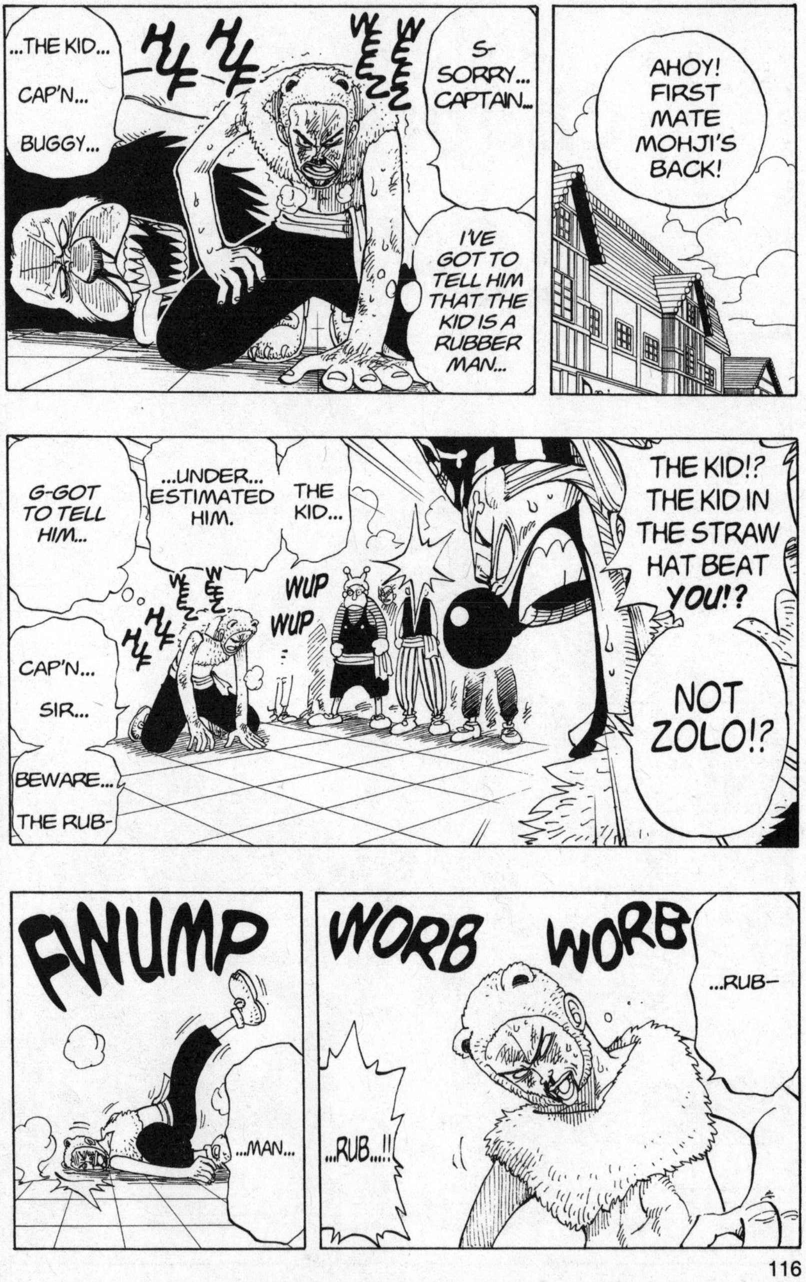
AHOY! FIRST MATE MOHJI'S BACK!
S-SORRY... CAPTAIN...
I'VE GOT TO TELL HIM THAT THE KID IS A RUBBER MAN...
WEEZE WEEZE
HUF HUF
...THE KID...
CAP'N...
BUGGY...
THE KID!? THE KID IN THE STRAW HAT BEAT YOU!?
NOT ZOLO!?
WUP WUP
THE KID...
...UNDER... ESTIMATED HIM.
G-GOT TO TELL HIM...
WEEZ WEEZ
HUF HUF
CAP'N...
SIR...
BEWARE...
THE RUB-
WORB WORB
...RUB-
...RUB...!!
FWUMP
...MAN...

READ THIS WAY

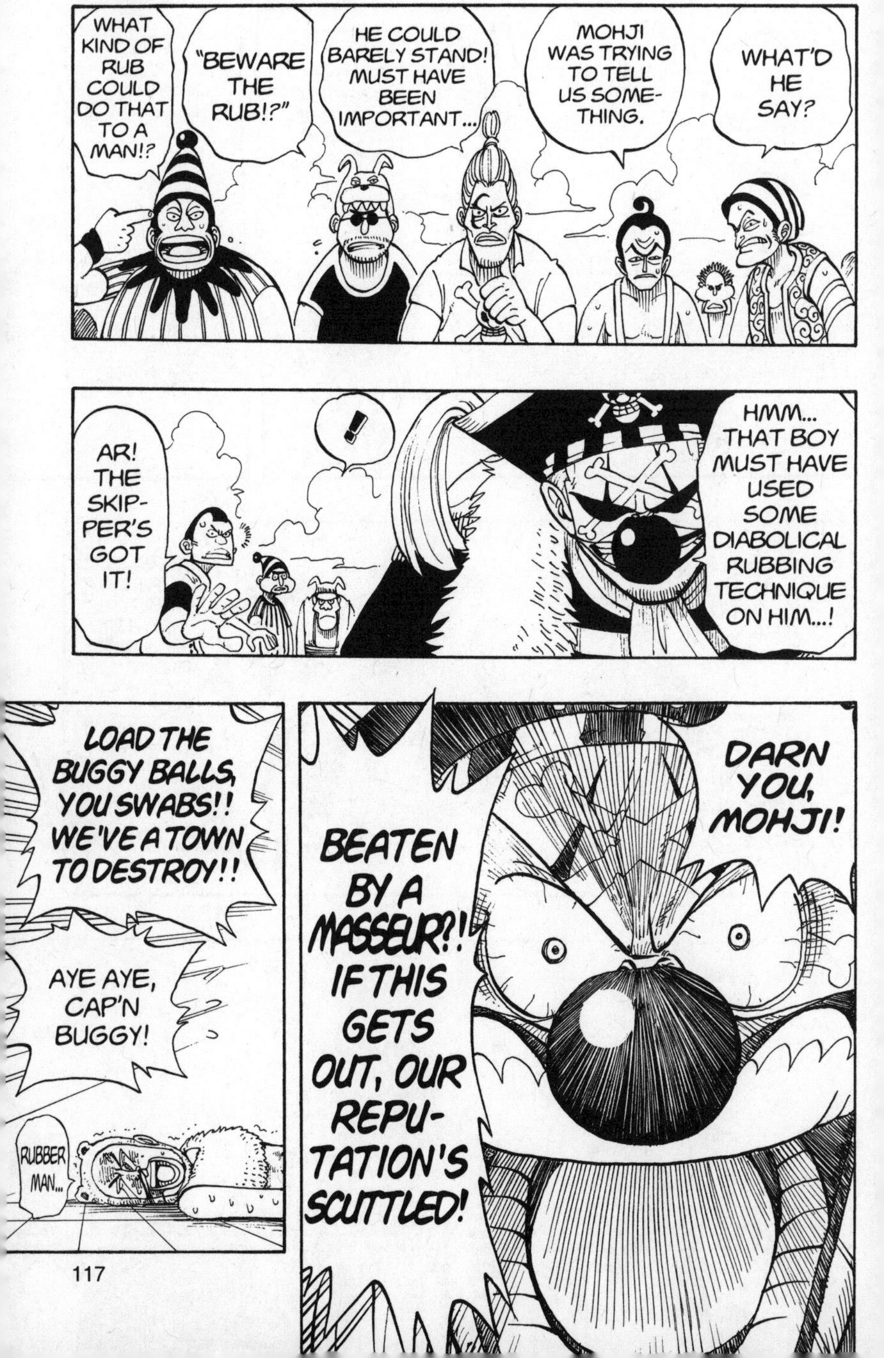
WHAT'D HE SAY?
MOHJI WAS TRYING TO TELL US SOME-THING.
HE COULD BARELY STAND! MUST HAVE BEEN IMPORTANT...
"BEWARE THE RUB!?"
WHAT KIND OF RUB COULD DO THAT TO A MAN!?
HMM... THAT BOY MUST HAVE USED SOME DIABOLICAL RUBBING TECHNIQUE ON HIM...!
!
AR! THE SKIP-PER'S GOT IT!
DARN YOU, MOHJI!
BEATEN BY A MASSEUR?! IF THIS GETS OUT, OUR REPU-TATION'S SCUTTLED!
LOAD THE BUGGY BALLS, YOU SWABS!! WE'VE A TOWN TO DESTROY!!
AYE AYE, CAP'N BUGGY!
RUBBER MAN...

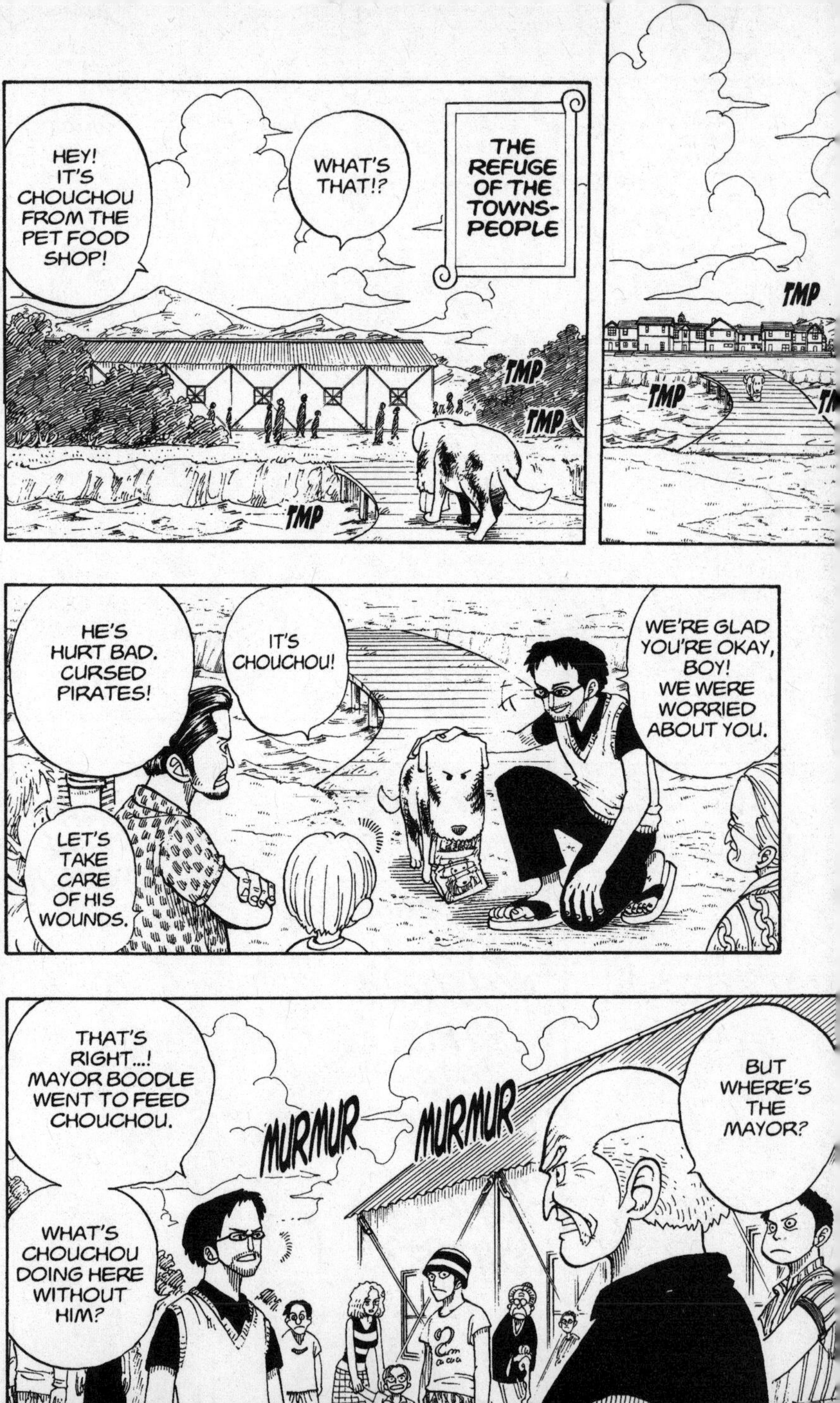
TMP
TMP
THE REFUGE OF THE TOWNSPEOPLE
WHAT'S THAT!?
HEY! IT'S CHOUCHOU FROM THE PET FOOD SHOP!
TMP
TMP
TMP
WE'RE GLAD YOU'RE OKAY, BOY! WE WERE WORRIED ABOUT YOU.
IT'S CHOUCHOU!
HE'S HURT BAD. CURSED PIRATES!
LET'S TAKE CARE OF HIS WOUNDS.
BUT WHERE'S THE MAYOR?
MURMUR
MURMUR
THAT'S RIGHT...! MAYOR BOODLE WENT TO FEED CHOUCHOU.
WHAT'S CHOUCHOU DOING HERE WITHOUT HIM?

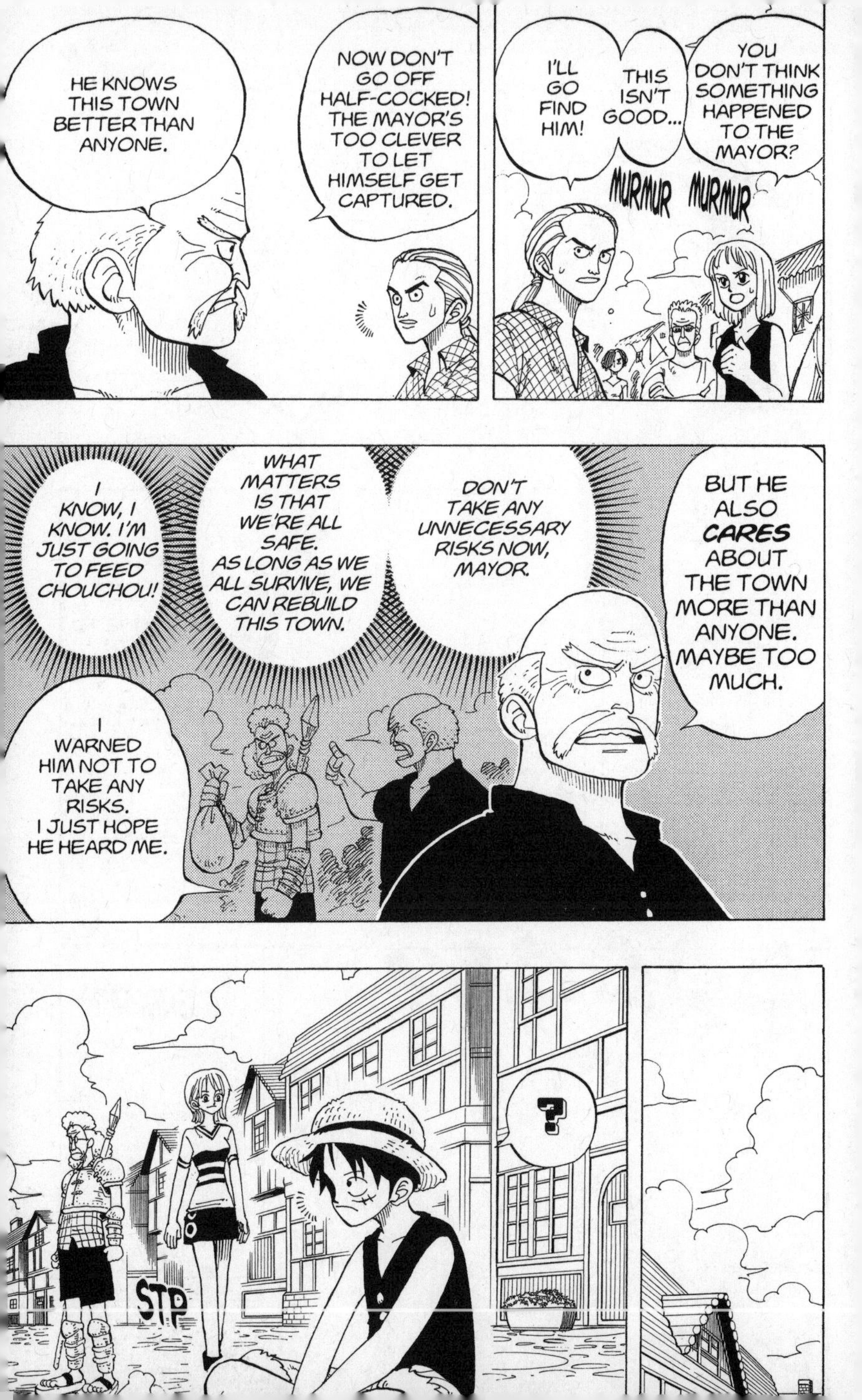

YOU DON'T THINK SOMETHING HAPPENED TO THE MAYOR?
THIS ISN'T GOOD...
I'LL GO FIND HIM!
MURMUR MURMUR
NOW DON'T GO OFF HALF-COCKED! THE MAYOR'S TOO CLEVER TO LET HIMSELF GET CAPTURED.
HE KNOWS THIS TOWN BETTER THAN ANYONE.
BUT HE ALSO **CARES** ABOUT THE TOWN MORE THAN ANYONE. MAYBE TOO MUCH.
DON'T TAKE ANY UNNECESSARY RISKS NOW, MAYOR.
WHAT MATTERS IS THAT WE'RE ALL SAFE. AS LONG AS WE ALL SURVIVE, WE CAN REBUILD THIS TOWN.
I KNOW, I KNOW. I'M JUST GOING TO FEED CHOUCHOU!
I WARNED HIM NOT TO TAKE ANY RISKS. I JUST HOPE HE HEARD ME.
?
STP

READ THIS WAY

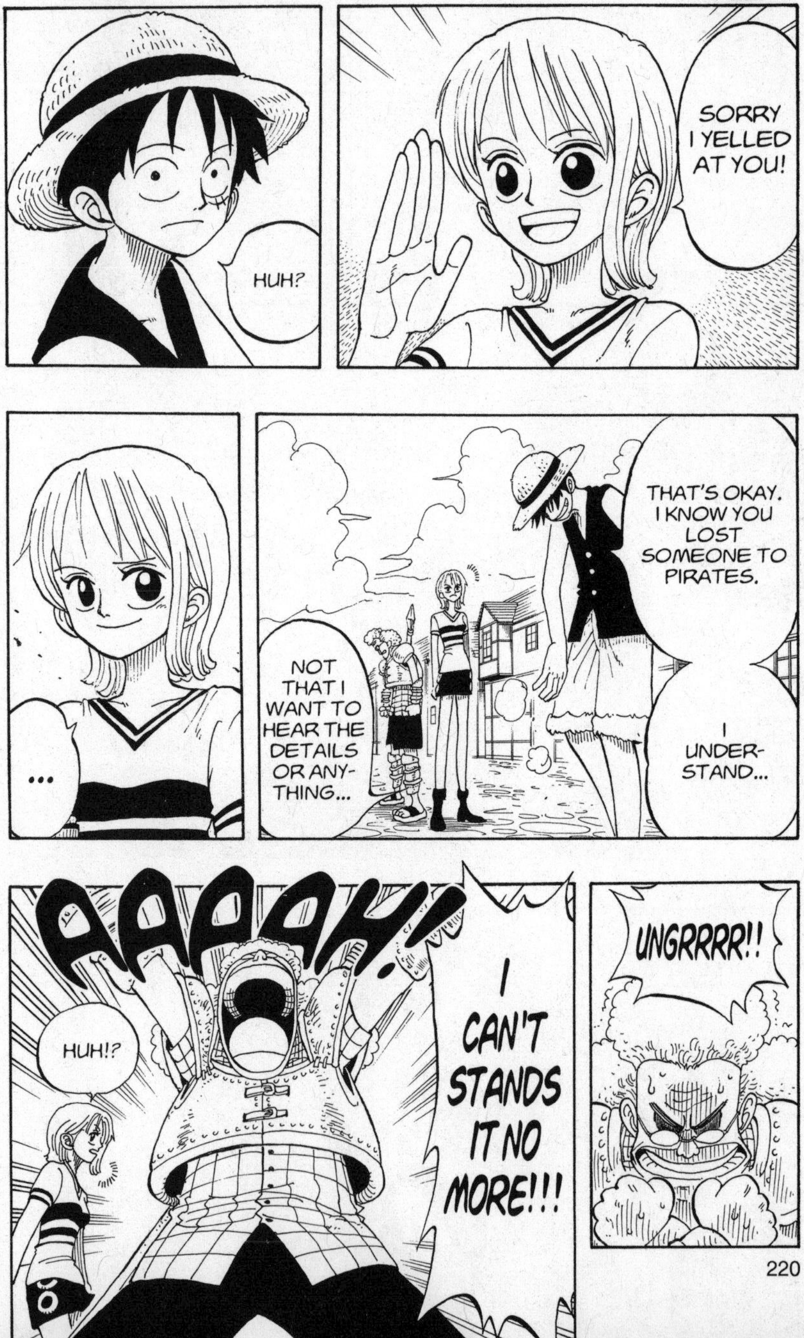
SORRY I YELLED AT YOU!
HUH?
THAT'S OKAY. I KNOW YOU LOST SOMEONE TO PIRATES.
I UNDER-STAND...
NOT THAT I WANT TO HEAR THE DETAILS OR ANY-THING...
...
UNGRRRR!!
AAAAAH!!
I CAN'T STANDS IT NO MORE!!!
HUH!?

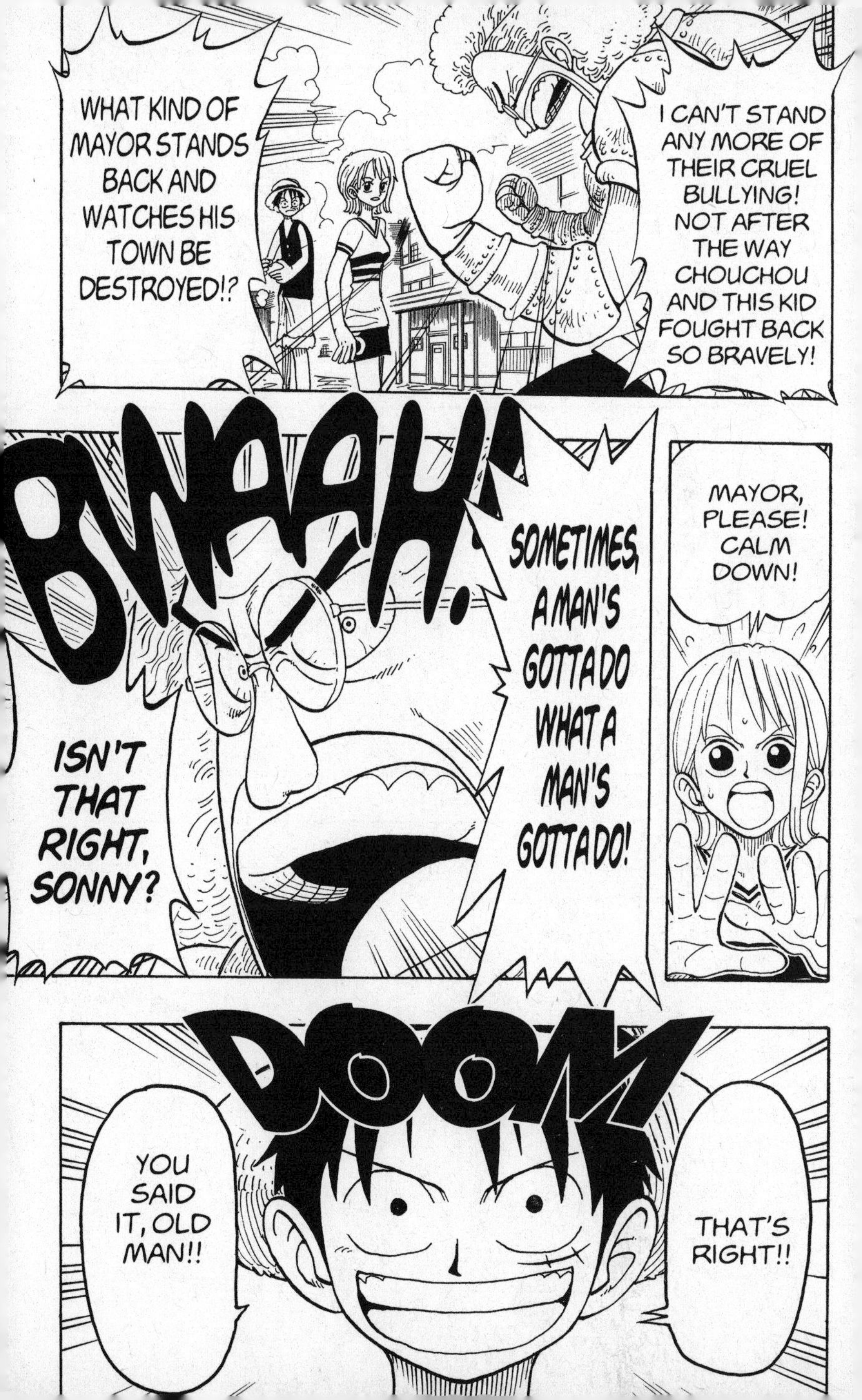
I CAN'T STAND ANY MORE OF THEIR CRUEL BULLYING! NOT AFTER THE WAY CHOUCHOU AND THIS KID FOUGHT BACK SO BRAVELY!
WHAT KIND OF MAYOR STANDS BACK AND WATCHES HIS TOWN BE DESTROYED!?
MAYOR, PLEASE! CALM DOWN!
BWAAH!
SOMETIMES, A MAN'S GOTTA DO WHAT A MAN'S GOTTA DO!
ISN'T THAT RIGHT, SONNY?
DOOM
THAT'S RIGHT!!
YOU SAID IT, OLD MAN!!

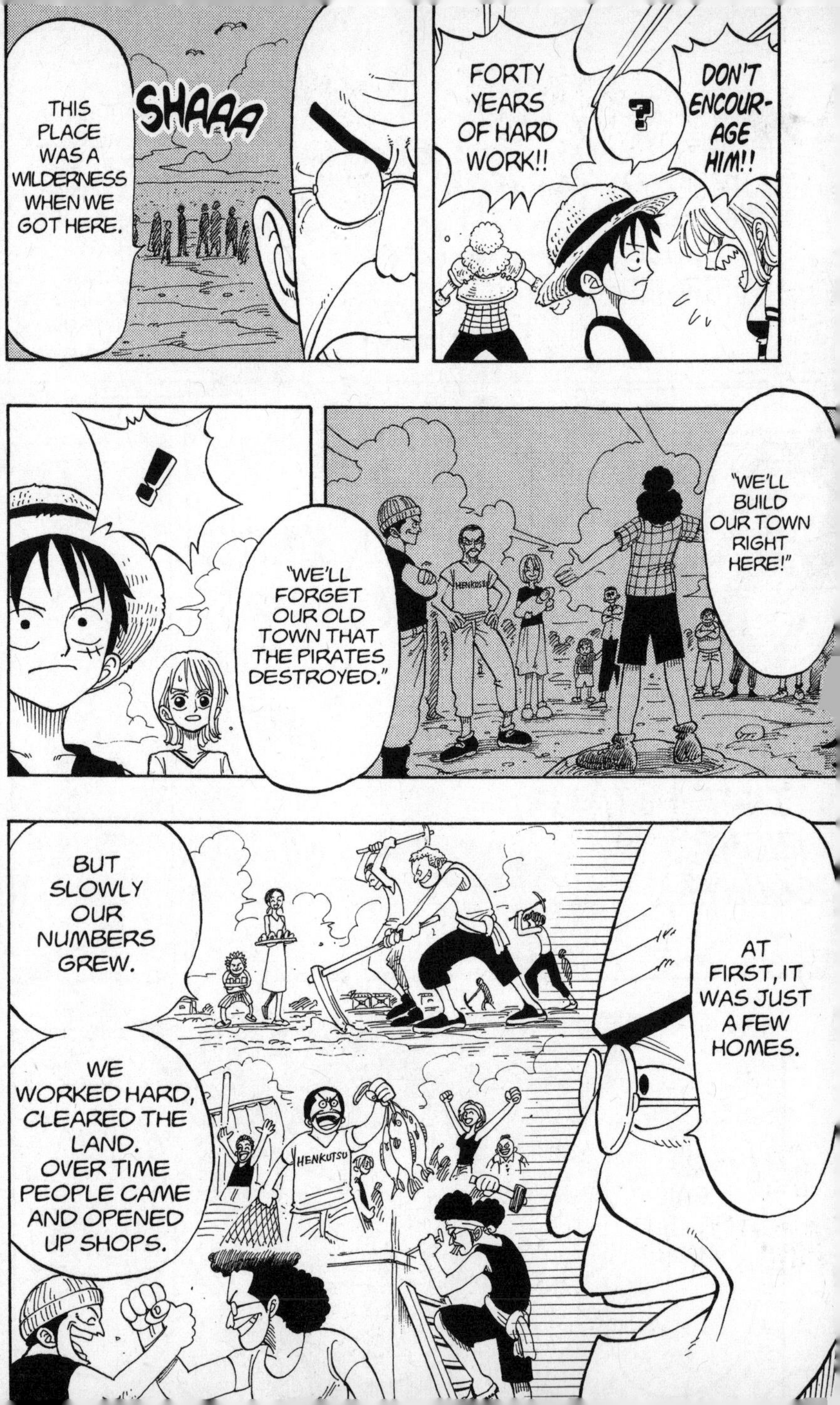
FORTY YEARS OF HARD WORK!!
?
DON'T ENCOURAGE HIM!!
THIS PLACE WAS A WILDERNESS WHEN WE GOT HERE.
SHAAA
"WE'LL BUILD OUR TOWN RIGHT HERE!"
"WE'LL FORGET OUR OLD TOWN THAT THE PIRATES DESTROYED."
HENKUTSU
!
AT FIRST, IT WAS JUST A FEW HOMES.
BUT SLOWLY OUR NUMBERS GREW.
WE WORKED HARD, CLEARED THE LAND. OVER TIME PEOPLE CAME AND OPENED UP SHOPS.
HENKUTSU

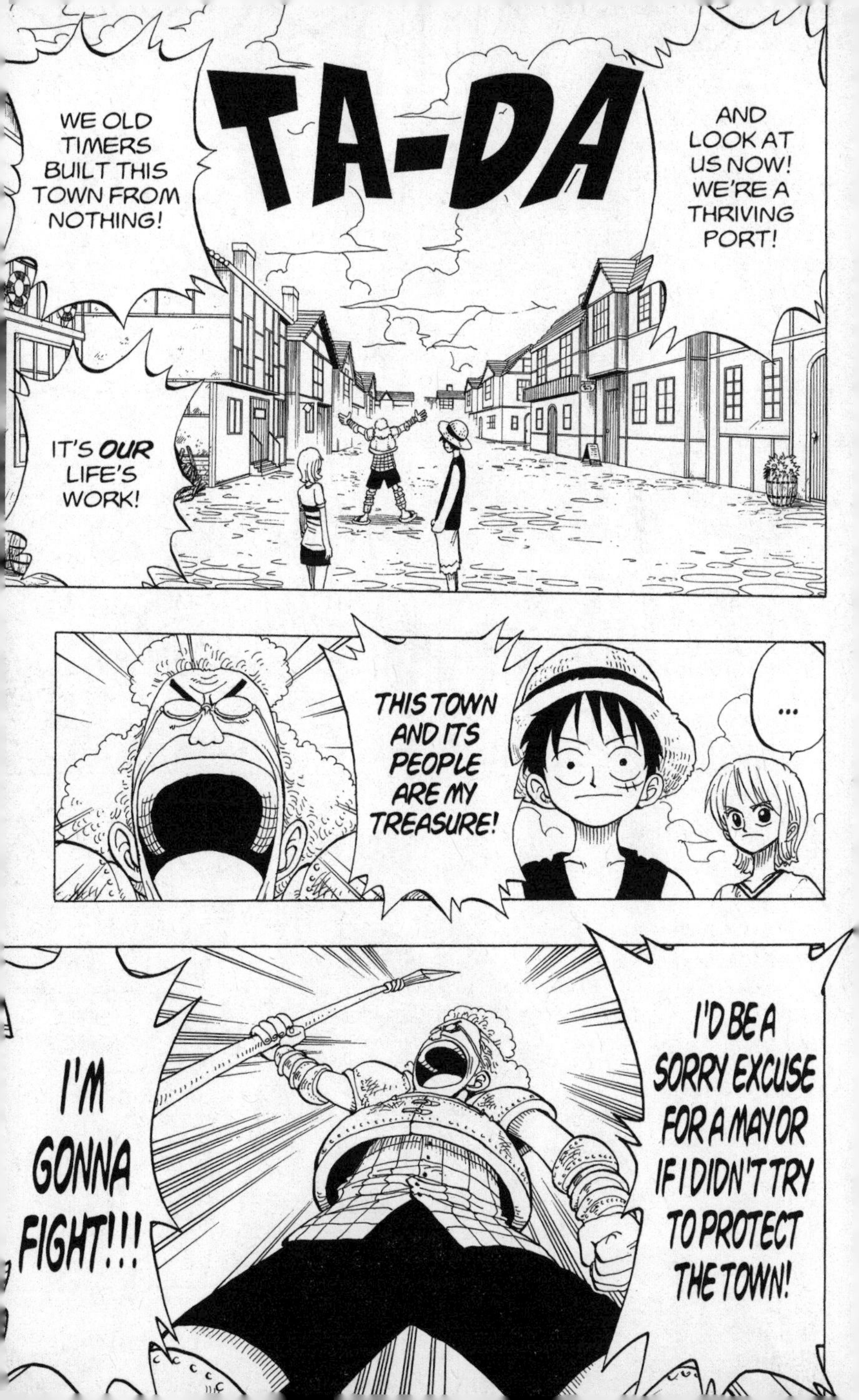
TA-DA
AND LOOK AT US NOW! WE'RE A THRIVING PORT!
WE OLD TIMERS BUILT THIS TOWN FROM NOTHING!
IT'S **OUR** LIFE'S WORK!
...
THIS TOWN AND ITS PEOPLE ARE MY TREASURE!
I'D BE A SORRY EXCUSE FOR A MAYOR IF I DIDN'T TRY TO PROTECT THE TOWN!
I'M GONNA FIGHT!!!

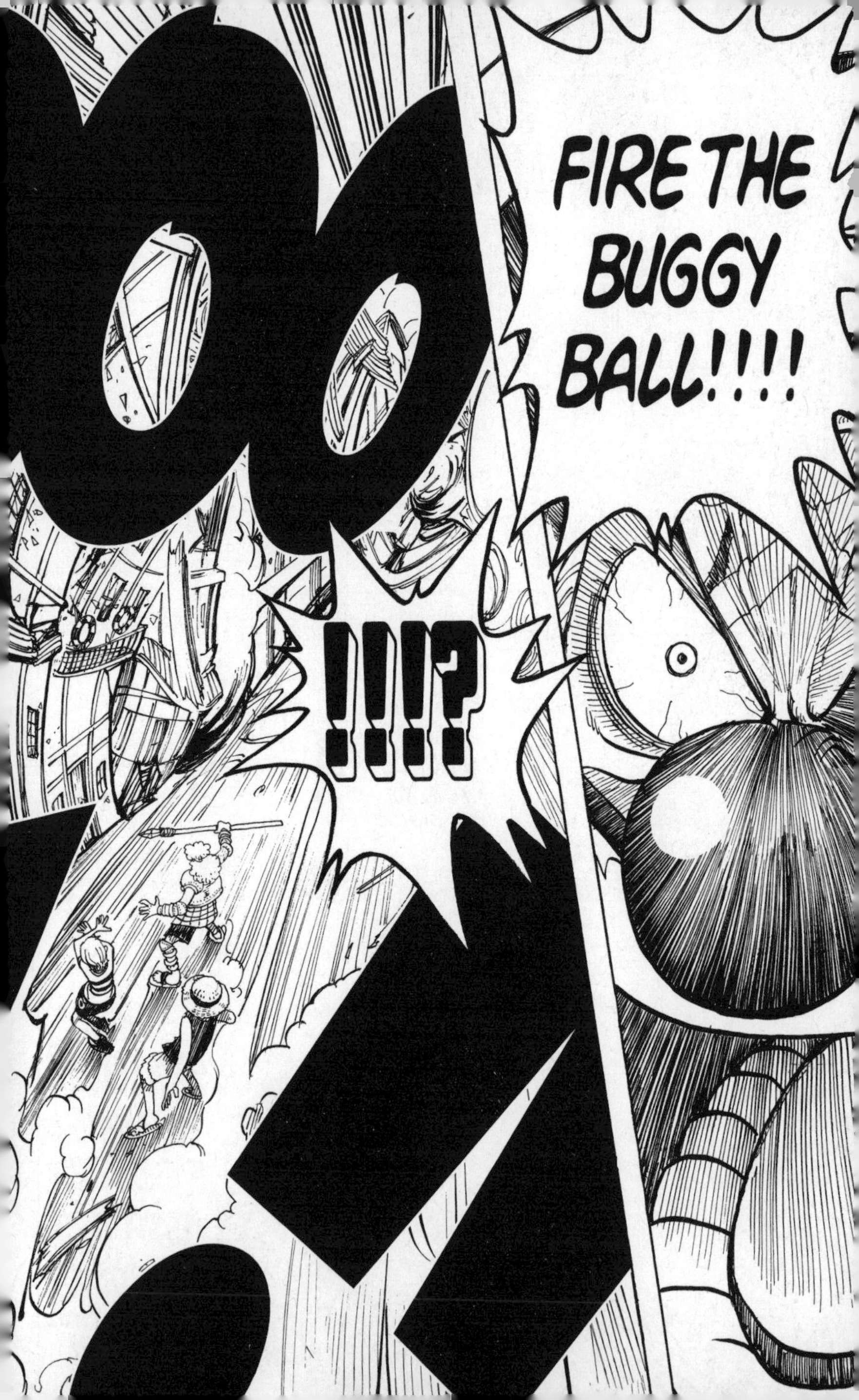
FIRE THE BUGGY BALL!!!!
!!!?

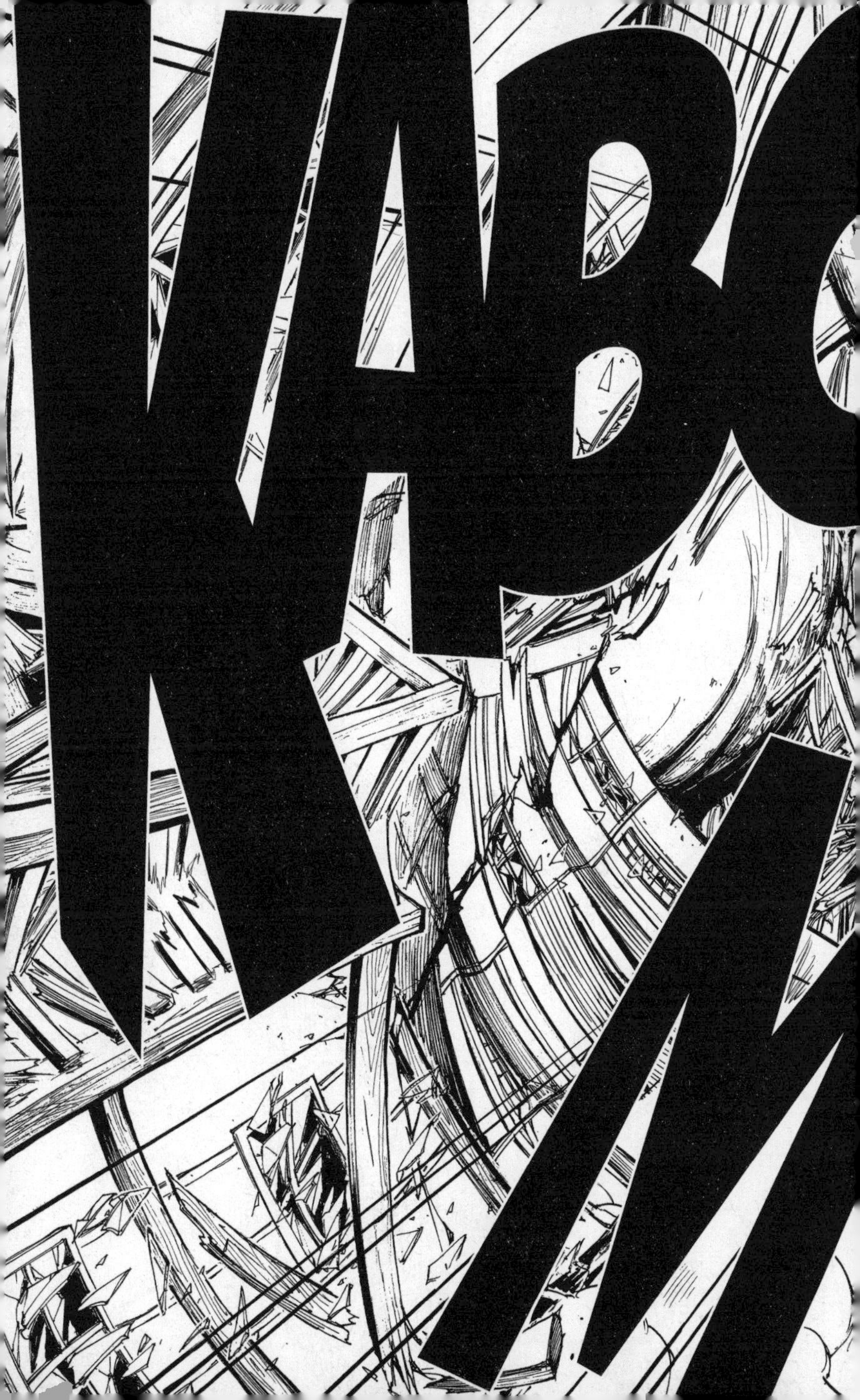
KAB

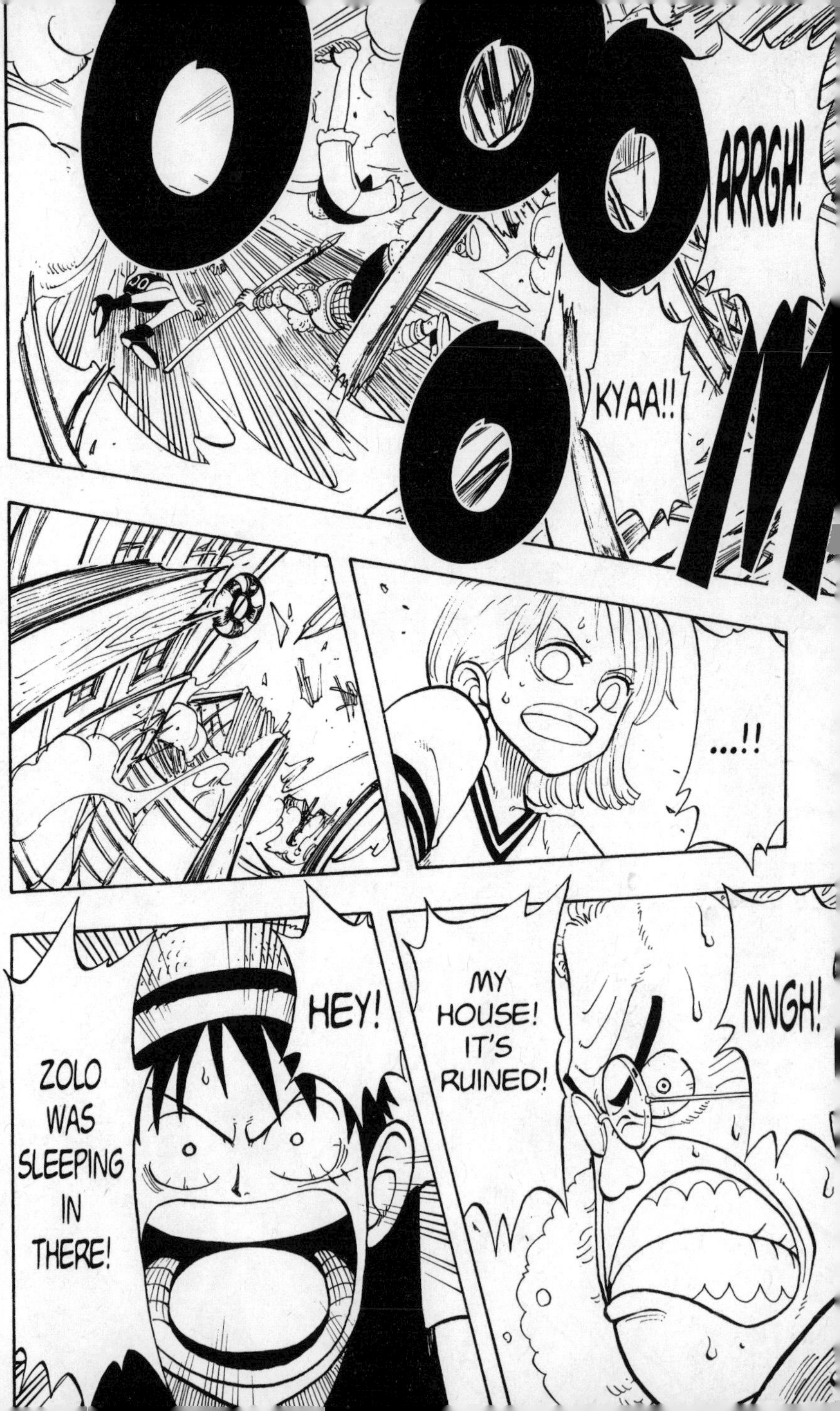
ARRGH!
OOOOM
KYAA!!
...!!
NNGH!
MY HOUSE! IT'S RUINED!
HEY!
ZOLO WAS SLEEPING IN THERE!

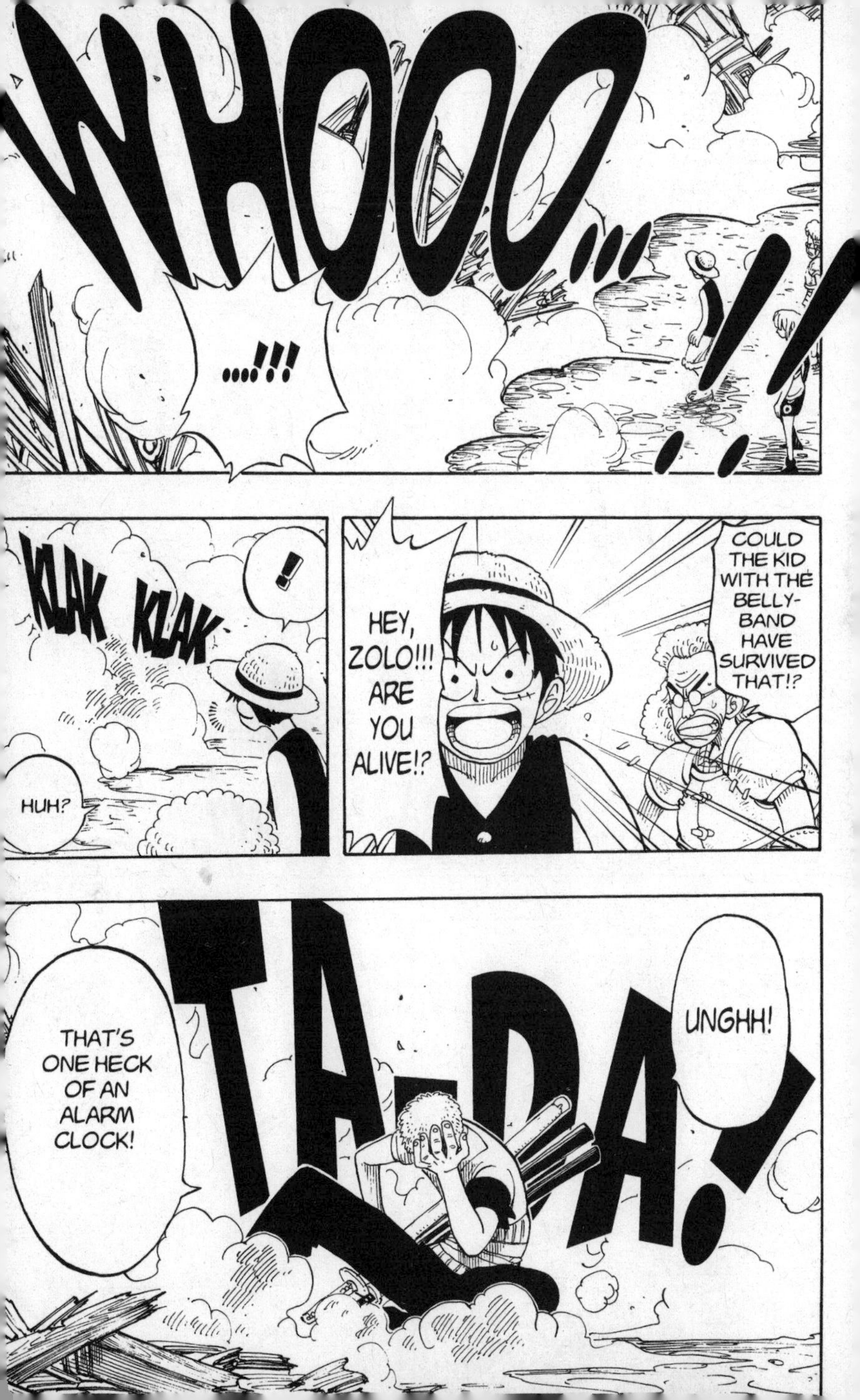
WHOOO...!!
....!!!
COULD THE KID WITH THE BELLY-BAND HAVE SURVIVED THAT!?
HEY, ZOLO!!! ARE YOU ALIVE!?
!
KLAK KLAK
HUH?
UNGHH!
TA-DA!
THAT'S ONE HECK OF AN ALARM CLOCK!

READ THIS WAY

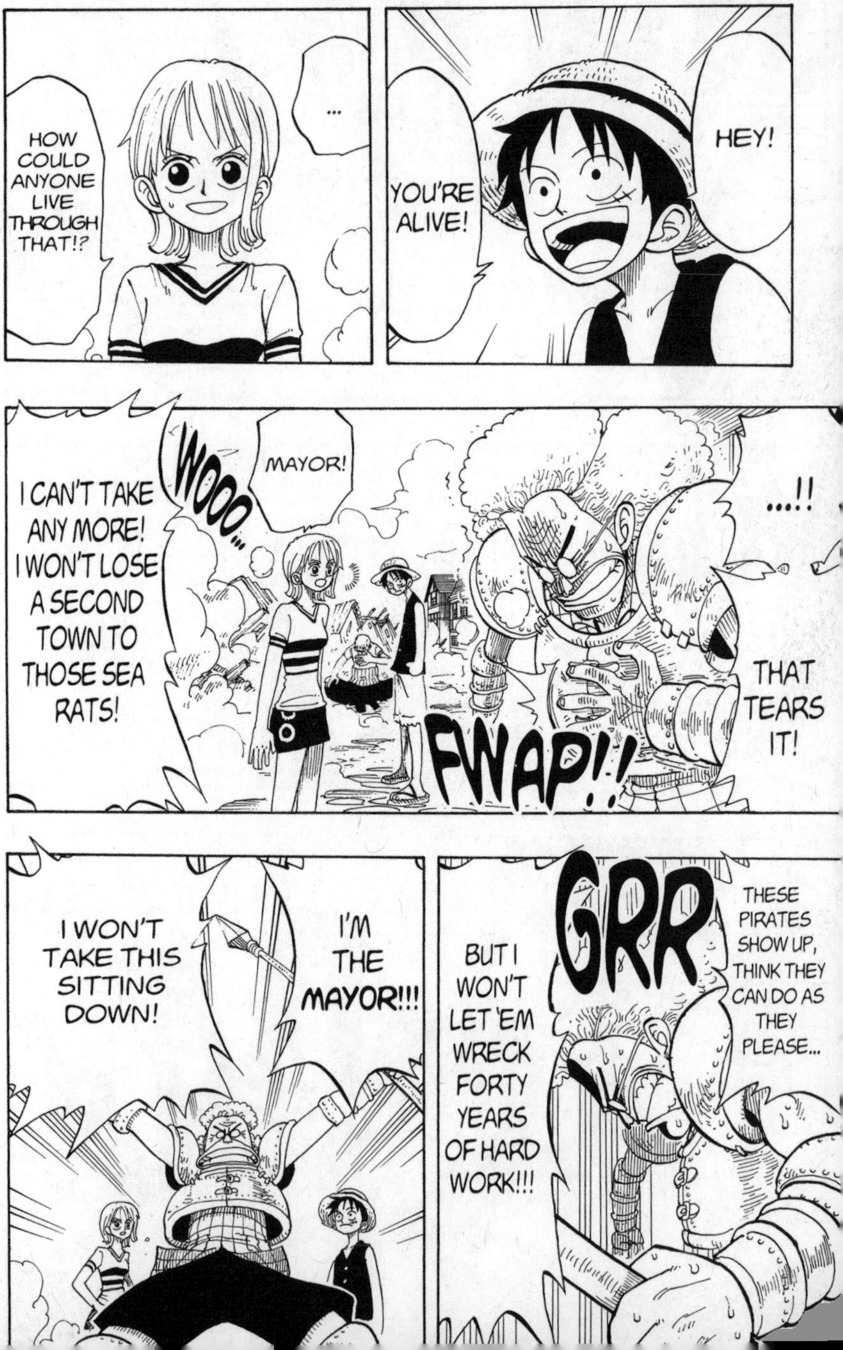
HEY!
YOU'RE ALIVE!
...
HOW COULD ANYONE LIVE THROUGH THAT!?
...!!
THAT TEARS IT!
FWAP!!
MAYOR!
WOOO...
I CAN'T TAKE ANY MORE! I WON'T LOSE A SECOND TOWN TO THOSE SEA RATS!
THESE PIRATES SHOW UP, THINK THEY CAN DO AS THEY PLEASE...
GRR
BUT I WON'T LET 'EM WRECK FORTY YEARS OF HARD WORK!!!
I'M THE MAYOR!!!
I WON'T TAKE THIS SITTING DOWN!

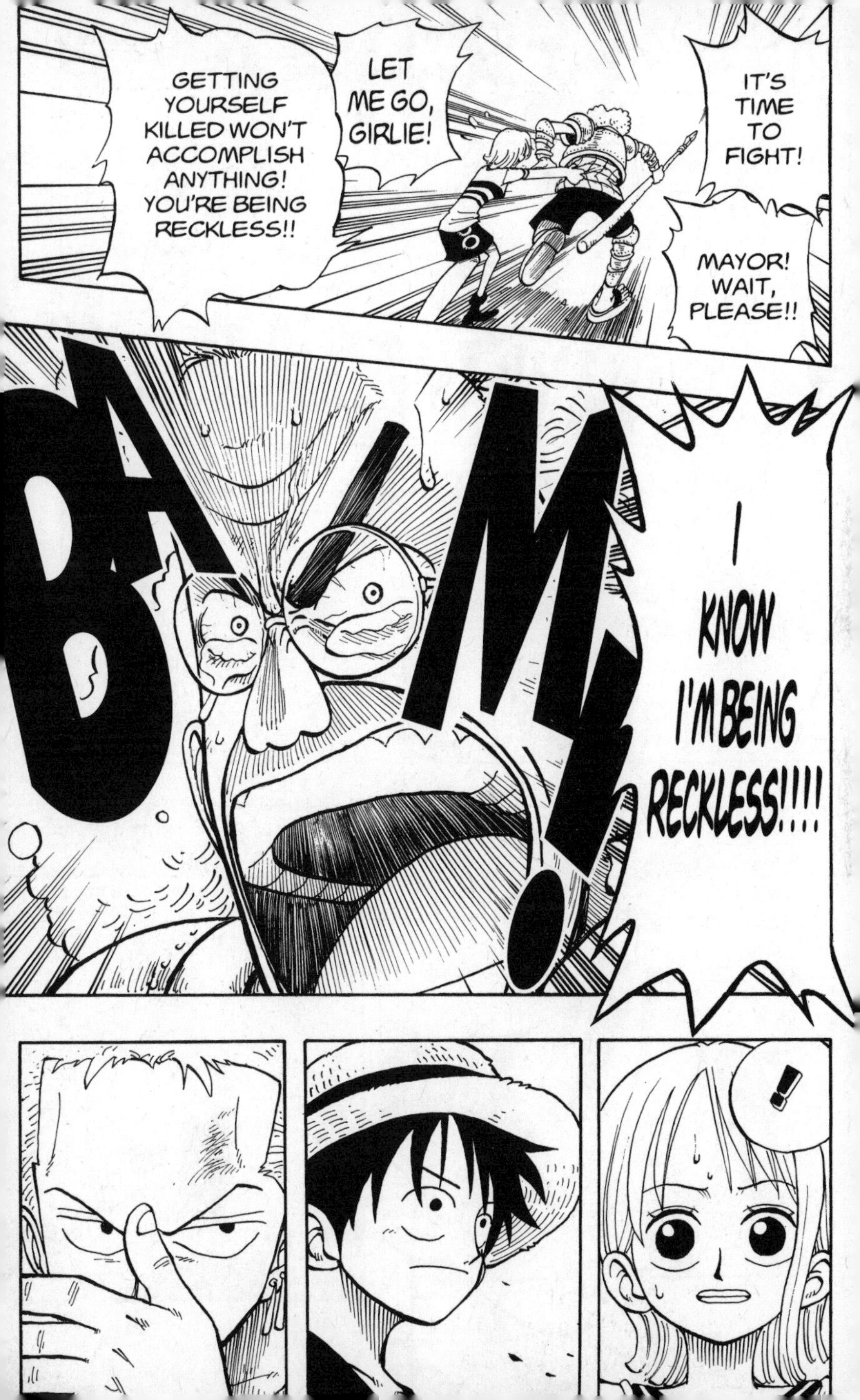
IT'S TIME TO FIGHT!
MAYOR! WAIT, PLEASE!!
LET ME GO, GIRLIE!
GETTING YOURSELF KILLED WON'T ACCOMPLISH ANYTHING! YOU'RE BEING RECKLESS!!
I KNOW I'M BEING RECKLESS!!!!
BAM!
!

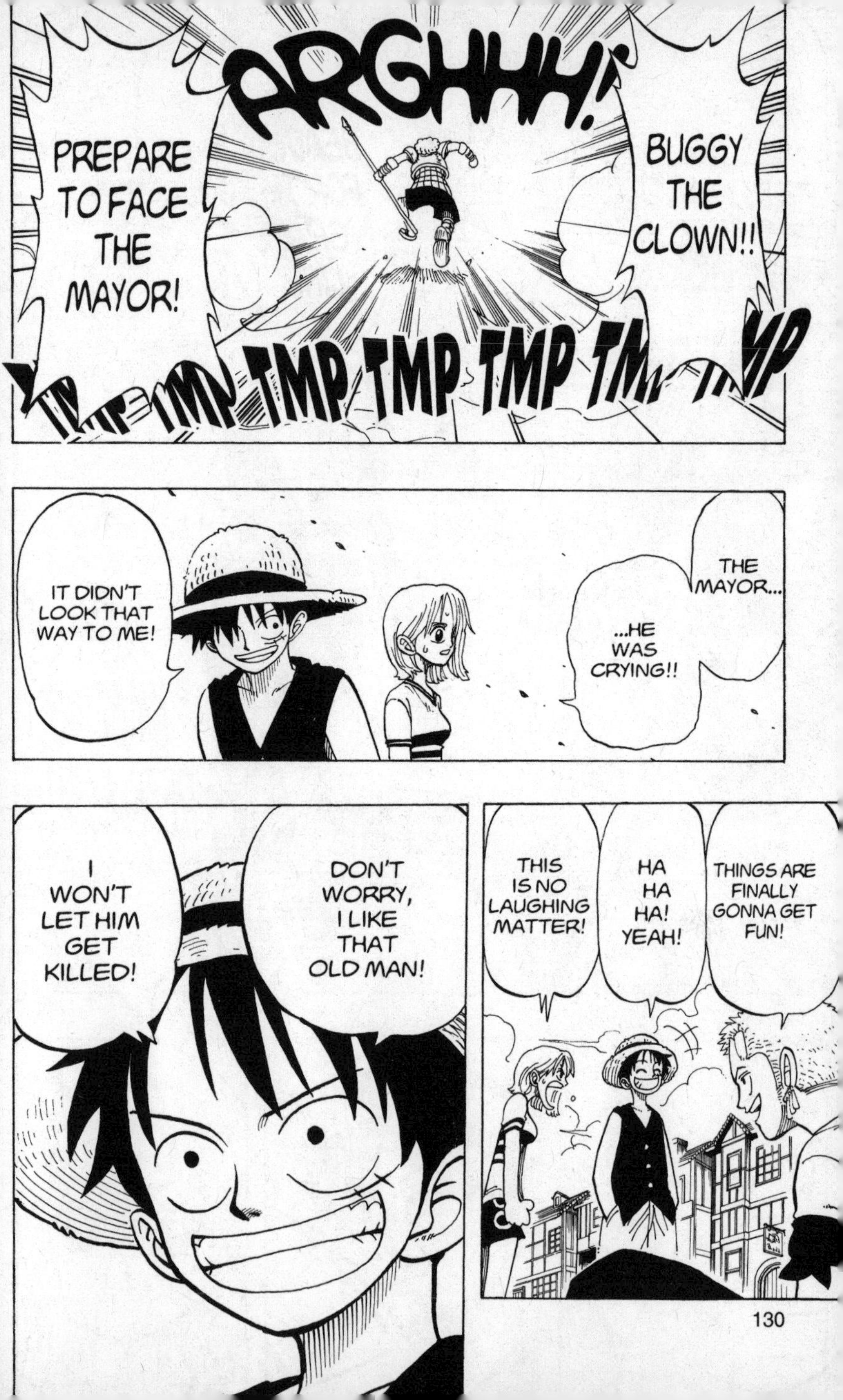
ARGHH!
BUGGY THE CLOWN!!
PREPARE TO FACE THE MAYOR!
TMP TMP TMP
THE MAYOR...
...HE WAS CRYING!!
IT DIDN'T LOOK THAT WAY TO ME!
THINGS ARE FINALLY GONNA GET FUN!
HA HA HA! YEAH!
THIS IS NO LAUGHING MATTER!
DON'T WORRY, I LIKE THAT OLD MAN!
I WON'T LET HIM GET KILLED!

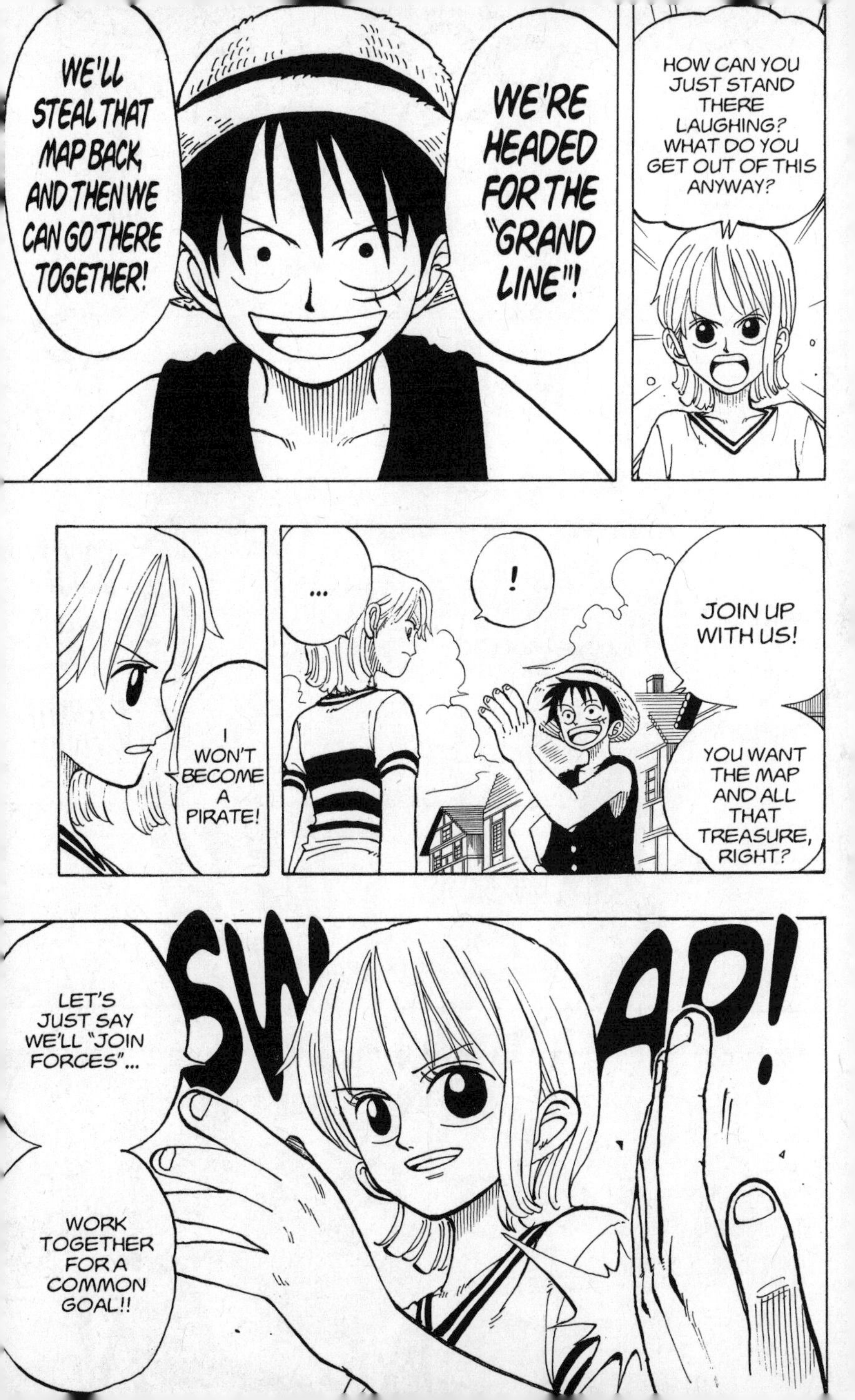
HOW CAN YOU JUST STAND THERE LAUGHING? WHAT DO YOU GET OUT OF THIS ANYWAY?
WE'RE HEADED FOR THE "GRAND LINE"!
WE'LL STEAL THAT MAP BACK, AND THEN WE CAN GO THERE TOGETHER!
JOIN UP WITH US!
YOU WANT THE MAP AND ALL THAT TREASURE, RIGHT?
!
...
I WON'T BECOME A PIRATE!
SW AP!
LET'S JUST SAY WE'LL "JOIN FORCES"...
WORK TOGETHER FOR A COMMON GOAL!!

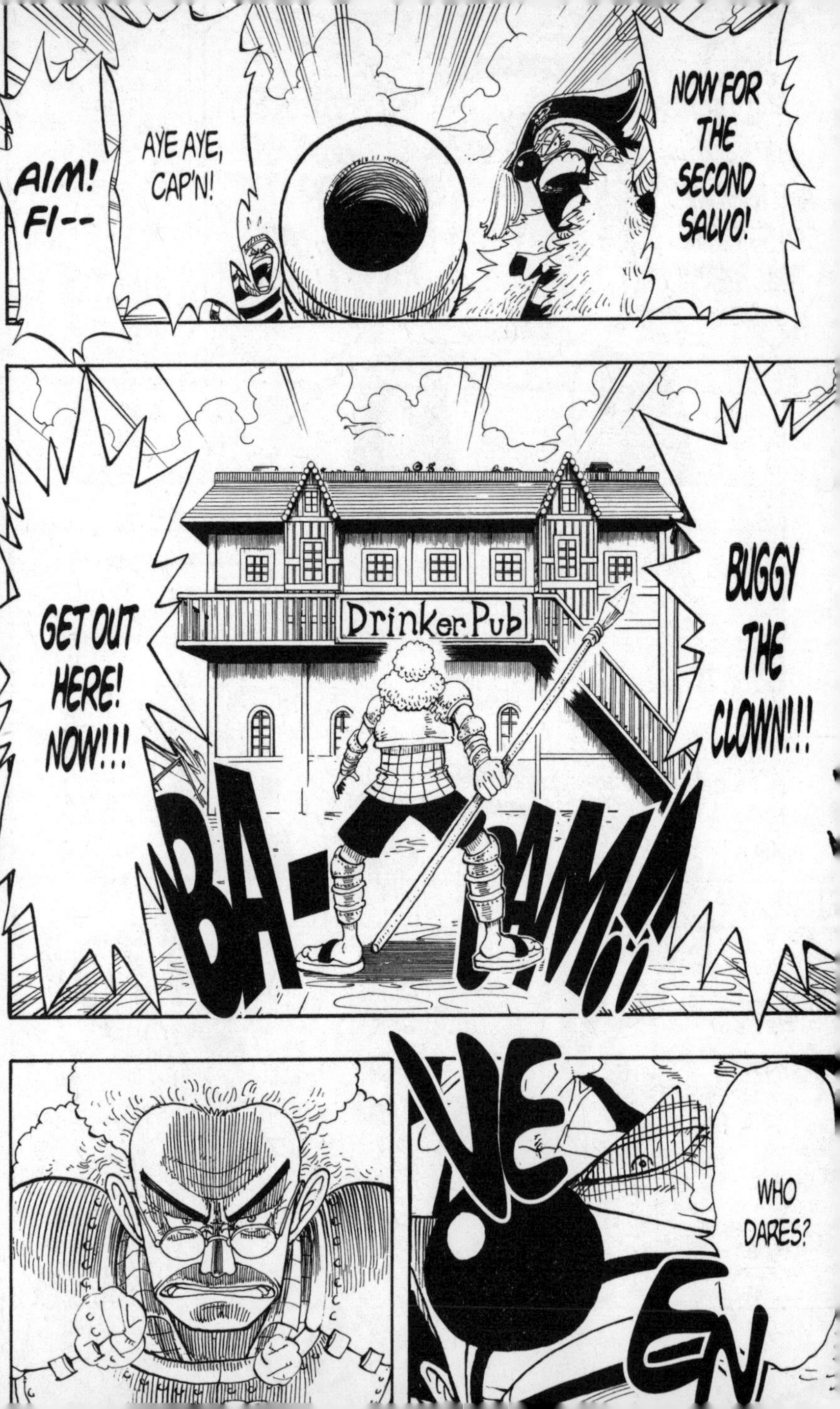
NOW FOR THE SECOND SALVO!
AYE AYE, CAP'N!
AIM! FI--
BUGGY THE CLOWN!!!
GET OUT HERE! NOW!!!
Drinker Pub
BA-CAM!!
WHO DARES?

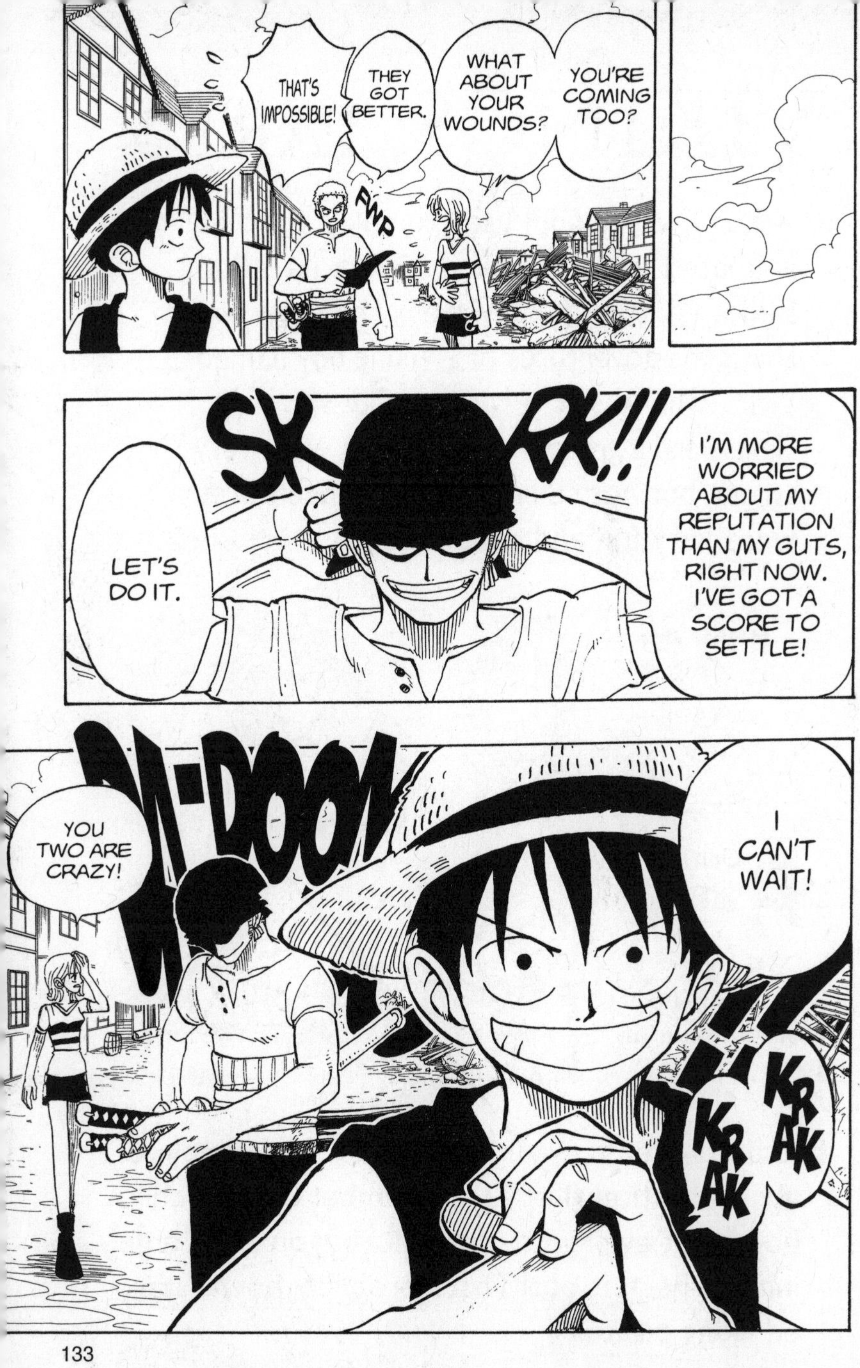

YOU'RE COMING TOO?
WHAT ABOUT YOUR WOUNDS?
THEY GOT BETTER.
THAT'S IMPOSSIBLE!
FWP
I'M MORE WORRIED ABOUT MY REPUTATION THAN MY GUTS, RIGHT NOW. I'VE GOT A SCORE TO SETTLE!
SK RK!!
LET'S DO IT.
I CAN'T WAIT!
KRAK KRAK
KRAK KRAK
-DOOM
YOU TWO ARE CRAZY!

VIKINGS, PART 3

✤ When I was a kid, I used to enjoy watching an animated tv seres called **Chiisa na Viking Bikke** ("Little Viking Vicke"). The show was about the adventures of a Viking boy named Vicke, who wasn't very strong but was very clever, and a group of Vikings who were very strong but not so smart. Their adventures were very fun and entertaining.

Mother Ylva

Vicke

Ga ha ha ha ha!

Vicke's father (the Captain)

Geh Heh heh!

Sven, the mean guy (enemy of Vicke and the others)

← Musician

He's always saying this.

That's impressive!

Merry Men

✤ It aired over 15 years ago, so a lot of people of my generation (I'm 23) remember it from childhood. If it ever gets rebroadcast, you should definitely check it out! That's probably how I started liking pirates.

Chapter 15:
GONG

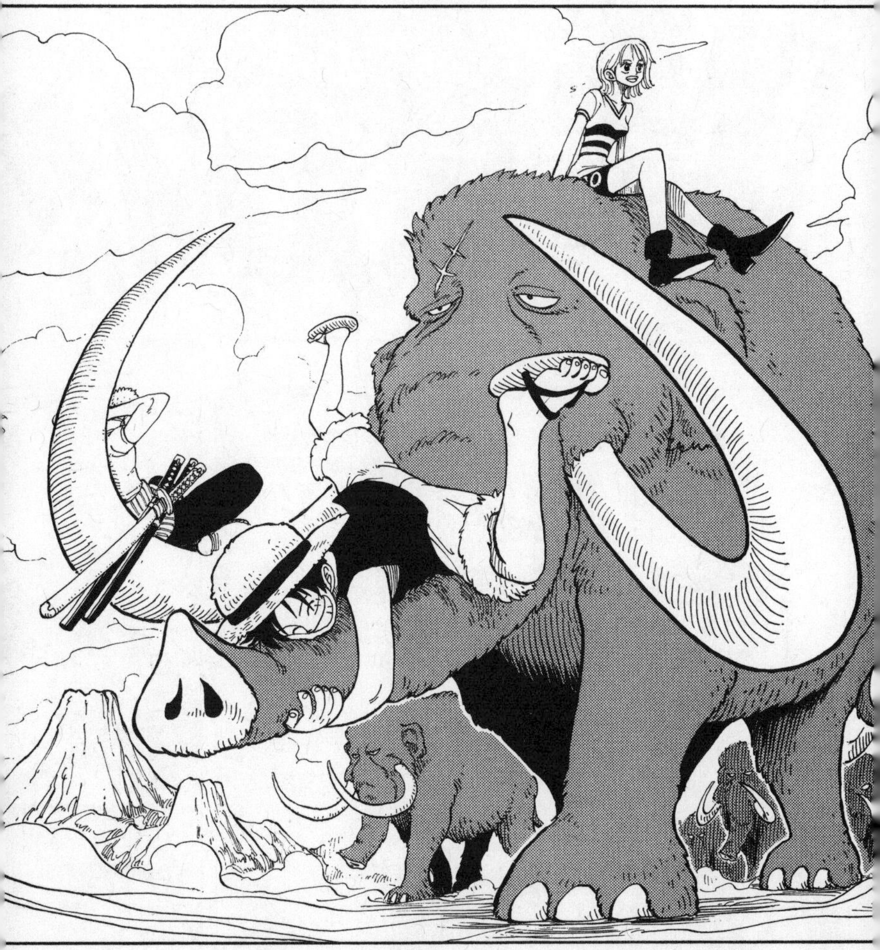

READ THIS WAY

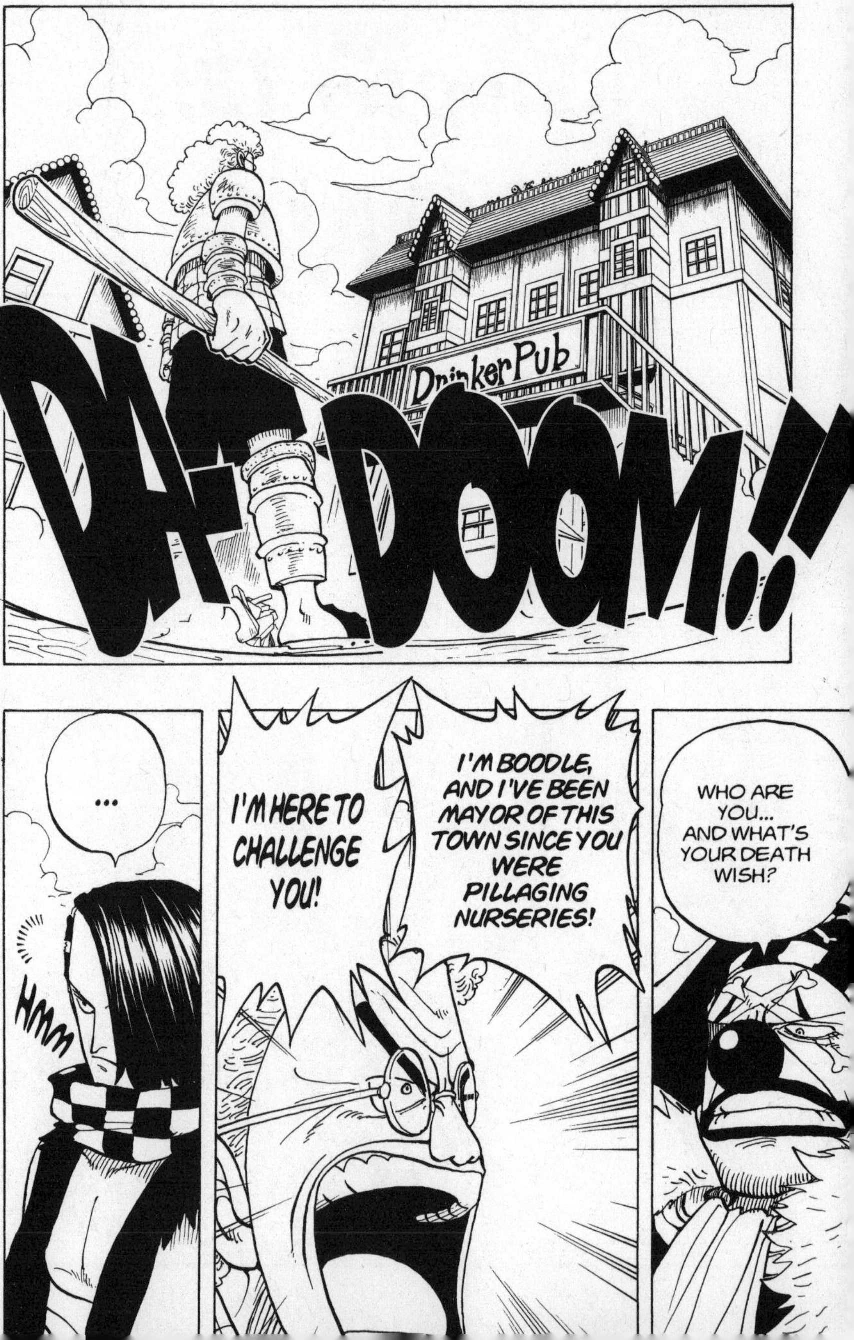
Drinker Pub
DA-DOOM!!
WHO ARE YOU... AND WHAT'S YOUR DEATH WISH?
I'M BOODLE, AND I'VE BEEN MAYOR OF THIS TOWN SINCE YOU WERE PILLAGING NURSERIES!
I'M HERE TO CHALLENGE YOU!
...
HMM

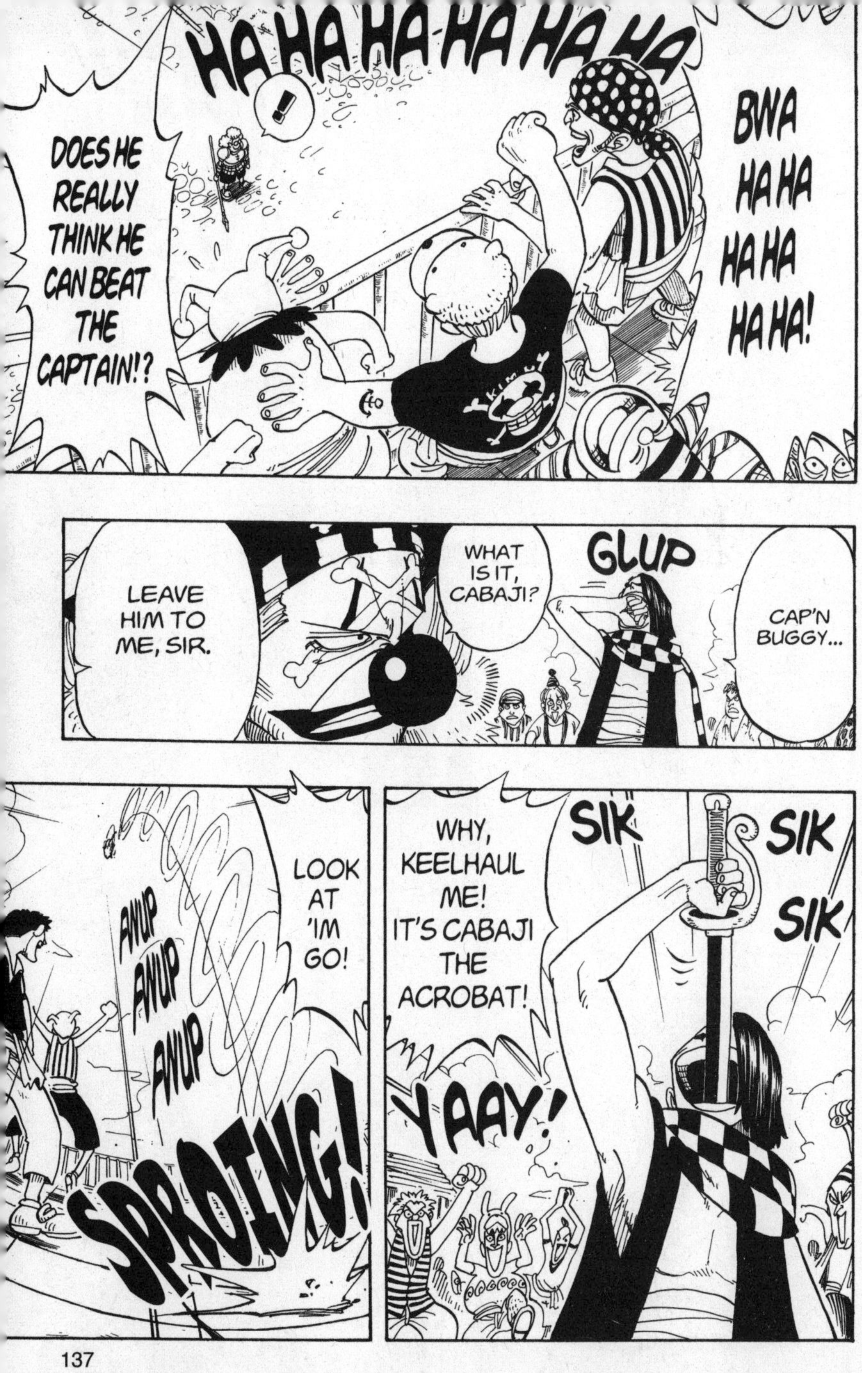
HA HA HA-HA HA HA HA
BWA HA HA HA HA HA HA!
!
DOES HE REALLY THINK HE CAN BEAT THE CAPTAIN!?
CAP'N BUGGY...
GLUP
WHAT IS IT, CABAJI?
LEAVE HIM TO ME, SIR.
SIK
SIK
SIK
WHY, KEELHAUL ME! IT'S CABAJI THE ACROBAT!
YAAY!
LOOK AT 'IM GO!
FWUP
FWUP
FWUP
SPROING!

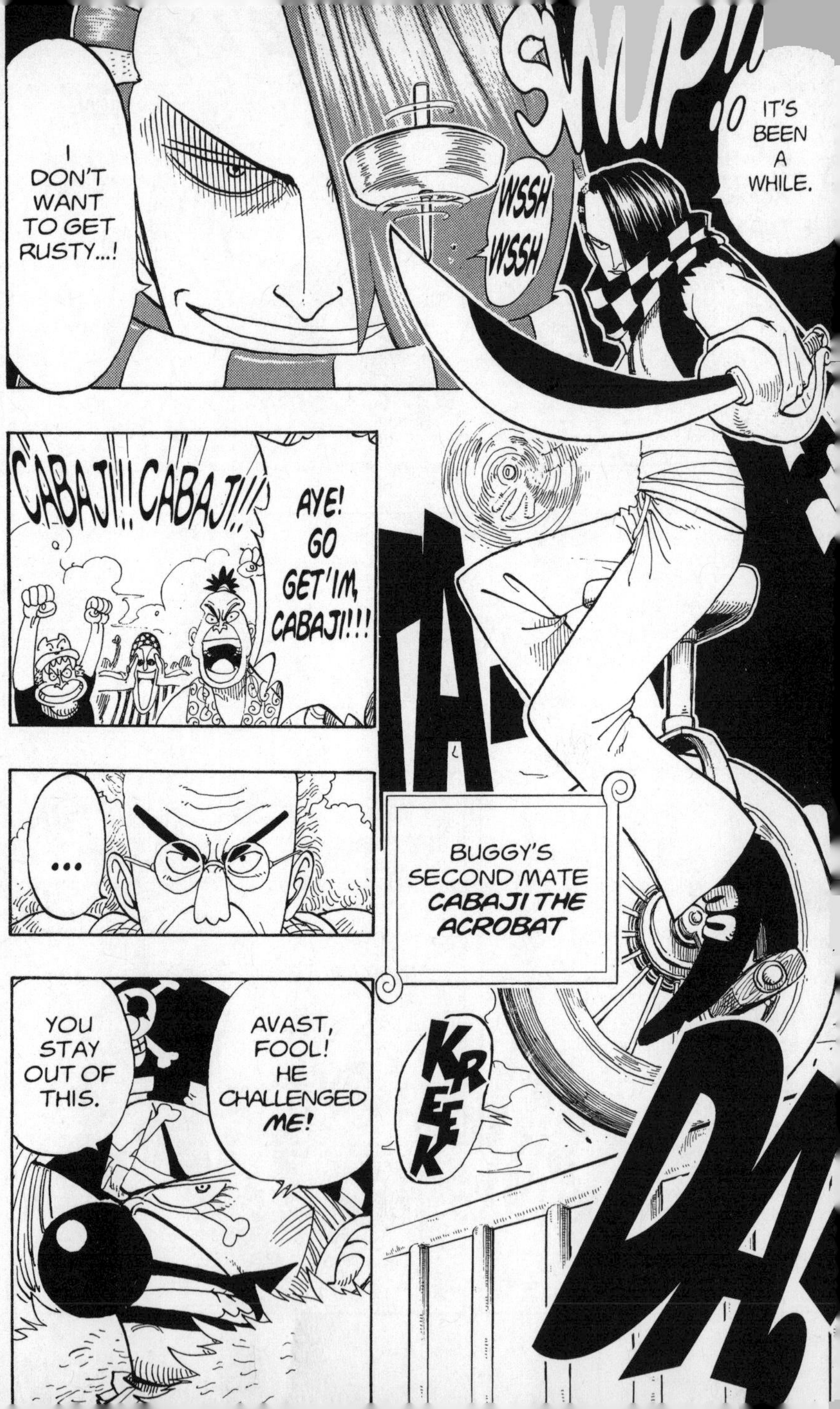
SNIP!!
IT'S BEEN A WHILE.
WSSH WSSH
TA
BUGGY'S SECOND MATE CABAJI THE ACROBAT
KREEK
DA
I DON'T WANT TO GET RUSTY...!
AYE! GO GET'IM, CABAJI!!!
CABAJI!! CABAJI!!
...
AVAST, FOOL! HE CHALLENGED ME!
YOU STAY OUT OF THIS.

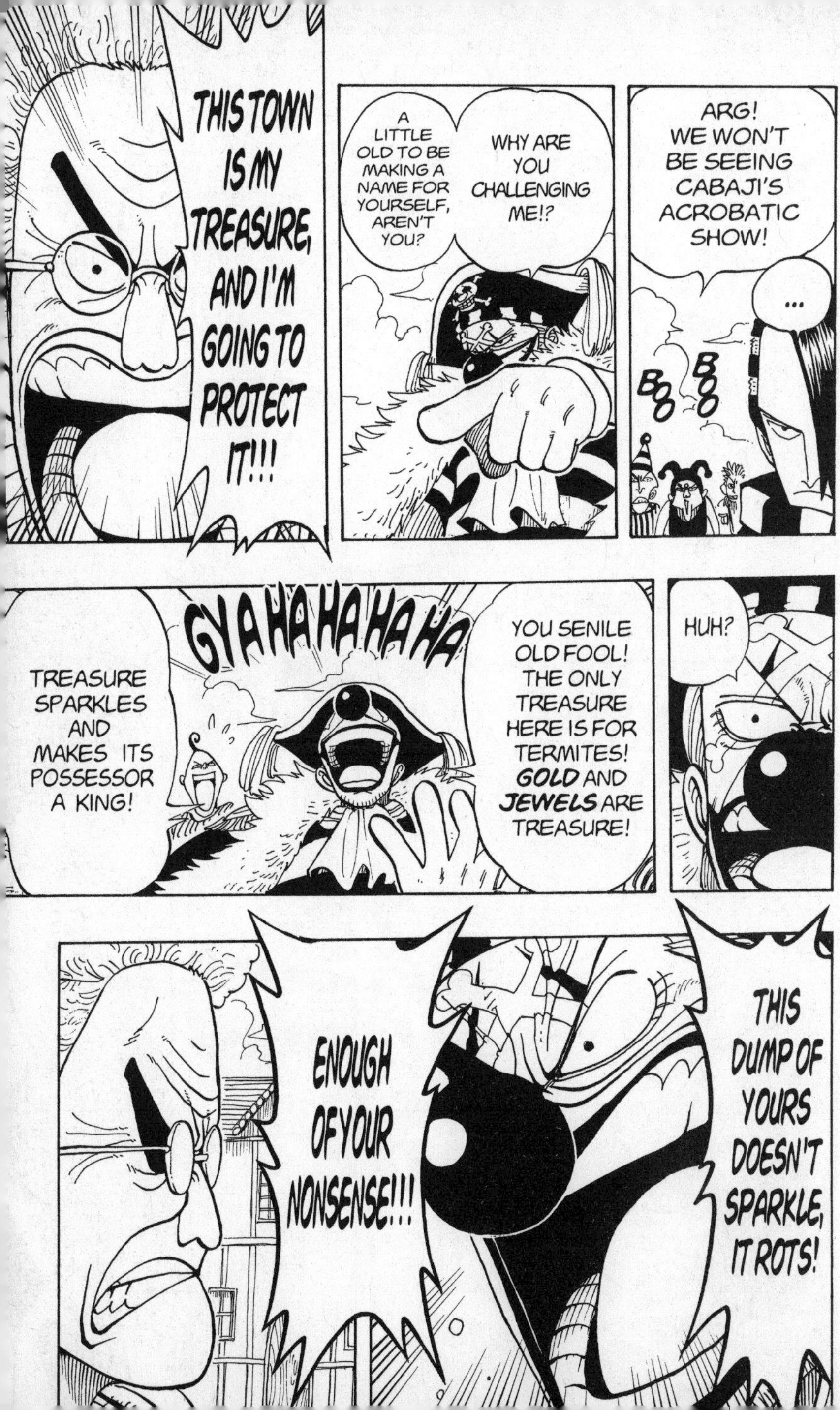
ARG! WE WON'T BE SEEING CABAJI'S ACROBATIC SHOW!
...
BOO
BOO
WHY ARE YOU CHALLENGING ME!?
A LITTLE OLD TO BE MAKING A NAME FOR YOURSELF, AREN'T YOU?
THIS TOWN IS MY TREASURE, AND I'M GOING TO PROTECT IT!!!
HUH?
YOU SENILE OLD FOOL! THE ONLY TREASURE HERE IS FOR TERMITES! GOLD AND JEWELS ARE TREASURE!
GYAHAHAHAHAHA
TREASURE SPARKLES AND MAKES ITS POSSESSOR A KING!
THIS DUMP OF YOURS DOESN'T SPARKLE, IT ROTS!
ENOUGH OF YOUR NONSENSE!!!

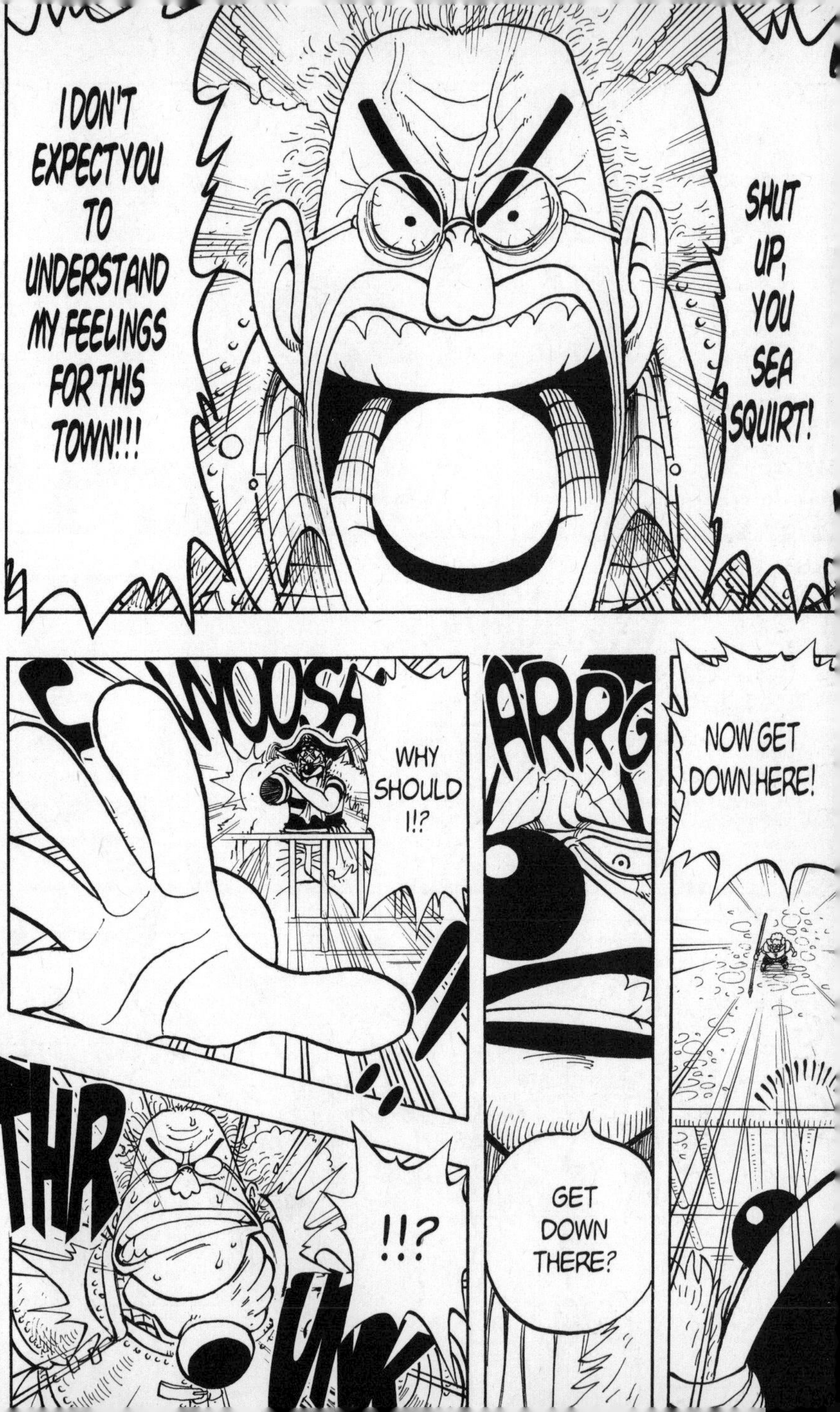
SHUT UP, YOU SEA SQUIRT!
I DON'T EXPECT YOU TO UNDERSTAND MY FEELINGS FOR THIS TOWN!!!
NOW GET DOWN HERE!
ARRG
GET DOWN THERE?
WOOSA
WHY SHOULD I!?
THR
UNK
!!?

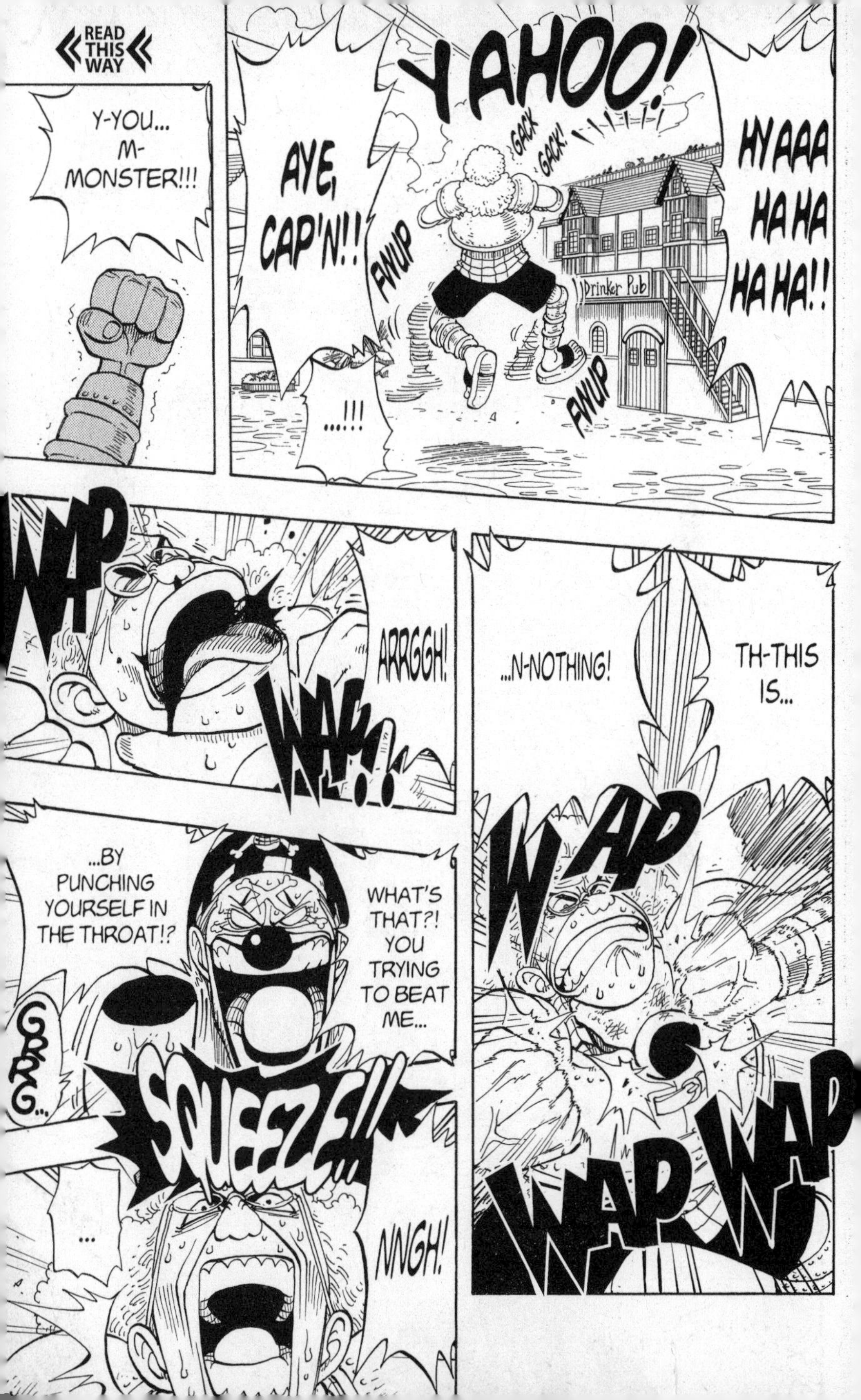
READ THIS WAY
YAHOO!
GACK GACK!
HYAAA HA HA HA HA!!
AYE, CAP'N!!
FWUP
FWUP
...!!!
Y-YOU... M-MONSTER!!!
TH-THIS IS...
...N-NOTHING!
WAP
WAP WAP
WAP
ARRGGH!
WAP!!
WHAT'S THAT?! YOU TRYING TO BEAT ME...
...BY PUNCHING YOURSELF IN THE THROAT!?
SQUEEZE!!
GORRG...
NNGH!
...

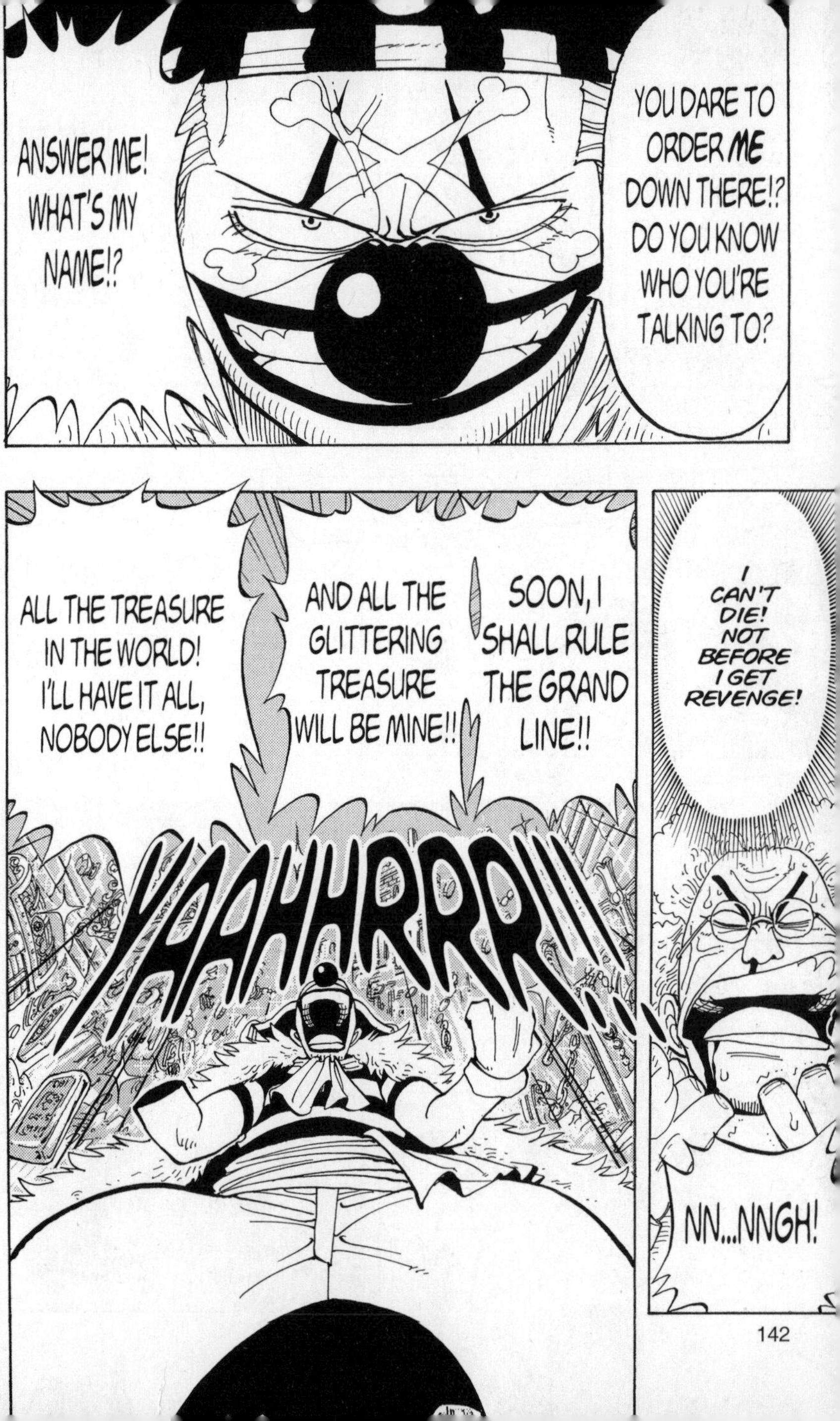
YOU DARE TO ORDER ME DOWN THERE!? DO YOU KNOW WHO YOU'RE TALKING TO?
ANSWER ME! WHAT'S MY NAME!?
I CAN'T DIE! NOT BEFORE I GET REVENGE!
NN...NNGH!
SOON, I SHALL RULE THE GRAND LINE!!
AND ALL THE GLITTERING TREASURE WILL BE MINE!!
ALL THE TREASURE IN THE WORLD! I'LL HAVE IT ALL, NOBODY ELSE!!
YAAHHRRRR!!!

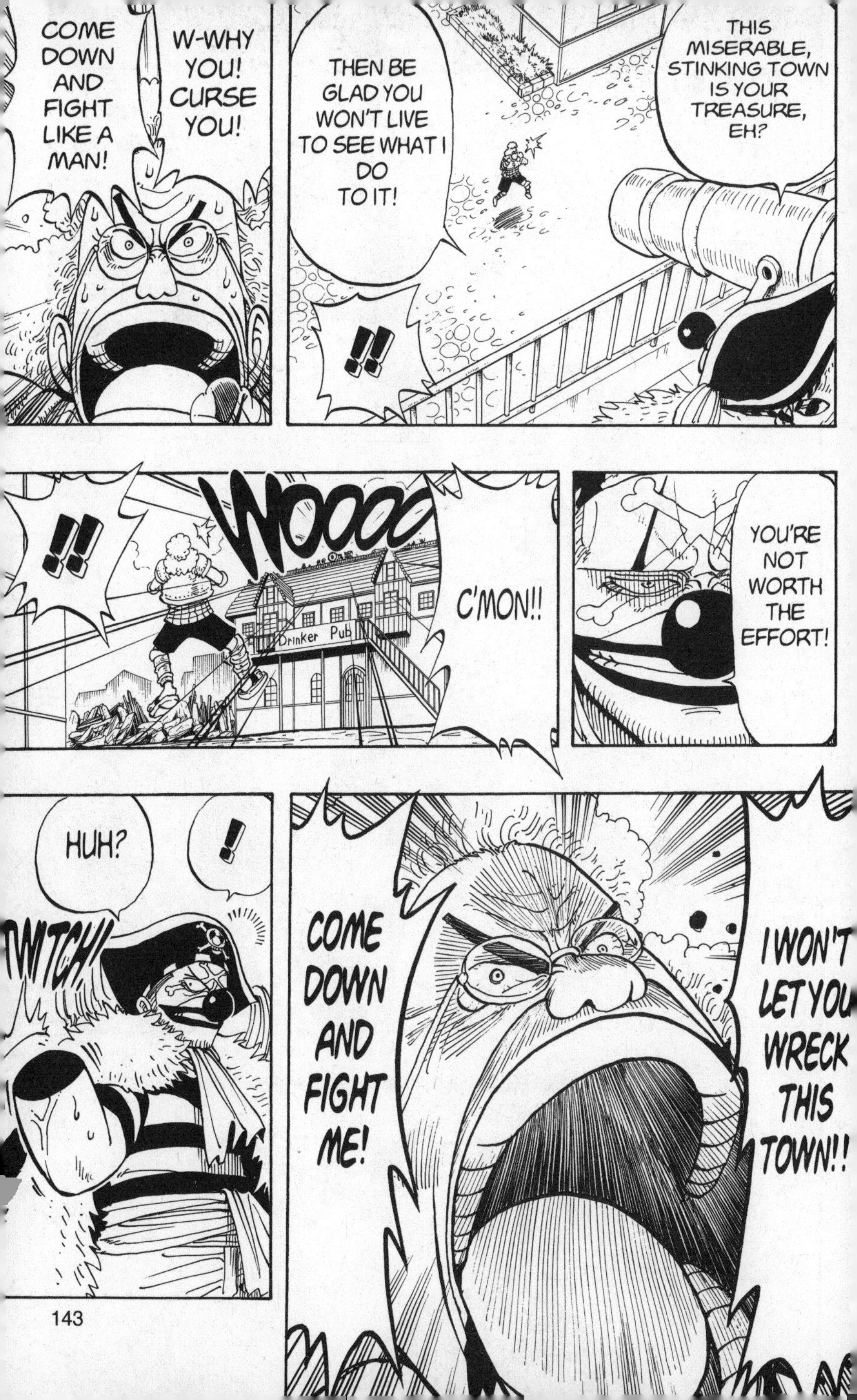
THIS MISERABLE, STINKING TOWN IS YOUR TREASURE, EH?
THEN BE GLAD YOU WON'T LIVE TO SEE WHAT I DO TO IT!
!!
W-WHY YOU! CURSE YOU!
COME DOWN AND FIGHT LIKE A MAN!
YOU'RE NOT WORTH THE EFFORT!
C'MON!!
WOOOO
!!
I WON'T LET YOU WRECK THIS TOWN!!
COME DOWN AND FIGHT ME!
!
HUH?
TWITCH

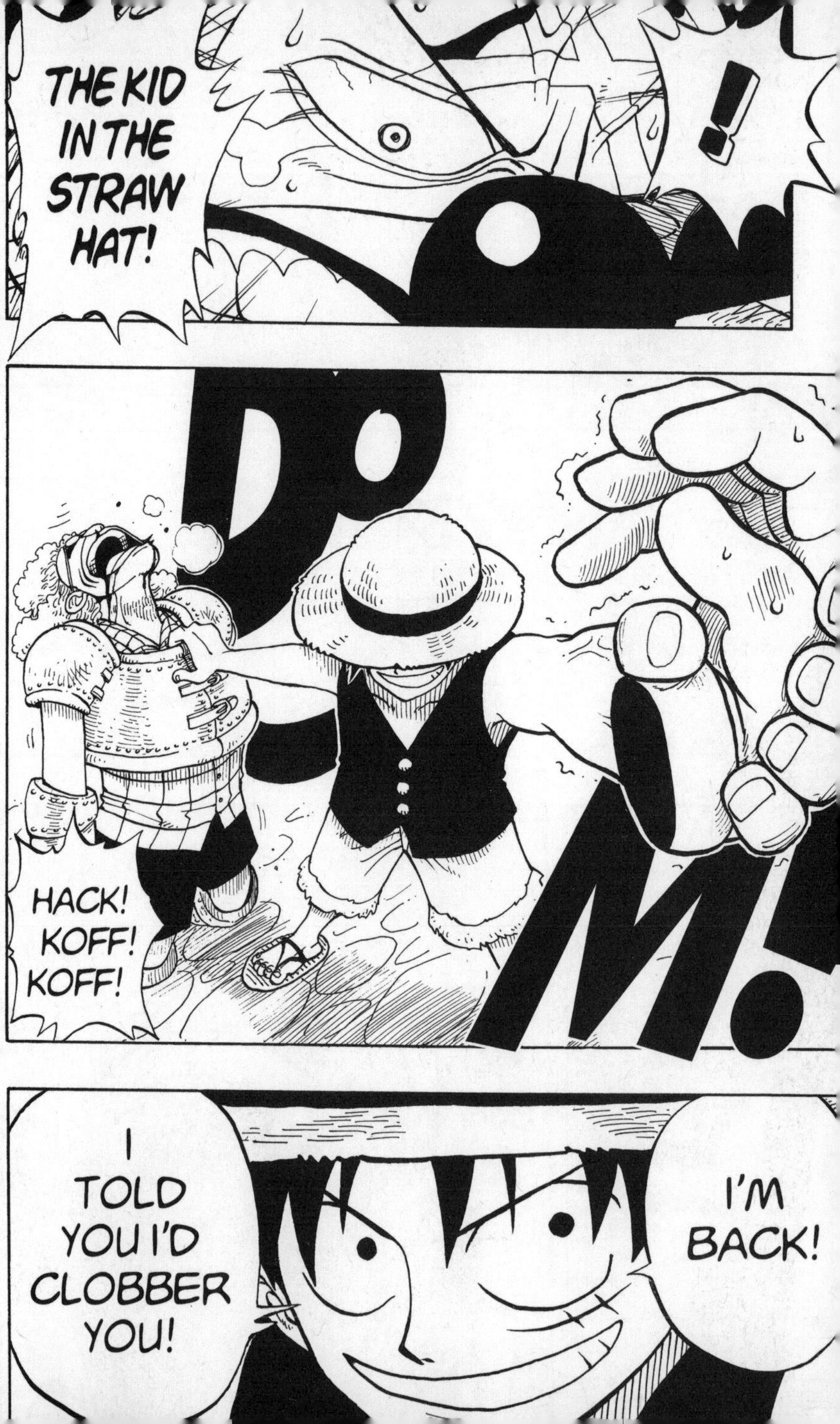
!
THE KID IN THE STRAW HAT!
HACK! KOFF! KOFF!
I'M BACK!
I TOLD YOU I'D CLOBBER YOU!

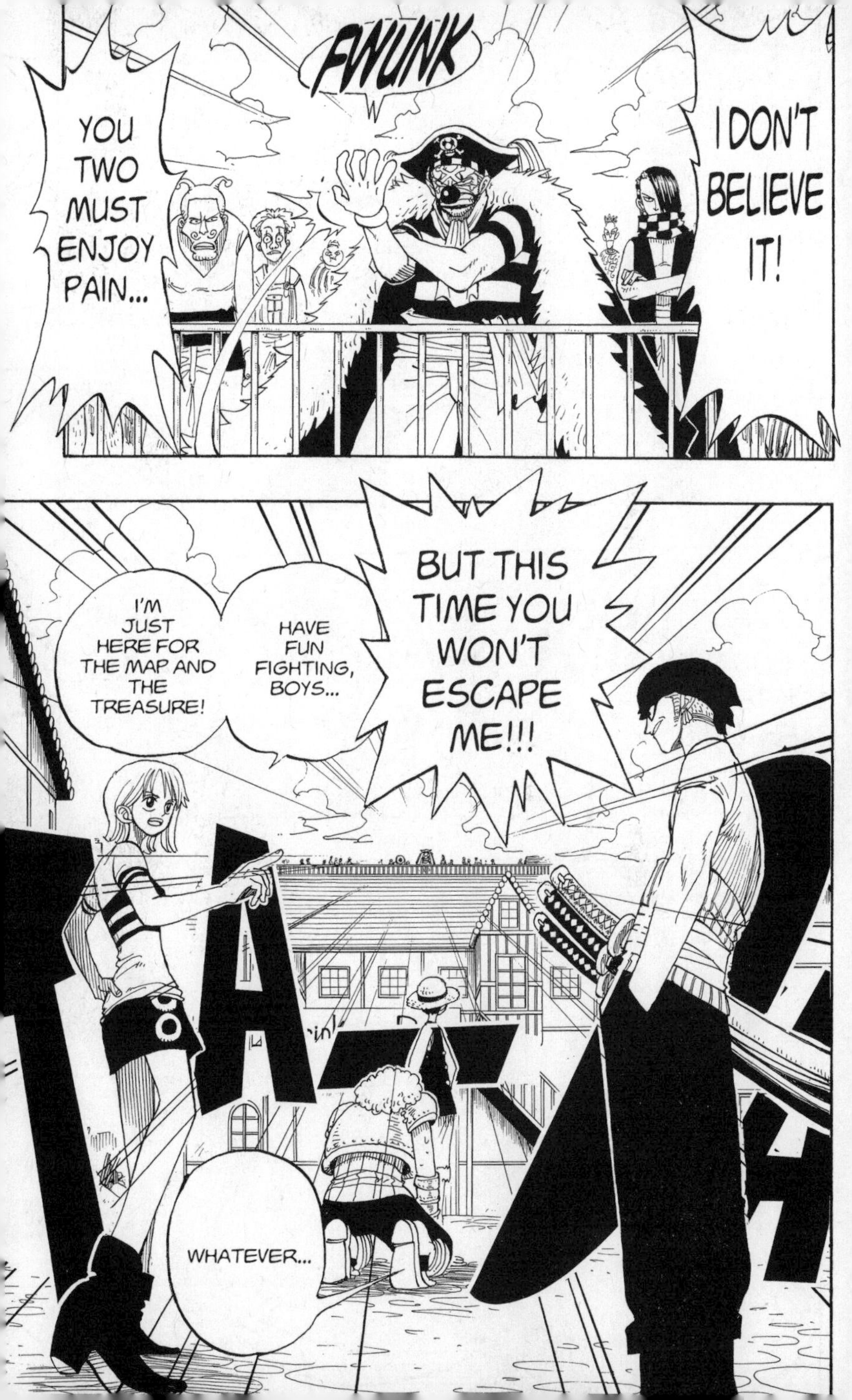
I DON'T BELIEVE IT!
FWUNK
YOU TWO MUST ENJOY PAIN...
BUT THIS TIME YOU WON'T ESCAPE ME!!!
HAVE FUN FIGHTING, BOYS...
I'M JUST HERE FOR THE MAP AND THE TREASURE!
WHATEVER...

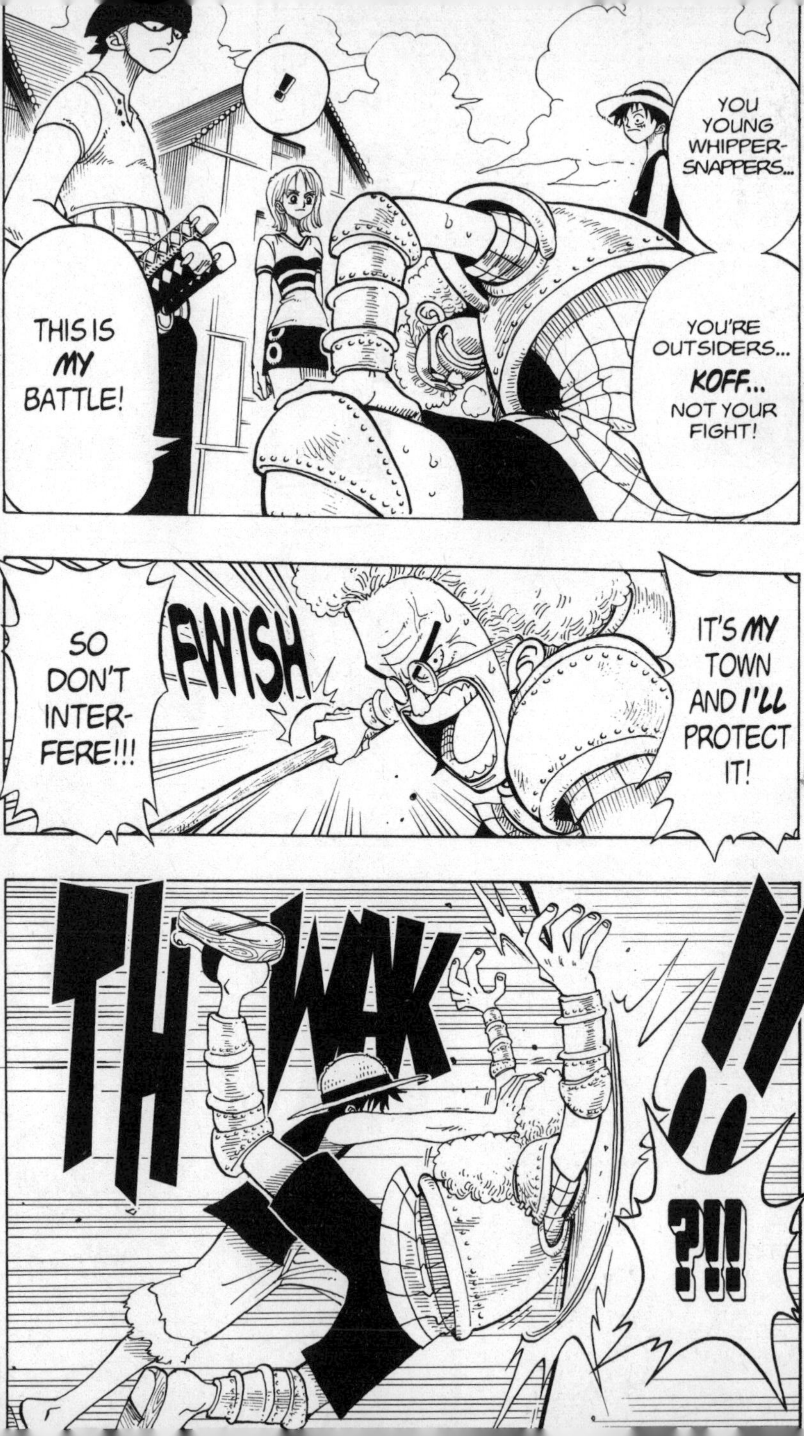
YOU YOUNG WHIPPER-SNAPPERS...
!
YOU'RE OUTSIDERS... KOFF... NOT YOUR FIGHT!
THIS IS MY BATTLE!
IT'S MY TOWN AND I'LL PROTECT IT!
FWISH
SO DON'T INTER-FERE!!!
!!
THWAK
?!!

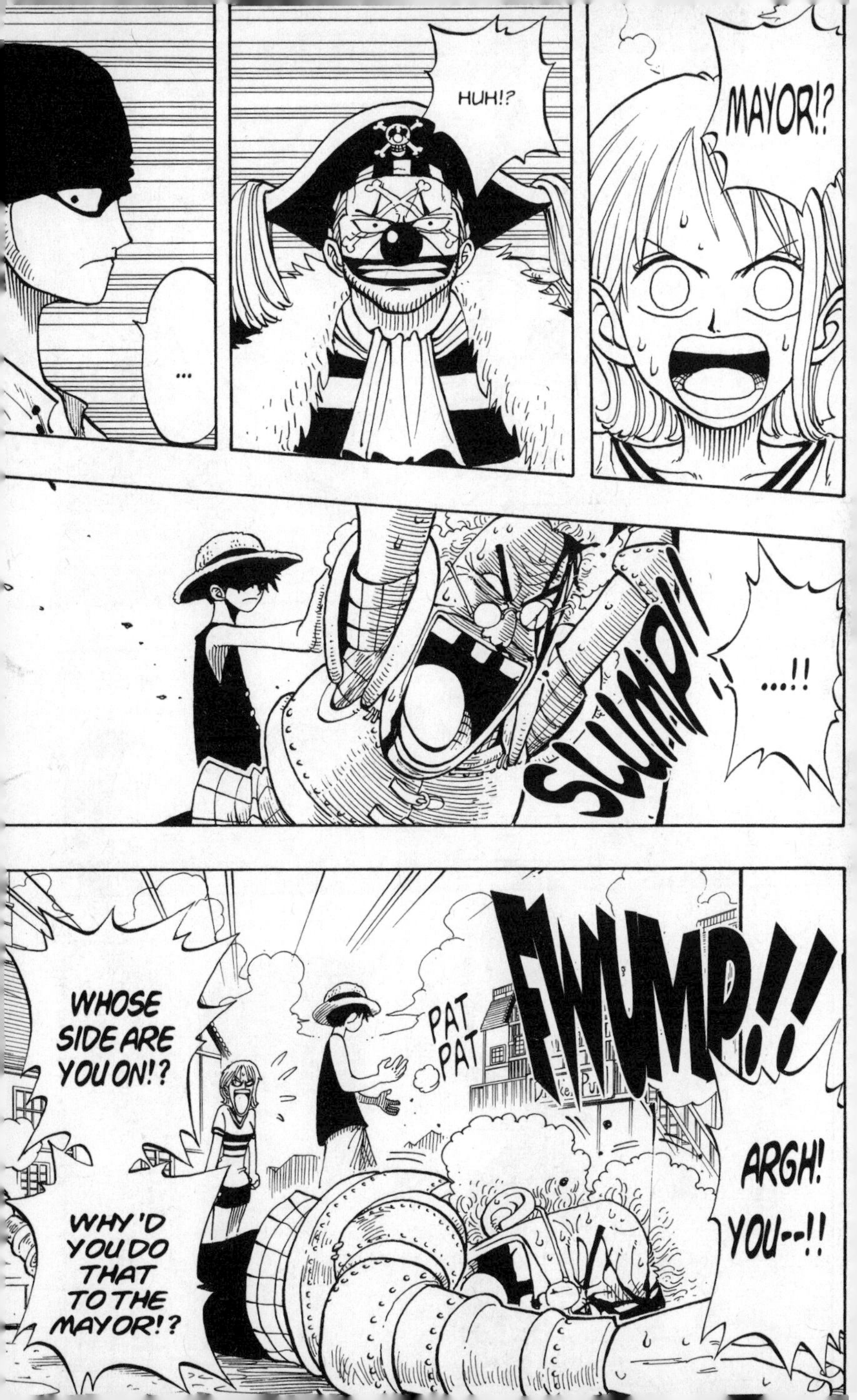
MAYOR!?
HUH!?
...
...!!
SLUMP!!
FWUMP!!
ARGH! YOU--!!
PAT PAT
WHOSE SIDE ARE YOU ON!?
WHY'D YOU DO THAT TO THE MAYOR!?

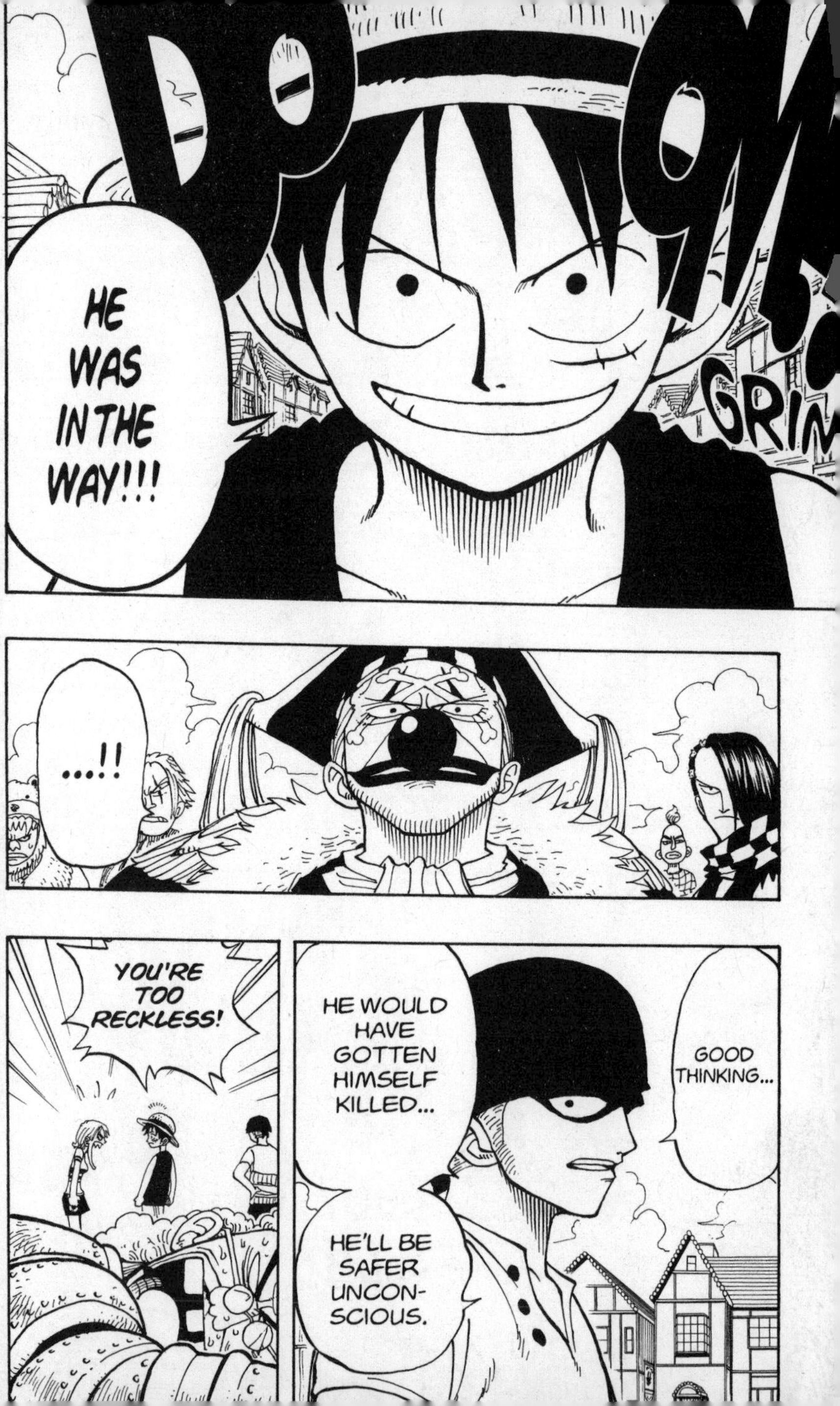
GRIN
HE WAS IN THE WAY!!!
...!!
GOOD THINKING...
HE WOULD HAVE GOTTEN HIMSELF KILLED...
HE'LL BE SAFER UNCONSCIOUS.
YOU'RE TOO RECKLESS!

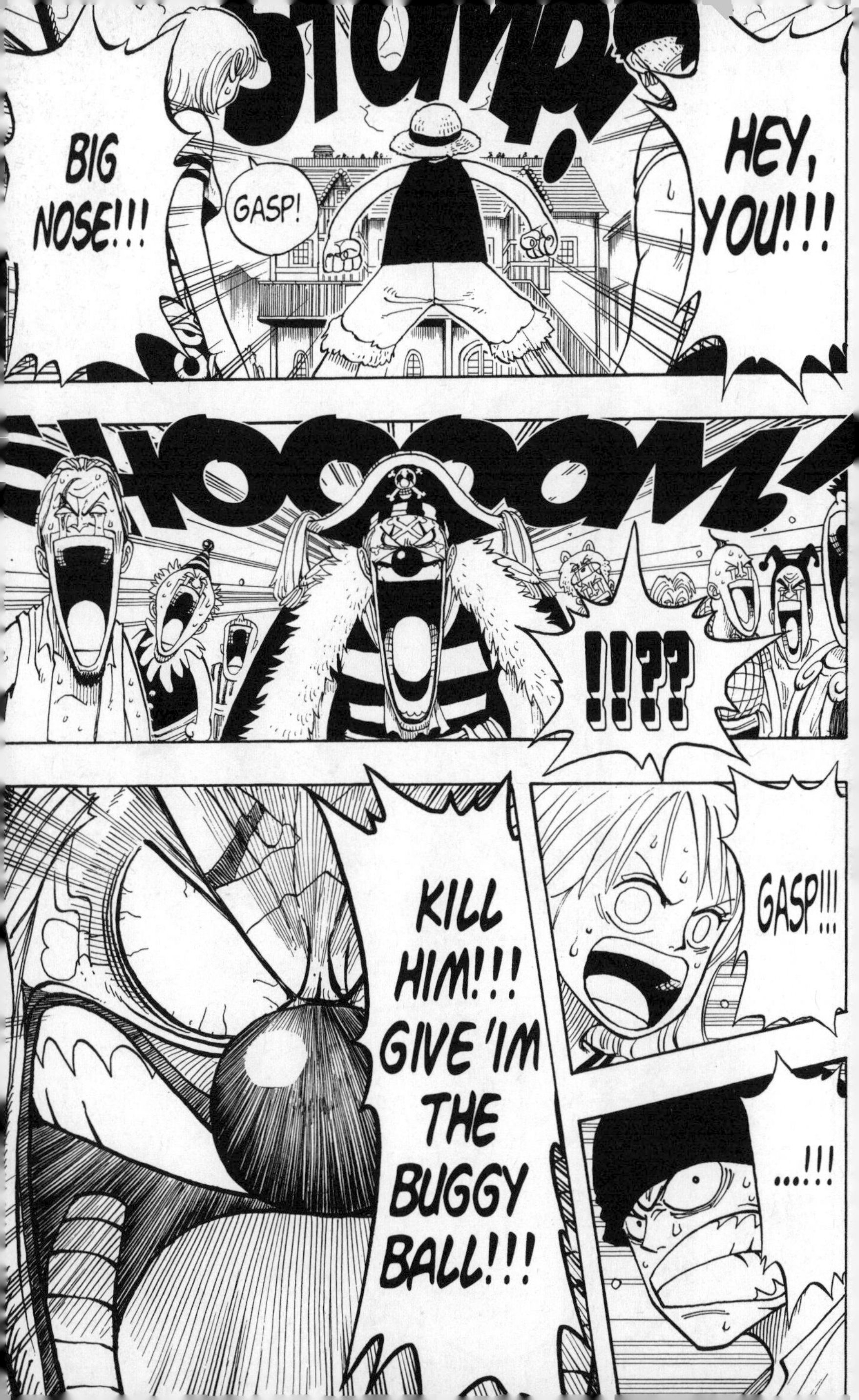
HEY, YOU!!!
GASP!
BIG NOSE!!!
!!??
GASP!!!
...!!!
KILL HIM!!! GIVE 'IM THE BUGGY BALL!!!

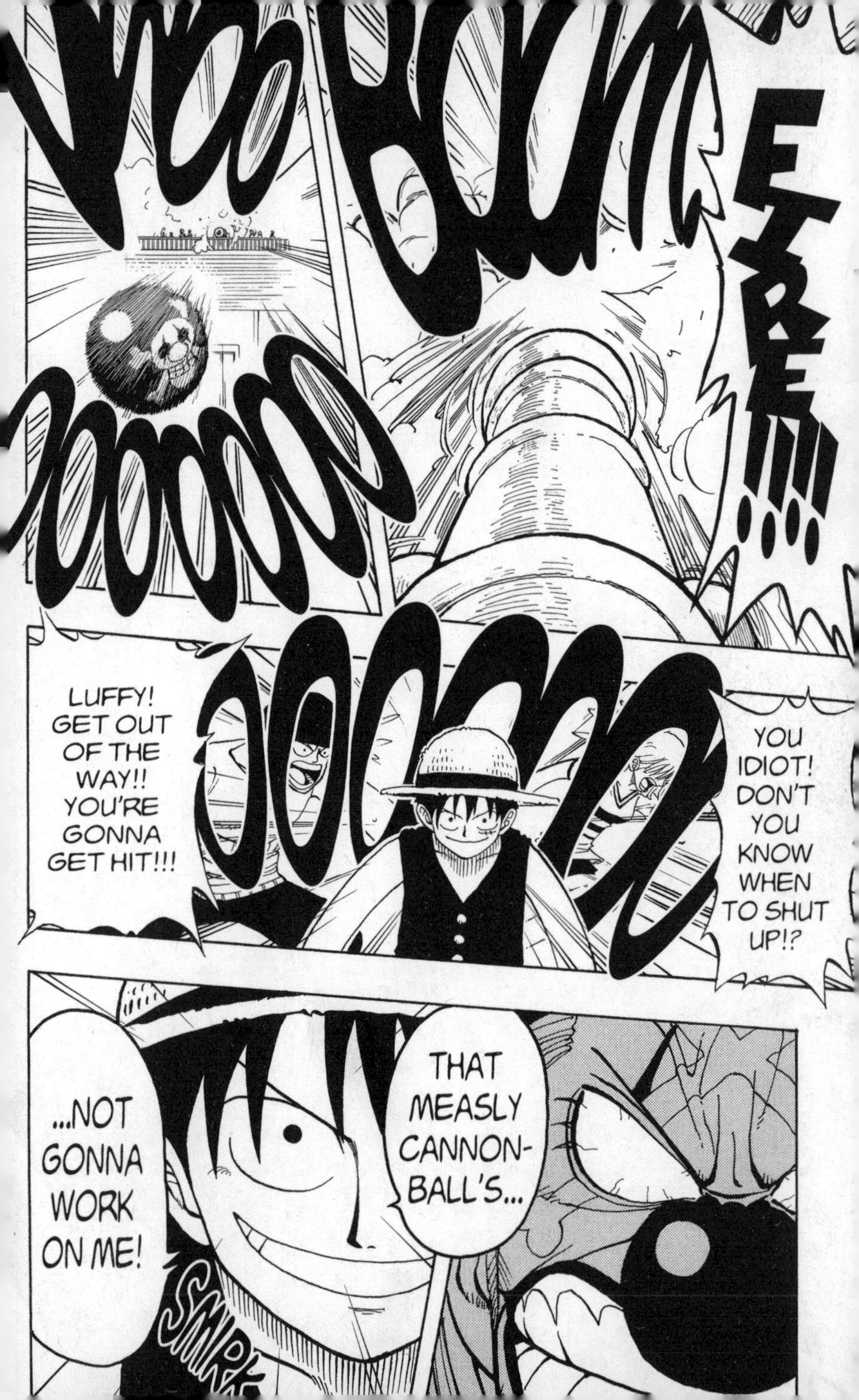
FIRE!!!
YOU IDIOT! DON'T YOU KNOW WHEN TO SHUT UP!?
LUFFY! GET OUT OF THE WAY!! YOU'RE GONNA GET HIT!!!
THAT MEASLY CANNON-BALL'S...
...NOT GONNA WORK ON ME!
SMIRK

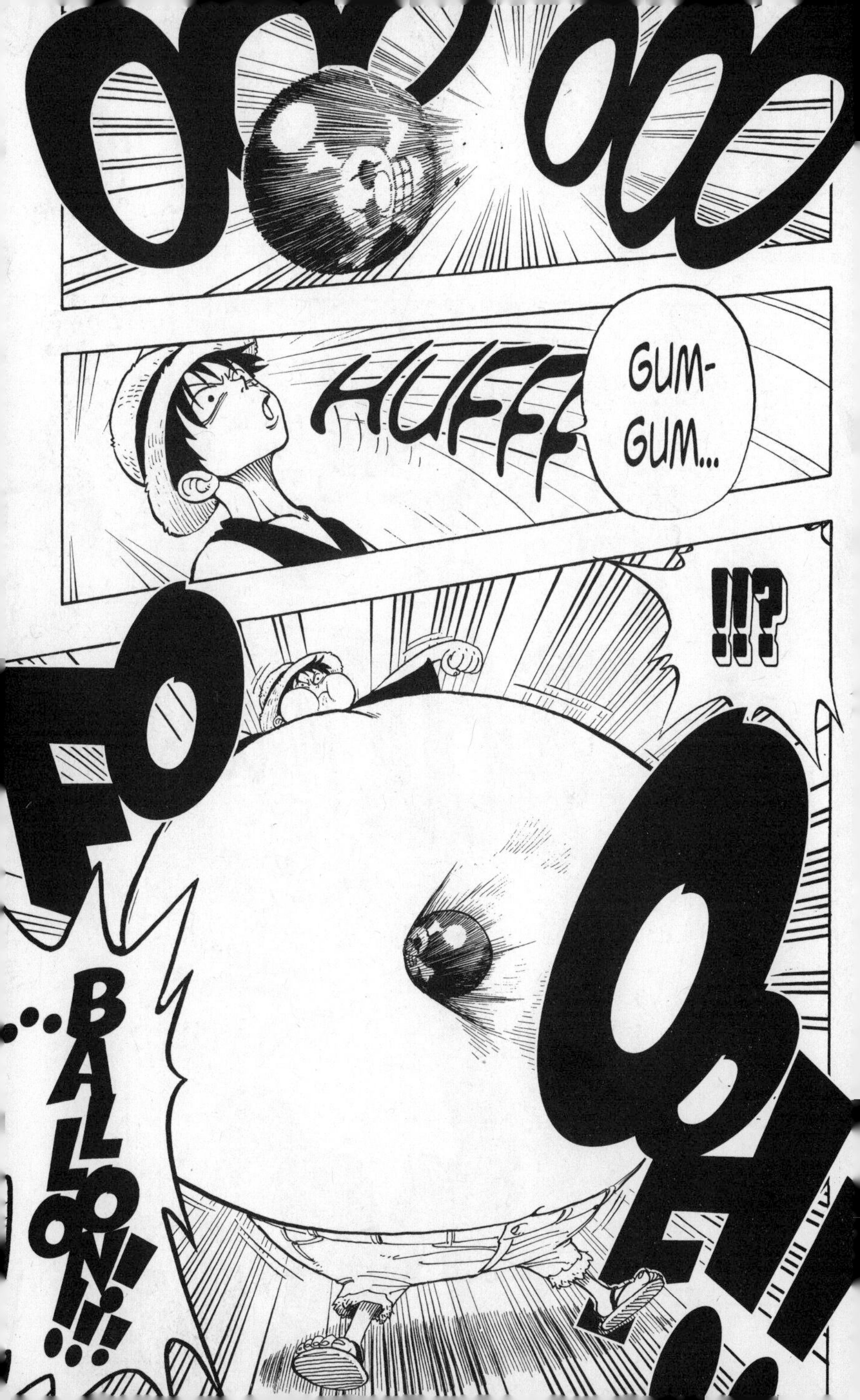
GUM-GUM...
HUFF
!!?
...BALLOON!!!

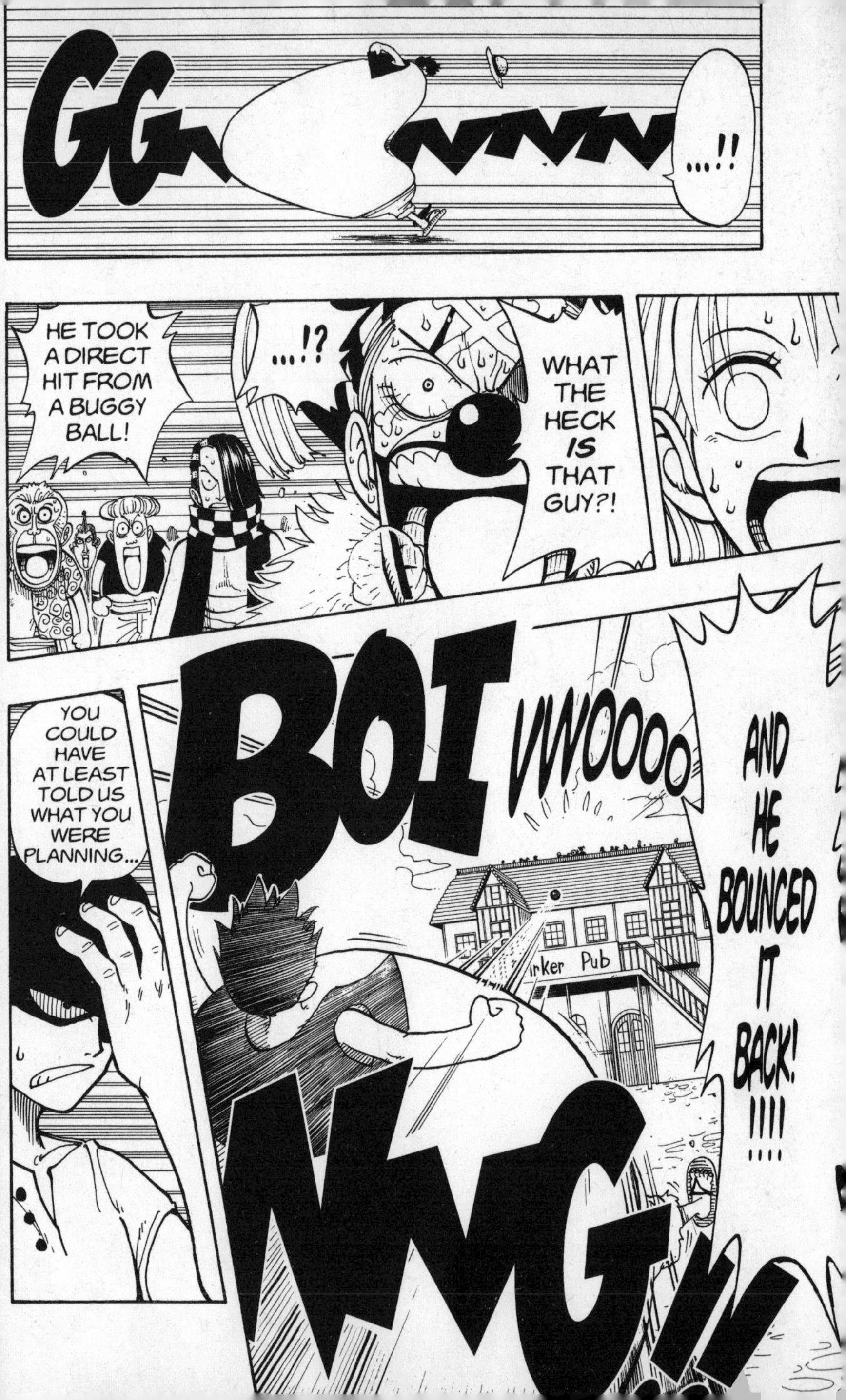
...!!
GGANNNNG
WHAT THE HECK IS THAT GUY?!
...!?
HE TOOK A DIRECT HIT FROM A BUGGY BALL!
AND HE BOUNCED IT BACK!!!!!
BOI VWOOOO
NNG!!
irker Pub
YOU COULD HAVE AT LEAST TOLD US WHAT YOU WERE PLANNING...

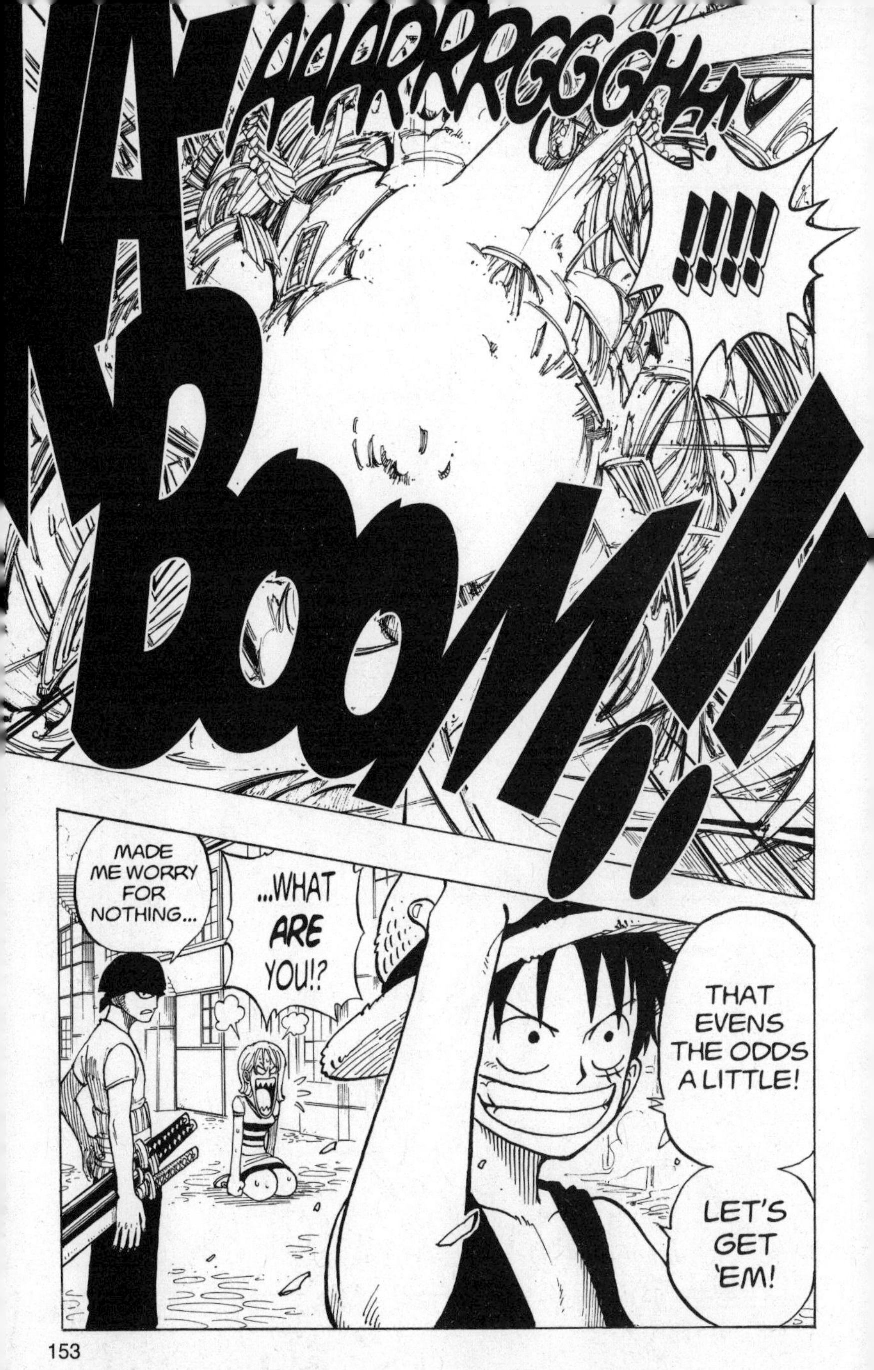
AAARRGGGH!
!!!!
KABOOM!!
THAT EVENS THE ODDS A LITTLE!
LET'S GET 'EM!
...WHAT ARE YOU!?
MADE ME WORRY FOR NOTHING...

One Piece Rough Sketch!

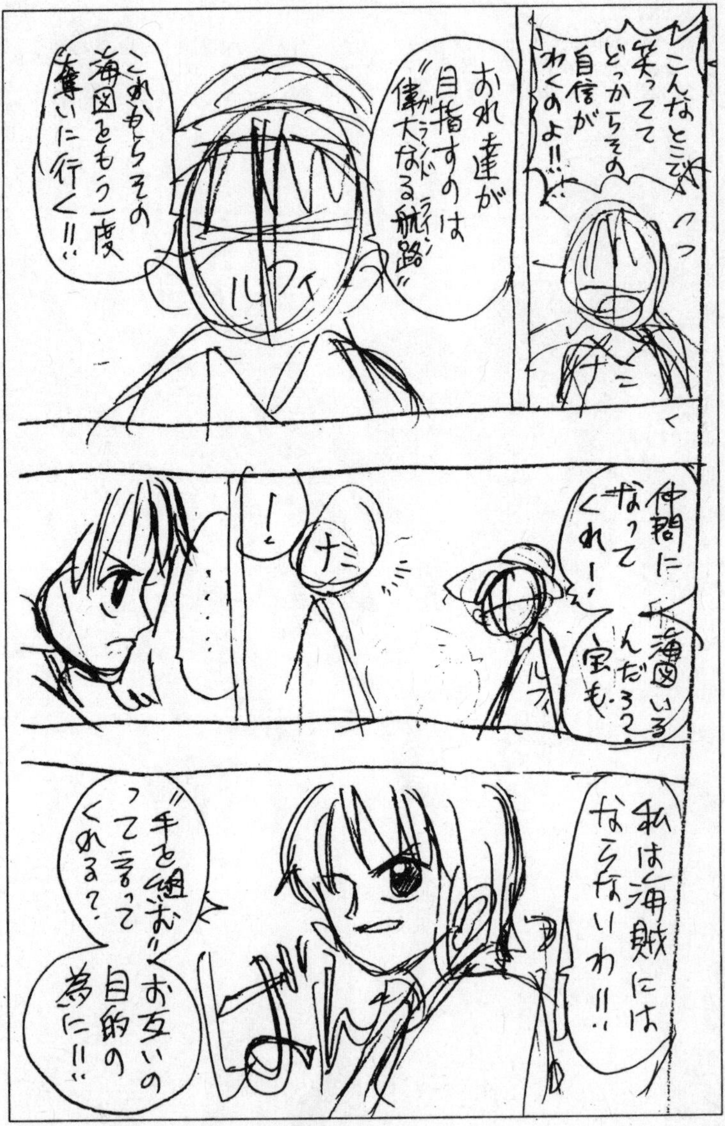
こんなとこで笑っててどっからその自信がわくのよ!!
おれ達が目指すのは"偉大なる航路(グランドライン)"
これからその海図をもう一度奪いに行く!!
仲間になってくれ!
海図いるんだろ? 宝も
!
……
私は海賊にはならないわ!!
ばん
"手を組む"って言ってくれる? お互いの目的の為に!!

Chapter 16:

VERSUS BUGGY'S CREW!

FIRST MATE
CAPTAIN
WANTED
MIKIO ITO
SECOND MATE

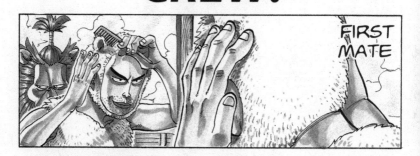

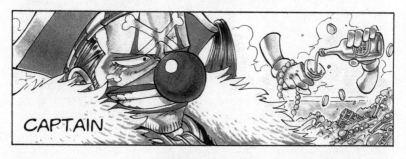

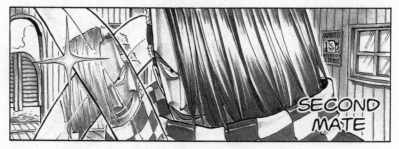

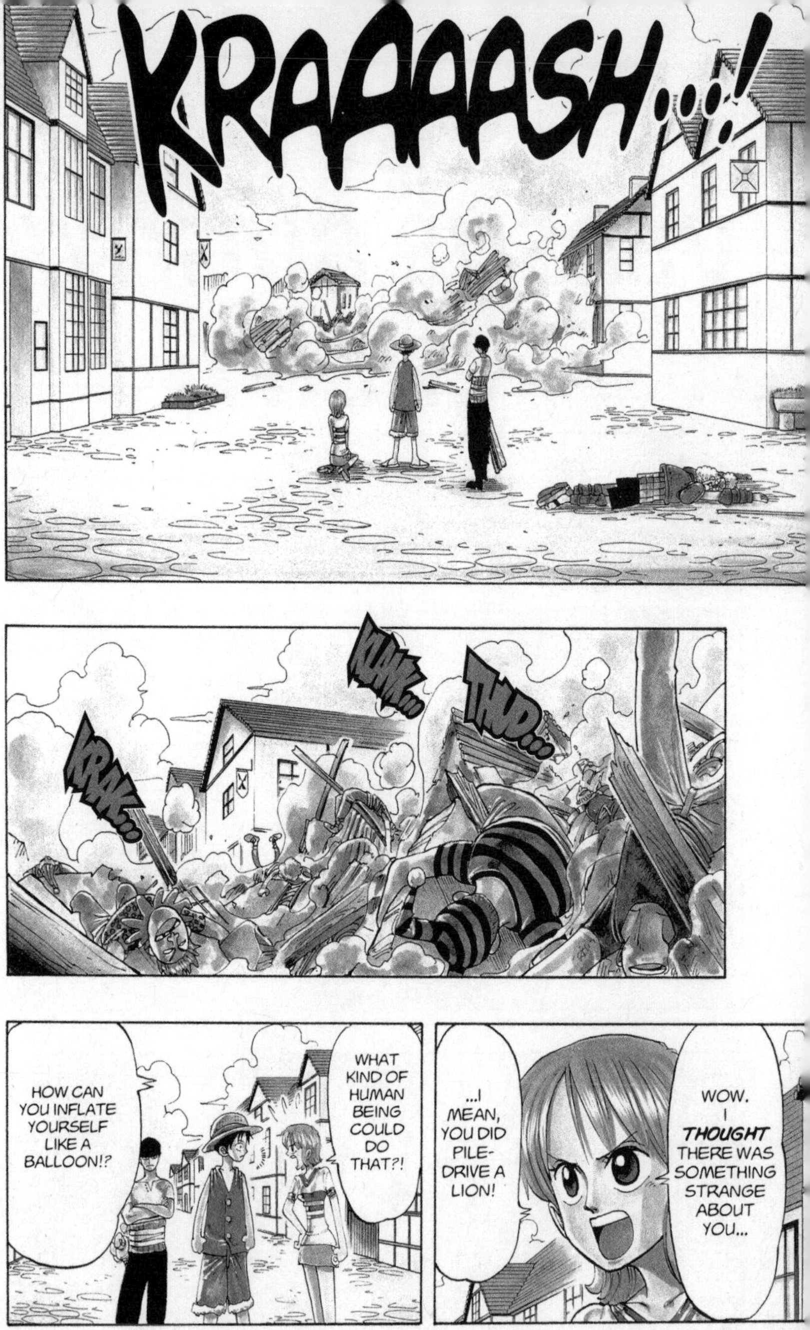
KRAAAASH...!!
THUD...
KLANK...
KRAK...
WOW. I ***THOUGHT*** THERE WAS SOMETHING STRANGE ABOUT YOU...
...I MEAN, YOU DID PILE-DRIVE A LION!
WHAT KIND OF HUMAN BEING COULD DO THAT?!
HOW CAN YOU INFLATE YOURSELF LIKE A BALLOON!?

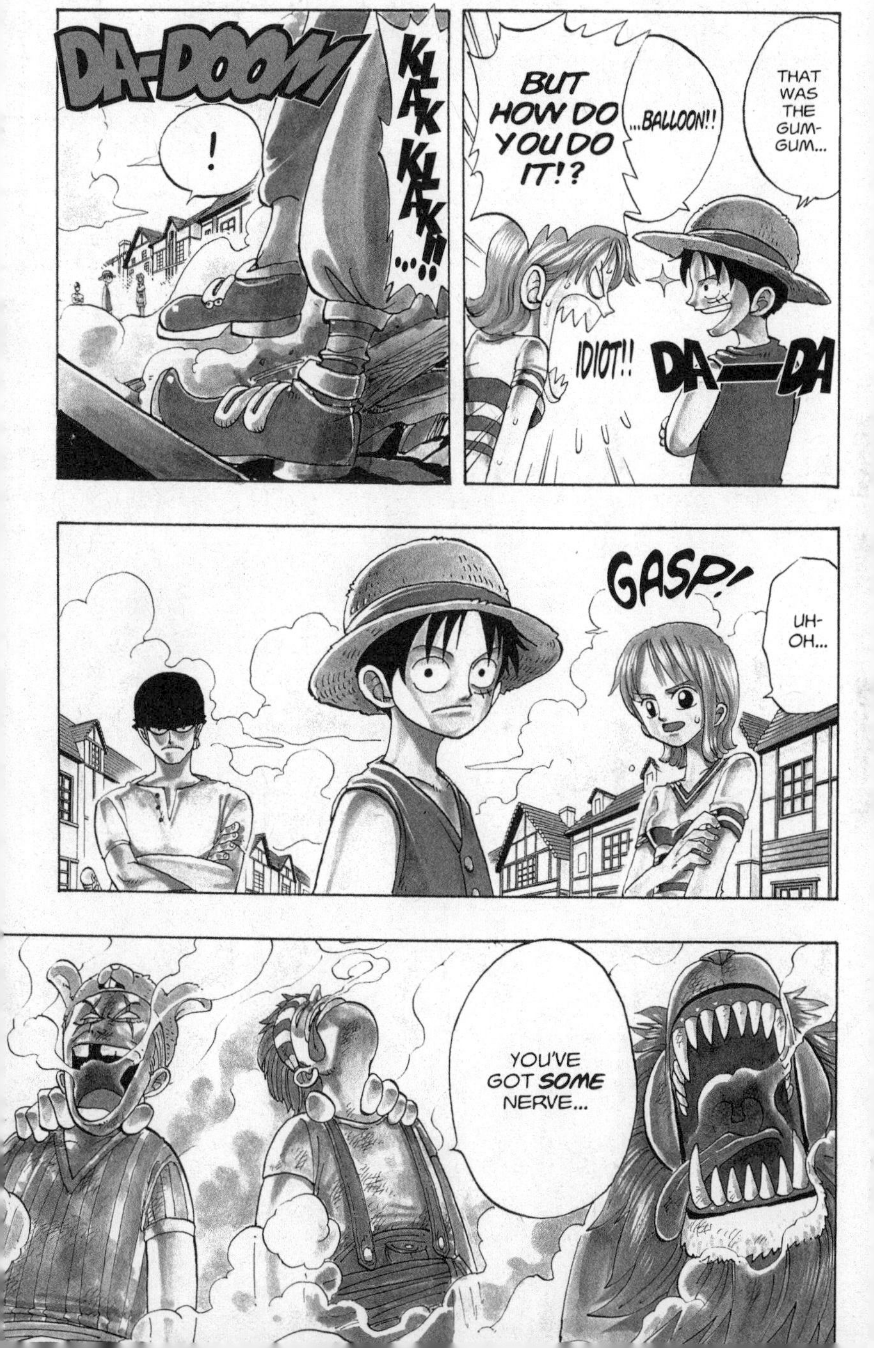

THAT WAS THE GUM-GUM...
...BALLOON!!
BUT HOW DO YOU DO IT!?
DA—DA
IDIOT!!
KLAK KLAK KLAK!!...
DA-DOOM
!
UH-OH...
GASP!
YOU'VE GOT **SOME** NERVE...

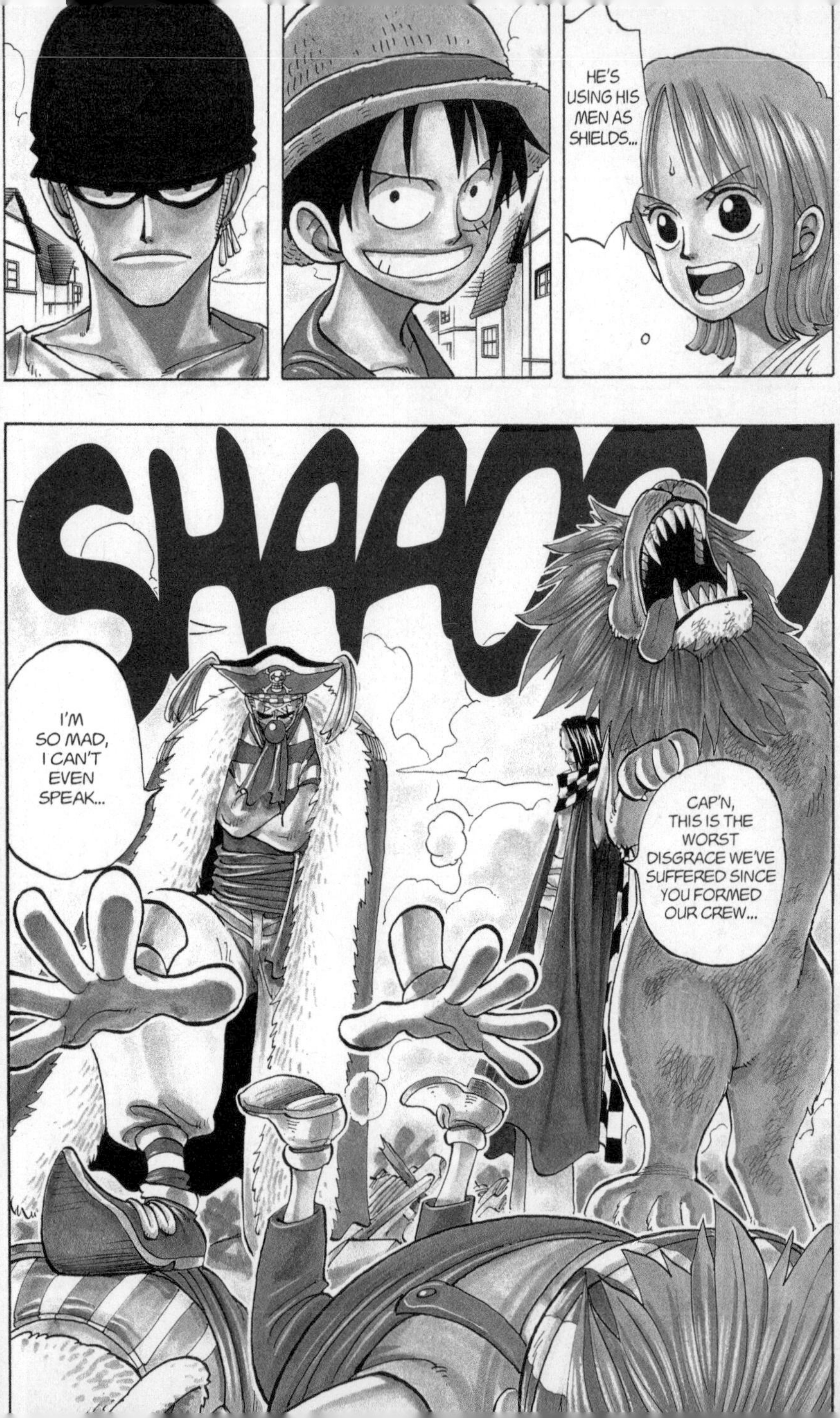
HE'S USING HIS MEN AS SHIELDS...
CAP'N, THIS IS THE WORST DISGRACE WE'VE SUFFERED SINCE YOU FORMED OUR CREW...
I'M SO MAD, I CAN'T EVEN SPEAK...

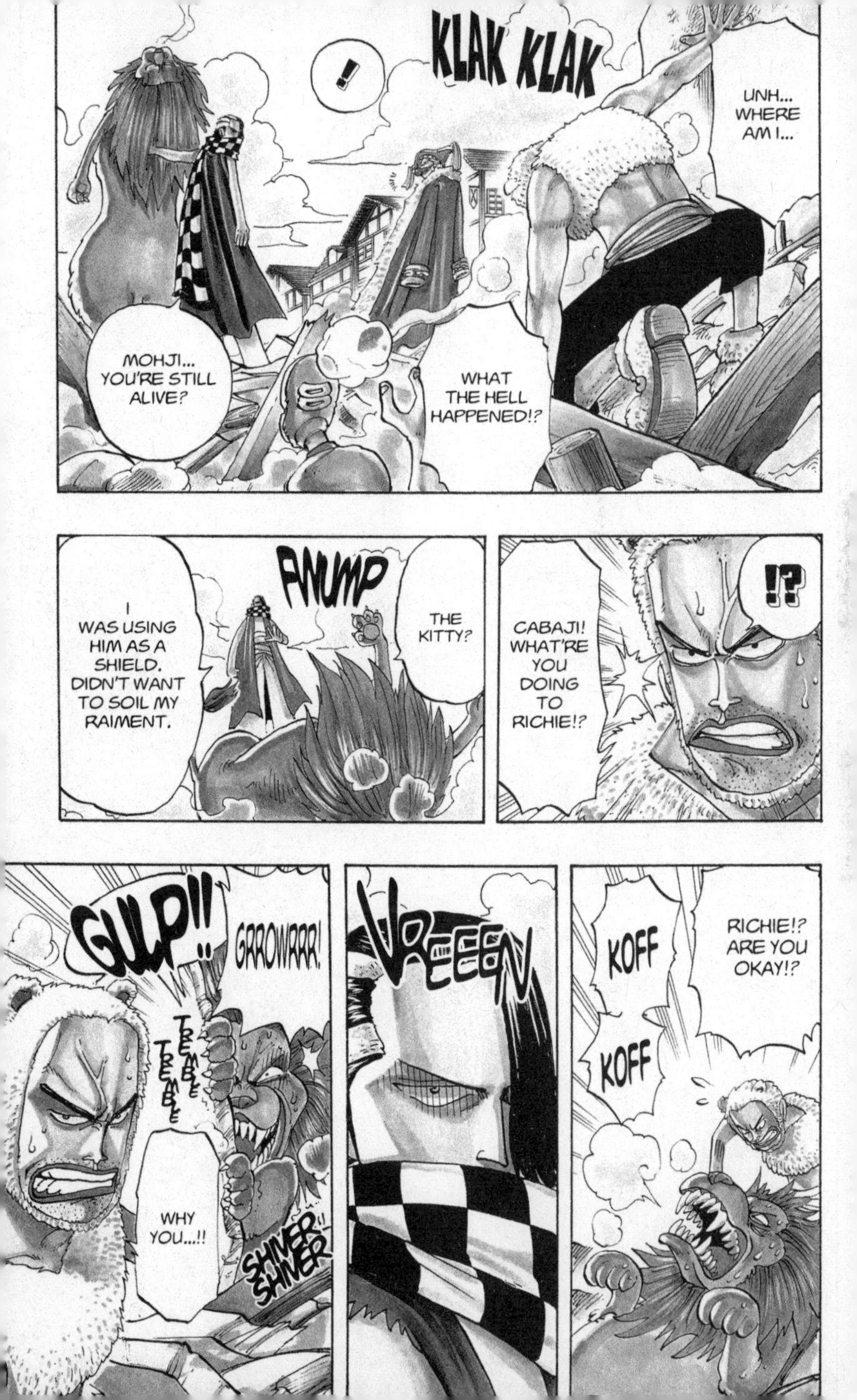
UNH... WHERE AM I...
KLAK KLAK
!
WHAT THE HELL HAPPENED!?
MOHJI... YOU'RE STILL ALIVE?
!?
CABAJI! WHAT'RE YOU DOING TO RICHIE!?
THE KITTY?
FWUMP
I WAS USING HIM AS A SHIELD. DIDN'T WANT TO SOIL MY RAIMENT.
RICHIE!? ARE YOU OKAY!?
KOFF
KOFF
VREEEN
GRROWRRR!
GULP!!
TREMBLE TREMBLE
WHY YOU...!!
SHIVER SHIVER

READ THIS WAY

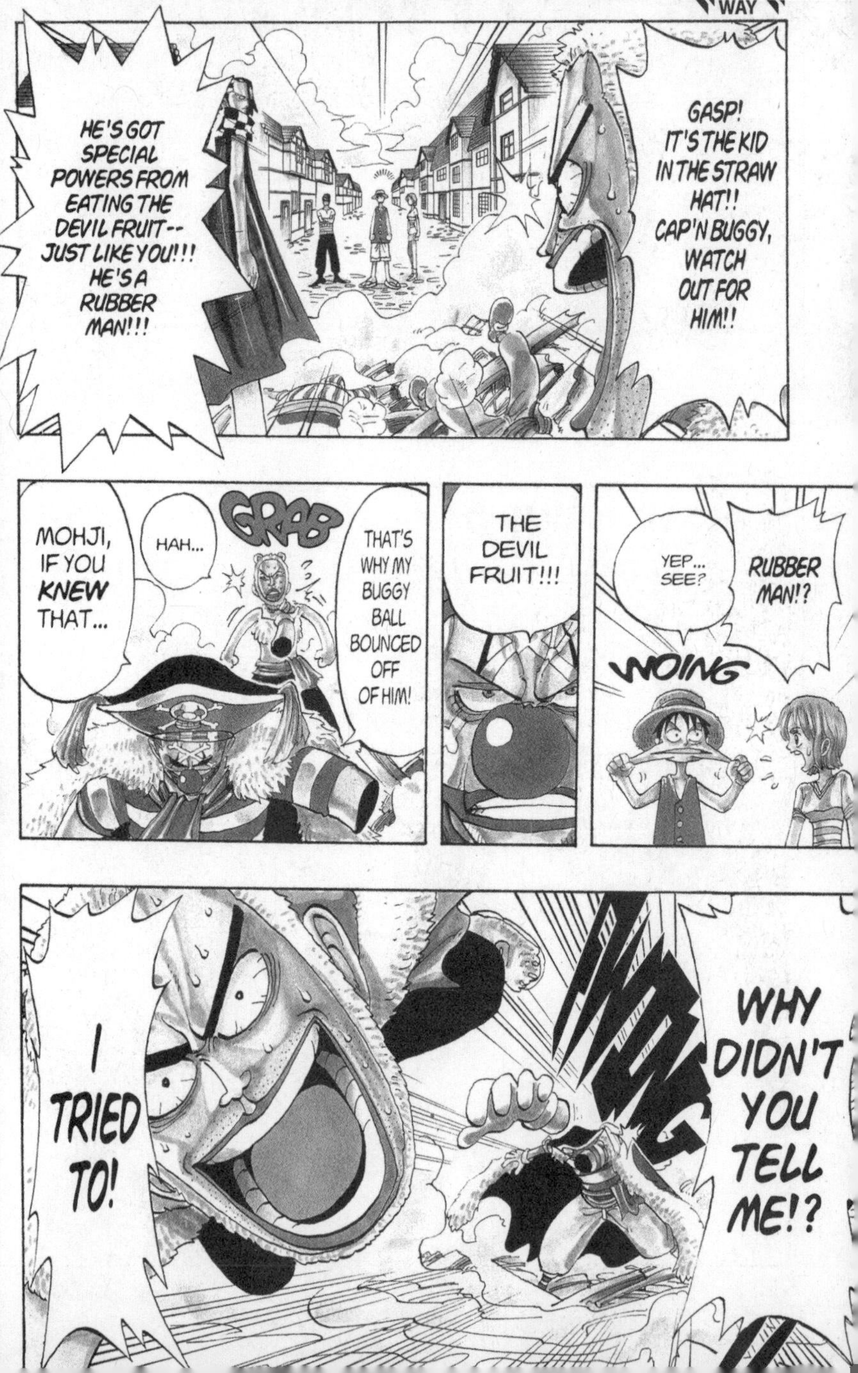
GASP! IT'S THE KID IN THE STRAW HAT!! CAP'N BUGGY, WATCH OUT FOR HIM!!
HE'S GOT SPECIAL POWERS FROM EATING THE DEVIL FRUIT-- JUST LIKE YOU!!! HE'S A RUBBER MAN!!!
RUBBER MAN!?
YEP... SEE?
WOING
THE DEVIL FRUIT!!!
THAT'S WHY MY BUGGY BALL BOUNCED OFF OF HIM!
GRAB
HAH...
MOHJI, IF YOU KNEW THAT...
WHY DIDN'T YOU TELL ME!?
I TRIED TO!

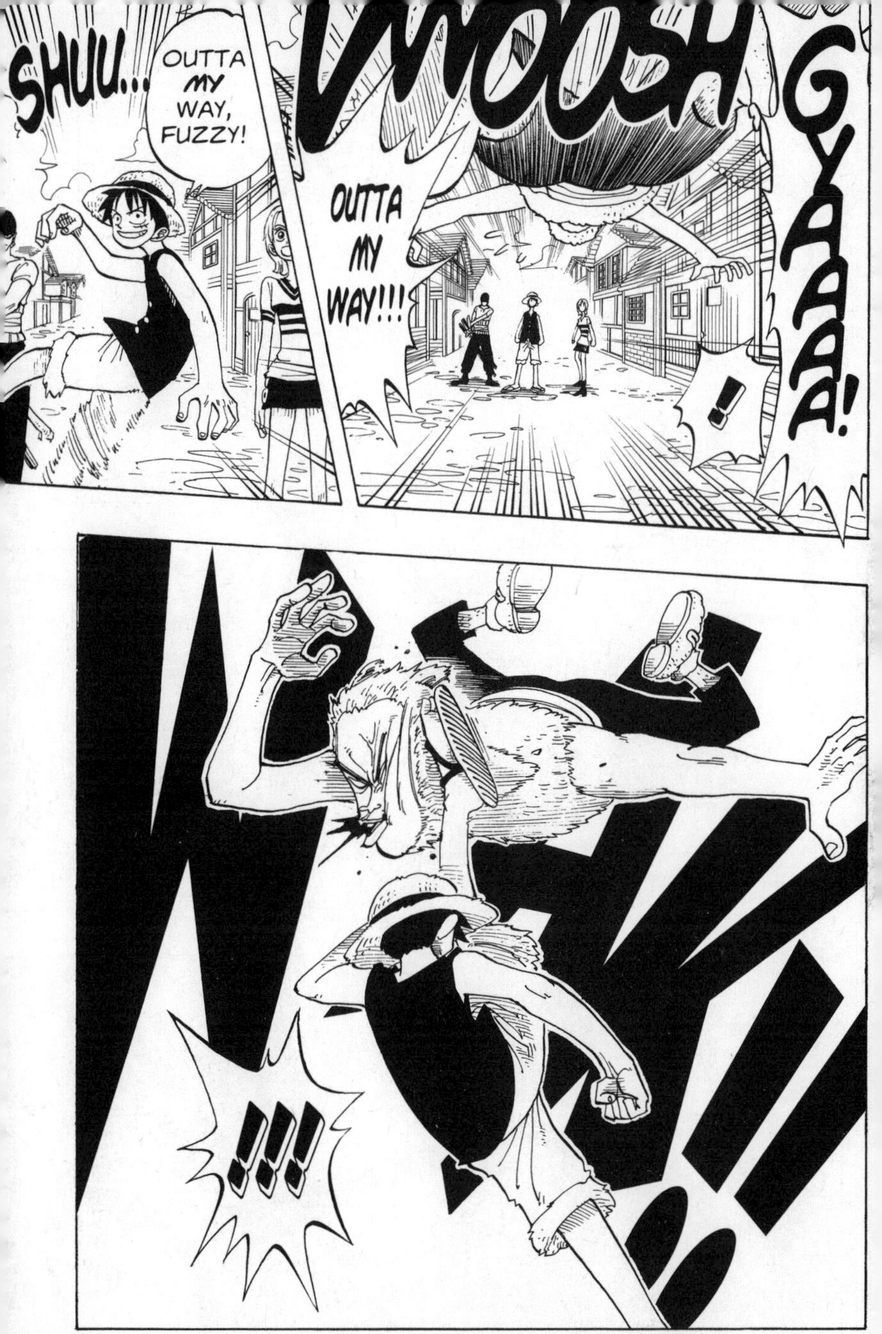
WHOOSH
GYAAAA!
OUTTA MY WAY!!!
!
SHUU...
OUTTA MY WAY, FUZZY!
!!!

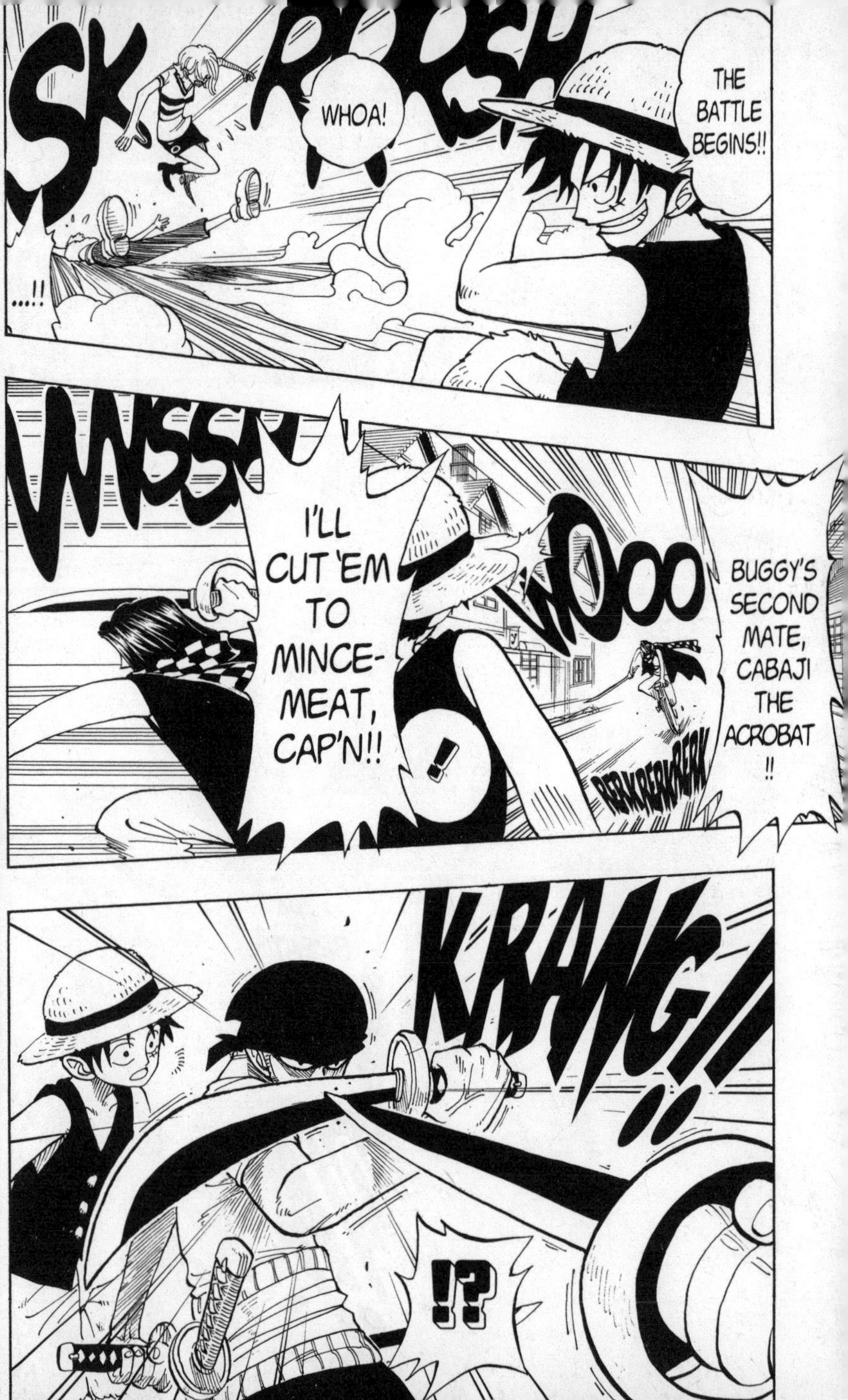
THE BATTLE BEGINS!!
WHOA!
....!!
BUGGY'S SECOND MATE, CABAJI THE ACROBAT !!
RERKRERKRERK
WOOO
!
I'LL CUT 'EM TO MINCE-MEAT, CAP'N!!
KRANG!!
!?

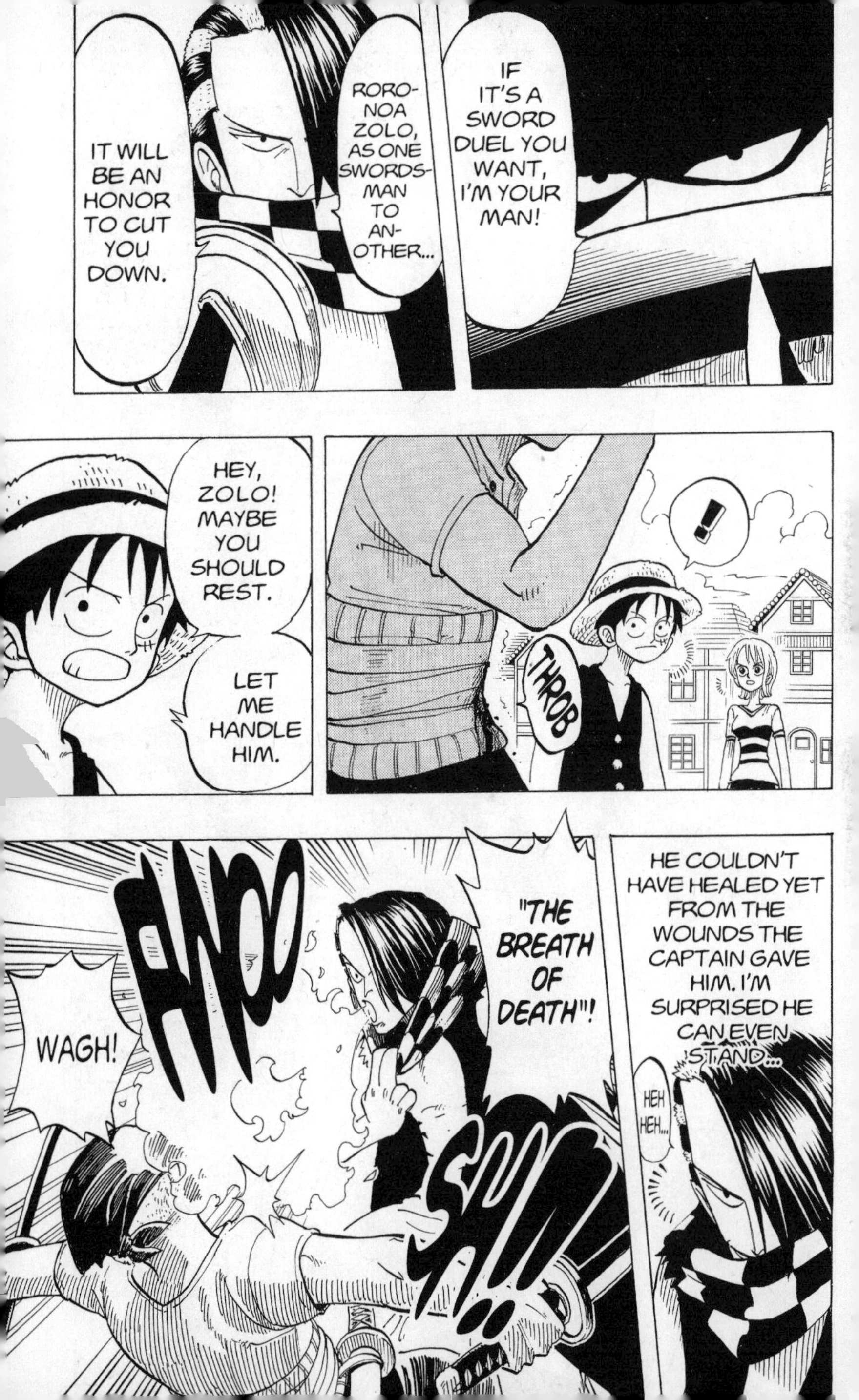
IF IT'S A SWORD DUEL YOU WANT, I'M YOUR MAN!
RORONOA ZOLO, AS ONE SWORDSMAN TO ANOTHER...
IT WILL BE AN HONOR TO CUT YOU DOWN.
!
THROB
HEY, ZOLO! MAYBE YOU SHOULD REST.
LET ME HANDLE HIM.
HE COULDN'T HAVE HEALED YET FROM THE WOUNDS THE CAPTAIN GAVE HIM. I'M SURPRISED HE CAN EVEN STAND...
HEH HEH...
"THE BREATH OF DEATH"!
FHOO
WAGH!
SPOO...

READ THIS WAY

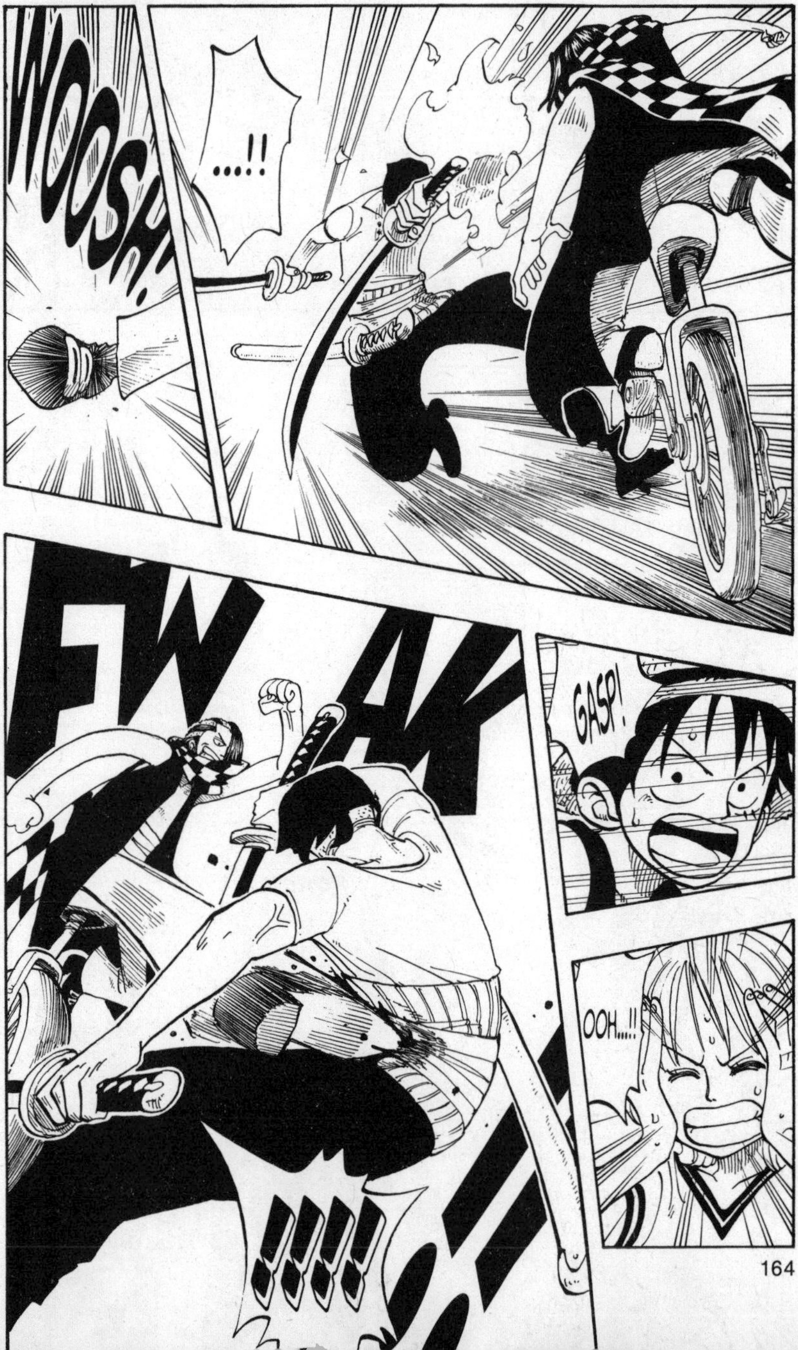
...!!
WOOSH!!
GASP!
OOH...!!
FWAK!!!!

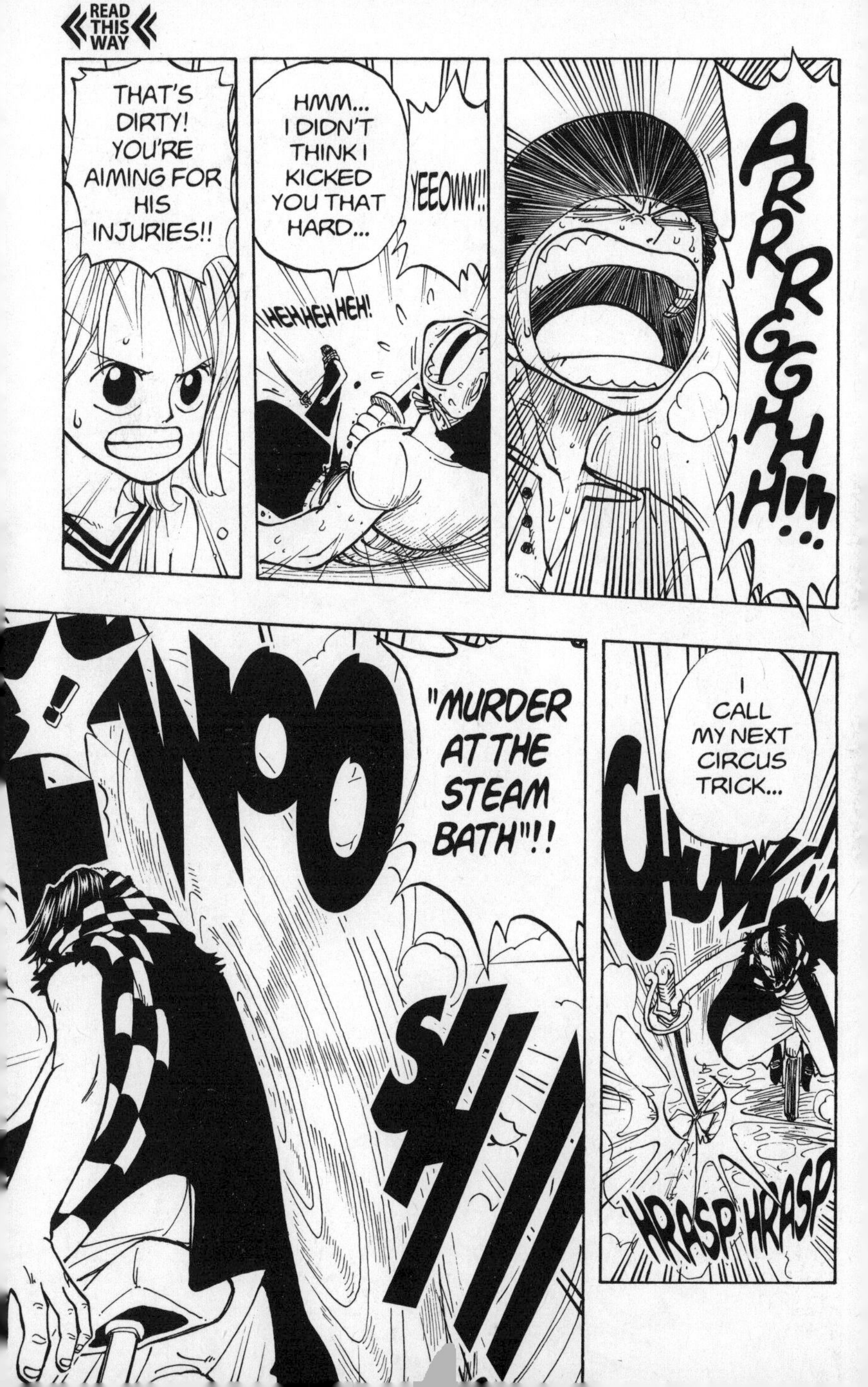
READ THIS WAY
ARRRGGHHH!!
YEEOWW!!
HMM... I DIDN'T THINK I KICKED YOU THAT HARD...
HEHHEHHEH!
THAT'S DIRTY! YOU'RE AIMING FOR HIS INJURIES!!
I CALL MY NEXT CIRCUS TRICK...
HRASP HRASP
"MURDER AT THE STEAM BATH"!!

READ THIS WAY

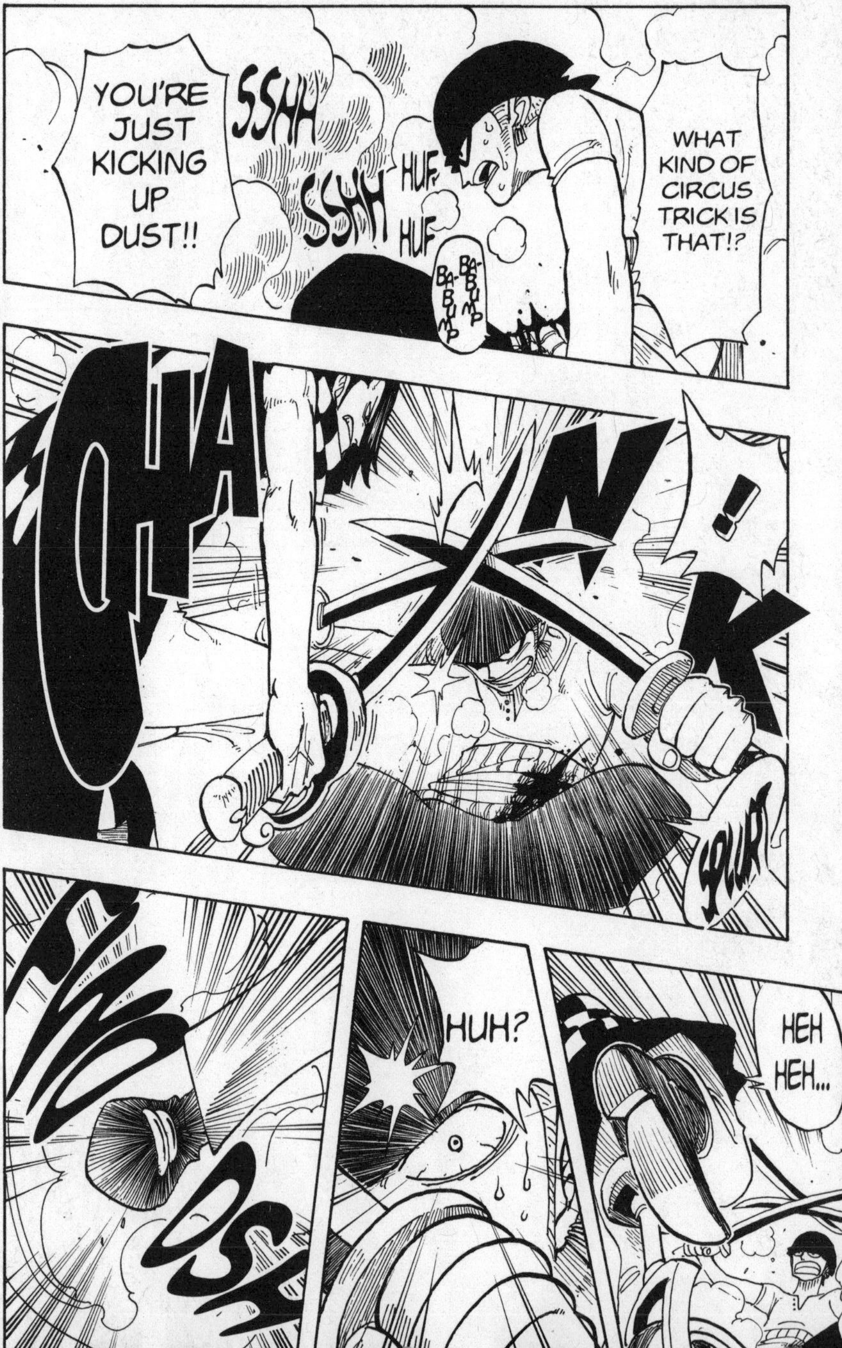
WHAT KIND OF CIRCUS TRICK IS THAT!?
HUF HUF
SSHH SSHH
YOU'RE JUST KICKING UP DUST!!
BA-BUMP BA-BUMP
CHANK!
SPLURT
HEH HEH...
HUH?

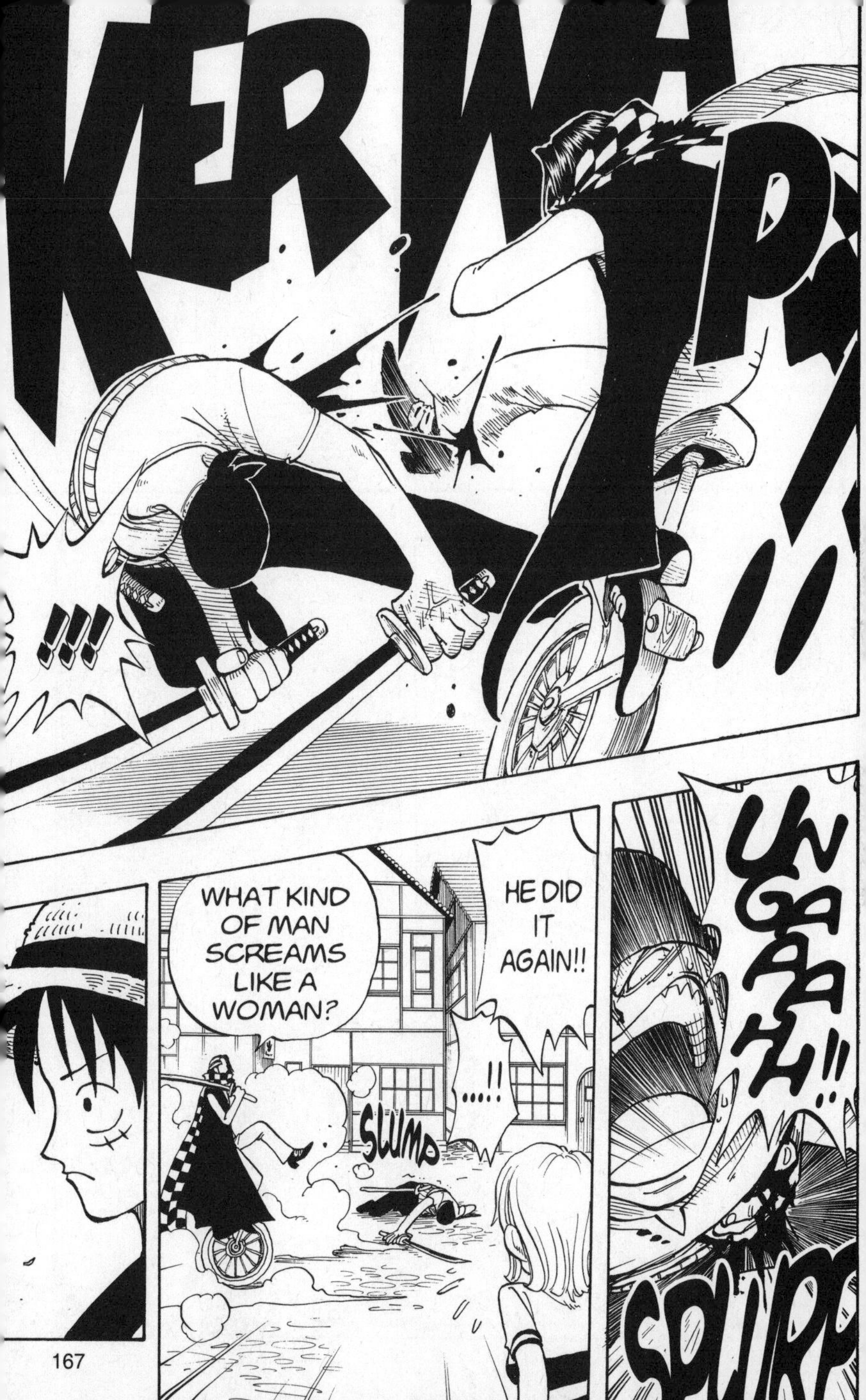
KERWAP!!
!!!
UNGAAAH!!
HE DID IT AGAIN!!
WHAT KIND OF MAN SCREAMS LIKE A WOMAN?
...!!
SLUMP

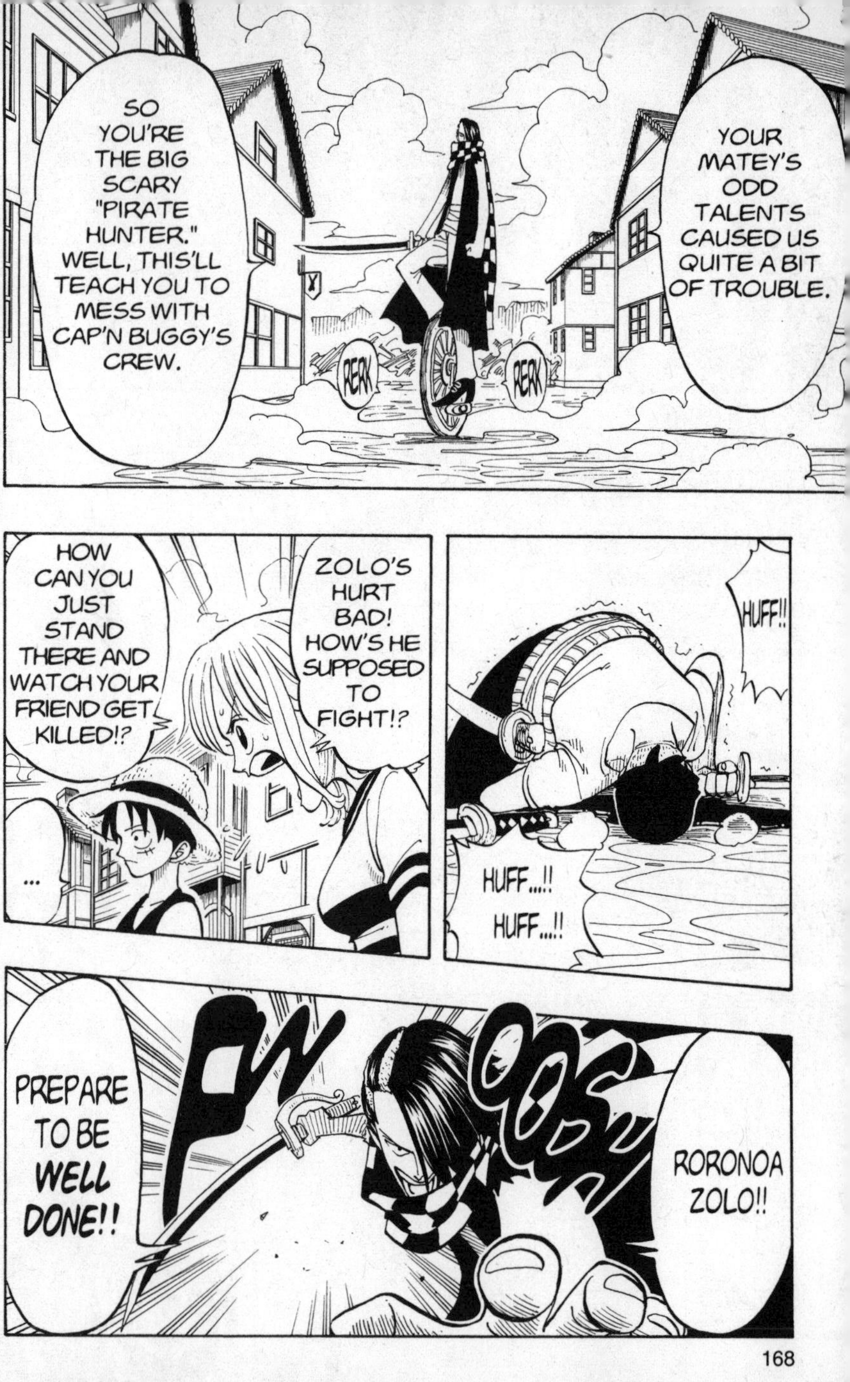
YOUR MATEY'S ODD TALENTS CAUSED US QUITE A BIT OF TROUBLE.
RERK
RERK
SO YOU'RE THE BIG SCARY "PIRATE HUNTER." WELL, THIS'LL TEACH YOU TO MESS WITH CAP'N BUGGY'S CREW.
HUFF!!
HUFF...!!
HUFF...!!
ZOLO'S HURT BAD! HOW'S HE SUPPOSED TO FIGHT!?
HOW CAN YOU JUST STAND THERE AND WATCH YOUR FRIEND GET KILLED!?
...
RORONOA ZOLO!!
PREPARE TO BE WELL DONE!!

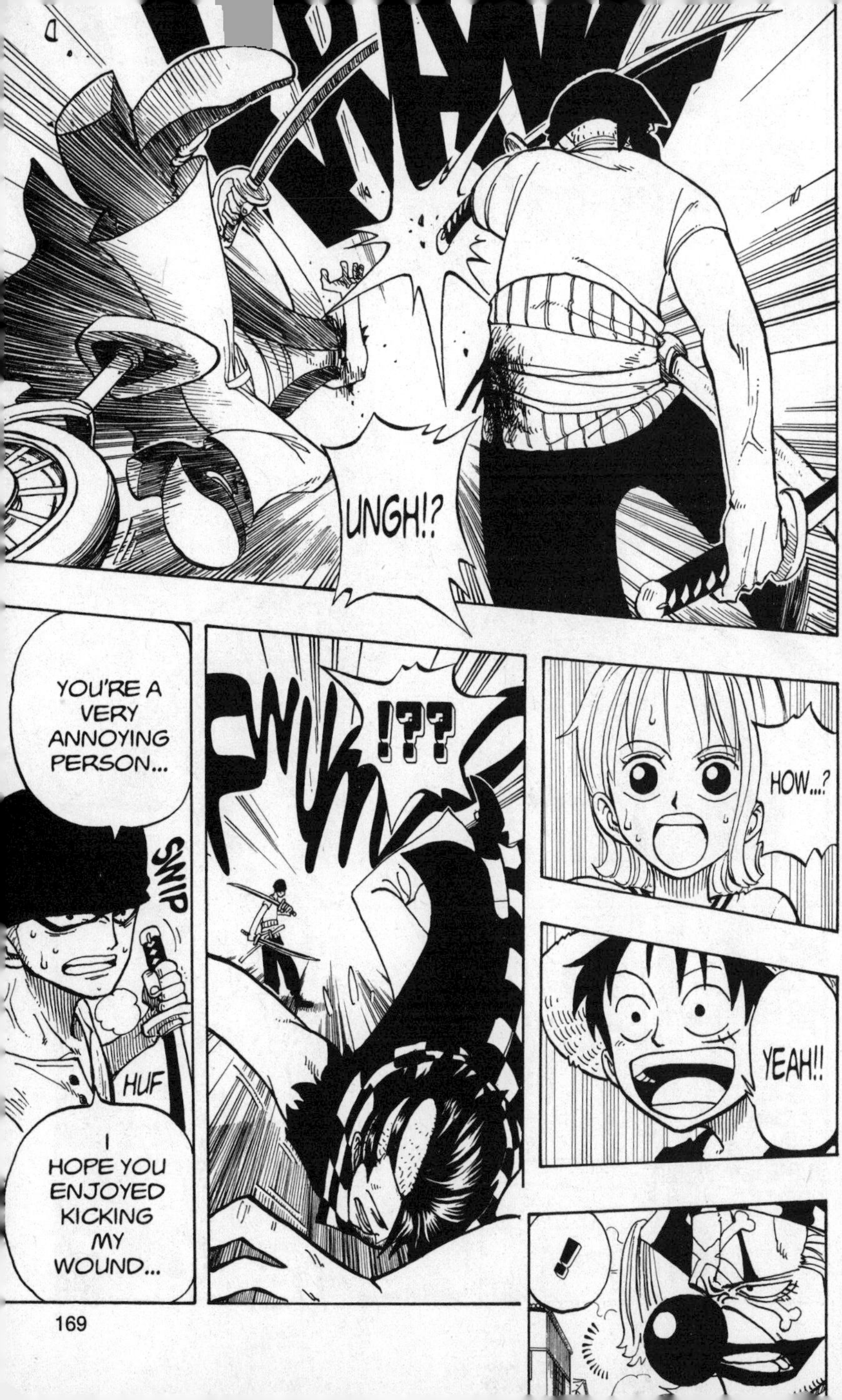

UNGH!?
HOW...?
YEAH!!
!
!??
YOU'RE A VERY ANNOYING PERSON...
SWIP
HUF
I HOPE YOU ENJOYED KICKING MY WOUND...

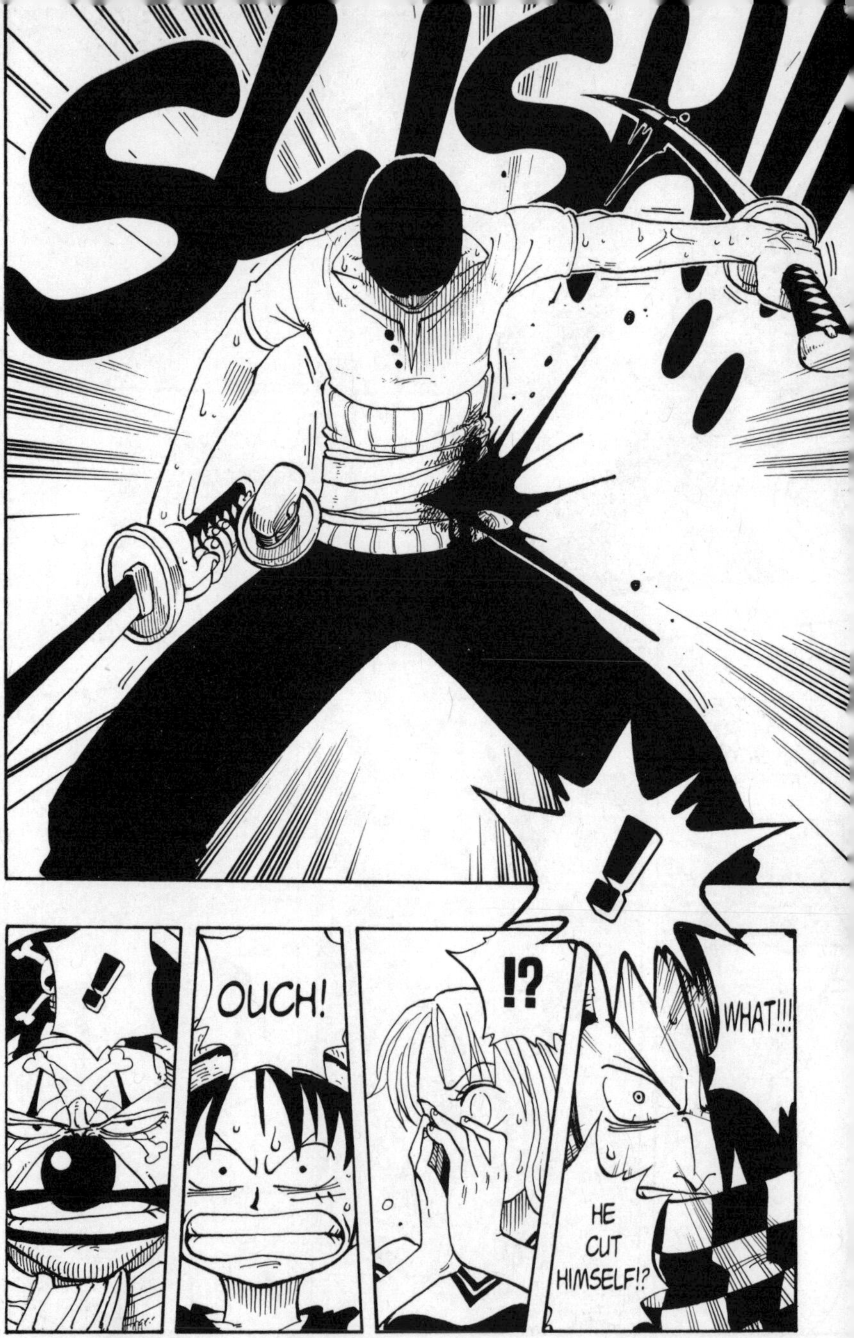
SLISH
!
WHAT!!!
HE CUT HIMSELF!?
!?
OUCH!
!

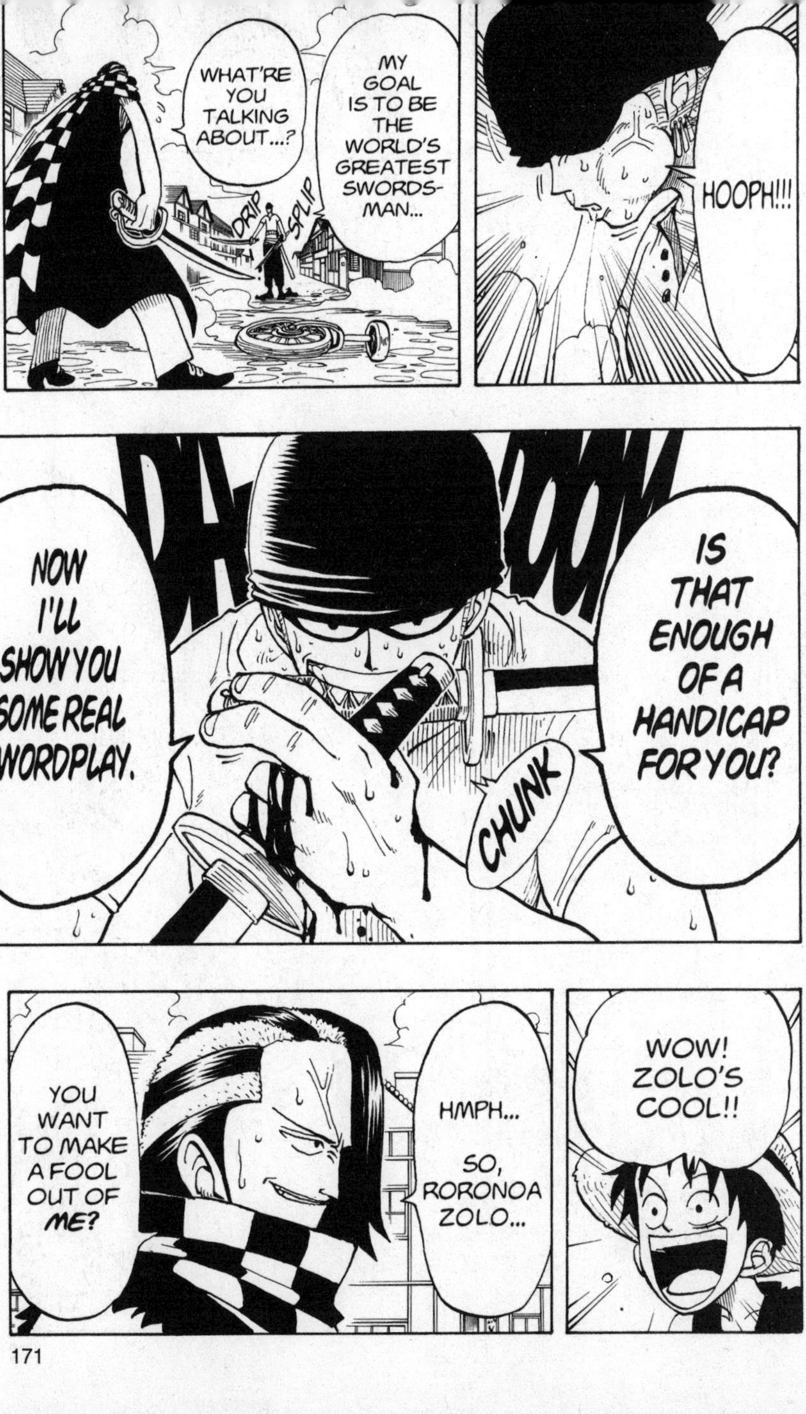
HOOPH!!!
MY GOAL IS TO BE THE WORLD'S GREATEST SWORDSMAN...
WHAT'RE YOU TALKING ABOUT...?
SPLIP
DRIP
IS THAT ENOUGH OF A HANDICAP FOR YOU?
CHUNK
NOW I'LL SHOW YOU SOME REAL SWORDPLAY.
WOW! ZOLO'S COOL!!
HMPH...
SO, RORONOA ZOLO...
YOU WANT TO MAKE A FOOL OUT OF ME?

One Piece Rough Sketch!

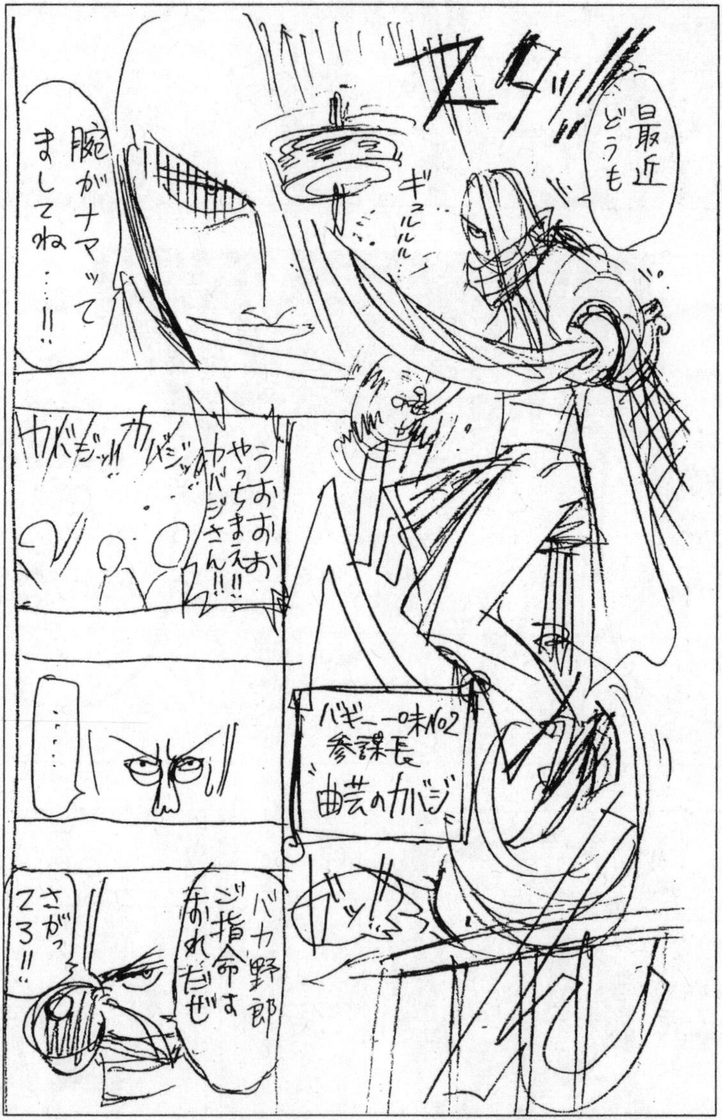

スタッ
最近どうも
ギュルル…
腕がナマッてましてね……!!
バギー一味No2
参謀長
曲芸のカバジ
ガッ!!
うおおお
やっちまえ!!
カバジさん!!
カバジ!!! カバジ!!
……
バカ野郎
ご指命は
おれだぜ
さがってろ!!

Chapter 17:

HIGH LEVEL, LOW LEVEL

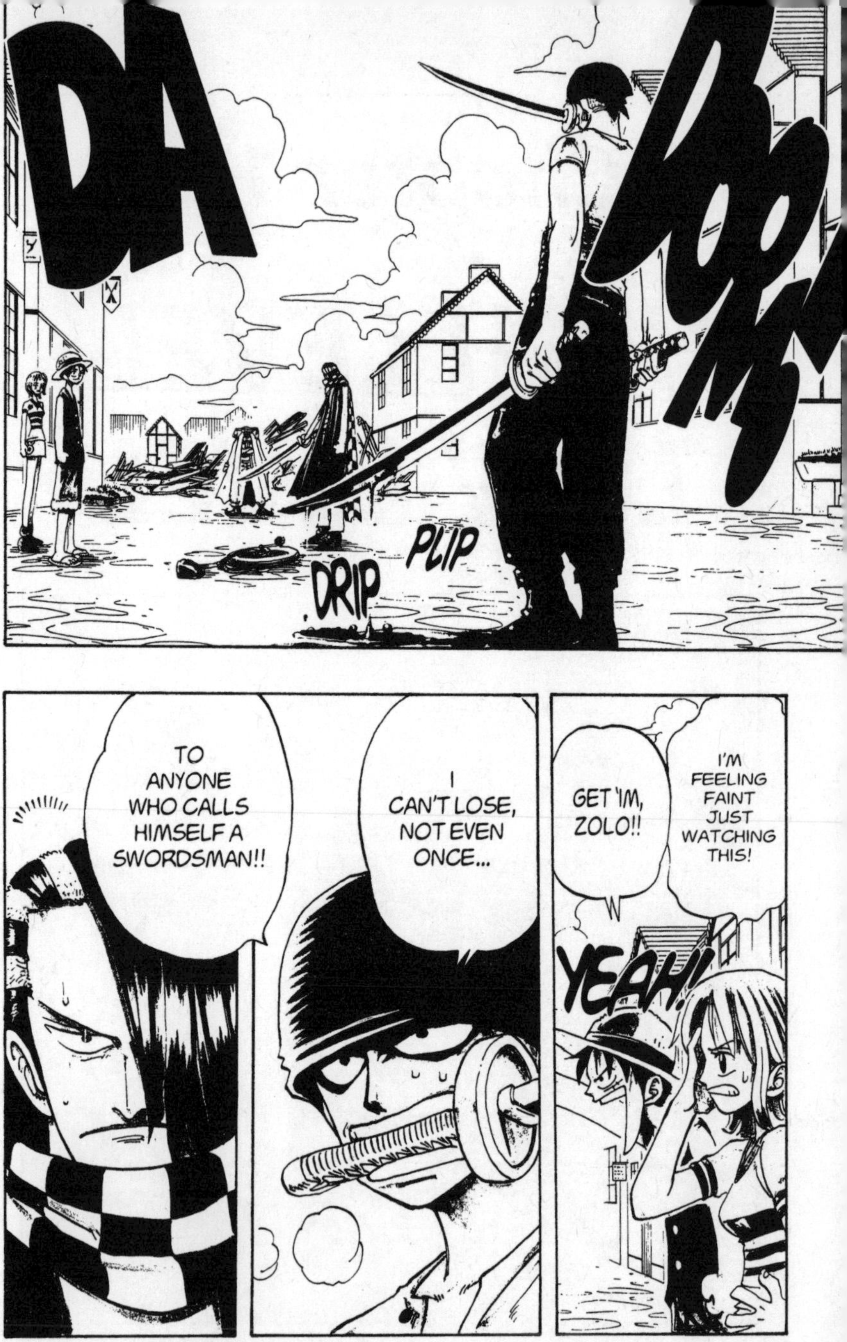
DA
PLIP
DRIP
I'M FEELING FAINT JUST WATCHING THIS!
GET 'IM, ZOLO!!
YEAH!
I CAN'T LOSE, NOT EVEN ONCE...
TO ANYONE WHO CALLS HIMSELF A SWORDSMAN!!

READ THIS WAY

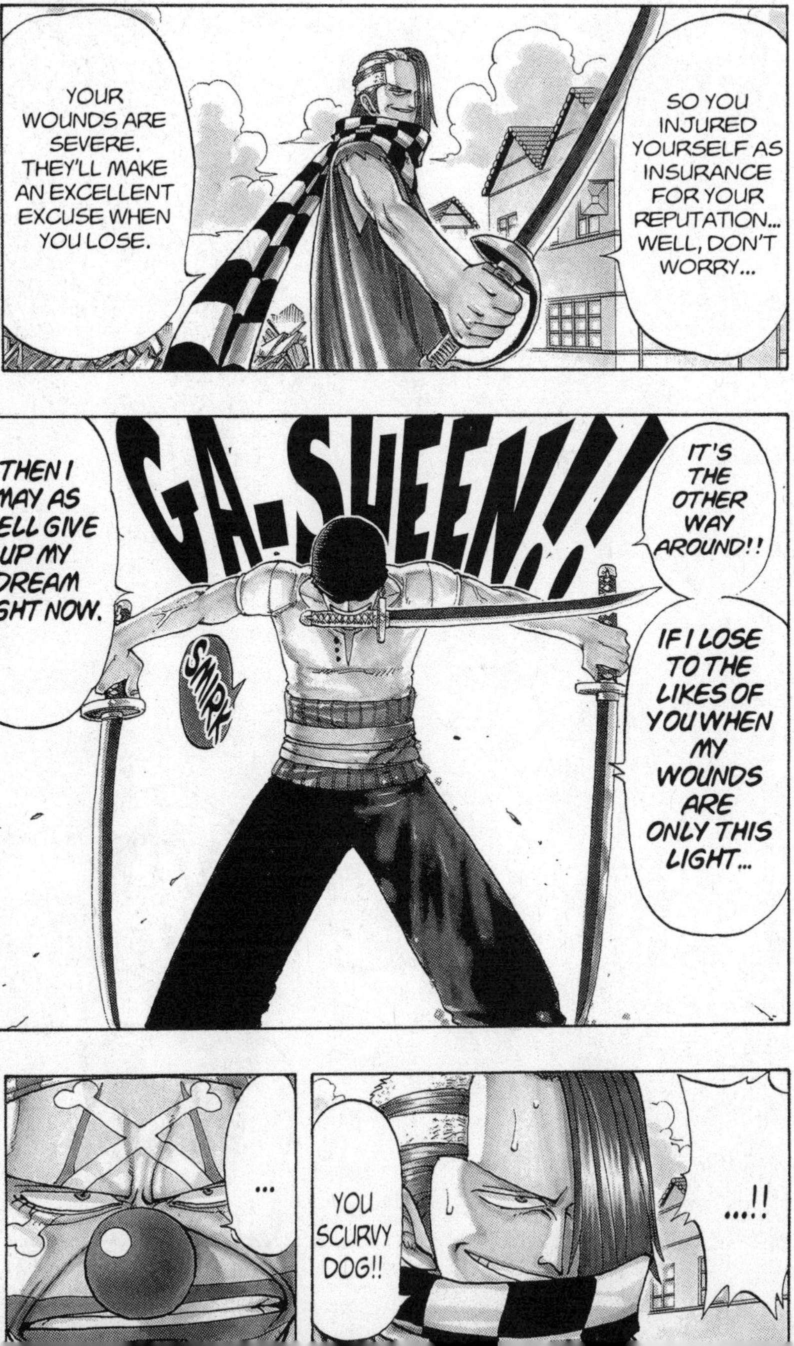
SO YOU INJURED YOURSELF AS INSURANCE FOR YOUR REPUTATION... WELL, DON'T WORRY...
YOUR WOUNDS ARE SEVERE. THEY'LL MAKE AN EXCELLENT EXCUSE WHEN YOU LOSE.
IT'S THE OTHER WAY AROUND!!
GA-SHEEN!!
IF I LOSE TO THE LIKES OF YOU WHEN MY WOUNDS ARE ONLY THIS LIGHT...
THEN I MAY AS WELL GIVE UP MY DREAM RIGHT NOW.
SMIRK
...!!
YOU SCURVY DOG!!
...

READ THIS WAY

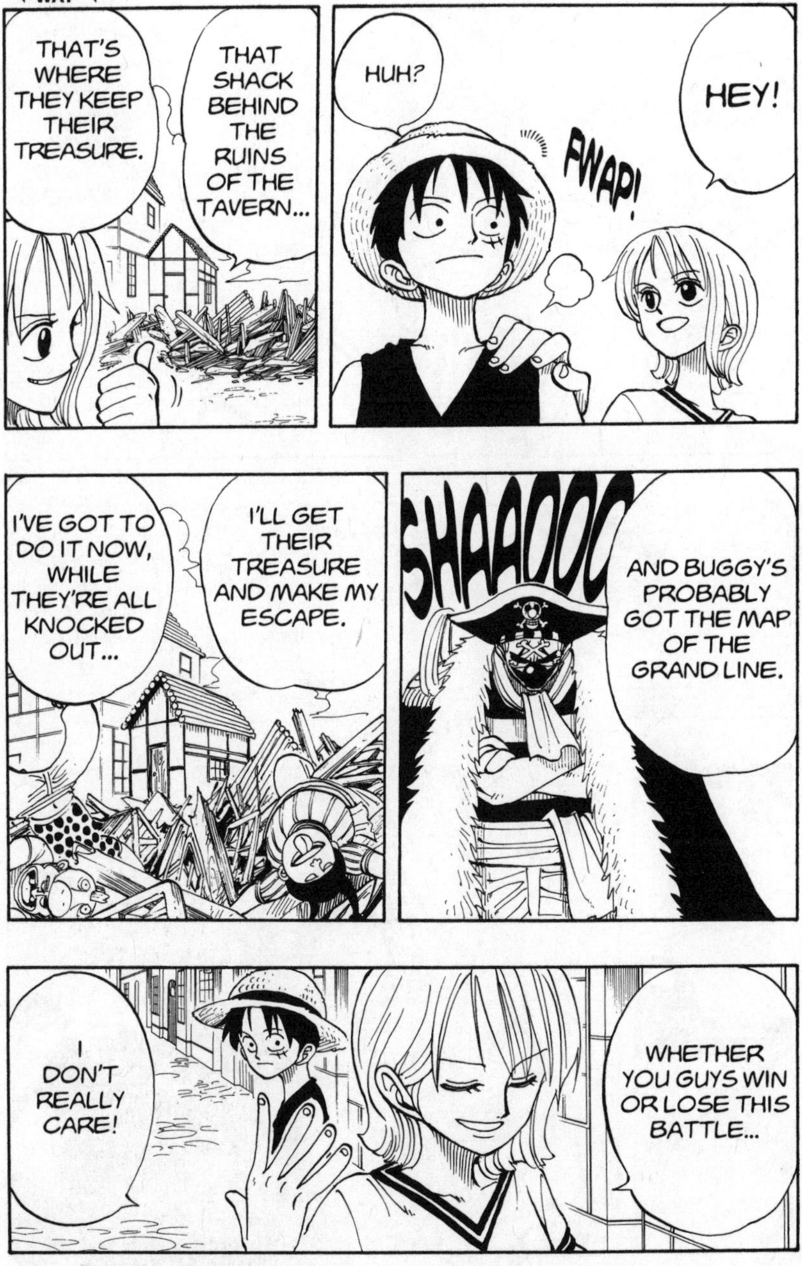
HEY!
FWAP!
HUH?
THAT SHACK BEHIND THE RUINS OF THE TAVERN...
THAT'S WHERE THEY KEEP THEIR TREASURE.
SHAADOO
AND BUGGY'S PROBABLY GOT THE MAP OF THE GRAND LINE.
I'LL GET THEIR TREASURE AND MAKE MY ESCAPE.
I'VE GOT TO DO IT NOW, WHILE THEY'RE ALL KNOCKED OUT...
WHETHER YOU GUYS WIN OR LOSE THIS BATTLE...
I DON'T REALLY CARE!

READ THIS WAY

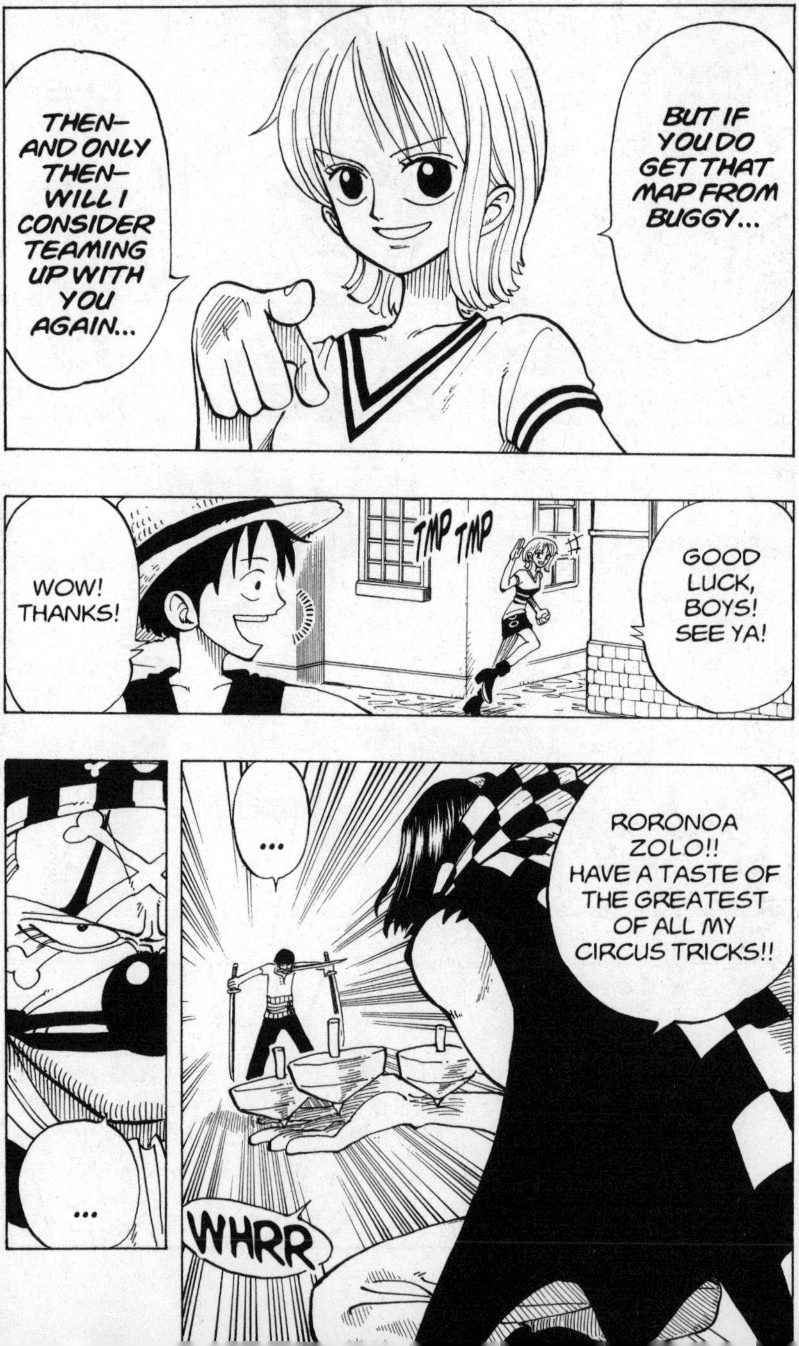

BUT IF YOU DO GET THAT MAP FROM BUGGY...
THEN—AND ONLY THEN—WILL I CONSIDER TEAMING UP WITH YOU AGAIN...
GOOD LUCK, BOYS! SEE YA!
TMP TMP
WOW! THANKS!
RORONOA ZOLO!! HAVE A TASTE OF THE GREATEST OF ALL MY CIRCUS TRICKS!!
...
WHRR
...

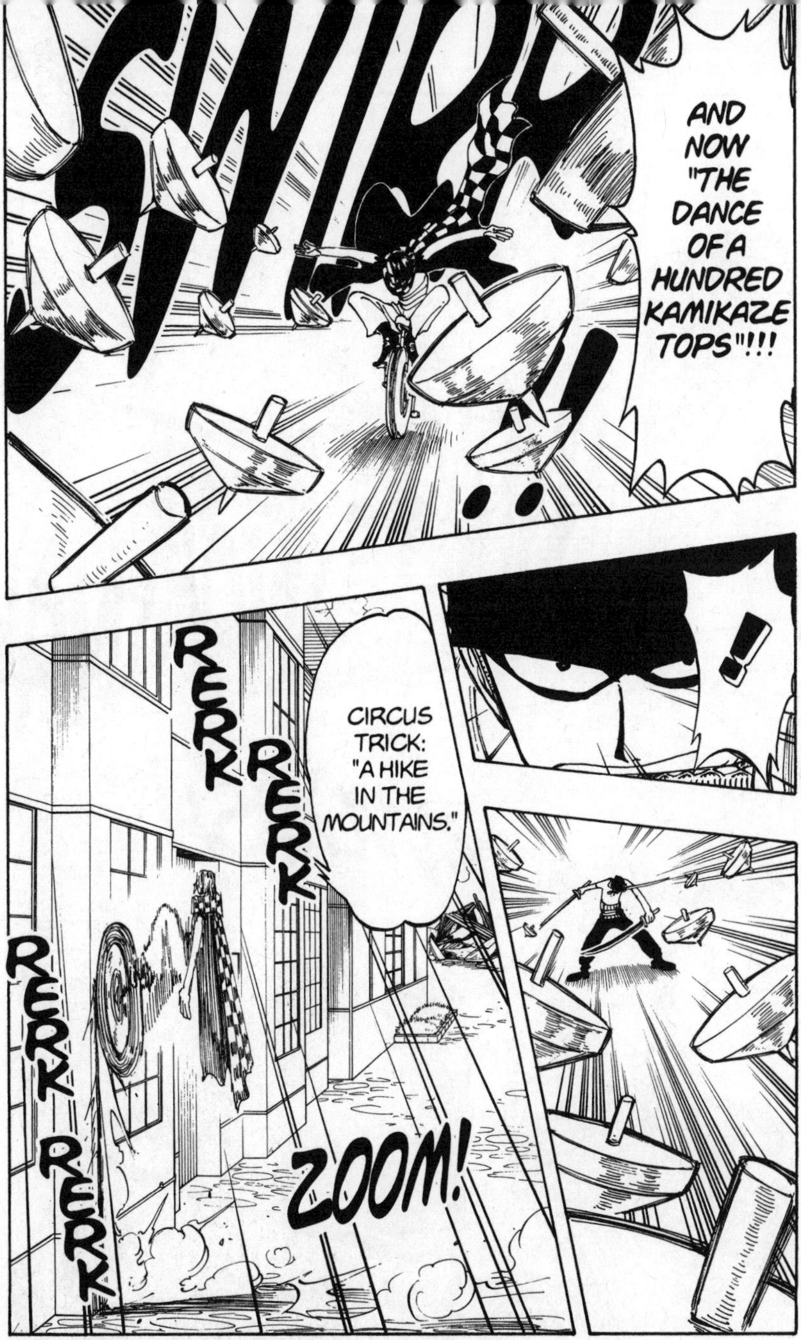
SWIP
AND NOW "THE DANCE OF A HUNDRED KAMIKAZE TOPS"!!!
CIRCUS TRICK: "A HIKE IN THE MOUNTAINS."
RERK RERK
RERK RERK
ZOOM!

READ THIS WAY

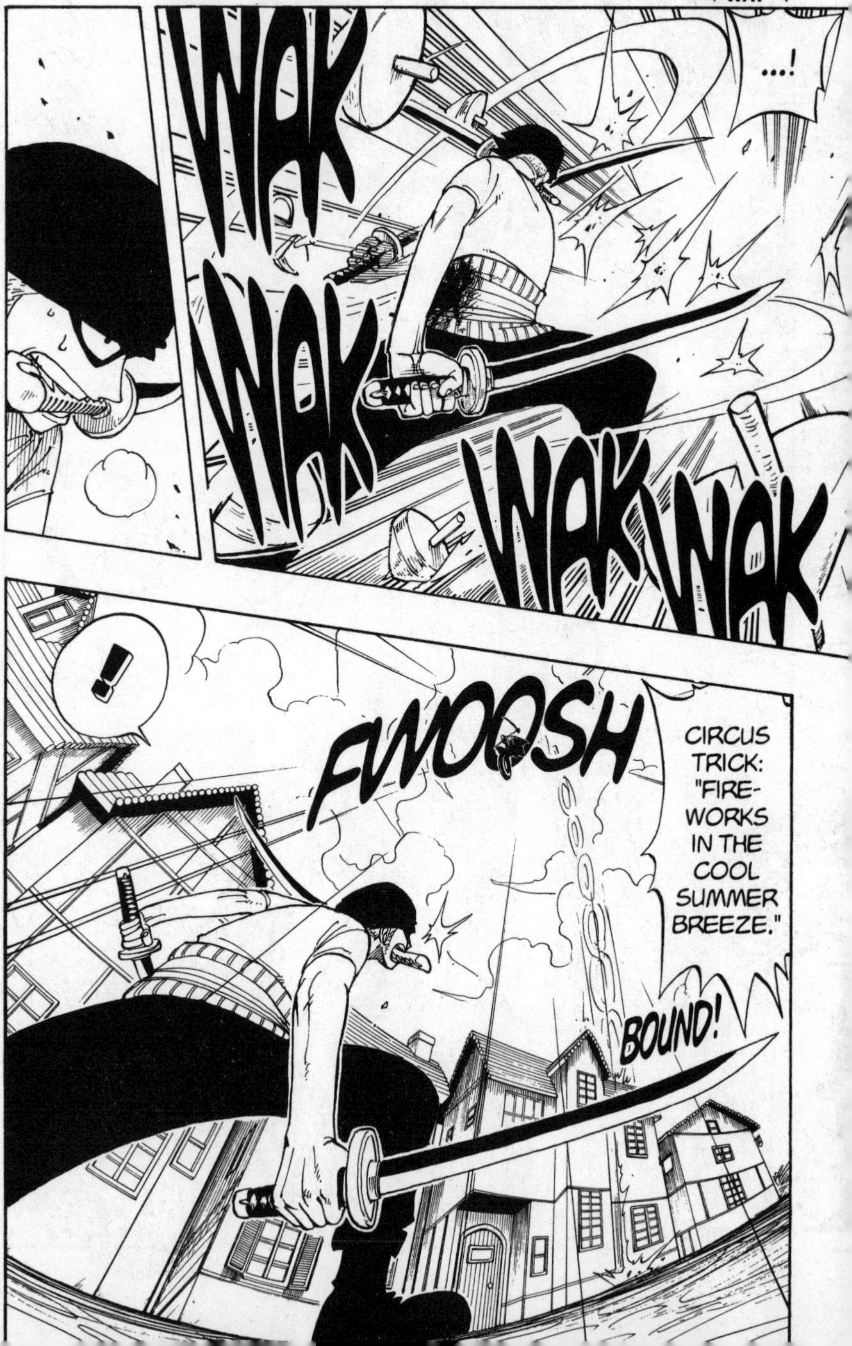
...!
WAK
WAK
WAK
WAK
CIRCUS TRICK: "FIRE-WORKS IN THE COOL SUMMER BREEZE."
FWOOSH
!
BOUND!

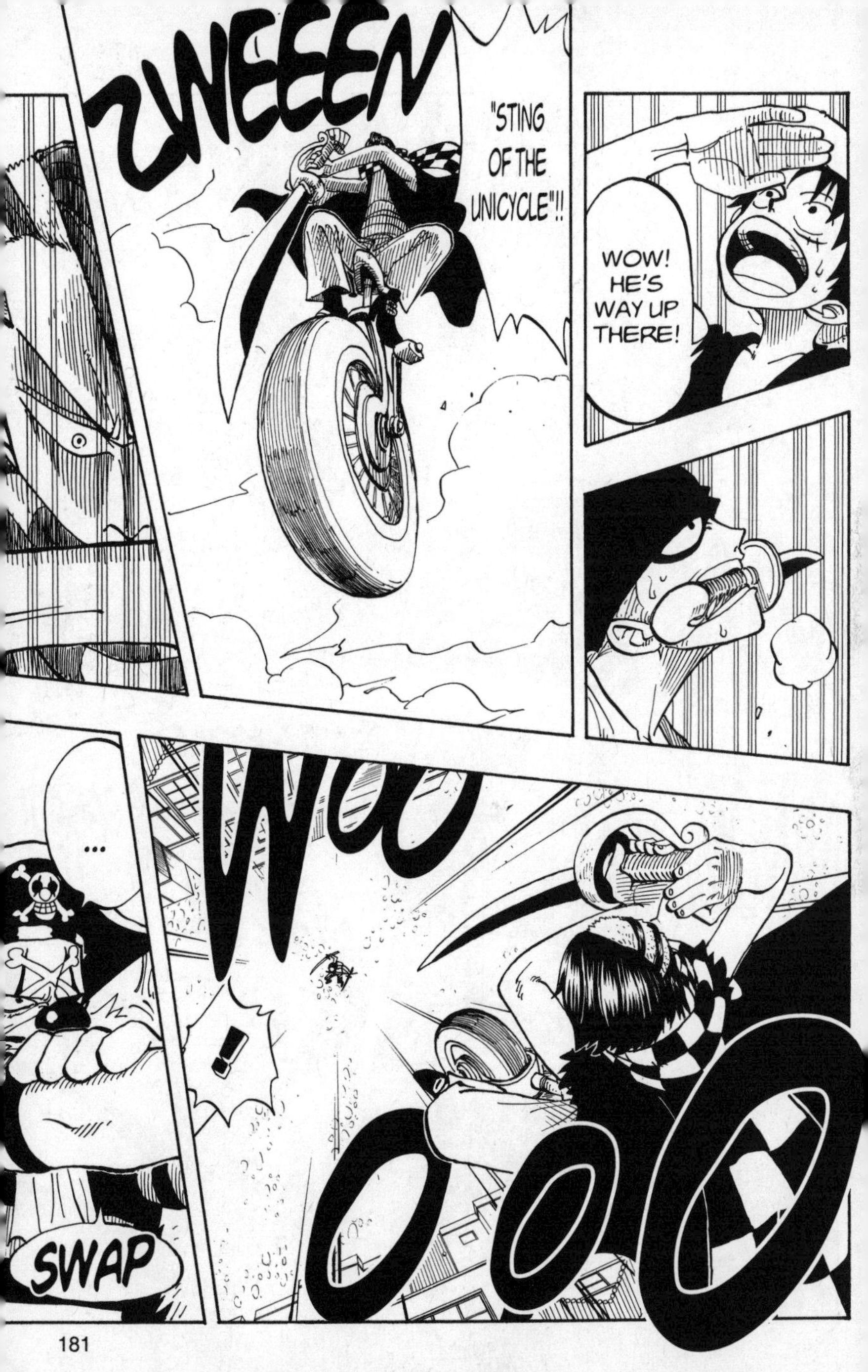
WOW! HE'S WAY UP THERE!
ZWEEEN
"STING OF THE UNICYCLE"!!
WOOO
!
...
SWAP

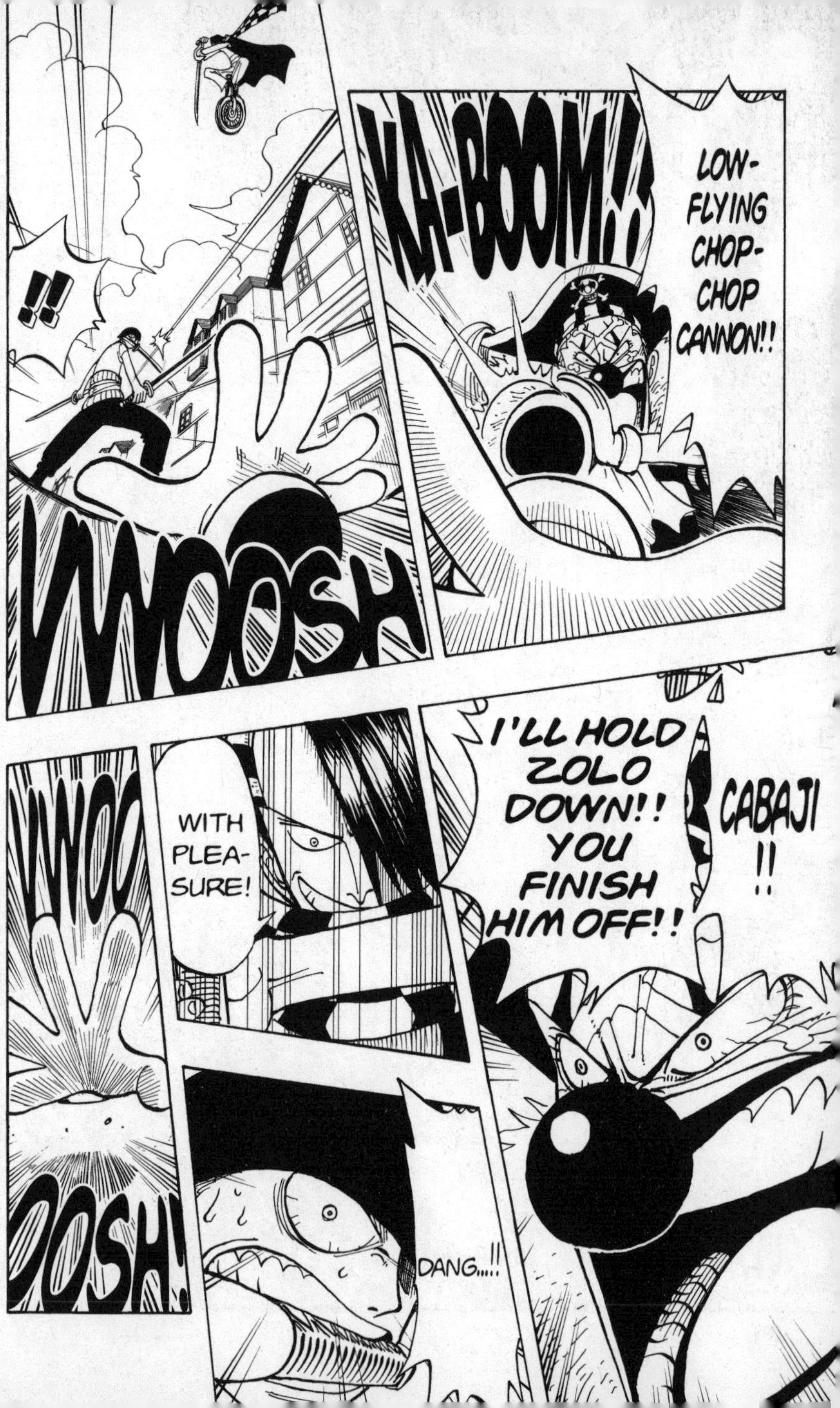
KA-BOOM!!
LOW-FLYING CHOP-CHOP CANNON!!
!!
WHOOSH
CABAJI!!
I'LL HOLD ZOLO DOWN!! YOU FINISH HIM OFF!!
WITH PLEASURE!
DANG...!!
WHOO
OOSH!

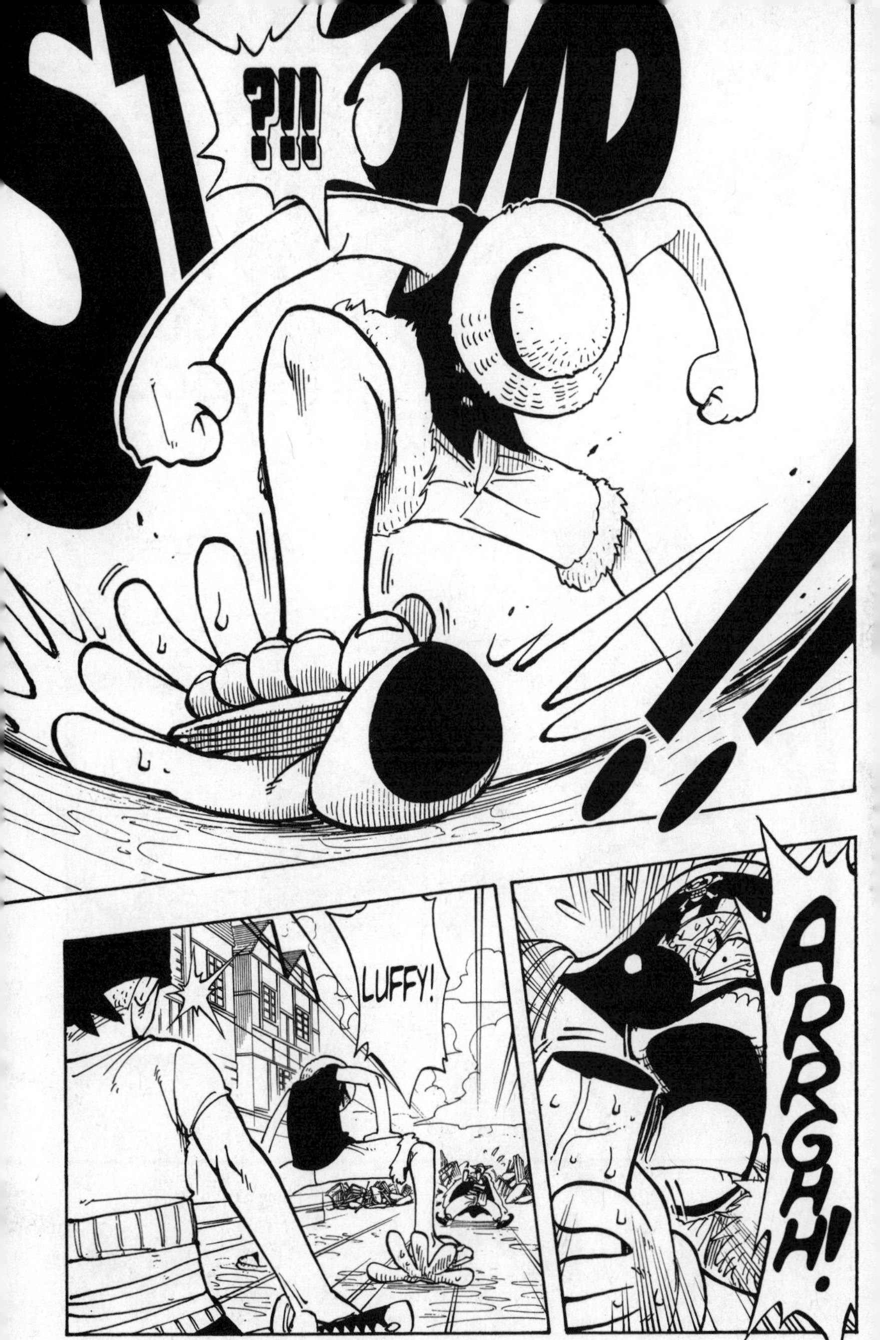
STOMP
?!!
ARRGH!
LUFFY!

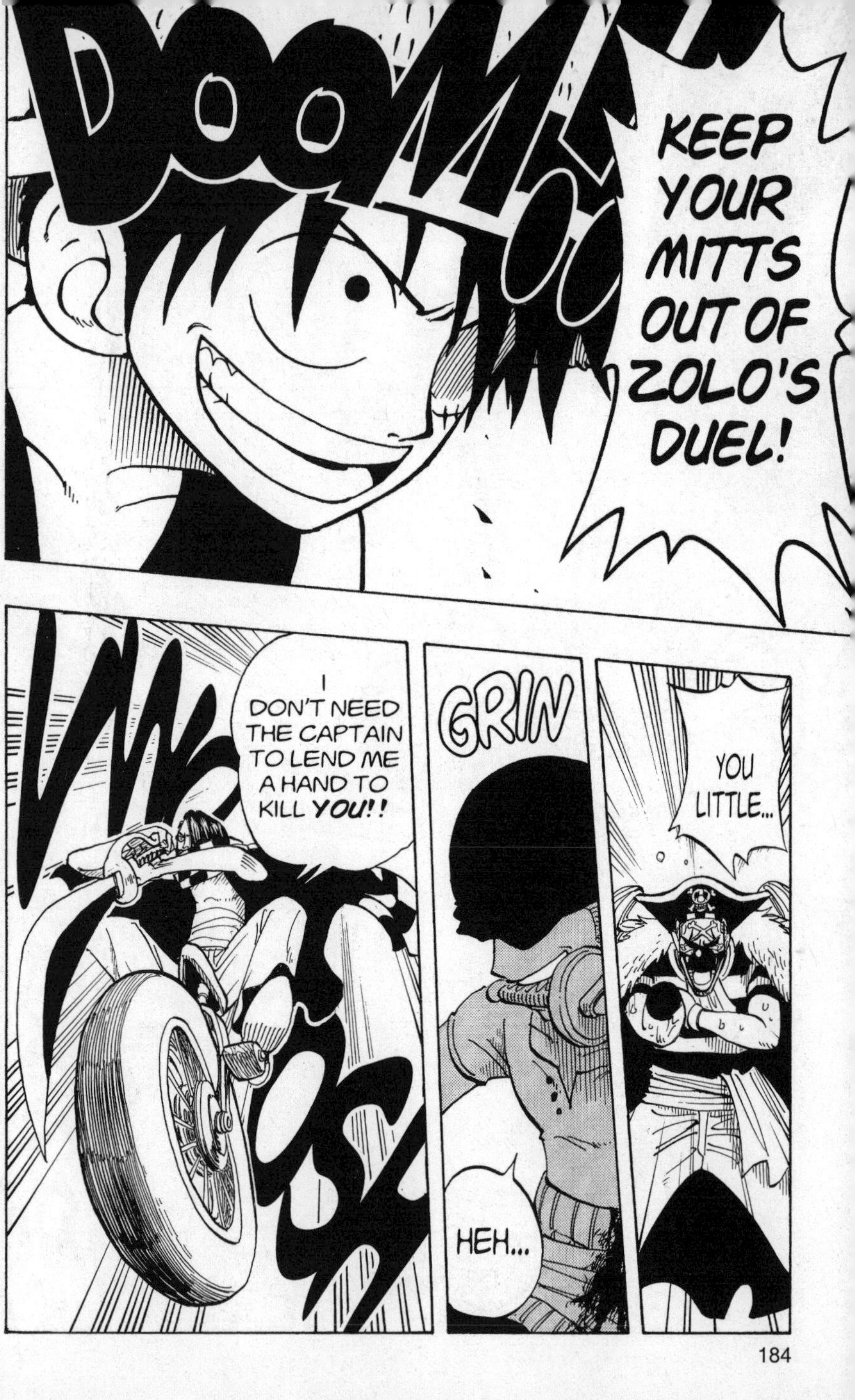
DOOM!
KEEP YOUR MITTS OUT OF ZOLO'S DUEL!
YOU LITTLE...
GRIN
HEH...
I DON'T NEED THE CAPTAIN TO LEND ME A HAND TO KILL YOU!!

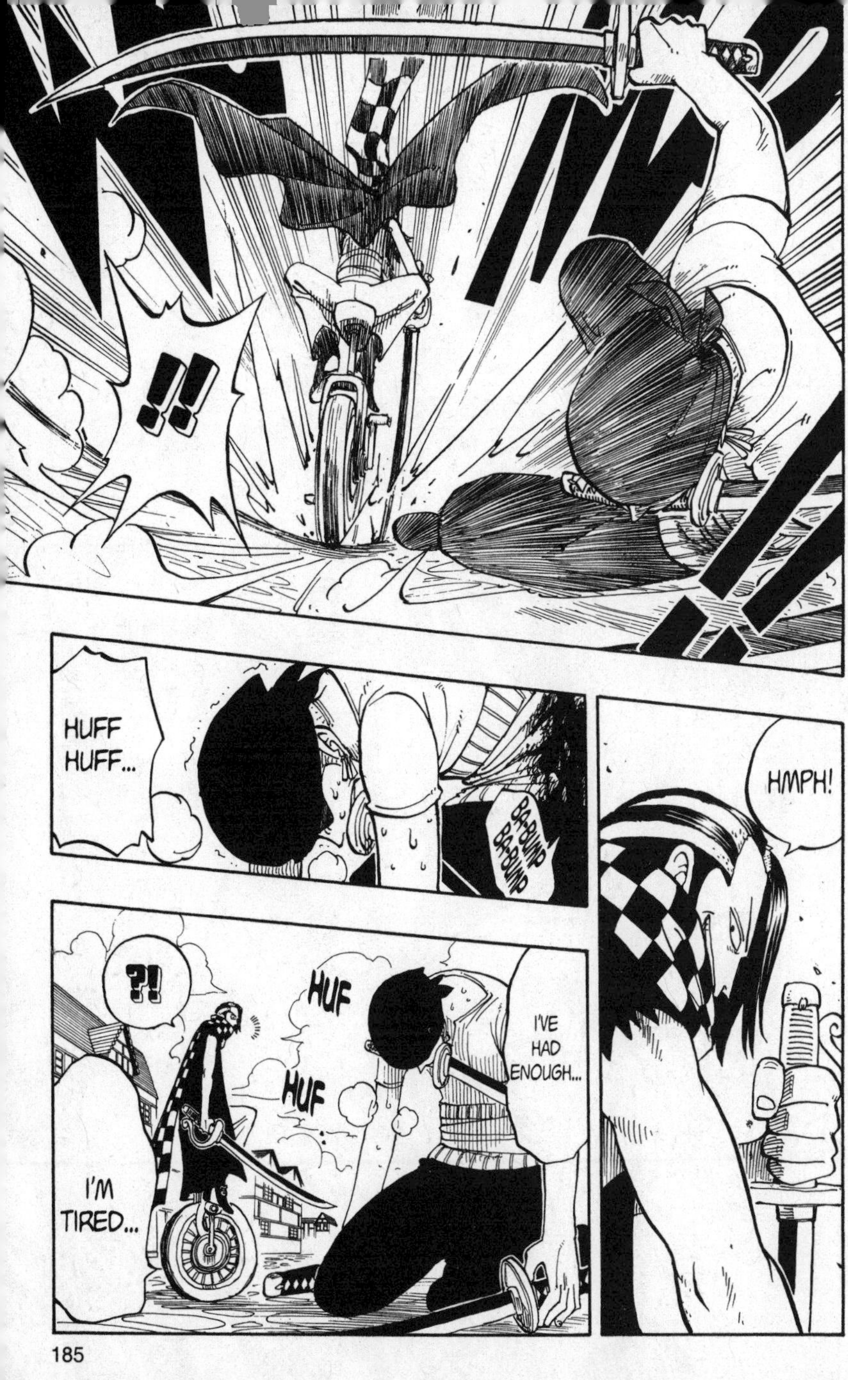
!!
HMPH!
HUFF HUFF...
BA-BUMP BA-BUMP
I'VE HAD ENOUGH...
HUF
HUF
?!
I'M TIRED...

READ THIS WAY

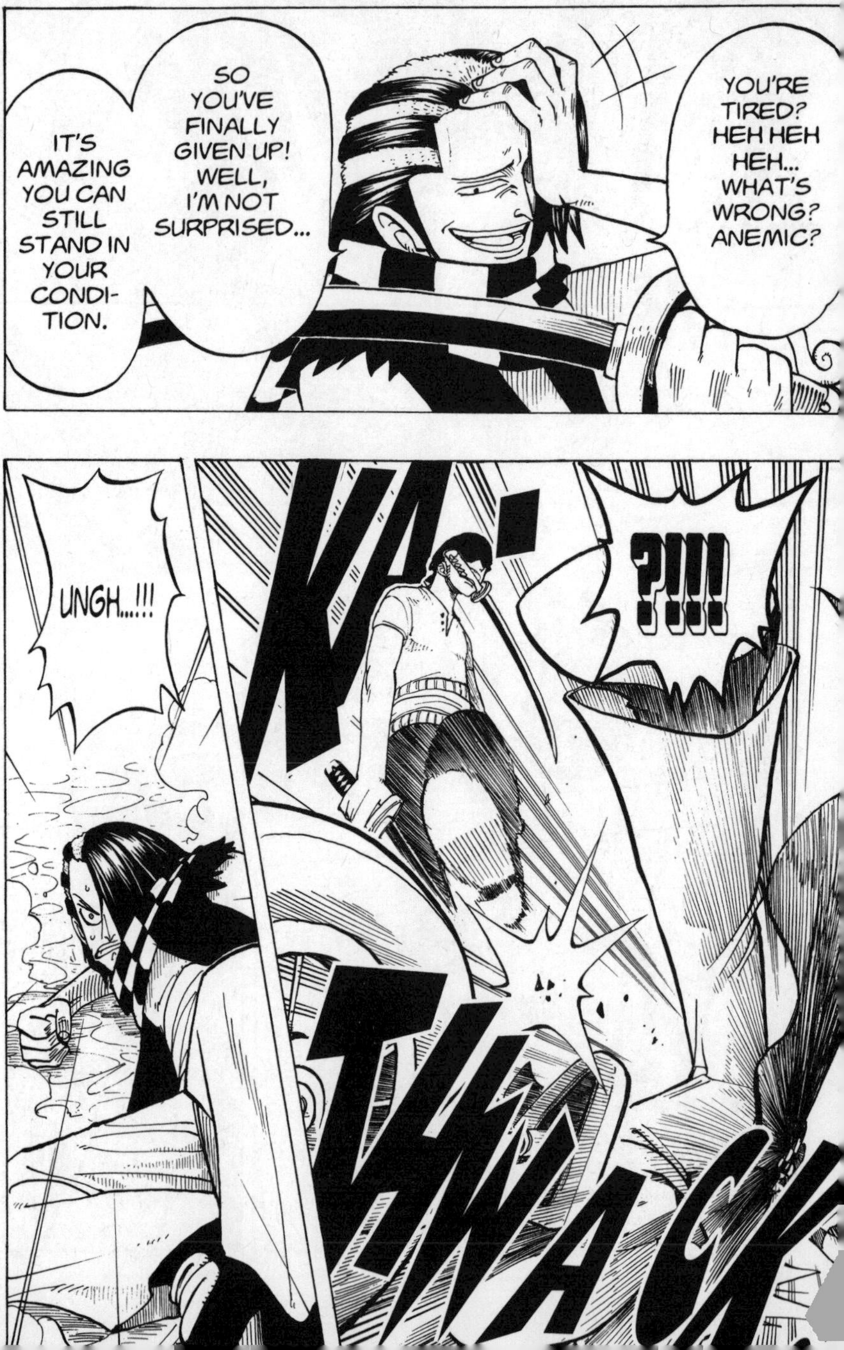

YOU'RE TIRED? HEH HEH HEH... WHAT'S WRONG? ANEMIC?
SO YOU'VE FINALLY GIVEN UP! WELL, I'M NOT SURPRISED...
IT'S AMAZING YOU CAN STILL STAND IN YOUR CONDITION.
?!!!
KA
UNGH...!!!
THWACK

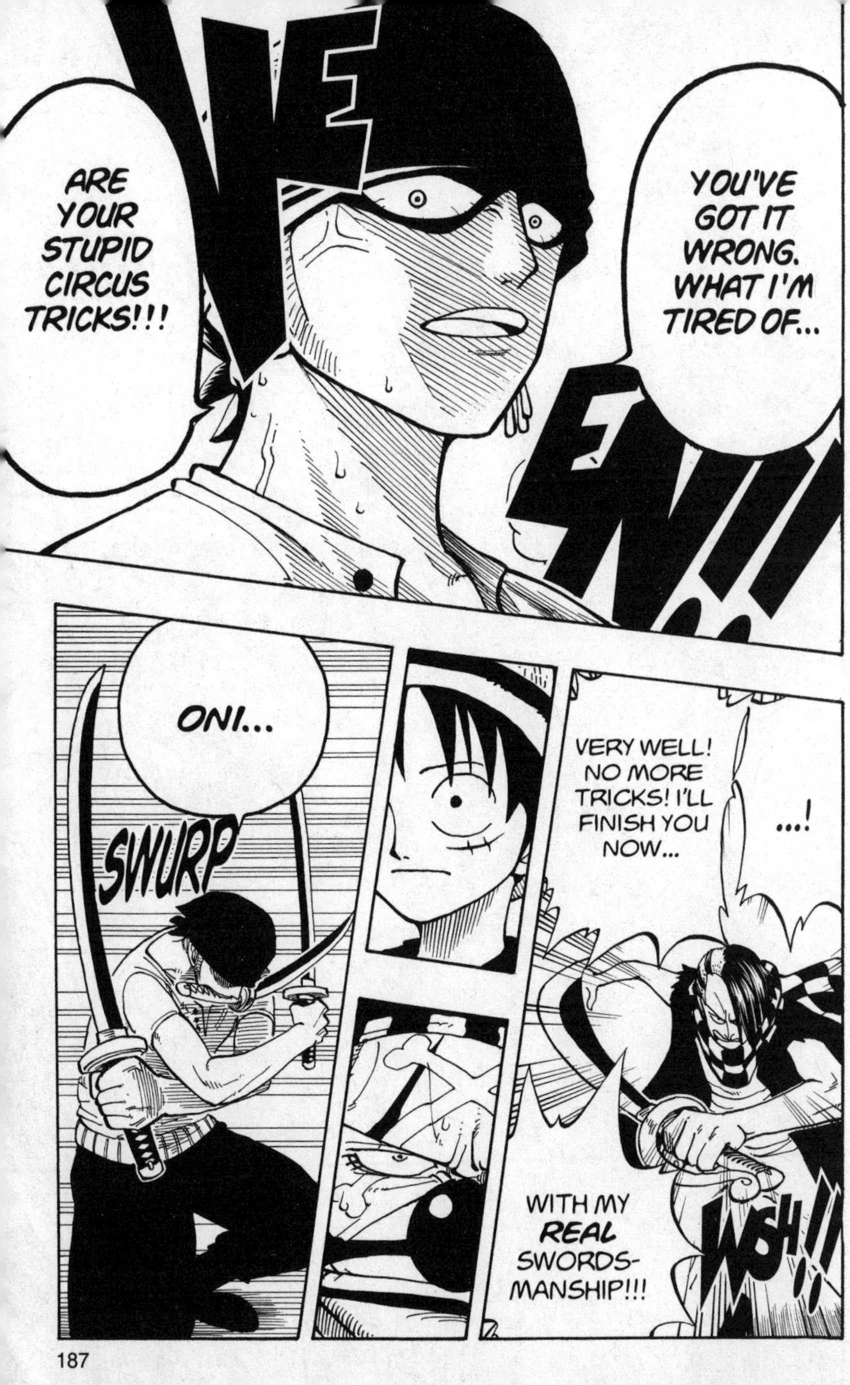
YOU'VE GOT IT WRONG. WHAT I'M TIRED OF...
ARE YOUR STUPID CIRCUS TRICKS!!!
VERY WELL! NO MORE TRICKS! I'LL FINISH YOU NOW...
...!
WITH MY REAL SWORDSMANSHIP!!!
WSH!!
ONI...
SWURP

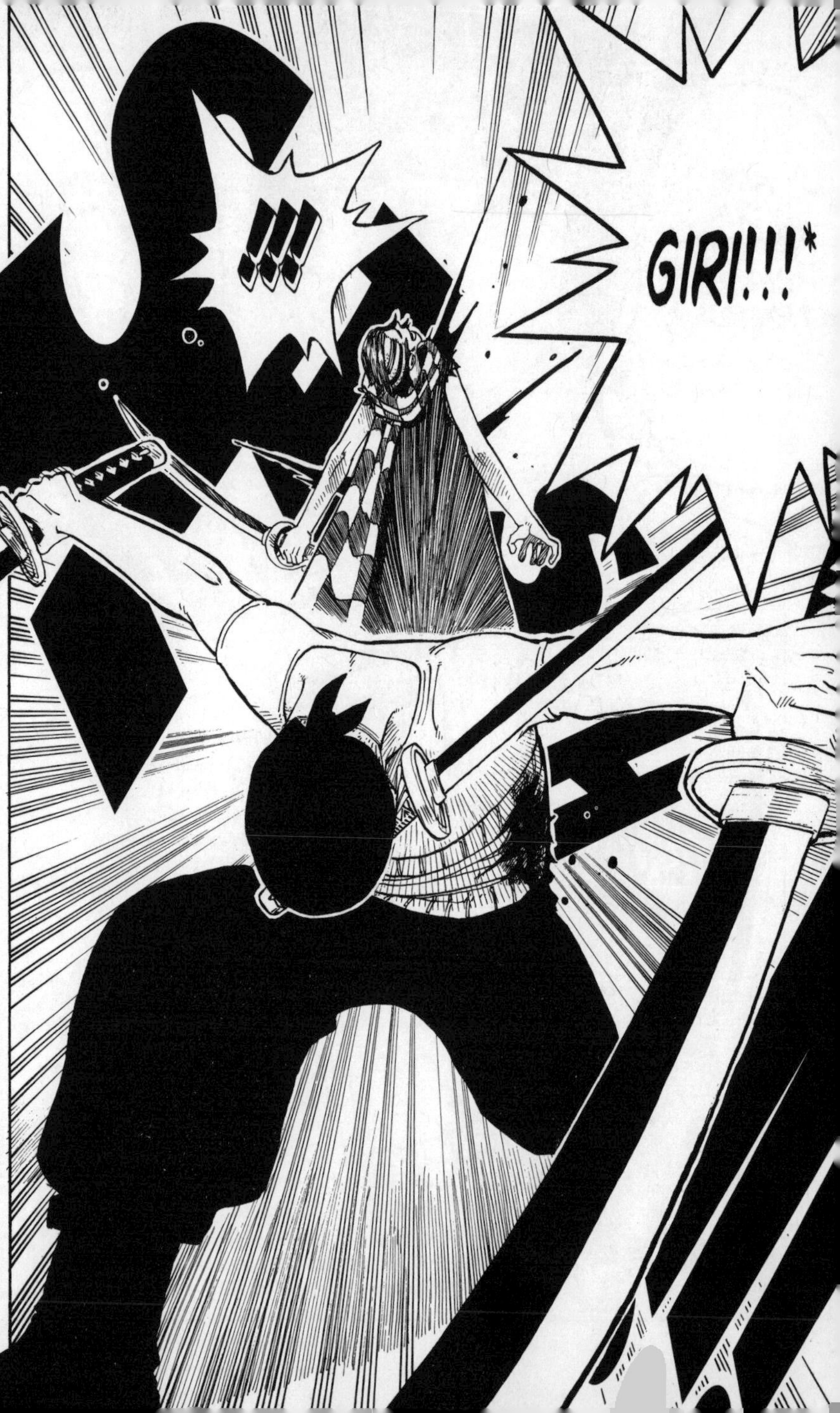
!!!
GIRI!!!*

* ONIGIRI = "DEMON SLASH!"

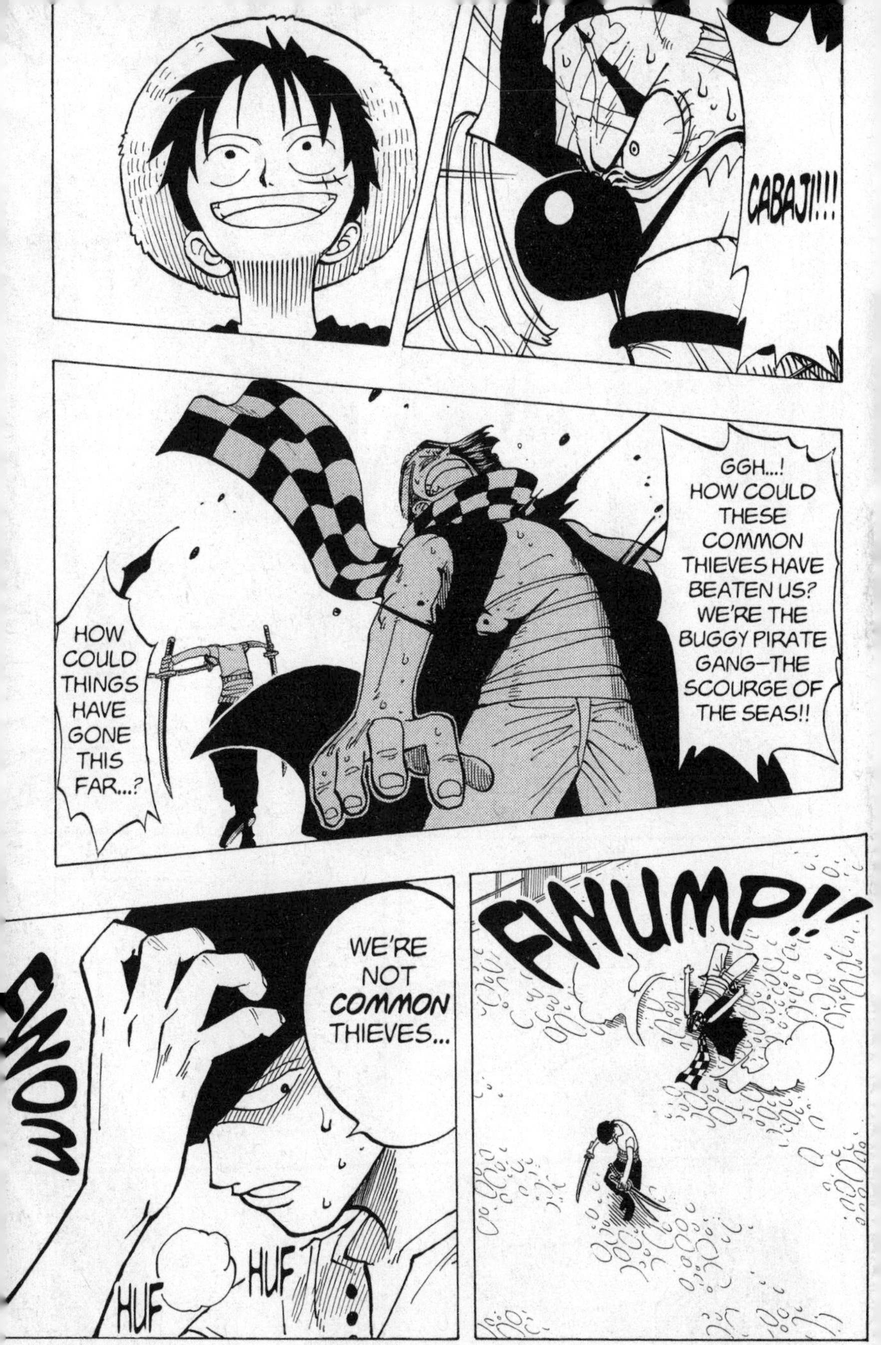

CABAJI!!!
GGH...! HOW COULD THESE COMMON THIEVES HAVE BEATEN US? WE'RE THE BUGGY PIRATE GANG—THE SCOURGE OF THE SEAS!!
HOW COULD THINGS HAVE GONE THIS FAR...?
FWUMP!!
WE'RE NOT COMMON THIEVES...
WOMP
HUF
HUF

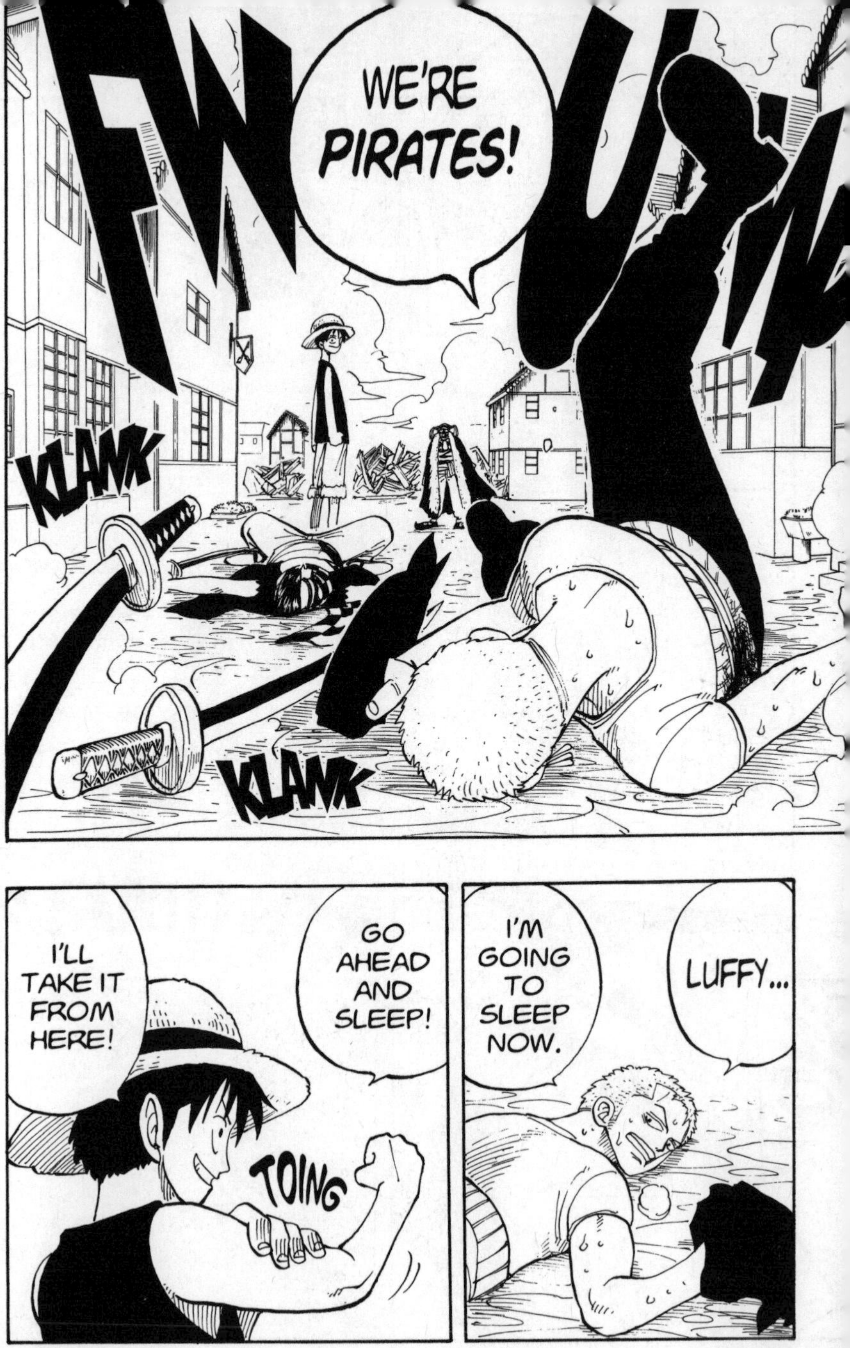

WE'RE PIRATES!
KLANK
KLANK
LUFFY...
I'M GOING TO SLEEP NOW.
GO AHEAD AND SLEEP!
I'LL TAKE IT FROM HERE!
TOING

READ THIS WAY

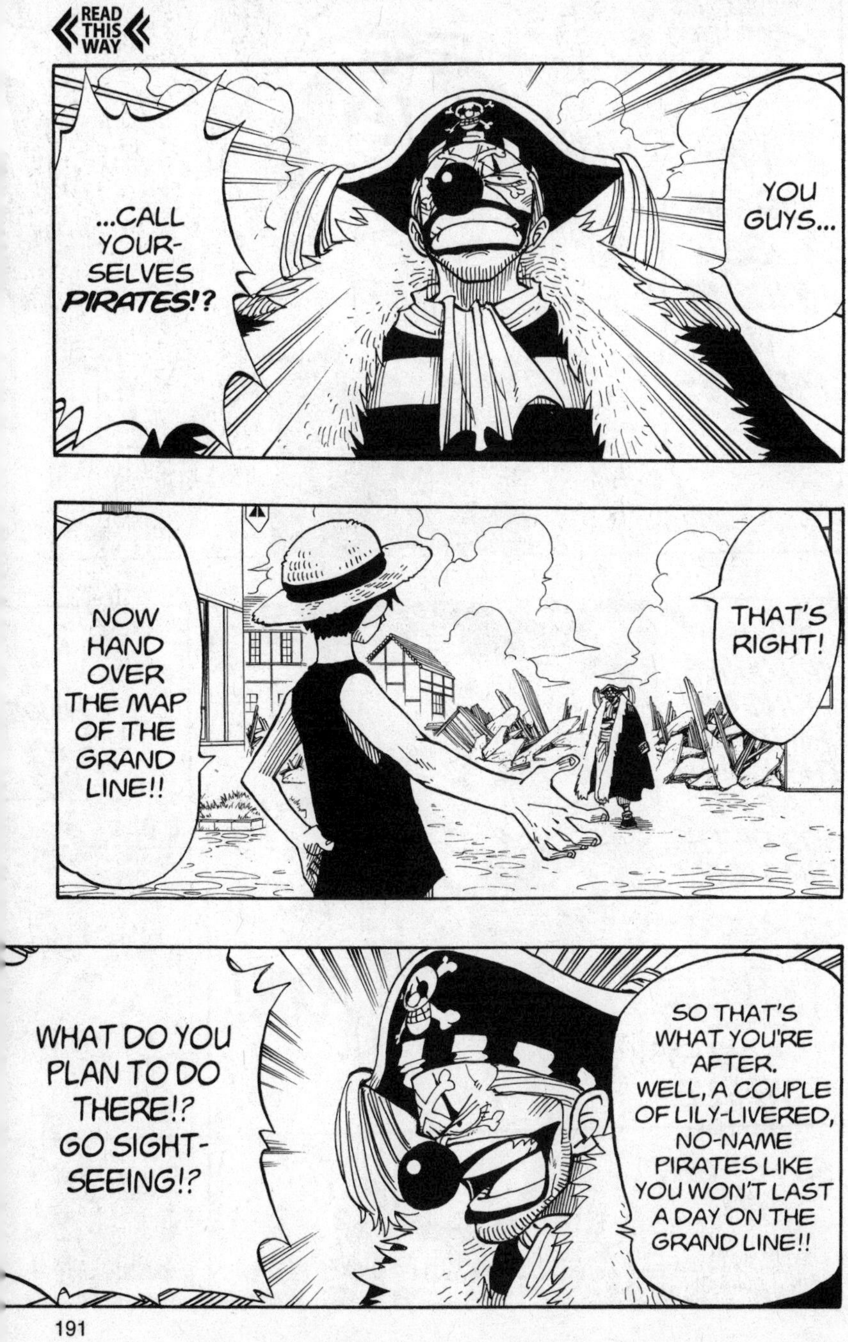

YOU GUYS...
...CALL YOURSELVES *PIRATES!?*
THAT'S RIGHT!
NOW HAND OVER THE MAP OF THE GRAND LINE!!
SO THAT'S WHAT YOU'RE AFTER. WELL, A COUPLE OF LILY-LIVERED, NO-NAME PIRATES LIKE YOU WON'T LAST A DAY ON THE GRAND LINE!!
WHAT DO YOU PLAN TO DO THERE!? GO SIGHT-SEEING!?

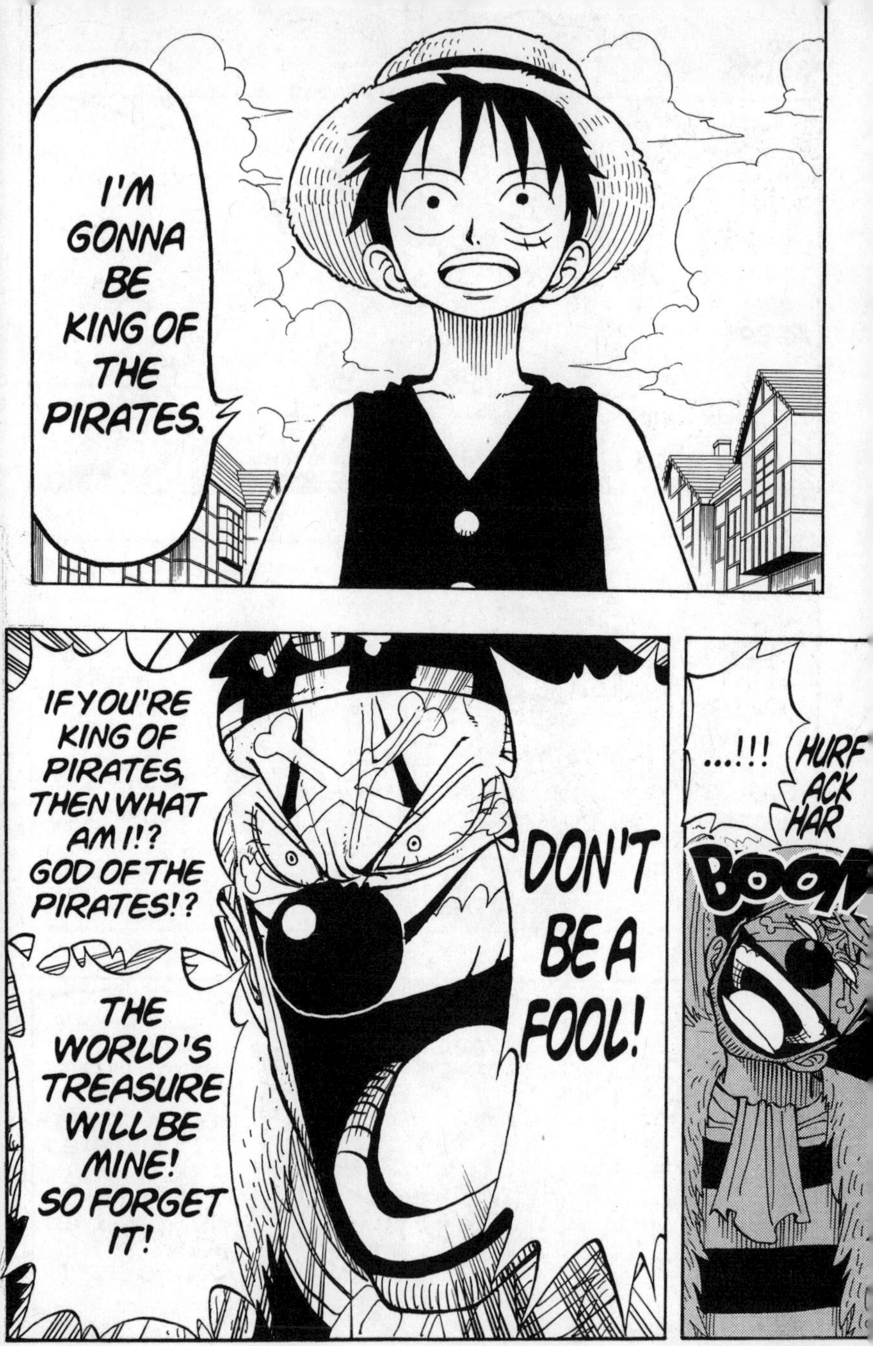
I'M GONNA BE KING OF THE PIRATES.
HURF ACK HAR
...!!!
BOOM
DON'T BE A FOOL!
IF YOU'RE KING OF PIRATES, THEN WHAT AM I!? GOD OF THE PIRATES!?
THE WORLD'S TREASURE WILL BE MINE! SO FORGET IT!

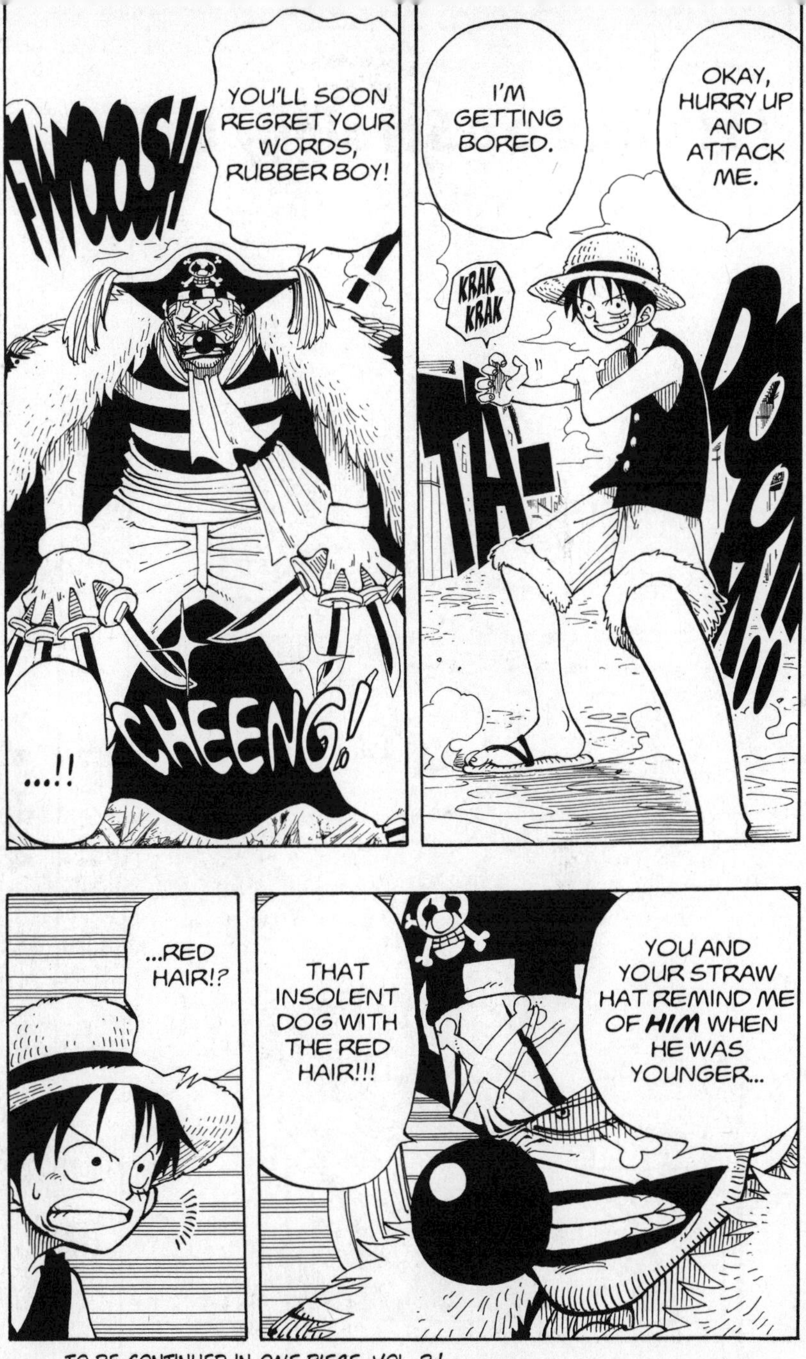
OKAY, HURRY UP AND ATTACK ME.
I'M GETTING BORED.
KRAK KRAK
YOU'LL SOON REGRET YOUR WORDS, RUBBER BOY!
FWOOSH
CHEENG!
...!!
YOU AND YOUR STRAW HAT REMIND ME OF *HIM* WHEN HE WAS YOUNGER...
THAT INSOLENT DOG WITH THE RED HAIR!!!
...RED HAIR!?

TO BE CONTINUED IN *ONE PIECE*, VOL. 3!

Let's make a Sproingy Luffy!

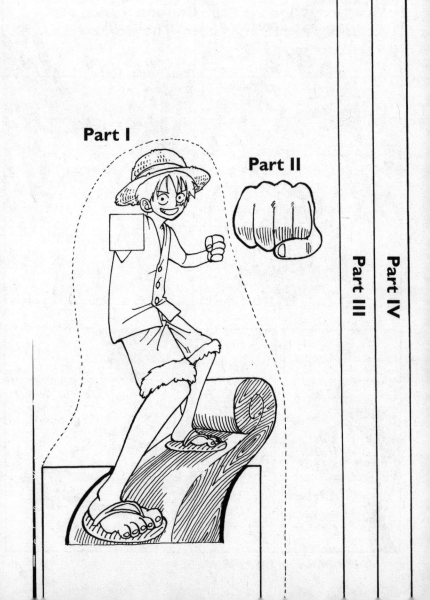

Part I

Part II

Part III

Part IV

How to make a Sproingy Luffy:

You need:
Scissors - Glue or paste - Crayons, markers, or colored pencils - Stiff paper - The strong will to make Sproingy Luffy

Instructions:

1.   Color! To start out, color the various parts of Luffy. (Have fun!) Use flesh color for Parts II, III and IV. People who don't like messing up their books can make a photocopy to color and cut out instead.

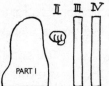

2.   Cut it out! Cut out Part I along the dotted line, and cut out the pieces for Parts II, III and IV, following the lines.

3.   Paste Part I onto a piece of stiff paper.

4.   Wait for the glue to dry. Act cool. You can dance while you wait, too.

Let it Dry!

5.   Cut out Part I (you'll be cutting the stiff paper, too), following Luffy's outline this time. Do it all powerful-like! Carefully cut the slots, following the thick lines around his legs, and make Luffy stand up.

Ta-Da!

Slots

6. Glue Part III and Part IV at right angles to each other, just at the tips!

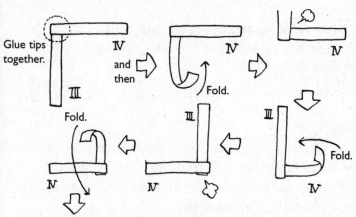

Glue tips together.

IV

and then

Fold.

IV

IV

Fold.

III

Fold.

III

III

IV

IV

IV

Fold.

And so on and so forth, folding them over and over each other like you're weaving.

← You should get something sproingy like this thing.

Glue the other ends together, and then you're done with this part!

7. Assemble (Rise, Luffy, Rise!) **8.** COMPLETION!

boiii-iing!

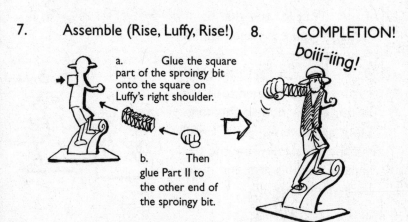

a. Glue the square part of the sproingy bit onto the square on Luffy's right shoulder.

b. Then glue Part II to the other end of the sproingy bit.

BORUTO
-NARUTO NEXT GENERATIONS-

CREATOR/SUPERVISOR **Masashi Kishimoto**
ART BY **Mikio Ikemoto** SCRIPT BY **Ukyo Kodachi**

A NEW GENERATION OF NINJA IS HERE!

Naruto was a young shinobi with an incorrigible knack for mischief. He achieved his dream to become the greatest ninja in his village, and now his face sits atop the Hokage monument. But this is not his story... A new generation of ninja is ready to take the stage, led by Naruto's own son, Boruto!

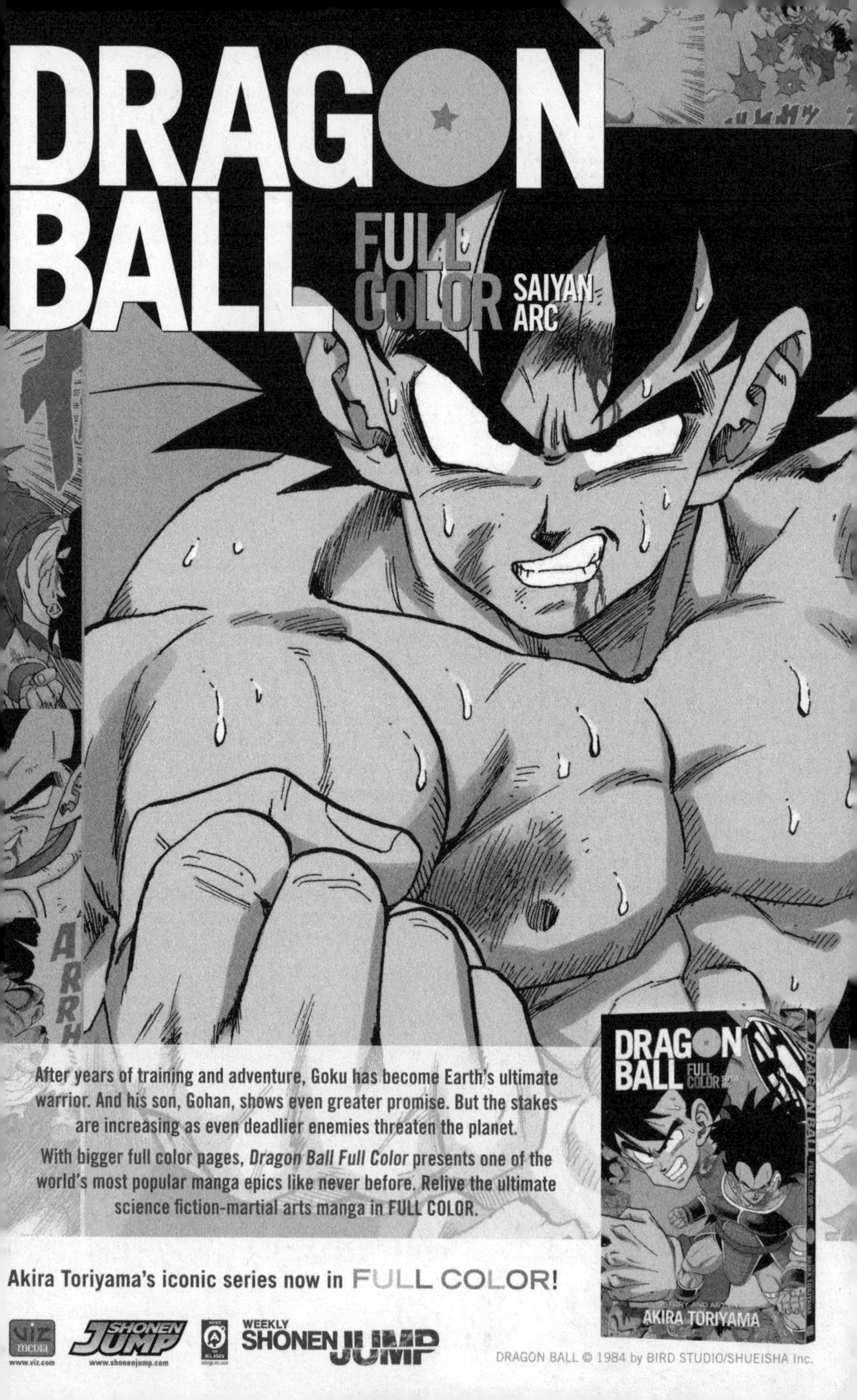
DRAGON BALL
FULL COLOR SAIYAN ARC
After years of training and adventure, Goku has become Earth's ultimate warrior. And his son, Gohan, shows even greater promise. But the stakes are increasing as even deadlier enemies threaten the planet.
With bigger full color pages, Dragon Ball Full Color presents one of the world's most popular manga epics like never before. Relive the ultimate science fiction-martial arts manga in FULL COLOR.
Akira Toriyama's iconic series now in FULL COLOR!
DRAGON BALL FULL COLOR
AKIRA TORIYAMA
viz media
www.viz.com
SHONEN JUMP
www.shonenjump.com
WEEKLY SHONEN JUMP
DRAGON BALL © 1984 by BIRD STUDIO/SHUEISHA Inc.

You're Reading in the Wrong Direction!!

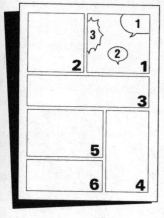

Whoops! Guess what? You're starting at the wrong end of the comic!

...It's true! In keeping with the original Japanese format, **One Piece** is meant to be read from right to left, starting in the upper-right corner.

Unlike English, which is read from left to right, Japanese is read from right to left, meaning that action, sound effects and word-balloon order are completely reversed...something which can make readers unfamiliar with Japanese feel pretty backwards themselves. For this reason, manga or Japanese comics published in the U.S. in English have sometimes been published "flopped"—that is, printed in exact reverse order, as though seen from the other side of a mirror.

By flopping pages, U.S. publishers can avoid confusing readers, but the compromise is not without its downside. For one thing, a character in a flopped manga series who once wore in the original Japanese version a T-shirt emblazoned with "M A Y" (as in "the merry month of") now wears one which reads "Y A M"! Additionally, many manga creators in Japan are themselves unhappy with the process, as some feel the mirror-imaging of their art skews their original intentions.

We are proud to bring you Eiichiro Oda's **One Piece** in the original unflopped format. For now, though, turn to the other side of the book and let the journey begin...!

—Editor